Allegories of History,

Allegories of Love

So we must turn to allegory, the method dear to men with their eyes opened.

PHILO JUDEUS

I am not unaware that many people have said many things about paradise.

SAINT AUGUSTINE

Allegories are empty speculations, and as it were the scum of Holy Scripture. . . . a sort of beautiful harlot, who proves herself especially seductive to idle men. . . . awkward, absurd, invented, obsolete, loose rays.

MARTIN LUTHER

The reader will find that personifications of abstract ideas rarely occur in these volumes . . . .

WILLIAM WORDSWORTH

In defense of allegory, (however, or for whatever object, employed,) there is scarcely one respectable word to be said.

EDGAR ALLAN POE

. . . allegory to my sense is quite one of the lighter exercises of the imagination. . . . It is apt to spoil two good things, a story and a moral, a meaning and a form. . . .

HENRY JAMES

I hated, even as a child, allegory . . . .

D. H. LAWRENCE

Allegories of History,

Allegories of Love

STEPHEN A. BARNEY

ARCHON BOOKS · 1979

© Stephen A. Barney 1979
First published 1979 as an Archon Book,
an imprint of The Shoe String Press, Inc.
Hamden, Connecticut 06514
All rights reserved
Filmset in Baskerville
by Asco Trade Typesetting Ltd of Hong Kong.
Lithoprinted and bound in The United States of America

This book has been published with the assistance
of the FREDERICK W. HILLIS PUBLICATION FUND
of Yale University

Library of Congress Cataloging in Publication Data

Barney, Stephen A
Allegories of history, allegories of love.

Includes bibliographies and index.
1. Allegory. I. Title.
PN56.A5B36   809'.91'5   78-15148
ISBN 0-208-01749-6

to Cherry

Contents

7

CONTENTS

9

Acknowledgments

My first debt is to the work of scholars who have preceded me in the field. All writers will know how easy it is to transform the memory of others' work into a figment of one's own imagination. I have tried to document specific borrowings in the bibliographical notes which follow each chapter.

I am grateful to Yale University for a Morse Fellowship and a series of summer research grants which gave me the leisure to pursue this work. Lord Annan kindly made available to me the facilities of University College, London, for the months I was there.

I wish to thank the students of a course in allegory which I taught for three years at Yale, for listening, provoking, and making it seem worthwhile. Traugott Lawler, Charlotte Morse, Morton Bloomfield, James Nohrnberg, Mark Rose, Bartlett Giamatti, Robert L. Kellogg, Theodore Leinbaugh, David Riggs, Anne Mellor, Barbara Packer, James McIntosh, Margie Waller, Bruce Stovel, Walter Reed, Jane Smith, Maureen Quilligan, Max Byrd, and Ronald Jager all read portions of this book in draft. Their advice has been invaluable; my inadequate thanks to them all.

To Robert Kellogg I owe my first interest in allegory, in Spenser, and in medieval literature, kindled sixteen years ago when I was an undergraduate at the University of Virginia; he has been my model of a good teacher. David Riggs performed the office of a friend by a particularly keen (his term was "savage") criticism of a chapter,

which was particularly helpful—we had some good talk. Traugott
Lawler, collegially, and my father, kindly, labored over the proofs,
and I am happy in their vigilance. James Nohrnberg has been my
scholarly confidant during the whole process, graciously sharing his
ideas, his learning, and his own work on Spenser. His daughter
Gabrielle helped me with the spelling of "Jiminy Cricket."

I dedicate this book with love to my wife.

New Haven   S. A. B.
December, 1977

CHAPTER ONE

Introduction

CHARACTERISTICS OF ALLEGORIES

The first piece I have handled is that of *Tom Thumb*, whose author was a Pythagorean philosopher. This dark treatise contains the whole scheme of the Metempsychosis, deducing the progress of the soul through all her stages.

The next is *Dr. Faustus*, penned by Artephius, an author *bonae notae*, and an *adeptus*; he published it in the nine hundred eighty-fourth year of his age; this writer proceeds wholly by reincrudation, or in the *via humida*; and the marriage between Faustus and Helen does most conspicuously dilucidate the fermenting of the male and female dragon.

Whittington and his Cat is the work of that mysterious rabbi, Jehuda Hannasi, containing a defense of the Gemara of the Jerusalem Mishna, and its just preference to that of Babylon, contrary to the vulgar opinion.

The Hind and the Panther. This is the masterpiece of a famous writer now living, intended for a complete abstract of sixteen thousand schoolmen from Scotus to Bellarmine.

JONATHAN SWIFT, *A Tale of a Tub*

By what authority dost thou these things? and who hath given thee this authority that thou shouldst do these things?

MARK 11:28

ABOUT THIS BOOK

The days are gone when the book by C. S. Lewis, *The Allegory of Love* (1936), held the field of allegorical studies for students of literature. A new book now needs special justification in a crowded court. My subject here is unique: to treat the best works of allegory, without chronological restriction, in themselves, and not in the service of the theory of allegory. I aim to sketch as briefly as possible the present state of the theory, and, along the way, to make some contribution to the theory; but my emphasis is practical criticism. Except in this introduction, I do not excerpt and paraphrase allegories in order to illustrate a principle of allegorical technique. Rather I introduce principles of allegory, others' and my own, in order to illuminate texts. It is too easy to shortchange or misrepresent an allegory by treating it too briefly. My argument in this book is that we are aided in the serious business of criticism by considering allegory as a special subject, not only for theoretical reasons, but for practical ones. There are traditions which allegories employ and upon which they reflect; more important, the very allegorical mode of a work often becomes part of its theme. The choice of allegorical fiction by an author implies something about the construction of his world.

The eight works to which I devote chapters seem to me, with two exceptions, the eight most important allegories we have. I have omitted prolonged treatment of Dante, partly because of A. C. Charity's *Events and Their Afterlife* and Robert Hollander's *Allegory in Dante's "Commedia"* (Princeton, 1969), books which are recent, intelligent, and thorough; partly because, not being a Dantist, I fear to rush in; mainly because I hope this book can serve as a prolegomenon to Dante, the greatest of allegorists. I have included one of Hawthorne's tales, rather than his more important masterpiece, partly because so much has been written about *The Scarlet Letter*, partly because I wanted to treat a short story, and partly because of my feeling that Hawthorne's longer works are expanded tales, so that for this author criticism of a short tale can be as extensive and illuminating as a more repetitive criticism of a more repetitive work.

With these exceptions, I have tried to select the works which can teach us most about the nature of allegory. I trust that my bias toward works in English will be shared by most of my readers. The translations from foreign tongues are throughout, unless otherwise noted, my own. The order of the book is not strictly chronological because I have divided allegories into two different kinds, each represented in one part of this book; within each part the order is chronological, the better to observe historical process.

Although this book aims to make it difficult to speak facilely about allegory, we should start with glosses on some of the special terms of the subject, and a few distinctions. Much has been written about allegory, but the understandable redundancy of the criticism makes it possible to review in short space the principal ideas which need to be borne in mind through this book. This chapter, like the others, concludes with a note intended to direct the reader to the best of the other studies on its particular topic. In this introduction I note some characteristics of allegory, chiefly of "classical" allegory as it appears before the Enlightenment. After that time allegorists became especially self-concious, and their parodies and inversions of the mode are not useful for a preliminary description.

To describe or define a thing, as the words' etymologies suggest, is to fix its boundary, which surely cannot be done until the thing is examined, and perhaps not even then. Descriptions tend to mechanize a subject, but in my experience good allegories refuse to submit to a scheme. At the beginning, then, I will try to open doors, not to close or unhinge them. As the epigraph from Swift suggests, the subject is liable to fancifulness of all kinds. I will try to draw some conclusions, but I keep in mind what a critic of Spenser writes: "As in so many areas of literary scholarship, the conclusions which men reach about the nature of allegory are a lot less interesting than the paths they follow to arrive at their conclusion." I accept this not as a counsel of despair, but as a challenge.

The process of arriving at conclusions must begin somewhere, and as I began my investigation with works which (to paraphrase Augustine) everyone, everywhere, has always called allegories, so I introduce the subject with the term "allegory" in its most popular use, in "ordinary language." Here and elsewhere it may be felt that I use the term too loosely: I plead guilty to the charge—I want to risk being too inclusive at first, and to discriminate as I go. The plan of chapters of the book imitates the plot of my ponderings: my own process of discovery has been painfully inductive. Finally I aim to be properly responsive to allegory, if not definitive of it. I should confess at the outset that at least one boundary of the study will not be fixed or trespassed. A complete study of allegory depends on a perfected theory of fiction itself, which I neither offer nor have.

INTIMATIONS OF ALLEGORIES

The word "allegory," "other-speech," *alieniloquium*, suggests that allegories present one thing by a customary route, and another thing more deviously. We will survey the various ways in which the presented and the deviously implicit are related, but we should first consider how a person becomes aware that he is in the presence of an allegory, and why he begins to look for signals which lead him toward the Other.

What probably stirs us to recognize a work as an allegory is its resemblance to works we customarily call allegories. A premise of this book is that allegories hold more than one trait in common; that is, that the presence of allegory usually entails (and is signalled by) the presence of a theoretically unlimited but practically finite bundle of forms, themes, and motifs. Certain traditional topics are signs of allegory: the choice of roads in a labyrinthine forest, the garden with interesting vegetation and a commandment, the vision of the other world, the decorated wall, conversation with an authoritative person. Many of these topics also occur in fictions which are not allegories, especially in romances, but this loose and potentially misleading recognition begins the process of drawing the reader's mind away from the flow of the text, as he ceases to respond to what he reads in the way that he responds to actual history. When we stop saying, "I have seen that," or "I know how he feels," and start saying, "I have read this sort of thing before," we begin to penetrate to the Other (we are alienated) and to sense the presence of allegory— we become distracted, "drawn aside."

When features of a text encourage us to be more particular, to say not only, "I have read this sort of thing before," but to add, "in Exodus," or "in the *Aeneid*," we call the text *allusive*. Our text "plays back" the former text. If the allusion is extensive, especially if it resides in the whole plot of the text, it tends towards allegory. The correspondence of the presented text to the old, authoritative text encourages the reader to look for a *tertium quid*, a principle of interpretation to which the correspondence points. Since the literary monuments—the Bible, Virgil, Ovid—have submitted to allegorical interpretations of their own, the *tertium quid* may not be far to seek. The fact that the antique text *has been criticized* makes it a fit support for allegory. The meaning of Exodus has been stated in a rationalized, discursive, philosophical language, and this language may easily be applied to the new text which alludes, by its narrative structure, to Exodus itself. In this case the rationalized language ("the Red Sea water means Baptism") is the Other.

This method of recognition is fraught with dangers. If the theory of archetypes has any validity, then all narratives may be considered allusive. Many overtly allusive texts are not allegories: the title page of *Joseph Andrews* mentions Cervantes's work, but few consider *Joseph Andrews* an allegory. Nevertheless, allusion, especially to the select body of most authoritative texts, can arouse the distracted kind of reading which precedes allegorical interpretation. The special case of typology—of which more later—is the subject of the first part of this book.

A second often remarked signal of the presence of allegory has to do with disruption of the reader's expectations. One definition of the term "form" calls it that quality in a work which draws from the reader a certain expectation about what he will experience in reading. This definition, depending on the reader, is—perhaps necessarily— extrinsic (can form be defined formally?). We expect an alexandrine at the end of a Spenserian stanza, combat in epic, attacks on the literate in satire. Most of all, when we meet a person in a narrative plot, we expect him to behave, or just maintain his being, with some kind of consistency; and when we find ourselves in a certain time and locale in a narrative, in a certain "world," we expect it to persist. Aristotle instructs us to look for a beginning, middle, and end which are continuous and causally related. When a fiction fails to fulfill the expectations aroused by its form—we thought we were in Paris and here we are at the gates of hell—we look for a cause, and we look for allegory. It is as if the alignment between the traditional fable and the imposed allegorical meaning were never quite true. Of course the distracted reader, confronted with a breach of form, may discover that no allegory explains it. The author may have been incompetent.. He may operate under a different aesthetic, one under which—as

Melville argues (with irony) in a chapter of *The Confidence-Man*—
out of a rage for mimesis he imitates the inconsistencies of reality.
For example, in Chaucer's Merchant's Tale we have a series of
discontinuities: Pluto and Proserpina are represented as king and
queen of Fairye, and they dispute about Solomon and Jesus ben
Sirach. But there is no hint, in these discontinuities, of allegory.

Nevertheless, discontinuities of form can intimate allegory. Two
other kinds of "discontinuity" have traditionally called forth allegorical interpretation, but they should be considered confusions of
interpretation rather than formal discontinuities. First, granted that
the Bible is the word of God, it has been felt to contain statements
which, unless interpreted allegorically, are inconsistent with what
we know of the divine mandates. Augustine made the classical
formulation of this point: if a text in the Bible is inconsistent with
the ultimate mandate, charity, then it is allegory. Jean Pépin has
collected sayings of the Church Fathers to the effect that literal
absurdity is a sign of allegory. These opinions have rather to do with
the origin of allegoresis than with the recognition of allegory, if
modern Biblical criticism is right. We now assume in the first instance
that nothing in the Bible is absurd or discontinuous with God's
utterance, so long as we understand such things as textual transmis-
sion, human frailty, cultural relativity, *Sitz im Leben*, and the Hebrew,
Aramaic, and Greek languages. The Bible is continuous with the
word of God, and in this matter therefore not allegory.

Far more pernicious is the second confusion, which assumes,
regardless of a work's overt form, that fictions *are* mimetic, that they
imitate in language what goes on in "real life" as it is perceived by
the "common sense," according to what Bertrand Russell called the
metaphysics of the Stone Age. (It may be more recent.) If fictions
imitate real life, then their discontinuity with real life becomes a
discontinuity in form, and the cause for the disruption is sought.
This gives to all of the less historical-looking genres—romance,
pastoral, satire, utopia, dream—a presumption of allegory of which
they may be innocent. All fantasy may be interpreted as allegory.

Here a problem of discrimination arises: how to judge when a
fiction is not an allegory. The fact that many allegories are clothed
in fantastic genres complicates the problem. Even though a romance
may contain no breach of its proper form, its separation from real
life will, often enough, point toward allegory. But fantasies can be

simply arbitrary constructions: that we are reading a fantasy does not necessarily imply that we are reading an allegory.

The special feature of fantasy is its imposture of fictional causes and motives which are, in our physics and psychology, both impossible and improbable. Fantasies admit into their realm beings which have no normal source, like demons, and events which have no cause, arbitrary and supernatural events. But fantasies usually abide by the principle of form: the unearthly beings (men from Mars, the Sans brothers) are articulated through fictional patterns and behave according to certain (arbitrary) laws. A saint, in an old legend, becomes supernatural when he is put to death. Stoning and boiling have little effect on him, but he can be killed by decapitation. The event is arbitrary, but systematic, because it follows from the pure mortification of the flesh which the saint has undertaken: no *outsider* can mortify his flesh, but only separate it. Saints' legends are fantastic, but they work out their own internal laws, they fulfill our trained expectations, they preserve continuity, they have form. They are arbitrary not in terms of themselves, but in terms of our commonsense notion of reality. A fantastic fiction which had no form would be truly unsettling, and would probably be reclassified as no longer fiction, be wrenched by interpretation into a semblance of formal fiction, or be dismissed as a hopeless piece of incompetence. Fantastic fiction cannot be removed very far from our normal categories of expectation.

We need to make a sharp distinction between fantasy and allegory. If truly self-contained fantasies could be written, without any reference to our physics or psychology, they would surely be liable to allegorical interpretation, but the interpretation would be utterly arbitrary, imposed by the interpreter. A highly systematic, deterministic fantasy, a highly formal fantasy, tempts the reader into allegoresis, simply because the presence of elaborate order looks so analogous to the order of our commonsense cosmos. The more perfect the fantasy, the more it looks like allegory, and the less allegorical it is. The paradox here is that the dominance of form, like discontinuity of form, intimates allegory. But the former, our allegoresis of pure fantasy, is a matter of interpretation, whereas the latter, the allegory signalled by discontinuous form, is often a matter which abides in the fiction and not in our heads. A fantasy requires other signals before we can legitimately label it allegory.

We recognize allegory, then, not in opposition to realism, the kind of fiction which seems to represent, as a historian represents, real life; rather, a certain amount of realism is necessary to allegory. From this point of view we can see why personification so distinctively signals the presence of allegory. (Here, and throughout this book, by "personification" I mean the labeling of a figure in a fiction with an abstract name, like "Killjoy," and not the attribution of human qualities to an object, as the dancing of daffodils.) Personification brings into a fiction a name from outside the autonomous world (unless the whole fiction constitutes a single personification). The name usually introduces a discontinuity of form, and distracts the reader as much as an inexplicable shift in locale. The disruption results from a breach in the fictionality of the work—we expect the names of fictional persons to be fictional, wholly arbitrary, and not "given" from some extraneous scheme. The person of a personification is fantastic—we never meet such persons in the real world of common sense—but the name of a personification is realistic in the sense that it affirms, it forcibly connects the fictional world to a world we might consider true. Sansjoy is a fictional knight whose name forces us to associate him with a real thing, despair. Sansjoy is more real, with respect to his name, than Redcrosse, perhaps less real than another person in the same allegory, named Despair. This dual nature of personification, that it is fantastic in terms of fictional form but real in terms of what we (may) believe, makes it the most trustworthy signal of allegory.

When we read something that contains traditional topics found in early allegories, that is strenuously allusive, that displays discontinuity of form, and that includes personifications, we feel that we are reading an allegory. Clearly these features are not conclusive or exclusive, but they set us on the road. They share a trait: all these signs of allegory distract us from that kind of absolute engagement in the flow of a text which I cannot define, but only point to, in the hope that what I refer to is a common experience. This distraction toward abstraction, when it does not result from our own or an author's ineptitude, nearly resembles the general process of criticism of a text, and it is often observed that allegories are works which embody their own criticism. Northrop Frye says "all commentary is allegorical interpretation." Fictions tend to seem allegories when they affirm as a critic affirms. I will return to this notion later.

In brief, we recognize allegories because they are allusive, distracting, discontinuous, realistic, and critical.

ALLEGORICAL NAMES

In this book I have found it profitable to treat allegories as whole fictions, to dismiss allegories contained in larger fictions, and to avoid detailed investigation of the complex and confused matter of the linguistics of allegory: the nature of metaphor, of symbolism, of word and meaning and naming. These are hard and serious topics, proper to philosophy, but certainly the business of literary criticism. I have chosen another road into the subject of allegories.

To *name* something, to *personify* it, to *abstract* from it, to *allegorize* it, to *symbolize* it, to make it *literal*, to *signify* something by it, *typify* it, all imply certain relations between phenomena and words, and between concepts and words, which have been cast into doubt, but which must be supposed in order to describe allegory. *Abstraction* can be taken as the paradigm for these various processes. We "draw away" from the phenomenon of spilt milk, we *abstract* ourselves from it, and *name* it Bad Fortune; the *name* has no substantial link to the phenomenon, but denotes a mental operation, a concept, whose *symbol* is spilt milk. We could make a fiction in which Bad Fortune entered the plot, and *personify* the concept as a human spilling milk, *named* Malsort or Dischance. People who spill milk are pretty much all alike. We class them under the *type*, the Unfortunate, and we can permit the name of the *type* to *personify* the concept in our fiction. Or we introduce a figure into our fiction who obsessively spills milk, and does nothing but spill milk, like a figure in a drawing, or a demon; the figure begins to *allegorize* itself, to be perceived less as a representation of what it is, a human spilling milk, and more as a representation of a concept, Bad Fortune.

The jumble of terms in this last paragraph needs to be untangled. Although the various processes to which they refer are related, the terms indicate aspects of these processes from radically different points of view. These terms are the bane of allegorical criticism, the most prolific source of confusion. Our task here will be to clarify and simplify, and to remain cognizant of the circularity involved in describing naming and abstraction in a language of names and abstractions. In what follows, which is provisional, I speak of "allegory" only in its aspect of naming.

The elements of allegorical relationships are: things (*res*); the common and proper names of things (words, "institutional" *signa*); the names of things as they appear in fictions; and the reader's apprehension of the names of things as they appear in fiction. Of this series—objects, language, fictions, consciousness—the first and last items are sheer hypotheses; and, notoriously, they are inextricably intertwined. Lying behind things are the dark and vexed sciences of ontology and physics; lying behind consciousness the equally problematic sciences of psychology and epistemology. The modernist ease with which we "bracket out" the problems of being and consciousness, so that we can continue with the middle ground of language and fiction, veils anxiety—the demons are still there. In my experience, most errors in treatments of allegory have their source here: a critic will, in the midst of a sophisticated discourse, suddenly remember the problem of being ("of course, *res* are mere phenomena"), and his argument slides away. It is well, then, to acknowledge our limits at the outset.

By its nature, fiction withdraws from the question of whether its names refer to things. This is not to say that fiction has nothing to do with life; merely to say fiction is not related to life by imitating life as history imitates it. In the presence of a thing, a name is merely a mental contrivance; in the presence of a name in a fiction, the thing to which it pretends to refer is merely a mental contrivance.

We could stop the investigation at this point and say that fiction is allegory, that the intensely self-aware pretense of reference, which is (representational) fiction, constitutes what we have meant by allegory all along. Again, I argue that we must discriminate further, and recognize another operation which is peculiarly allegorical. *Allegory*, in its referential aspect, *pretends to name, not things, but whatever lies under things*—substances, relations, intentions, faculties, categories, powers, ideas. Plotinus's defense of literature, against Plato's charge that fictions were delusory shadows of shadows, was that fictions could be shadows of ideas: fictions can be allegories. Plato himself speaks of the *hyponoia*, the "underlying intelligence," of fictions, as we would speak of allegory. I am simply restating the argument that allegory is realistic, but now I am using the older definition of the real, not as the imitative and commonsensical, but as the substantial, in Platonic terms. Allegory assumes, and imposes on us, the idea that there is something underneath. Does this proposal make sense of the issues normally encountered in treatments of allegory in this area of language?

We speak of a name as "concrete" when it urges our consciousness to nestle close to the thing (milk), and "abstract" when it urges us to think of classes or aspects of things, perhaps no longer of physical things at all (nutriment). Of course the term "abstract name" is shorthand for the term "name of an abstract thing." We are to imagine a hierarchy of names, ranging from the most sensuous and material, most accidental, to the most inclusive and spiritual, most substantial, from milk to the idea of the good. The idea of the good, either deep within us or away behind things, may be considered merely the name of the ultimate class whose members are the names of good things (Nominalism), or the name of a transcendent but existent entity (Realism). Ultimate or transcendent names are members of the class of abstract names.

Allegorical names are not concrete, but abstract. The simplest and most characteristic class of allegorical names is applied to personifications, and when asked to list some personifications we first think of abstract words—Nature, Greed, Christian, Goodman. More challenging and interesting allegories often augment the list of abstract names with names one step removed from them. So we have foreign words—Natura, Sansjoy, Liberum-Arbitrium, Sortini—or words drawn from names formerly proper but reduced to abstract words— Urania, Cupid, Lucifera, Peter (their etymologies often suggest that these new-minted abstractions were abstractions in origin)—or words phonologically jumbled and enigmatic—Hawthorne's Aminadab (Bad Anima spelled backwards?), Kafka's K., Arthegall, and perhaps the group Demogorgon, Orgoglio, George. These names operate like secret causes: when they are understood, the activities of the persons who are named are understood. The more enigmatic the name, in competent hands, the freer the range of possible activity within the fiction, and the more illuminating the final disclosure of the name's referent.

It is not the pure abstractness of a name in a fiction which makes us call it personification. Proper names are the extreme of concreteness, yet arbitrary proper names happen also to be, sometimes, formally abstract words (Ecglaf, Michael, Justin), and all proper names can become abstract as they form adjectives, lose their initial capitals, or take the indefinite article (Quisling, Falstaff, Newton). Furthermore, with more difficulty, one can imagine a normally concrete name applied to a personification in an allegory. "Milk," in the fictional setting of a flier for the Dairy Association, may come to name not the thing but a commodity, or a universal good. The rarity of this kind of personification implies that it is a boundary condition, and hence that our analysis, along the lines of abstract and concrete, proper and common names, cuts the right way.

The identifying characteristic of personification is most easily grasped negatively. If, in a fiction, a person "behaves" (as agents in fictions behave) in a way contrary to what his name leads us to expect, we sense either the absence of personification, or incompetence. If we understand the name "Malecasta" correctly, we feel that we are misled if she behaves chastely. Usually a personification signals itself by its abstract name, but it always signals itself by the conformity of its behavior to its name. This identification derives from the concept of form as that which defines our expectations. We may err in understanding a fictional person's name or his behavior, and thereby fail to know whether or not he is a personification; but these matters of critical discernment have no bearing on the status of personification.

That the names given to personifications are usually abstract names follows from the fact that they imply a certain kind of behavior. Concrete names do not possess the verblike, predicative force of abstract names. "Milk" suggests, normally, only the thing milk, whereas "Pride" suggests being proud and "Nature" suggests *naturans* or *naturata*. Further, as Angus Fletcher has noted, the strict congruence of a personification's behavior with its name lends it an obsessive, demonic character, which may point to the origins of personification.

When we give a person a name, in fiction or out, we capitalize its initial; but only in fiction do we expect a person to behave in accordance with some principle resting within the name—unless we hold, as many peoples do, opinions like those of Walter Shandy. Because, as we have noted, a proper name is radically concrete—it points to a unique thing, a class with one member—a personification merges the abstract (and real) and the concrete (and fictional). The merger, secure enough within the fiction, unstabilizes the reader's mind as his apprehension is drawn in two directions at once. A skillful allegorist exploits this division.

The peculiar property of personification, the merging of the concrete and the abstract, brings us to two terms, symbol and metaphor, which have to be considered as received problems in the criticism of allegory. While it should first be observed that neither a symbol (necessarily) nor a metaphor is a name, and hence neither is identical to a personification, the terms are related to personification and to allegory. Treatments of the relation of symbolism to allegory may be traced to Goethe and Coleridge, and I refer the reader to C. S. Lewis's and Edwin Honig's books on allegory for comment on these matters. In the Romantic period, there existed a tendency to speak of good allegory as symbolism, and bad allegory as allegory. Very likely the reason for this is the abuse of personification by lesser poets of the eighteenth century.

When Blake writes, "O rose, thou art sick," the grammar of the rhetorical address, the invocative apostrophe, nearly turns the word "rose" into a personification. But not quite: the rose is a "thou" only rhetorically, because it does not behave as a person in the fiction. Yet something draws us away from the object named by "rose" as we read this and the rest of the lines of the poem. Roses, the objects, are traditional sumbols of love. We normally speak only of animals and abstractions (people, governments) as being sick. Both the tradition and the discontinuity suggest that the word "rose" in this poem refers to more than an object, a rose.

In this respect, symbols are like personifications. The differences should be noted. The word "rose" is neither an abstract nor a proper name. As a common, concrete name it draws attention immediately to the object. We consider that it is the object, and not the name (word) "rose," which is the channel of our attention as we draw toward the concept "love." It makes no difference whether we consider the word or its object the channel—by any other name it smells as sweet. Furthermore, we sense no radical merger of disparate entities when we associate the word "rose" with the thing, a rose, whereas we do when we associate the name "Pride" with a fictional woman. On the other hand, when presented with the word "rose," our minds have to go far to arrive at the concept "love," and the further we go the less sure we are that we have arrived at the right place. When presented with the woman named Pride, our journey is controlled, and the goal present at the beginning: personifications skip a step.

The boundary cases between symbol and personification are of two sorts. First, a personification may be also a symbol. Spenser's creature Lust is a personification, but he is described as resembling the male genitalia, and as such he works as a symbol (of lust). As if to recognize him as a boundary case, Spenser names him only in the lemma of the canto (4.7) in which he appears, and there in lowercase letters. He is not a knight, not even a wild man, but still not quite the thing itself. More complex but related cases are of the second sort, in which fictional persons seem scarcely to be personifications, yet their proper names enigmatically hint at less than arbitrary qualities. The Old Testament has many of these cases. Hawthorne's Coverdale suggests the concealed or muffled heart; his Aminadab may suggest the bad part of the soul; his Herkimer may jumble the word "America."

In this book I seldom use the term "symbol," for two reasons. The term is often confused with the more general term "sign," and people speak of "anything that refers" as a symbol. But along with symbols, names and personifications are also signs, as are parts of wholes and temporally or causally related phenomena (natural signs). Also, the term "symbolism," as distinct from "allegory," has acquired an aesthetic value, especially in Romantic and post-Romantic thought. The reasoning has been that symbols maintain their concrete (and appreciated) sense while they simultaneously refer to what they symbolize; or even that symbols do not refer at all, at least not to any concept, but simply, full of implication, glow. In contrast—so this theory holds—allegory—for which we must read, "personification"—mechanically lays down the whole system of reference, provides no room for the play of the imagination, kills the object in favor of the concept (compare, "the letter killeth . . . "), grabs us by the lapels. I share Coleridge's (and Hawthorne's!) distaste for the thinness, preachiness, and dullness of which personification is capable, but I notice that I am immersed in a tradition of leaden, hectoring symbolism just as he was immersed in a tradition of abused personification. Symbols do refer; if a literary object looks as if it were going to refer, if it has a referential form, and does not refer, we should give it another name than symbol. Our inability to be precise and confident about the things referred to by symbols does not oblige us to give up the idea of reference. The rose of Blake's poem may refer to innocence or the imagination, instead of (or together with) love, but it refers.

Some modern cant has it that "symbols" refer merely to themselves, or to silence. If a symbol refers only to itself, then the thing to which it refers has become both itself and a referent, a thing symbolized (we murder to dissect). This is analogous to abstraction. This kind of reference is interesting—Wordsworth may be thought to have achieved it—just as the separation of an object from a homogeneous mass and the illumination of it by a critical consciousness is interesting; but self-reference is not the abolition of reference. If silence is an entity (*res*), then reference to it is the usual kind of reference. If silence is not an entity, then I fail to see why we call the object which refers to silence a symbol, or for that matter, what we are talking about at all. To speak of symbolism as a "poetry of silence" is to confuse the science of reference with the science of phenomenology. I suspect the villain here is the preference, which everyone feels on occasion, of silence to talk, of immediate and sensuous apprehension to language, of music to poetry. But neither symbolist poetry, nor criticism, lacks words.

Finally, I would argue that the merging of concrete and abstract in a symbol differs in form from the same merging in a personification, but that the difference gives no intrinsic aesthetic syperiority to a symbol. Confusion here is rife, because of failure to maintain discriminations between name and thing, concrete and abstract, and proper and common. What is usually forgotten is that personifications are concrete in that they are persons. A. D. Nuttall, in his interesting study of allegory in terms of the British empiricist tradition, observes that the term "idea," which etymologically suggests "visual emblem" as well as "concept" or "form," compasses in itself the dual nature of allegorical images. The aesthetic question is illegitimately raised with regard to the issue of concreteness, when one should raise it with regard to the response which a fiction elicits. It is not the presence or absence of personifications which allows us to evaluate fictions, but the presence of things stirring, of whatever sort. The maker of a fiction imposes an interpretation, it is true, when he labels a person with an abstract name, but this labeling is not the only phenomenon which the fiction presents, except in the case of incompetence (or our misunderstanding). The room for the free play of our critical

27

imaginations is as great in fictions which include personifications as in those which include only symbols, or neither. We go wrong here when we take the use of a personification or a symbol as the grounds for judging a whole fiction.

Like symbols, metaphors are not exclusive signs of the presence of allegory, but only local tropes. We will treat the classical rhetoricians' idea of "extended metaphor" later, but here let us glance briefly at the relation of metaphor to symbol and personification. The obvious distinction is that metaphors are relations of two (explicit) terms, whereas symbols and personifications are composed of one term. Some metaphors resemble personifications in their explicit yoking of a concrete fictionalized object (flame) with an abstract name (love) as in "I burn with the flame of love." One might find a personified flame labeled "Love" in a fiction. The difference, obviously, is that the two terms of metaphors are not essential parts of the fictional form—they are not part of the pretense but, as it were, commentary. A fictional agent cannot be burned with a flame of love as long as the flame remains metaphor, but can only talk about it. We say, oddly, that the fictional person cannot *literally* be burned. When both the terms of a metaphor become perceptible to the (fictional) senses, causative, and active in a fiction, they cease to be terms of a metaphor, and become personification, or, if left implicit and unlabeled, symbol. Either term of a metaphor can be proper or common, abstract or concrete. Like personification, and in opposition to symbol, the immediate term of a metaphor, the "tenor" (love), is usually abstract, in comparison with the "vehicle" (flame).

The explicitness of metaphor and the grammatical machinery which signals it (especially in the case of simile), make its technique of reference overt. Hence metaphors are temporary phenomena in a fiction: visible in them is the deliberate decision by narrator or character to assert a comparison, which can prove wrong or go away at will. Chaucer's narrator may decide that the comparison of Troilus to a lion no longer serves his purpose, and so relinquish the metaphor, but personifications and symbols cannot be banished so easily from a fiction. Personifications and symbols are not, like metaphors, meditations upon fictional characters, objects, and events, but rather they *are* fictional characters, objects, and events. Once posited, they are inalienable if continuity is preserved. The medieval exegetes were right not to treat metaphor and its kindred tropes as part of the "spiritual" level of meaning of the Bible.

Still to consider are two terms connected with the linguistic apparatus of allegory: "type" and "literal." These are treated in other sections. Here I have tried to bring out the distinctions which our lexicon of allegorical terminology is capable of making. The critical instruments of this analysis have been simple: the distinctions between fiction and reality, abstract and concrete, proper and common, name and thing, and the ideas of substance and of discontinuity. I find with some relief that I have avoided, except incidentally, the concepts of "meaning" and "intention."

KINDS OF ALLEGORY

We distinguish "an allegory," which has a plural, from "allegory." The latter, often called a "mode," is the stumbling block of allegorical theory. The very inclusiveness of the term "mode" poses the problem; in the proposition "allegory is a mode," the predicate scarcely escapes from the subject. The word "allegory" refers to a way of *speaking* (agoreuein), so we could accept the description of the process of allegorical naming, in the last section, as a provisional index of the content of "allegory" as such. But this equates the mode with what I consider among the signs of the mode, allegorical names —the reasoning is circular. We need to back off, to look at works which we call "allegories," and to return to this problem later.

For the remainder of this book, I consider the term "an allegory" to refer, unlike the terms "symbol" or "personification," to a whole fiction. I take narrative fiction, as epos or as drama, to be primary. Although it is easy to imagine a lyric which includes personifications, it is not easy to imagine a pure lyric, a lyric without a story, which we would comfortably call "an allegory." Allegories require persons engaged in events—beginnings, middles, ends. The boundary case would be a description of a static scene, laden with personification, like an emblem or triumph. If we can call such a description an allegory, I propose that we conceive of the scene as a stilled moment in a moving narrative. The archetypal description of this sort, the pageant, contains the very vehicle of motion—the triumphal car. Pictures like Dürer's which we call "allegories" are moments of narrative, and we "read" them. Allegorical names pose a state of being, but allegories have a temporal dimension. We can reserve the adjective, "allegorical," for the kinds of things which pertain to allegories; but an allegory is a whole fiction.

Narrative fictions may be analyzed into their form and their content. Form, that which governs a reader's expectations concerning the whole fiction, is classified into genres; content consists of the particular persons, things, and events, and the particular words, which we find in a particular fiction. Along these lines we can discern two kinds of allegories which, as far as I can see, are fundamental. They are typology and reification (thing-making). Lying under each is a sort of proto-allegory. Under typology lies a myth (a story), full of mystery and authority, laden with potential significance. Under reification lies a literary trope, often personification. When a trope of this sort, an allegorical name, ceases to be merely a part of a fiction, or as Marc-René Jung puts it, when it becomes no longer an *ornatus*, a decoration of the rhetorical surface of the fiction, but an autonomous agent, the fiction becomes an allegory. The kind of allegory which is typology seizes upon a form, a genre; reification seizes upon content, a thing. Let us take up these two in turn.

When a narrator wishes to explicate his own discourse, among the devices to which he may resort, such as repetition, wordplay, and metaphor, is the exemplum or parable (from *parabola*). This is a story, told by way of illustration, whose elements correspond to some elements of the narrator's principal theme, which I will call "the frame," as the two segments of a parabola correspond. (This is not, by the way, an allusion to the actual etymology of the geometric term "parabola.") In use we roughly distinguish an exemplum—an *old* story, the narrative analogue of many proverbs, old metaphors—from a parable, a story composed *ad hoc*. In fact both forms often present themselves as old stories, bits of popular or learned culture. Exempla and parables are figures, rhetorical tropes.

If we could imagine an exemplum or parable removed from its narrative or discursive frame, as a narrative standing alone without such signals as "The kingdom of heaven is like . . . ," then we would have a simple and whole fiction. Let us further imagine that this whole fiction elicits, by some means, an interpretation, and that the interpretation amounts to the same discourse or narrative as the original context which we imagined as framing the exemplum. Now we can call the whole fiction an allegory of the kind called typological.

The relation of a typological allegory to its interpretation, its framing discourse, is analogous to the relation of a symbol to the "tenor" of the suppressed metaphor which the symbol implies. (Compare *parabola* and *symbolon*.) A rose is to love as the action of the parable of the sower is to the action of judgment. A typological allegory need bear no grammatical signal of its relation to its "interpretation" (the implied narrative discourse, fictional or not, which would frame the allegory if it were an exemplum); the relationship is discovered when the similarity is perceived. In the first section of this chapter we looked at how this discovery may take place.

I hasten to offer the traditional definition of typology, and to accommodate these proposals to it; I think my notion of typology includes, and extends the implications of, the traditional view. In Biblical hermeneutics, typology is defined as the recognition of Old Testament persons or events as foreshadowings of persons and events in the New Testament. A. C. Charity formulates it: "the science of history's relation to its fulfilment in Christ." David, the Tree of Life, are types; Christ, the Cross, are antitypes. In the last few years, especially since the appearance of Erich Auerbach's essay "Figura," the term typology has also been used in non-Biblical criticism, where it is defined, again in Charity's words, as "either the broad study, or any particular presentation, of the quasi-symbolic relations which one event may appear to bear to another—especially, but not exclusively, when these relations are the analogical ones existing between events which are taken to be one another's 'prefiguration' and 'fulfilment.' "

At first it appears that my definition of typology is much broader than these traditional ones, but note that the traditional definitions of typology go far beyond my proposal in one important respect: they do not limit themselves to fiction. In traditional Christian hermeneutics, of course, there is no question of fiction, as the Bible merely records what is God's action of prefiguration and fulfillment in history. My use of the term typology must avoid the idea of history on this level, because in this book I speak of allegory, which is a kind of fiction, and fiction has nothing immediately to do with history. The consequence of this difference bears on the matter of allusion, which, in any definition, will be the principal sign of typology. For us, the recognition of an allusion will not imply the recognition of anything in the historical past. Strictly speaking, I assume, there is

31

nothing about the *Aeneid* which makes it a part of the historical past, or at least nothing which restricts it, as a fiction, from being as present as anything else we conceive of as being present. We can use the term "old fiction," if we keep in mind that we refer to the time of composition of the fiction, and often to the accumulated weight of its authority, but not to its presence or absence from our time.

We have set aside the notion of typology as a relation in time. Still, our proposed definition of typological allegory differs from the usual definition of typology. In our definition the form of the allegory elicits the text which might have been its frame, as an exemplum elicits the homily in which it is inserted. It may be objected that a typological allegory—that is, a narrative which presents a type—is not enclosed in its interpretation—its antitype—nor is the antitype a discourse, it is (the narration of) an event. Neither the story of Christ's entombment nor "The Rime of the Ancient Mariner" encloses the story of Jonah and the whale; nor is the story of Jonah and the whale a type of a sermon on death. Again, I have extended the usual definition in order to be more inclusive. The usual typological relation, when it is taken as a relationship in fiction, sets one story against another; I go a step further, and propose that the second, "alluded to" story, the antitype, either is or implies a discursive, nonfictional interpretation as well. The account of Jonah does imply a discourse on death, especially (for a Christian audience) by way of the account of Christ's burial, and that sermon may be said to enclose the story.

I have two motives for introducing this perplexity. First I want to put all the narratives which, by their form, reveal themselves as allegory into one category, for the sake of a simplicity which I hope is heuristic. Second, I want to set aside questions of temporal priority, such as "which is the type and which the antitype?" as misleading. A common feature of typology, including the four typological allegories which we are to treat in the first part of this book, is the presentation of the "type," the presented fiction, *after* the fact of the antitype. When we deal with post-New Testament allegories, we have to speak of relations of authority or of interpretation, not of history.

If we understand a typological allegory as an unframed exemplum, we grant that either a discourse or a story can act as the implied frame, so to speak, of the allegory which we read. A story may interpret another story. The first story may be authoritative, because of the antiquity of its composition, its cultural importance, its perfection, its presumed inspiration. When one story alludes to another by resembling its form, our attention is drawn to the form itself, the *tertium quid*. All descents to the underworld in fictions delineate a collective frame of interpretation. We tend to speak of a fictional descent to the underworld as a typological allegory if it draws us inevitably to the most authoritative one (Christ's, for example), and hence to the accumulated discursive interpretations of the Harrowing of Hell. It might also be argued that discursive interpretations of stories depend ultimately on stories, for instance on a philosophical myth or a creation myth.

The case of the Bible, if we may conceive of it as fiction, most clearly presents typology. Once the exegete has discovered the similarity between the Old story and the New, he scarcely feels a need to offer more in the way of interpretation. The relationship is the meaning; for the exegete, there is no meaning beyond the story of Christ. The story of Christ is the "other-speech," and in medieval exegesis the typological interpretation was usually called the "allegorical." In Charity's terminology, the other fictions which resemble the form of the New Testament narrative can be only, for the Christian, "subfulfilments" of the ultimate antitype, the life of Christ. Further, the various fictional forms which imitate the central, most authoritative, form are not only interpreted by the central form (before or after the date of composition), but interpret it. We understand Christ's heroism and kingship better if we see him through the form of David; St. Paul's vision of the heavens acquires some of its value for us when we see its form repeated by Dante.

I said before that typological allegories reveal themselves as allegories through their form. Of course other signals may draw us to look at a typological allegory as such—resemblance to other allegories, personification, discontinuity of form. But it is the formal resemblance of a fiction to its interpretation, its frame or antitype, that forges the link. We feel that we are taught most authoritatively when a typological relation is established between a fiction and the Ur-form of that fiction, the most important text in the genre. Hence typology works most powerfully, as typology, when it brings a traditional genre into relation with the Bible, or the Virgilian texts, or Greek myths, or folk tales. If allegory may be said to have a standard

33

form, it would be the comic form of the Bible set in terms of the individual narrative, a Bildungsroman: an unbalanced man quests for salvation, endures adventures, and sees the city. Northrop Frye might conceive of this as the complete genre, and the other genres as fragments of it.

That more can be said about typology, the succeeding chapters will show. Likewise the other kind of allegory can be briefly described here, but I develop the idea of reification at length in the second part of this book. By "reification" I mean the posing, in a fiction, of a palpable thing (*res*), in place of (where, in another kind of discourse, we would expect) an abstraction, an idea, or another thing. The similarity of reification to personification and symbolism will be apparent; we will need to clarify the relations among these terms.

Reification includes personification and is like it in "making literal," in introducing among the physical and causative presences of a fiction something which otherwise would remain a figure of speech, a metaphor. It differs from personification in its extensiveness; unlike personification, a reification allegory affects the whole operation of a fiction, in that it "permanently" affects the nature of the literal itself.

For example, in the story of Pinocchio, the moral condition of the central character enters the fiction, no longer merely as an ethos or submerged cause, but as a physical presence. Three clichés dominate the story, as I remember it: "if you tell a fib your nose will grow"; "listen to your conscience"; "be a good boy." Each of these clichés (that is, idiomatic types) contains a metaphor, of progressively more abstract tenor: the nose as measure of truth; the conscience as audible agent; goodness as humanity. Each metaphor, in the fantasy, is reified. Pinocchio's nose grows. His conscience is personified as that (often) invisible, but audible creature whom Walt Disney called Jiminy Cricket. Finally, having become good, Pinocchio turns into a real boy: his humanity reifies his morality. Without these reifications, the story could no longer persist in recognizable form. The literal level is not only dominated by, but composed of, reified metaphors; the third one, that a good puppet is (fictionally, will become) a boy is difficult and serious, and gives the story its poignancy.

34

Furthermore, the interpretation of the story consists primarily of discovering the metaphors and the original clichés which contain the metaphors. The interpretative process resembles that of typology, but where a typological allegory usually points to a story, a reification allegory points to a single metaphor. In the case of the Pinocchio story, the excitement of interpretation arises out of the critical insight that this popular fiction is that kind of allegory, rather than out of critical insight into the ontological relation of morality to humanity. In other less popular fictions, the excitement of discovery of literary kind may be overshadowed by the excitement of discovery of the imperatives embedded in the reified metaphors.

A reification allegory like the Pinocchio story often involves the metamorphosis of the whole being of a person. Its archetypes include the Resurrection, the Circe myth, and the Pygmalion myth—I will concentrate on the last of these in this book. A particularly instructive example is that of Malbecco, treated in chapter seven, who undergoes Circean transformations until finally he is abstracted into a pure personification-without-the-person, that is, a proper name, with a ghostly crabbedness. The process Malbecco undergoes may be called reification, but it is so extreme that at last the *res*, the human creature, vanishes. Spenser gives us, in the appropriate book, a lesson on the procedure of reification allegory. At the opposite extreme from Malbecco's de-reification is the case of Pinocchio, in which the human boy at the end of the story likewise is not particularly a reification of anything, probably because integrated humans are not exactly *res*. Both Malbecco and Pinocchio virtually leave the realm of allegory, and when they do their stories are over.

Reification allegory need not involve personification. A metaphor which provides the ethos of a story may simply be embodied in the physical matter of the story, without use of abstract names. Examples, which we will meet again later in this book, are metaphors such as "the wound of love" or "her poisonous beauty," which can be literalized as wounds and poison. This kind of reification is often so pervasive in a fiction that it is difficult to perceive.

A more common kind of reification, perhaps the most common kind of allegory of all, may be called literal expressionism, or projection allegory. This is akin to hypostasis, the materializing of the divine substance (God walking in the garden), and may be defined as the reification of abstractions which are thought to be part of a complex whole. A part of the soul (a faculty), a part of the physical universe (an element), a part of the philosophical cosmos (an angel, an emanation of the Demiurge, Nature), a part of the body (a humour, the heart), a part of a pantheon (a mythical deity), a part of a social order (a class, a profession), a part of a temperament (a vice, an instinct, a passion) are given concrete status in a fiction. We can imagine creatures named Reason, Genius, Venus, and False-Seeming meeting in the same fiction, and we can ascribe this mixture of levels to the possibility of multiple reference of reification allegory.

The typical case is the projection of a character's faculty or disposition outside of himself—it is ex-pressed—onto a fictional person or object. A lascivious woman meets a person called Luxuria; an angry knight enters the Castle Irate. Fletcher observes that many of the fragmentations and realignments of the psyche which are characteristic of psychotic states have counterparts in reification allegories of projection, doubling, demoniacal persistence, dwarfishness, giganticism, and the various other forms of monstrous bewitchment. That mental states have physical components is characteristic both of psychopathology and of allegory. We observe change in a central character in an allegory, as he responds differently to similar situations, but we seldom enter him to see the process of change itself because so much of his interior is expressed by the persons and landscapes which surround him in projected reifications which cannot change. Hence the central person in a reification allegory often appears to be passive and naif, and often, in modern allegory, a mechanical clown. The moral obligation of a central character may simply be, as it surely is in the first book of *The Faerie Queene*, to pull himself together.

The form usually taken by reification allegory is personification. Personification is the local signal of reification allegory; that is, an allegorical name is the sign of this kind of allegorical narrative. A special kind of personification deserves mention here, which I call "analysis and categorization." An allegorist may apply to the various parts of a complex image—a chariot, a garden, a temple—names derived from some single parallel system. (The words "parallel" and "category," it happens, derive from the two Greek roots which form the word "allegory.") The system—for example, the philosophical terminology of ethics—is analyzed into its constituents, and these constituents are applied, one by one, to appropriate parts of the complex image—the chariot's wheels, bed, horses, driver, attendants, and so forth. The presentation of an emblem of analysis and categorization need no more dominate a whole fiction than a single personification; but the potential for elaboration of parts can imitate, locally, the thoroughgoing extension of personification in a reification allegory as it works itself out in the temporality of a whole fiction. So Langland's and Spenser's great "scenes" seem to reflect, as it were vertically, the horizontal development of the allegory. Normally, though, a reification allegory involves a person who meets reified fragments of himself and of the various orders of his world, in temporal sequence. Allegories without central persons may be treated as deviations from this norm.

Fundamental to reification allegory is the central figure himself, as he is fragmented, and as he undergoes entire ontological change. The metamorphoses of Malbecco and Pinocchio give these figures their significance. The Christian doctrine of the afterlife gives us the most powerful form of this kind of reification. Charity has described how in Dante's poem the principle of *contrapasso*, the appropriateness of the punishment to the sin, signifies that Dante's shades are reduced versions, reifications, of the moral nature of the living. A Dantesque shade is a reification of a human's moral teleology, rendered fictionally in the temporal state, "after." (We might compare Pope's sylphs, the reified afterlives of female vanities.) The play *Everyman* dramatizes the stripping away of everything but the core moral state, the presence of death and its attendant reification of the spirit. As Dante's *Comedy* is the essential moral vision, *Everyman* is the essential moral drama.

The obsessive, changeless nature of reifications, especially of the more demoniacal personifications, indicates that they are radically typical. If a person typically behaves greedily, an allegorist reifies greed and confronts the person with it in a hyperbole (compare *parabola, symbolon*) of his own state. His throat is elongated, or he meets a beast named Gula. This term "typical" resembles the term "typological." If these two kinds of allegory could be clearly related to each other, perhaps the term "allegory" could be explained. This project requires examination of several full-blown examples of allegory, such as the succeeding chapters of this book undertake.

In this book I have gathered the two kinds of allegories, typological and reification allegories, under the rubrics "allegories of history" and "allegories of love." I attempt to explain these rubrics further

37

in the Proems to each part. One kind of allegory operates by a relation, usually chronologically expressed, between one discourse and another; the other kind of allegory operates by a relation, often spatially or linguistically (paradigmatically) expressed, between names and things. The terms are not strictly parallel—hence my distinction. This technical distinction has its counterpart in two human enterprises: the social reflection on history—remembering, recording, hoping—and the personal reflection on one's self, one's relation to nature, and one's connection with others, which is love. The central image of allegories of history is likely to be the book, where records outlive marble monuments, and names are things; the parallel image is the mirror, the fleet trap of apparent images, where the self is the other.

THE ORIGIN OF ALLEGORY

A full treatment of what can be said about the origin of allegory lies much beyond my scope, but we should examine the subject briefly for the light it may shed on the nature of allegory. Literary studies commonly associate the original with the primal, hence the prior and fundamental. To arrive at the origins of allegory, even in our Western culture, very likely involves entering into a state of mind—represented, for instance, in the Pyramid Texts and perhaps some early Indian poetry—which does not acknowledge certain distinctions which we assume, distinctions between self and other, between cause and effect, between part and whole, between magic and science. So far as I can see, we cannot enter here, but only speculate.

Coleridge held that the late classical legend of Cupid and Psyche was the "first allegory completely modern in its form." He put his finger on a commonplace of the criticism of allegory, which his chief follower, C. S. Lewis, has popularized: the notion that allegorical agents developed historically from the classical divinities or daimons. The historical evidence is the ambivalent late Roman pantheon, whose deities waver in character (as the contemporary Stoic critics of Homer would expect) between gods and personifications: Psyche, Fama, Fortuna, Caesar, Discordia. This view assumes that allegorizing springs from a cast of mind which believes that the gap between

38

rational knowledge and the whole truth of things is peopled by steadily diminishing ignorance (or by things impossible of knowing), but not by angels or demons. In this view, the scientific attitude caused allegory as it removed the mana from daimons, but maintained the pantheon of daimons and reinterpreted them as personifications. James Nohrnberg terms this source of allegory "partially decomposed animism." The process, of course, is still under way among us, as is a counterprocess, a remythologizing.

This view may be partial, in that it may not account for the whole phenomenon of allegory, and of course it may articulate the right facts in the wrong way. Still, the notion of allegory as a more or less accidental by-product of the cultural process of demythologizing helps us to understand the special power of allegory in less science-ridden cultures than our own. A man in the old days of "mythical consciousness" would believe (can this be the right word?) that a stone falls because of a daimon force which he calls Weight. He makes a humanoid idol, calls it the idol of Weight, and worships it. At some point Aristotle, say, teaches him that Weight is not a daimon force, but simply a final cause, a category of the stone's entelechy. This rearrangement of terminology passes for science. Armed with this new consciousness, the new man reinterprets, "rationally," the idol he had made, and considers it a fiction which represents, as personification, a part of the new science. The difficulty of "scientific" rationalization of the soul and its faculties may account for the prominence of psychological allegory in our culture, at least up to about the time of Locke. The Enlightenment bore witness to a profound change in the nature of allegory, whose effects we will see in later chapters. In any case, the first allegorist would be the man who respected the old gods, but turned mythography into fiction. The origin of allegory in mythology may explain a complete allegory's comic form, since myths seem by nature reposed, "green," vital, and integrated.

The problem here is our ignorance of prehistorical Western culture. I find no compelling reason to assume that allegory is not as old as storytelling itself. The capacity to make metaphors very likely accompanies the capacity to speak, and allegory requires by way of mental equipment, I think, only the idea of fiction and the capacity to make metaphors. One can imagine a culture in which very much of what we would consider metaphorical expression ("I am a tiger") would not be considered metaphor ("But I *am* a tiger"); but it is hard to imagine a culture in which there is no rational, scientific thought at all, no ability to make comparisons while maintaining a knowledge of difference. For instance, political science seems to be necessary to the survival of our species; perhaps prehistoric, storytelling humans had political allegories, like Aesop's fables.

The classical rhetoricians defined allegory as continued metaphor, and included it among the tropes. Since this definition denies discontinuity, presumably, of both tenor and vehicle, it cannot suffice; nor does it imply any necessity for the continued metaphor to pervade the whole fiction. In fact the rhetorician's examples—for instance, elongated comparison of the state to a ship—are always ornaments included within a larger discourse, usually an oration. The classical definition of allegory defines one sort of what we would call a framed exemplum. The rhetoricians may be allies of, but are surely not the progenitors of allegory.

Their recognition of metaphor at the heart of allegory is just. The epistemological source of allegory is the same as the source of metaphor: the application of the Other, often the better known or more palpable, to the mystery at hand. The necessary condition of both metaphor and allegory is a recognition of the fictionality of the application; both implicitly deny any ontological identification of the Present and the Other, any homeopathic animism. A metaphor which refuses to distinguish tenor from vehicle is not a metaphor, but a magical identification; an allegory which fails to acknowledge its fictionality is not an allegory but a myth. Obviously the relationship between allegory and myth is very close. I withhold treatment of the topic until the second part of this book.

Christianity helped to eradicate classical mythology. The Bible presents only one divine myth. Monotheism and daimonism are incompatible. In the Scriptural view, the work of God in the world is accomplished not in magic and mana, in physical dislocations and transformations, but in history, in the favor and purpose which God steadily reveals to his people. To Jew or Christian, paganism is systematic idolatry. The kind of allegory which conforms to Biblical thought is typology, and typological allegoresis is found first among exegetes of the Bible. Modern exegetes, especially Protestants, are unwilling to speak of Biblical typology as allegory, and since our definition of allegory has proposed that it is fiction, we would agree—

that is, we will not consider the "allegory of the theologians" here. Nevertheless the model of typological allegory may be found in the Bible. There, historical events bear the same kind of formal resemblances, because of divine purpose, that are posed in typological allegories. As Thomas Aquinas observed, things signify under God as words signify under man (*S.T.* 1.1.10). In this sense, the Bible presents both typology and reification. Jewish and Christian worship does not consist of recognizing the Bible as allegory, but of reenacting and commemorating those events, God's things, and continuing the history.

For our subject, it is the allegoresis of the Bible, by more or less uncomprehending critics, which is most influential, but since allegoresis is a matter of critical response rather than a work's intrinsic nature, even though some allegoresis is contained in Scripture itself, the topic falls properly in the next section of this chapter. Setting this aside, the Bible presents two kinds of discourse which bear on allegory: prophetic parable and apocalypse.

Both forms tend to be political and enigmatic. The parable spoken by Jotham, in the ninth chapter of Judges, may be taken as representative. Jotham mounts upon a high place, like a prophet, speaks a dangerous parable about the choice of kings, points the parable with bitter irony at the murderous king his brother, and flees into exile. In the parable, the fruitful trees refuse to reign over the other trees, but the useless bramble accepts the throne, promising a fiery curse if the trees disobey. As is typical of parables, this one pretends to be a puzzle, an enigma; but the fact that Jotham flees after speaking it demonstrates that the application is not difficult. It is safe to say that parables (and allegories) pretend to be enigmas in order to reinforce the sense that there is a community of endangered critics who conspire in understanding. The pretense of enigma is a kind of critical fiction, which in some circumstances, for instance in the political atmosphere of modern Russia, can become also a legal fiction. "Dark conceits" and veiled allegories are not obscure to their audiences, but pretend to be obscure. A truly obscure parable or allegory must be a contradiction in terms; we can speak of allegory as retarding or redefining our recognition of the Other, but surely not as veiling it. Perhaps I beg a question which I cannot answer, but it seems to me that a description of allegory as puzzle by no means accounts for the aesthetics of allegory. Observing the pretense of obscurity, the classical rhetoricians and their followers often linked allegory with enigma, irony, and satire—the modes of speaking the thing which is not.

In an earlier section we noted that parables are not allegories, being framed fictions and not complete in themselves. The harder a parable becomes, the less frame which interprets it, or the more distant the parable itself stands from its interpretation, the closer it approaches to allegory. The process surely represents no historical progress; the clearly framed parable of the mustard seed (Matthew 13) derives from the more enigmatic, centuries older vision of the eagle and the tree of Ezekiel 17. The extreme case is the book of Revelation, which claims to describe the things which John of Patmos saw, and the things he learned when he ate the book. The claim is that Revelation is no fiction, but vision, truly recounted but surreal. The Apocalypse looks like a series of unframed parables, but still it is not quite allegory because of the claim that it is not quite fiction. As parables are not allegory because of the grammar of simile which surrounds them, so Revelation is not allegory because of its representational claim. Both forms, of course, present materials for allegory which later, deliberate, and autonomous fictions will exploit. For example, when the claim of vision which the Apocalypse makes became associated with the late classical idea of visionary dreams, its symbols and methods became available to the great series of medieval allegories, the dream visions.

The early centuries of the Christian era are among the most exciting in intellectual history, because of the ferment of ideas which grew out of the decay of the antique religions, the continuity of the literary, philosophical, and rhetorical traditions, and the vigorous, polemical righteousness of the new religion as it advanced among the literate populace. Present, in amorphous variety, were the conditions of allegory: the demythologizing of the classical pantheon, the sophisticated understanding of figures of speech like metaphors and personifications, the idea of typology, the tradition of quasi-enigmatic satire, and the polemical and philosophical allegoresis of the Bible and the classics. In retrospect it seems that Prudentius's *Psychomachia*, which unites all these potentials into an actual, pure allegory, was almost inevitable.

ALLEGORESIS

A work of literature can be mistaken for an allegory, and commented upon as such, or it may be an allegory, and receive a critical interpretation which attempts to expose its technique and its meaning. Both of these processes are called "allegoresis," and are distinguished from the process of making allegory, "allegorizing." To know which of the two kinds of allegoresis a reader is practicing, we have to decide, case by case, whether the work he is treating is an allegory. The difficulty of deciding this is the difficulty of understanding what a literary work is "in itself," in its intention as displayed in its form and content. Fortunately, the history of mistaken allegoresis is so long that we can find in it consistent motives for consistent kinds of error. Errors in allegoresis are interesting in themselves, and often provide a model for allegorizing.

The most abundant body of allegoresis is found in Biblical commentary. Since, according to our definition, there is little if any allegory in the Bible, most Biblical allegoresis is not based on the actual allegorical character of the Bible, and needs to be explained by the principle of "accommodation." This word has two senses. The first sense, which Dante terms "condescension" (*Par.* 4.43–45) and Thomas Aquinas terms "convenience" (*S.T.* 1.1.9, cited by Charity, p. 186), is God's graceful accommodation of his intelligible substance to the limitations of the human sensorium, as when he appears with hands and feet. I will not speak of this as "accommodation," but as above, as "hypostasis." The other sense is relevant here, the modernizing reinterpretation of old literature which has become for some reason no longer comprehensible or dignified (if it ever was), in spite of its canonical centrality. As certain prescriptions of the Torah became, over the centuries, alien to the mores of the Jewish community, became Other, or as certain prophecies seemed to go unfulfilled, or as a transforming sensibility of religious dignity made texts like the Song of Songs a problem, Jewish haggadic commentators began to concoct allegorical interpretations. The Strack-Billerbeck commentary on the New Testament from the Talmud and Midrasch fully reveals the influence of these commentaries on allegoresis within the New Testament, especially on the idea of typology. The interpretations which we find in the epistles, of the oxen threshing grain as the ministers of the Gospel, of Sarah and Hagar as the two Testaments, of Adam and the rock in the wilderness as prototypes of Christ, are founded on old Jewish interpretations.

In the Helleno-Roman world a parallel development had taken place with respect to the central texts—especially Homer—of mythography. The difference, of course, is great: while Jewish and Christian commentators tried to reconcile Scripture with itself, with more modern but still Scriptural revelations of God, late Greek and Roman commentators tried to reconcile their accounts of the gods with "modern" monotheism and atheism. Hence Hellenic allegoresis is more thoroughgoing. By the first century after Christ, we have a Heracleitus, cited in R. P. C. Hanson's book on early allegoresis up to Origen, interpreting the story of Athene's pulling Achilles' hair as an allegory of the state of his mind. Pure reification allegoresis of this sort goes beyond the accommodations which the Jews and the authors of the New Testament felt they needed. Moreover, Hellenistic science and theosophy in the Pythagorean tradition yielded rich and fanciful interpretations of the classical mythology. The most bizarre cosmological theories and the most obscene mysteries could be justified by an allegorical understanding of the mythographic canon. By the Christian era, accommodation could also be polemics.

The city in which the Jewish and Hellenic strands of allegoresis were most likely to meet was Alexandria, and Philo Judeus, probably a contemporary of St. Paul, reveals the consequences of that meeting in his vast allegorical interpretations of the Old Testament, particularly Genesis. His Greek affiliation is shown in a single example: explaining why God took six days to create the world, he says "the things which were created needed order" (*Leg. Alleg.* 1,2). The Greek principle of cosmic order justifies the Hebrew account of the creation, and lays the basis for the tradition of the hexameron in Biblical commentaries. Philo was willing to give up the Bible's claim to historical verity for the sake of his interpretation of the Bible as the mysterious repository of Hellenic philosophy. In this, the later Christian commentators, most authoritatively St. Augustine, differed from Philo.

The mystery religions and the hermetic speculations of the Hellenic world survived late into the Roman Christian era, but we know as little about their teachings as we know about the Jewish cabbala of the period. Much of our information about these traditions, which we may loosely group under the term "Gnostic," comes from anti-

Gnostic polemics by orthodox Christians. It is too little recognized how close was the struggle, on the one hand against the agnostic or atheistic Stoics, and on the other against the Gnostics, by the orthodox line of Christian thought up to the time of the empirical establishment of the Church and the great Fathers of the fourth century. During this period we find evidence among the preserved sources of an intensity and range of allegorical criticism of sacred and secular texts unapproached until the Italian Renaissance. The orthodox idea of the sacredness of history, and the fundamentally typological reading of the Bible, which preserved its literal level, barely won the day.

The most important fact about the early allegoresis of the Bible is its sheer magnitude. Virtually every object, every proper name (the Old Testament authorized this), every event in Scripture was yoked with others of its kind, in vast concordances compiled by commentators who seem to have known the whole Bible by heart. Once certain principles of interpretation were established, according to the dictum that "whatsoever was written, was written for our learning" (Romans 15:4), which Thomas Aquinas quotes as justification for a strained typological argument (*S.T.* 3.5.2), interpretations which seem to us mannered, surreal, and offensively antiliteral became commonplace. The things of the world could be, under the influence of Biblical commentary, taken symbolically, as the standard interpretations were applied outside of the confines of Scripture. Hence derives the common medieval metaphor of the world as God's book, in which one can read God's purpose. The symbolic view of the world has its roots in Platonic philosophy, but we may say that its plenitudinous foliage is the work of Scriptural exegesis.

Henri de Lubac has studied the responses to a need, which was felt by the Church Fathers and their medieval successors, to bring order into the morass of exegetical interpretation. It was early recognized that there were different classes of interpretations, and sophisticated thinkers like Augustine were able to associate these classes with different modes of understanding— in categories like corporeal, intellectual, spiritual. The same object or name or event could be (because it had been) interpreted in several ways, according to the design of the exegete. A word in the Bible had its own ("proper"), literal sense, and it could refer as well, "spiritually" or "mystically," or "allegorically," to the Church, to the nature of the soul, to the origins and causes of things, to the physical material and construction

45

of the universe, to the body, to Christ and the events of the New Testament, to the moral situations and crises of life, to the afterlife. These classes of interpretation may be called respectively ecclesiologi-cal, psychological, etiological, physical, anatomical, Christological or (in a narrow sense) typological, tropological, and anagogical. This list is not exhaustive, and it could be simplified according to several methods of classification.

Far the most widespread method of arranging these classes of interpretation is the "four-fold method," made famous by Dante's letter to Can Grande della Scala, and familiar to us in the medieval mnemonic:

> Littera gesta docet, quid credas allegoria,
> Moralis quid agas, quo tendas anagogia.

"The literal teaches events, the allegorical what you believe, the moral what you do, the anagogical whither you are bent." In these verses, and elsewhere in the medieval discussions of the multiple meanings of Scriptural objects and names and events, the term "level" is not used: the standard terms (as in *S. T.* 1.1.10) are "significatio" and "sensus." The metaphor of "level" implies notions of both stratification and continuity which are simply not present in medieval thought. Much modern criticism of medieval allegory has gone astray by taking its own term "level" too seriously, and looking for multiple and hierarchically arranged continuities of signification.

The four senses named in the distich usually have the less confusing names "literal" (historical, proper), "typological," "tropological" (moral), and "anagogical." Since the three last, the "spiritual" or allegorical senses, do not clearly include all the kinds of interpretations which the exegetes made, we may ask why they became so prominent as a description of the whole exegetical method. I believe Charity has the best explanation: he observes that the typological sense refers the presented object (or event or name) to the past; the tropological sense refers the presented object to our own moral present; and the anagogical sense refers the presented object to our own and the world's future—the last things. Compare historical, affective, and religious criticism. So in the example used by Dante, the "allegorical" (typological) sense of the exodus of the Israelites is its prefiguration of Christ's redemption in our past; correspondingly, the moral sense

46

of the exodus is its signification of our own individual and contemporaneous conversion to grace; correspondingly, the anagogical sense of the exodus is its figuration of our future liberation in eternal glory.

From this it may be gathered that the fundamental principle of the fourfold method of interpretation is typological, having to do with the relation of patterned events in time. This conforms to our observation that the essence of orthodox exegesis is typological, to the salvation of history. The other senses, the physical and psychological and etiological and the rest, could never become as important. If it seems useful, we can classify these minor senses under a more general term, "signification of things as they are" (their causes, material, status, membership in the body or the Body of the Church) as opposed to the "signification of things as they were" (typology) and "signification of things as they will (ought to) be" (anagogy). Surely the *Divine Comedy* perfectly embodies, in its general conception, the fourfold method.

Implicit in our argument is an assumption which C. S. Lewis did not hold, that the allegoresis of the Bible, as influenced by Hellenic allegoresis, had a part in the origins of allegory. In *The Allegory of Love*, Lewis set aside the tradition of commentary,'and focussed his attention on the tradition of personification as preserved in classical narrative up to Statius. There is no denying the importance of classical personification as an influence on Prudentius and his followers, but criticism of allegory since Lewis has tried to right a balance by recognizing more influence from patristic sources on early allegorizing. In the next chapter, for instance, I argue that the *Psychomachia* reconciles Virgilian demonism with the Biblical view of history— classical personification with exegetical typology. Inattention to either source would fail to account for the peculiar nature of allegory in our culture. As the beautiful lies of mythology, in the antique Hellenic world, were transformed into deliberate fiction, so the beautiful errors of early Christian allegoresis were transformed into deliberate allegory.

WHAT IS ALLEGORY?

We have considered now the question of how one recognizes allegory, the characteristics of names in allegory, the kinds and origins of allegory, and some early forms of allegoresis which influenced the making of allegory. It remains to offer a working definition of allegory.

We immediately meet questions of degrees and boundaries: does the domain of allegory have a fixed limit? Many would consider Kafka's *The Castle*, which I treat in this book, an allegory, and many would not. The criterion of ordinary language defines the subject's center, not its edges. Practical criticism, and certainly discussion in the classroom, can leave the question unsettled, since the application of a given term to a work is less important there than an accurate description of that work. Still, we need to make the theoretical effort.

We can say what is *not* allegory. Allegory is not accidental or irrational. Neither fantasy, as we observed before, nor naturalism, insofar as naturalism properly imitates the apparently random flow of history, can be allegory. Hence allegory is deliberate and structured according to certain principles. Allegory is an artifice, and bears the same relationship of control to the whole world of discourse that a laboratory experiment bears to nature. Variables are carefully restricted, and insofar as results appear natural, knowledge is acquired. Allegory is a *knowing* sort of literature.

Much fiction shows signs of artificial control—one may say all poetry does. Allegory (as always, I mean "allegorical narrative") controls, not a fiction's length or phonological form, but the nature of its characters—especially their names—and the particular events of its plot. Ficino observed that when motion is orderly, we see that it is directed; the same argument from design applies to allegory. Allegory is rational in the old sense derived from *ratio*: measured, proportionate. Its plot cannot be free, as in fantasy, or wholly subsumed in wayward experience, as in naturalism. As a fiction moves toward the typical, through and beyond realism, or toward the ideal, through and beyond romance, it approaches allegory. Like satire, allegory tends to be encyclopedic, and like romance, it tends to be simple of plot and character.

The typical and the ideal can be described without reference to fiction. It is peculiar to allegory to seem to elicit descriptions of the typical and the ideal—the abstract—as if they were *applicable* to the fiction, as criticism or explanation of intention. Three terms we have noticed—"symbol," "hyperbole," "parabola"—all have to do with allegory, and all contain a metaphor of placement, of "throwing" things together, or juxtaposition. Any fiction can lead its reader toward reflection upon things, or toward introspection; but only allegory leads its reader toward a particular discourse or idea, or fails if it does not. Allegory, either typology or reification, signals the Other. Like a sacrament or a dream, or like such mysterious experiences as ecstasy, love, inspiration, or death, allegory draws two worlds together: the world expressed by the fiction, and the implicit world of authoritative myth or abstract statement. If fiction holds the mirror up to nature, allegory holds the mirror up to the ordering forms of the mind—old stories and ideas. In allegory, mental experience is made concrete, and physical experience is made abstract. What I said above about allegorical names may be said of allegory in general: it is at once arbitrary and autonomous, affirming nothing, connected and referential. Allegory, like intelligence itself, respects both the different and the same.

Allegory is hard to define because one wishes to avoid making it seem forbidding. The visible control of characters and events which allegory exerts may have its source in the author, but its force is felt on the reader. Allegory is, after all, didactic in impulse, even if not simply so. Allegory can enforce certain interpretations, or at least prohibit certain ones. Sansjoy may not be Despair, exactly, but he is certainly not Faithlessness. This control may be felt as unattractive imposition, especially if the allegory is poorly wrought or if the reader is ignorant and perplexed. At its best, the puzzle solving which is part of the reader's experience amounts to a re-creation of the allegorist's world, but it can be also merely irritating. Allegory is, in literary terms, conservative because it relies on special knowledge of language and it alludes to old literature. As the poet says, it must be abstract. Allegory loses in coldness and intellectualism what it gains in freedom and knowledge. All fiction works by indirection, but allegory refuses to conceal its artifice and its scheming. After all, allegory may be considered relatively artless.

The idea of allegory is more profoundly disturbing. It seems to know too much, to overmanage fiction; and it seems not to know the perfect thing, that absolute merger of form and content which characterizes the greatest fiction. It is (one may feel) bullying and narrow. Against these charges I can only point to the consummate allegories themselves: how the first book of *The Faerie Queene* poses the humanist fiction that the arbitrary and the contingent are not of this world; how the third and fourth books of *The Faerie Queene* finally relinquish allegory; how Dante collapses the unfurled cosmos of *Paradise* behind his pilgrim; or how Kafka in *The Castle* challenges, by allegorical form, the principles of reference, analogy, and allusion which are the basis of allegory.

For two reasons I suspect that the categories "reification" and "typology" constitute the fundamental, and inclusive, division of kinds of allegory. *Probet lector.* The first reason is historical. In the Judaic tradition of allegoresis of the Bible, typology predominates as a method for a variety of reasons: the respect for history, the repeated ritual celebrations of important events, the distrust of hypostasis, the distrust of a symbolic view of the world. The Hellenic tradition of the allegoresis of Homer is predominantly in favor of reification, again for a number of reasons: the sophisticated theories of ideas and forms and emanations, the complex vocabulary of psychology, the relative disinterest in history, the dissolving pantheon. The two traditions have divided the world of allegory between them.

A second reason, already mentioned, for the basic division of the kinds of allegory is its correspondence to a fundamental division of aspects of fiction, usually labelled "form" and "content" (more fashionable recent terms might be metonymic and metaphoric, or syntagmatic and paradigmatic). The form of a narrative involves its temporality: the chronology of its events, the sequence of the narration, its correspondence with received earlier forms, the process of apprehension by the reader. When any of these times of a narrative becomes reflexive—recalling, juxtaposing, or repeating material in interesting ways—there is a potential for the establishment of that broad relation of events called typology. The content of a narrative consists of its elements considered, as it were, spatially—as objects, as bits of language, landscapes, persons, sounds. When an object in a narrative shows signs of having acquired its place there because of some idea, it begins to look like a reification. In the case of both typology and reification, of both the allegory of form and the allegory of content, it is the sense that fictional elements are present for a reason, that they have taken on unusual interest, that leads us to allegory.

Bibliographical Note

Like the other notes in this book, this aims to document borrowings and quotations which appear in the chapters, and to list the studies by modern scholars which I have found most interesting and useful. The orientation is toward works in English, recent works, and works with bibliographies that can guide the reader further. I have in general excluded reference to unpublished theses. Abbreviations of journal titles are those listed in the *1975 MLA International Bibliography*.

The most general books on allegory are those of C. S. Lewis, *The Allegory of Love: A Study in Medieval Tradition* (London, 1936); Edwin Honig, *Dark Conceit: The Making of Allegory* (Evanston, Ill., 1959); Angus Fletcher, *Allegory: The Theory of a Symbolic Mode* (Ithaca, N.Y., 1964); and Gay Clifford, *The Transformations of Allegory* (London and Boston, 1974). Books somewhat more specialized in scope are Michael Murrin, *The Veil of Allegory: Some Notes toward a Theory of Allegorical Rhetoric in the English Renaissance* (Chicago, 1969); Rosemond Tuve, *Allegorical Imagery: Some Medieval Books and Their Posterity* (Princeton, 1966); Ellen Douglas Leyburn, *Satiric Allegory: Mirror of Man* (New Haven, 1956); Paul Piehler, *The Visionary Landscape: A Study in Medieval Allegory* (London, 1971); John MacQueen, *Allegory*, The Critical Idiom 14 (London, 1970); Peter Berek, *The Transformation of Allegory from Spenser to Hawthorne* (Amherst, Mass., 1962); A. D. Nuttall's stimulating study, *Two Concepts of Allegory: A Study of Shakespeare's "The Tempest" and the Logic of Allegorical Expression* (London, 1967); John M. Steadman, *The Lamb and the Elephant: Ideal Imitation and the Context of Renaissance Allegory* (San Marino, Calif., 1974); and Judson B. Allen, *The Friar as Critic: Literary Attitudes in the Later Middle Ages* (Nashville, Tenn., 1971). The remarks and practice of our best critic are collected in Bernard L. Einbond, *Samuel Johnson's Allegory*, DPL, ser. pract. 24 (The Hague and Paris, 1971).

Almost every book on literary theory has some remarks about allegory. Books on special topics which have important material for the study of allegory are Walter Benjamin, *Ursprung des deutschen Trauerspiels* (Berlin, 1928); A. Phillip Damon, *Modes of Analogy in Ancient and Medieval Verse*, U. Cal. Publ. in Class. Philol., vol. 15, no. 6, pp. 261–334 (Berkeley and

L.A., 1961, 1973); Johan Chydenius, *The Theory of Medieval Symbolism*, CHLSSF 27, no. 2 (Helsinki, 1960), Fr. trans. in *Poétique* 23 (1975): 322-41; Hans Robert Jauss, *Genèse de la poésie allégorique française au moyen âge* (*De 1180 à 1240*) (Heidelberg, 1968); Marc-René Jung, *Etudes sur le poème allégorique en France au moyen âge*, Romanica Helvetica 82 (Bern, 1971); Reinhart Hahn, *Die Allegorie in der antiken Rhetoric* (Tübingen, diss., 1967); and Helen Gardner, *The Limits of Literary Criticism: Reflections on the Interpretation of Poetry and Scripture* (London, 1956).

The "Robertsonian" controversy over the allegoresis of medieval literature may be traced in D. W. Robertson, Jr., *A Preface to Chaucer: Studies in Medieval Perspective* (Princeton, 1962); Robertson, "Some Medieval Literary Terminology with Special Reference to Chretien de Troyes," *SP* 48 (1951): 669-92; and Dorothy Bethurum, ed., *Critical Approaches to Medieval Literature*, Sel. Papers from the Eng. Inst., 1958-59 (New York and London, 1960). Jean Pépin wrestles with the fundamental problems of allegory with his customary learning, lucidity, and common sense in *Dante et la tradition de l'allégorie* (Montreal and Paris, 1970-71).

General articles include John Hughes, "An Essay on Allegorical Poetry," included in his edition of Spenser, 6 vols. (London, 1715), I:xxv-lvii, and printed in Willard H. Durham, ed., *Critical Essays of the Eighteenth Century: 1700-1725* (New Haven and London, 1915), pp. 86-104; Paul de Man, "The Rhetoric of Temporality," in *Interpretation: Theory and Practice*, ed. Charles S. Singleton (Baltimore, 1969); de Man's essay "Lyric and Modernity," which appears in *Blindness and Insight: Essays in the Rhetoric of Contemporary Criticism* (New York, 1971); Jean-Charles Payen, "Genèse et finalité de la pensée allégorique au Moyen Age," *RMM* 78 (1973): 466-79; Northrop Frye, "Levels of Meaning in Literature," *Kenyon Review* 12 (1950): 246-62; William K. Wimsatt, Jr., "Two Meanings of Symbolism: A Grammatical Exercise," *Renascence* 8 (1955): 12-24; Morton W. Bloomfield, "Symbolism in Medieval Literature," *MP* 56 (1958), 73-81; Bloomfield, "Allegory as Interpretation," *NLH* 3 (1972): 301-17; Walter J. Ong, "From Allegory to Diagram in the Renaissance Mind: A Study in the Significance of the Allegorical Tableau," *JAAC* 17 (1959): 423-40; Sheila Delaney, "Substructure and Superstructure: The Politics of Allegory in the Fourteenth Century," *Science and Society* 38 (1974): 257-80; Martin Price, "Form and Discontent," *NLH* 4 (1973): 381-87; E. A. Bloom, "The Allegorical Principle," *ELH* 18 (1951): 163-90; W. T. H. Jackson, "Allegory and Allegorization," *RS* 32 (1964): 161-75; Aldo Vallone, "Personificazione simbolo e allegoria del medio evo dinanzi a Dante," *Filologia e Letteratura* 10 (1964): 189-224. I quoted from Humphrey Tonkin's intelligent review, "Some Notes on Myth and Allegory in the *Faerie Queene*," *MP* 70 (1973): 291-301. On the patristic method of recognizing allegory see Jean Pépin, "A propos de l'histoire de l'exégèse allégorique: l'absurdité, signe de l'allégorie," *Studia Patristica*, ed. Kurt Aland and F. L. Cross, TUGAL, 63:ser. 5, vol. 8 (Berlin, 1957), pp. 395–413. Learned and thoughtful on Renaissance views of the relation of allegory to Aristotle's ideas of the possible and probable in poetics is Robert L. Montgomery, Jr., "Allegory and the Incredible Fable: The Italian View from Dante to Tasso," *PMLA* 81 (1966): 45–55. John Burrow's lecture on "The Literal Level" is beginning to be cited in print: I hope he will publish it soon. Some of its ideas are echoed in Marcia L. Colish, "Medieval Allegory: A Historiographical Consideration," *ClioW* 4 (1975): 341–55.

Typology is a science whose literature is as vast as that of astronomy. The best introduction to the whole field is A. C. Charity, *Events and their Afterlife: The Dialectics of Christian Typology in the Bible and Dante* (Cambridge, Eng., 1966). Other books in the field worth consulting are Jean Daniélou, *Sacramentum futuri: Etudes sur les origines de la typologie biblique* (Paris, 1950), trans. D. W. Hubbard as *From Shadows to Reality* (London, 1961); Robert M. Grant, *The Letter and the Spirit* (London, 1957); G. W. H. Lampe and K. J. Woollcombe, *Essays on Typology* (London, 1957): Hartmut Hoefer, *Typologie im Mittelalter: Zur Übertragbarkeit typologischer Interpretation auf weltliche Dichtung*, Göppingen Arb. z. Germ., no. 54 (Göppingen, 1971); Karlfried Grunder, *Figur und Geschichte: Johann Georg Hamanns "Biblische Betrachtungen" als Ansatz einer Geschichtsphilosophie* (Freiburg and Munich, 1958); Leonhard Goppelt, *Typos: Die typologische Deutung des Alten Testaments im Neuen* (Gütersloh, 1939); the issue of *SLitI* devoted to "Typology and Medieval Literature," ed. Hugh T. Keenan, vol. 8, no. 1 (1975): and especially for seventeenth-century thought, William G. Madsen, *From Shadowy Types to Truth: Studies in Milton's Symbolism* (New Haven, 1968).

Articles on typology include Rudolf Bultmann, "Ursprung und Sinn der Typologie als hermeneutischer Methode," *Theologische Literaturzeitung* 75 (1950): 205–11; Robert Hollander, "Typology and Secular Literature: Some Medieval Problems and Examples," in *Literary Uses of Typology from the Late Middle Ages to the Present*, ed. Earl Miner (Princeton, 1977); and the influential essays by Erich Auerbach, "Typological Symbolism in Medieval Literature," *YFS* 9 (1952): 3–10, and "Figura" (1944), trans. Ralph Mannheim in *Scenes from the Drama of European Literature* (New York, 1959), pp. 11–76. The notes to C. A. Patrides, *The Phoenix and the Ladder: The Rise and Decline of the Christian View of History* (Berkeley, 1964), rev. as *The Grand Design of God: The Literary Form of the Christian View of History* (London, 1972) are rich in bibliography; so is Sacvan Bercovitch, ed., *Typology and Early American Literature* (Amherst, 1972).

On personification see Robert Worth Frank, Jr., "The Art of Reading Medieval Personification-Allegory," *ELH* 20 (1953): 237–50; Bertrand H. Bronson, "Personification Reconsidered," *ELH* 14 (1947): 163–77; Charles Muscatine, "The Emergence of Psychological Allegory in Old

INTRODUCTION

French Romance," *PMLA* 68 (1953): 1160–82; Karl Reinhardt, "Personifikation und Allegorie," wr. ca. 1937 and publ. in *Vermächtnis der Antike*, ed. Carl Becker (Göttingen, 1960, 1966), pp. 7–40; Robertus Engelhard, *De personificationibus quae in poesi atque arte Romanorum inveniuntur* (Göttingen, diss., 1881); and the fine study of personification from the linguistic point of view, Paolo Valesio, "Esquisse pour une étude des personnifications," *Lingua e Stile* 4 (1969): 1–21. To the studies of symbolism already mentioned add Susanne K. Langer, *Philosophy in a New Key* (Cambridge, Mass., 1942, 1951), and her mentor Ernst Cassirer's *Philosophie der symbolischen Formen*, 3 vols. (Berlin, 1923–29).

Scarcely distinguishable from studies of typology are the treatments of Biblical allegoresis and patristic and medieval exegesis and hermeneutics. Outdated but still pleasant to read is Frederick W. Farrar, *History of Interpretation* (London and New York, 1886). On the term hermeneutics see Jean Pépin, "L'Herméneutique ancienne: les mots et les idées," *Poétique* 23 (1975): 291–300. Also see Isaak Heinemann, *Altjüdische Allegoristik*, Bericht der Jüdisch–Theol. Seminars (Fraenkelsche Stiftung) (Breslau, 1935); Adolf Jülicher, *Die Gleichnisreden Jesu*, part 1 (Freiburg i. B., 1888); Joachim Jeremias, *The Parables of Jesus*, trans. S. H. Hooke (London, 1954, rev. from the 6th German ed., New York, 1963); C. H. Dodd, *The Parables of the Kingdom*, rev. ed. (New York, 1961); Maxime Hermaniuk, *La Parabole evangélique: Enquête exégétique et critique* (Paris and Louvain, 1947); Eta Linneman, *Jesus of the Parables: Introduction and Exposition* (New York, 1966); C. H. Dodd, *The Interpretation of the Fourth Gospel* (Cambridge, Eng., 1953); Jean Daniélou, *Les Symboles chrétiens primitifs* (Paris, 1961); Harry Austryn Wolfson, *Philo* (Cambridge, Mass., 1947); Wolfson, *The Philosophy of the Church Fathers*, vol. 1 (Cambridge, Mass., 1956, rev. 1970), esp. chaps. 2 and 3, extremely good on early Christian allegoresis; Joseph Bonsirven, *Exégèse rabbinique et exégèse paulinienne*, (Paris, 1939); R. P. C. Hanson, *Allegory and Event: A Study of the Sources and Significance of Origen's Interpretation of Scripture* (London and Richmond, Va., 1959); Henri de Lubac, *Exégèse médiévale: Les Quatre Sens de l'Ecriture*, 2 parts in 4 vols. (Paris, 1959–64); Beryl Smalley, *The Study of the Bible in the Middle Ages*, 2d ed. (Oxford, 1952); P. C. Spicq, *Esquisse d'une histoire de l'exégèse latine au moyen âge*, Bibliothèque Thomiste, 26 (Paris, 1944); Raymond E. Brown, *The Sensus Plenior of Sacred Scripture* (Baltimore, 1955).

Articles which touch on allegorical exegesis are Hermann Kihn, "Ueber θεωρία und ἀλληγορία nach den verlorenen hermeneutischen Schriften der Antiochener," *Theologische Quartalschrift* 62 (1880): 531–82; H. N. Bate, "Some Technical Terms of Greek Exegesis," *JTS* 24 (1923): 59–66; Matthew Black, "The Parables as Allegory," *BJRL* 42 (1959–60): 273–87; Raymond E. Brown, "Parable and Allegory Reconsidered," *Novum Testamentum* 5 (1962): 36–45; M. -D. Chenu, "Les Deux Ages de l'allégorisme

54

scripturaire au moyen âge," *RTAM* 18 (1951): 19–28; M. -D. Mailhot, "La Pensée de St. Thomas sur le sens spirituel," *RThom* 59 (1959): 613–63; Armand Llinares, "Théorie et pratique de l'allégorie dans le *Livre de contemplacio* de Raymond Lulle," *AHDLMA* 39 (1972): 109–36.

The art historians have been in the forefront in understanding the uses of myth in allegory. I can only name the exemplars of the Warburg school: Panofsky, Saxl, Klibansky, Cassirer, Wittkower, Yates, Gombrich, and Ghisalberti and Edgar Wind and Jean Seznec—their works are voluminous. For full bibliography see Don Cameron Allen, *Mysteriously Meant: The Rediscovery of Pagan Symbolism and Allegorical Interpretation in the Renaissance* (Baltimore and London, 1970). A few important studies are Roger Packman Hinks, *Myth and Allegory in Ancient Art* (London, 1939); the articles on Homeric allegoresis by John Tate in *ClassQ* 23 (1929), 24 (1930), 28 (1934); Jean Pépin, *Mythe et allégorie: Les Origines grecques et les contestations judéo-chrétiennes* (Paris, 1958); Hugo Rahner, *Griechische Mythen in christlicher Deutung* (Zurich, 1945), trans. B. Battershaw (London, 1963); Alain Le Boulluec, "L'Allégorie chez les Stoïciens," *Poétique* 23 (1975): 301–21; F. Wehrli, *Zur Geschichte der allegorischen Deutung Homers in Altertum* (Leipzig, 1928); and Hans Robert Jauss, "Allegorese, Remythisierung, und neuer Mythos. Bemerkungen zur christlichen Gefangenschaft der Mythologie im Mittelalter," in *Terror und Spiel: Problem der Mythenrezeption*, ed. M. Fuhrmann (Munich, 1971).

PART ONE
Marking Time

Allegories of History

The harvest is past, the summer is ended, and we are not saved.

JEREMIAH 8:20

Proem to Part One

IN part one we are to consider four allegories of the sort I have described as typological. All four are unmistakably allegories, and they seem so quintessentially characteristic of the mode as to suggest that the structure of Biblical history (*Heilsgeschichte*) to which their plots conform most distinctly elicits allegorical treatment. They are "high" fictions, summations not only of the possibilities of allegory in their respective eras, but of the central ideas of the cultures from which they spring. Their forms are radically experimental; their passion is religiously intense; their ambition is to record what is permanent and universal.

The selection of these four for study was a simple matter: each concludes with obtrusive allusions to the Apocalypse and the imagery of the last book of the Bible. This observation guides our criticism toward constant retrospection, so we look at the works from the point of view of their ends. I have compared these four works in order to make out the main features of typological allegory, to discover the historical movements of thought and the formal matters of genre which make the four different from each other, and to treat each work in itself, in terms of the present state of criticism of each as an allegory and as a fiction. We want to see what is constant, what is conditioned by genre and intellectual history, and what is unique. The four allegories endlessly repeat the same story, and we look for what is the same and what is different.

59

The most remarkable constant feature of the four, spread in time over a millennium and a half, is the expression of the sense that the end of time is present and yet not present. The works are all decidedly linear in impulse and directed toward the final disclosure of the apocalypse, but each permits a disruption of the steady line of development toward revelation by inclusion of a figure who gives the lie to the optimism of Christian history. I call this figure the liar, the *mendax*, and trace his origin to the Fury Alecto in the *Aeneid*. His power conspicuously increases as we move from work to work until, with Melville, he takes over the fiction, rivaling the author.

Starting at the turn of the fifth century, with the *Psychomachia*, which is all personification, we find less and less strict personification allegory until, again with Melville, there is almost none. Doubtless this has to do with a change in taste; primarily it is a paradoxical function of the progressive interiorization of character in fiction. The "inside" of the *Psychomachia* is technically full—there is a complete complement of vices and virtues—but the experience of the poem is all external, of discrete warriors in combat on a plain. As allegorists become more sophisticated in their researches into the *bellum intestinum*, their devices of exposition become more fluid and less easily identified. The reader's role as interpreter becomes more strenuous, and pure personifications are pushed aside.

Finally, it may be noted that the recognition of the incompleteness of history, which the epigraph from Jeremiah conveys, is taken in all four allegories to lay a moral burden upon the reader to bring about a final revelation within himself. Although they are apocalyptic, none has the air of sublime removal from the things of the world which the term "visionary" can imply. But the works are not equally fervid in temper. One would have thought the hotter genres of epic and novel, used by Prudentius and Melville, would be particularly turbulent and passionate, and that Langland's dream vision and Spenser's romance would be cool and distant. But not so: nothing is more striking among these four than the moral, prophetic rage of Melville and Langland, to the extent that their forms nearly disintegrate, in contrast to Prudentius and Spenser. This seems to be less a matter of the allegorical mode or the circumstances of genre or era than of individual temperament. My effort to deal with such characteristics in their own terms, even when they run against the course of my argument, has given the book its length, but, I hope, a respect for fact.

CHAPTER TWO

The Siege of Paradise

PRUDENTIUS'S *Psychomachia*

Luctificam Alecto dirarum ab sede sororum,
Infernisque ciet tenebris . . . .

Aeneid 7.324–25

sic expugnata Vitiorum gente resultant
mystica dulcimodis Virtutum carmina psalmis.

Psychomachia 663–64

. . . Quoniam in furorem versus est.

MARK 3:21

THE *Psychomachia* commands the attention of the student of allegory
as the first long Christian allegory and the first extensive work which
everyone would call an allegory. Its primary force has been, I suspect,
not to teach us of "corporei latebrosa pericula operti / luctantisque
animae . . . casus" (the hidden dangers of the recesses of the body, and
vicissitudes of the struggling soul), but rather to establish the lineaments of one kind of allegorical fiction for the medieval and modern

worlds.* Its effect, though perhaps not its intention, has been literary rather than moral, in spite of the Carolingian comment that "totus liber est moralis."

REDUCTION

The plot of the *Psychomachia*, its articulation of the succession of events, is universally acceptable and useful, a virtue which has far outweighed certain defects, at least during the Middle Ages, when it was popular and influential. Prudentius represented in a simple and peculiarly *literary* form a quality of experience which we meet more often in the midst of flux and ambiguity and a demanding variety of possibilities, in life and in more mimetic fictions. The experience is that of learning to be good or, in Prudentius's terms, of receiving Wisdom and Christ's temple in the heart. There are various ways of depicting the acquisition of experience; part of the simplicity which we sense in the *Psychomachia* is Prudentius's choice almost exclusively of combat as the vehicle of experience, at least in the first part of the poem (up to line 639). The poet claims victory for the reader who can mark ("notare") the virtues in combat at close quarters (18–20). Conflicting figures meet on a battlefield: the good ones win. Literature which is episodic, especially when the episodes are structurally parallel, always seems simpler and more fundamentally fictional than complicated plots, and the presentation of successive episodes of single combat as the expression of any agon is a most usable artifice.

The *Psychomachia* also displays another kind of literary reductiveness: Prudentius presents no human protagonist. The opponents are segments of a whole person, personifications of virtues and vices. The lack of a single human figure in conflict has led, in fact, to difficulty among commentators who attempt to explain the poem's title: whether it be the battle *of* the soul against vices, which are then usually located in the members of the body; or whether it be the battle *in* the soul of vices and virtues seen as segments of the soul. Aside from any theological importance, this issue would be a trivial

---

*Citations refer to the Loeb Library edition, ed. and trans. H. J. Thomson (Cambridge, Mass., and London, 1949), here lines 892–93. Other bibliography is appended in a note at the end of this chapter. Unless otherwise noted, translations are my own.

one for a literary critic, if it were not understood that the important question is where to locate the protagonist, the "center of consciousness" of the action, or, more broadly, how to treat a fiction which presents no whole human protagonist. The major successors of Prudentius—the authors of *Le Roman de la Rose*, *Piers Plowman*, *The Faerie Queene*, and *Pilgrim's Progress*—have all provided human persons who are more or less complete. Readers of Spenser are familiar with the problem of whether Guyon or Redcrosse is, or represents, or manifests, or acquires his virtue of temperance or holiness.

Reinhart Herzog, in his study of Prudentius's allegory, compared the technique of the *Psychomachia* to the kind of personification allegory in Prudentius's (probably) earlier poem, the *Hamartigenia*. In his account of the origin of evil, the poet there depicted an "angelus degener" (debased angel), a "praedo potens" (powerful robber) who urges vices into combat against men's souls—Ira, Superstitio, Maeror, Discordia, Luctus, Sanguinis Sitis, and several more (389 ff.). According to Herzog, the *Psychomachia* represents a technical advance over the *Hamartigenia* by introducing personified virtues, rather than the soul of man in general, in combat with these vices, thus avoiding the fictional problem of illustrating a man and a personified abstraction in a single action, a problem analogous to "mixing levels" in philosophical discourse.

This genetic explanation can help us understand the absence of a whole man in the center of the *Psychomachia*, and can even clarify certain anomalies in the fictional level of the poem. The allegory that personifies virtues and vices as warriors fails to "square" absolutely. For instance, the poet introduces a whole historical man into its action—Job clings near Patience as she fights (163–64)—and a series of quite human opponents of Avarice, apparently Prudentius's favorite vice, including the "sacerdotes Domini" (priests of the Lord—498). Prudentius has not completely allegorized the action or, to speak more precisely, personified the experience he renders. Although, as we shall see, he has developed methods for introducing human history into his poem without marring the consistency of his fiction, nevertheless the pressure to refer inconsistently to men rather than personifications occasionally overcomes the poet. If one thinks of other allegorists—Dante, Jean de Meun, and Langland, for example—it appears that the urge to express disenchantment with the holders of sacerdotal offices is common in large allegories. This

63

is understandable, as the priests and friars were supposed to do the work the allegorist felt the need to do, especially, as learned men, to bring allusion to the sacred past to bear on men's present moral state. In our time the analogue is satire directed against academe. That Prudentius, inconsistently, also included a warning to priests scarcely complicates his reductive exclusion of humans as *personae*.

Another consequence of the carefully, if not completely, sustained fiction of warring personifications is an occasional lapse in the locus of action in the poem, which has been studied by Christian Gnilka and, more broadly, by Charles Muscatine, who describes the space of the poem as suggesting "values static, formal, ideologically fixed," characteristically early medieval, dealing with "moral rather than with physical space." The place of action is usually described in the poem as a field ("campus") near which is the camp ("castra") of the virtues, to which they finally retire after their victory. The locale of the action is inconsistent. On the one hand the battlefield seems to encompass the whole world, with the Jordan river nearby (99), and with Luxuria arriving from the western bounds of the world (Rome? Tartarus?—310). Avarice slaughters "per populos" (among the peoples) and seizes "omne hominum ... genus" (every race of men). She is conqueress of the world ("victrix orbis"—480-81, 493), and Hope, watched by the virtues, flies up to heaven (305–306). On the other hand, the poet is careful to locate the action, as is appropriate for his allegory, within the psyche, as in Pride's boast that his forces occupy "totum hominem" (the whole man—217). One perhaps unhappy effect of this triply conceived space—field, world, and soul—occurs in Concord's speech near the end, in which she exhorts the virtues themselves to put aside Discord, "quia fissa voluntas / confundit variis arcana biformia fibris" (for a divided will makes discord, a double interior in a heart at variance—760–61). One would have thought the virtues were irreducible segments of the psyche, but here Concord—obviously thinking of the locus as the heart and not as the fictional victory camp—warns her soldiers not to admit faction into *their* hearts. It is the poet who "confundit": it is likely that personification fictions and discontinuous conceptions of character and space are inseparable.

FIGURE AND ALLUSION: THE TIME OF THE ACTION

The *Psychomachia* reduces the degree to which fiction can imitate the world because it restricts the action to successive motives of combat and eliminates from the center of the action a complete human being. But Prudentius has given up certain customary forms of mimesis for a purpose. Prudentius is capable, as the *Hamartigenia* and *Apotheosis* show, of writing long, Lucretian poems which scarcely tell a story at all: the *Psychomachia* is for him a poem eminently narrative and unusually full of action. In fact it is his only complete fiction, his only representation of successive events which are not in the historical sense true. We are dealing, then, with a poet moving away from his normal literary modes—theological, often polemical, essays in verse and retellings of "true" Biblical and historical events—in order to achieve some other end. I take Prudentius's attempt to be, at the expense of consistency of space, to represent the process of time, and therefore time, more than any other dimension of narrative, is particularly under his control.

A plot is an imitation of history. An author can provide more or less material within and around his plot to make the reader conscious of this fact, primarily by referring the reader to other, either more traditional or less fictional history. Prudentius conveniently establishes this reference at the outset of his poem, in the preface, set apart in iambic trimeters from the dactylic body of the poem. The first word of the preface sets the theme: "Senex," the old one, the patriarch, Abraham, the man of faith, the great exemplar for Prudentius of the battle for good, old in years and old in Biblical history. Prudentius summarizes the contents of Genesis 14, in which Abraham rescues the captive Lot by going to battle with his household servants as his troop, and in which he is blessed and given bread and wine by Melchizedek. The poet also refers to the sacrifice of Isaac, the hospitality extended to the "triformis angelorum trinitas" (three-personed trinity of angels), and the conception of Isaac in Sarah's old age. Abraham is an "exemplum," says Prudentius, of the need to war against the "portenta cordis servientis" (monsters of the enslaved heart). The poet elaborates:

> haec ad figuram praenotata est linea,
> quam nostra recto vita resculpat pede:

65

vigilandum in armis pectorum fidelium,
omnemque nostri portionem corporis,
quae capta foedae serviat libidini,
domi coactis liberandam viribus;
nos esse large vernularum divites,
si quid trecenti bis novenis additis
possint figura noverimus mystica.
mox ipse Christus, qui sacerdos verus est,
parente inenarrabili atque uno satus,
cibum beatis offerens victoribus
parvam pudici cordis intrabit casam,
monstrans honorem Trinitatis hospitae.
animam deinde Spiritus conplexibus
pie maritam, prolis expertem diu,
faciet perenni fertilem de semine,
tunc sera dotem possidens puerpera
herede digno Patris inplebit domum.

50–68

[This picture has been marked down beforehand as a figure, which our life should trace again with rightful foot; that we must be vigilant in the armament of faithful hearts; that we must set free every part of our body which is enslaved by foul desires, set it free with forces gathered at home; that we are generously wealthy in domestic servants if we know what 318 can do by a mystic figure. Then Christ himself, who is the true priest, begotten of a father inutterable and one, offering food to the blessed victors, will enter the little house of the chaste heart, doing it the honor of having the Trinity as a guest. Then by embraces of the Spirit he will make the soul, piously married but for a long time lacking offspring, fertile with eternal seed, and then the woman (soul) having a dowry, giving birth late in life, will fill the house of the Father with a worthy heir.]

We scarcely need more than the cue-words "figuram," "figura," to see that Prudentius intends a typological explanation of Abraham's story. Philo and Origen had helped make the world receptive to typological exegesis—Philo seeing types of psychological faculties in Old Testament narrations, and Origen finding types of Christ and Christian doctrine there—but Prudentius need not have gone further than the seventh chapter of Hebrews for the suggestion of this little allegory: the author of the epistle wrote that Christ was the "verus sacerdos" of the order of Melchizedek. Prudentius tells us that Christ will perform three tropological functions in fulfillment of the "linea" of the story of Abraham: he will aid in the psychomachia, he will nourish the soul with the sacrament of bread and wine, entering it as a guest, and he will fertilize the soul through the agency of the Holy Spirit.

This preface, then, interweaves the two kinds of allegory—typology and reification, in the form of personification. Christ himself is the fulcrum of the two kinds of allegory: it is he whom Abraham adumbrates, and he will enter "parvam pudici cordis casam." Christ likewise serves as the "real" author of the poem, as the first lines of the narrative proper suggest: "Christe, graves hominum semper miserate labores / . . . dissere, rex noster" (Christ, always compassionate of the severe trials of men . . . say, our king). Christ's role for Prudentius is threefold: to render the poem authoritative as a divine muse (fictional role), to sum up the meaning of history (typological role), and to act presently on our soul's behalf (tropological role), in so far as the fictional psychomachia takes place continually in its readers' hearts.

These three roles correspond to the three schemes of space Prudentius mingles: the fictional space of the battlefield, the expanded space of the world seen in its historical dimension—a notion which the ecclesiastical use of the Latin word *saeculum* comprehends; and the interior space of the psyche. The three versions of space might be seen as three versions of the poet's (or reader's) point of view: the view of the fiction of the poem, the view looking outside at the world in the process of history, and the view looking within himself. The point of this complication is that Christ is at the center of each field of vision. That Prudentius was particularly concerned to postulate Christ's multiplex nature we know from his polemical insistence, especially in the *Apotheosis*, upon the orthodox view of the dual nature of the single person Christ against various rampant heresies. In the *Psychomachia* he takes care to explain that Christ is both Word and flesh (78–86); and, later, in the speech of Concord to which we have referred, she urges soul and body to unite, on the model of "mortale" (mortal being) uniting with God through the mediation of Jesus

67

(764–68). Christ unites divinity with matter, and history with the present: he is essential to Prudentius's scheme, and hence its author. The duplex Christ is the divine analogy for the double nature of those special fictional persons, personifications, who join the matter of their humanoid persons to the spirit of their names.

A shifting reference to time outside of the main course of narratives, what in general I call "allusion," is less perplexing or irritating to the reader than a shifting reference to other space: in the latter we generally see confusion, inconsistency, and incompetence (with, of course, great exceptions, such as the references to Britain in *The Faerie Queene*), while in the former we see enrichment and intelligence. It is easy to allude from within a fiction to history and literary tradition without jarring inconsistency, whereas to point suddenly to another locus of action disrupts our flow of reading. For Soberness to implant the spike of her battle standard (348) makes us, literal minded as we are, flinch when we think of the field as the heart, but a reference to Goliath does not.

The cause of this distinction may be our habit of thinking of unorthodox complications, overlappings, cycles, syncopations, and foreshadowings of time, and our habit of conceiving of space as single, eternal, and simple. Time is a river, space a rock. Another reason is aesthetic: that certain actions in fiction, for example, battles, are often localized in space for the sake of mimesis, but include no specific factor of time, as this may be unnecessary. More precisely, the duration of a fiction is often specified, but its absolute time in human history, its "aevum," can remain vague. The medieval romances are a most striking example. Our perception of time—our memory, our historiography, our rituals, our philosophy of time—is much more like fiction than is our perception of space, which (we feel) can constantly be compared to sensory data. In any case, Prudentius confuses the spatial locus of the *Psychomachia* for the same reason he elaborates its temporal dimension.

The *Psychomachia* alludes first of all to the Bible, then to the *Aeneid*. The modes and methods of these allusions will repay investigation, for they shed light not only on the art and meaning of the poem but also on its genesis: these two summations of their respective cultures are "sources" for Prudentius in the fullest sense.

The most obvious Biblical allusions are to Old Testament figures, complements to Abraham as he appears in the preface, who exemplify various virtues and vices. We have seen Job accompanying Patience (163); Adam (226) and Goliath (291) are exempla of Superbia in the speeches of Superbia and Spes; David ("puer"—300) of Mens Humilis; David and Samuel and Jonathan are called upon as exemplars by Sobrietas (386–400); the priesthood is of the "gentis Levitidis" (502); Avaritia alludes to Judas Iscariot (530) and Achar (537: Joshua 7); the narrator compares the victorious virtues to Israel after the Red Sea crossing (651); Discord names Belial her preceptor (714).

The first example after the preface of this overt typological association is most interesting: the connection of Pudicitia (Chastity) with Judith, slayer of Holofernes (58 ff.). Pudicitia, after bloodily dispatching Sodomita Libido, wonders that such Lust is still operative after Judith's accomplishment, as if the single event in history might have stopped foul desire for all time. This is an unusual demand to make on the power of typology, and of course it is wildly "inconsistent" in the fiction. The virtue continues to address the vice:

> at fortasse parum fortis matrona sub umbra
> legis adhuc pugnans, dum tempora nostra figurat,
> vera quibus virtus terrena in corpora fluxit
> grande per infirmos caput excisura ministros.
> numquid et intactae post partum virginis ullum
> fas tibi iam superest?
>
> 66–71

[But perhaps a matron struggling still under the shadow of the law had too little strength, even as she prefigured our times, in which the true power has flowed into earthly bodies to sever the great head with weak ministers. And after the virgin intact gave birth, is there any right remaining to you?]

Pudicitia goes on to show how the passing of the divine word into flesh has made flesh pure, so "occide, prostibulum" (die, whore), because "post Mariam" lust is ineffectual. She concludes by washing her sword, bloody from Lust's throat, in the Jordan, "abolens baptismate labem" (removing the stain by baptism). Pudicitia piles sacramental symbol (baptism) on material symbol (the unsheathed sword suggests libido) on typological symbol (Judith and Mary) onto her own personification.

From our present perspective the special interest of Chastity's monologue is the contorted passage of time it presents. The type of Judith has found its antitype in the "vera virtus" of the Incarnation. The term "verus," which we have seen twice now, is the technical term in the Vulgate for describing Christ's fulfillment of ancient figure: Christ is the "true" manna or "true" vine. Judith, in the shadow world under the Old Law, was not capable of slaying the vice. She was only an example, and the death of Holofernes has exemplary, not effective, force on man's psyche. Compare the line in the conclusion of Chaucer's Clerk's Tale, "Griselde is deed, and eek hire pacience." The power of the event of the virgin birth, however, is real; its effect is more than typological.

We are dealing with a paradox, because the action of the *Psychomachia*, since it alludes back to the narration of Christ's career, is presumably "post partum virginis" itself, yet clearly Sodomita Libido is not in every sense dead. We are in an age of grace ("virtus") very like the prelapsarian state, in which vicious potential is present but not able to operate freely in time or through time. It is as if time did not proceed at all: the space between Pentecost and Advent of the Church's calendar is a gap in which experience—conflict—takes place only in the abstract, if at all. We, after the event of Christ's life, are shadows (from this point of view) as much as were men before Knowledge in the form of fruit came to men at all. These dark notions require serious qualification, and we shall have to return to them.

THE TWILIGHT OF TIME

The historical allusions treated so far have all been to the Old Testament, with only two exceptions: Christ, of course, and Judas Iscariot, who is in a special sense the last inhabitant of the age of law. Allusions to the New Testament which involve temporal perspective are fewer but more significant. They may be divided into three categories: reference to the life and nature of Christ, to the sacraments, and to the present and future state of the Church. The first category has already been discussed in sufficient detail: the main text is

Pudicitia's consideration of the virgin birth and Christ's dual nature.

Baptism is mentioned, as it were, incidentally and for its psychological, not typological, significance. The sacrament for which Prudentius shows most concern is the Eucharist. The passage brings to a climax one of the best parts of the poem, the combat of Luxuria and Sobrietas. Luxuria has arrived on the battlefield:

> ac tunc pervigilem ructabat marcida cenam,
> sub lucem quia forte iacens ad fercula raucos
> audierat lituos, atque inde tepentia linquens
> pocula lapsanti per vina et balsama gressu
> ebria calcatis ad bellum floribus ibat.
>
> 316–20

[And then languishing she belched up her all-night feast, for it happened that she had heard at dawn the raucous clarion signal while lying before her dishes, and leaving the warm cups, her step slippery in the wine and perfume, drunk she went, trampling the flowers, to war.]

This uncouth warrior proceeds to do battle with flowers, which allure and destroy her enemy with venom. Sobrietas exhorts her debilitated forces to battle, and picks up the banquet motif the narrator has introduced. She asks if Luxury's wiles, her drunken feasts in the night, will enfeeble them, and expands the field of reference, as a good homilist must:

> excidit ergo animis eremi sitis, excidit ille
> fons patribus de rupe datus, quem mystica virga
> elicuit scissi salientem vertice saxi?
> angelicusne cibus prima in tentoria vestris
> fluxit avis, quem nunc sero felicior aevo
> vespertinus edit populus de corpore Christi?
> his vos inbutos dapibus iam crapula turpis
> Luxuriae ad madidum rapit inportuna lupanar,
> quosque viros non Ira fremens, non idola bello
> cedere conpulerant, saltatrix ebria flexit!
> state, precor, vestri memores, memores quoque Christi.
>
> 371–81

[Has thus the thirst of the wilderness left your minds, has it gone, that spring given to your fathers from a rock, which the mystical rod brought leaping from the top of a split stone? Did not angelic bread flow for your forefathers in their tents long ago, which a happier people in their twilight eat now in a later age from the body of Christ? Now wicked drunkenness snatches you, filled with this latter banquet, to the dripping brothel of Luxury, and you men whom no raging anger nor idols forced to yield in war, a besotted dancing woman bows! Stand, I pray you, be mindful of yourselves, and be mindful of Christ.]

The three times—Old and New Testaments and the present—are brought together here, and the present is near its end ("vespertinus"). Prudentius has connected the sacred feast with the antinomian feast of Luxury, so that historical type and antitype (manna and Eucharist) become likewise counterimages of moral failure. Prudentius's virtue is not his descriptive power (C. S. Lewis has observed this, and agrees that Luxuria and Sobrietas make the best fight), but he is good with typology: when typology merges with universal symbolism, as it does in the sacraments, he is at his best. The fourth Gospel and the epistles in particular gave Christian allegorists sanction to use imagery in this historical way; not only were Sarah and Hagar the Testaments, but the rock in the wilderness was Christ (I Cor. 10:4).

The last kind of allusion to Christian history refers to "the present state of Christ's Church," specifically to two subjects which were of great interest to Prudentius, martyrdom (the subject of his *Peristephanon Liber*) and heresy. The references occur within one section of the poem in which, the virtues having achieved victory, the vice Discord, in disguise, stabs Concord. "Discordia dicor," she puns, "cognomento Heresis" (I am called Discord, my cognomen is Heresy —709–10), "domus et plaga mundus" (my home and country, the world). She is appropriately defeated by dismemberment. Concord begins her long speech and, describing Peace, asserts that if "Christi pro nomine martyr" (a martyr in the name of Christ—775) should leap into fire, but be not peaceful in spirit, it would avail him nothing. In conclusion she refers to the serpent concealed in feathers, the wolf in sheep's clothing, Discord, here specified as a pair of arch-heretics, Photinus and Arius (794). Laura Cotogni, in her study of the

Psychomachia, had allusions such as this in mind when she wrote of the double reference of Prudentius's allegory, on the one hand to the soul, and on the other to the body of Christians in their collective struggle. The allegory, in this view, is both ecclesiological and psychological.

The unrealized apocalypse embarrassed the Church after the first century of our era. Of the several ways to handle this problem, one was to couple the progress of the soul—whose end in mortal state is real—with the progress of the Church: Cotogni cites the classical example, the allegorical reading of the Song of Songs as developed by Origen and later commentators. As human life ends and does not end, so the Church. A series of minor, individual apocalypses (that is, deaths), or an enduring ecclesiastical apocalypse, an "age of grace," bides time until the Apocalypse proper and the end of time. The greatest expression of these old ideas appeared soon after the *Psychomachia* in the *De Civitate Dei* of Saint Augustine: the whole question of time and providence was in the air. For Prudentius, the Church in battle with heretics is the final receptacle of God's sacred history before the end; the deed of Discord is the penultimate (and continuous) event in the whole grand poetic metaphor of typos and ethos, history and the soul. History both before and after the fulcrum, the Incarnation, is delineated in the poem.

THE FURY

Augustine's image of the second history, the history of the age of grace in the world, is Rome, the city of the world. Prudentius's allusions to the *Aeneid* create, in effect, a secular typology: the establishment of a "pax Concordiae" at the end of the *Psychomachia* recapitulates as it criticizes the institution of Rome. Like Rome, and in keeping with the paradoxes of the temporary, ephemeral apocalypses of the Christian world biding time before the end, the city founded by the virtues in the poem is not free from dissension, and the forces of evil have not finally been destroyed. It is a temporizing end, a shadow of apocalyptic perfection which is roughly parallel to those apocalypse-oriented communities, the monasteries, which were making their presence felt in the West.

Virgil did not describe, but only foreshadowed, Aeneas's founding

73

Rome: the last action of the poem is the conquest of the last enemy, not the building of the new citadel. Prudentius's borrowings from Virgil, which have been studied by Christian Schwen, Macklin Smith, and others, are primarily from episodes of battle. Allusions to the second half of the *Aeneid* are much more common. Almost every combat of virtues and vices includes some echo of the battles of Turnus, Camilla, or Aeneas. The great model of Roman valor provides Prudentius with a secular type, in his own language and in the epic style, of conquest and the establishment of peace.

The allusion is pointed in the first hexameter line: "Christe, graves hominum semper miserate labores" (Christ, always compassionate of the severe trials of men), an imitation of Aeneas's address to the Cumaean Sibyl and her god: "Phoebe, graves Troiae semper miserate labores" (*Aen.* 6.56). Virgil sets forth the prophecy of the Sibyl carefully in terms of the parallel of Aeneas's adventures and those narrated in the *Iliad*—it amounts to a summary of the second half of the *Aeneid* and alludes to those books' great source. The sibylline prophetess of history is analogous to the muse of poetry: she foretells the future at the same time she recalls the literary past. Prudentius presents a similar situation—although in this case Christ is the prophet and muse, and the seeker after knowledge is the poet, not the hero (the *Psychomachia* has no hero). As the sibyl foretold war and alluded to the *Iliad*, so Christ will inform the poet of the soul's war, and so the first line alludes to the *Aeneid*. Both invocations bespeak an encompassing view of history.

Prudentius alludes often to one character in the *Aeneid*, the Fury Alecto, whom Virgil modeled on Ennius's Discordia, and on an old idea that the Furies were an allegory of a tormented conscience (see Cicero, *De leg.* 1.14.40). Alecto first appears in the *Aeneid* after another grand knitting up of time, as irate Juno curses Aeneas; he will be a second Paris, and Rome will have its beginnings in a war parallel to the seige of Troy. Juno summons Alecto from Tartarus for her purpose, to instigate war between the Trojans and Turnus's Rutulians. Schwen has located Prudentius's specific borrowings from the account of Alecto: they are especially evident in the treatments of Avaritia and Discordia. Both Greed and Alecto are called "Erinys" (*Psych.* 566; *Aen.* 7.447); they both transform themselves deceptively in almost the same words, Greed into Frugi (Frugal), and Alecto into the mild priestess Calybe:

74

Greed: dixerat et torvam faciem furialiaque arma
    exuit inque habitum sese transformat honestum . . . .
        551-52

[She spoke, and doffs her savage look and hellish arms, and
transforms herself into a respectable appearance.]

Alecto: Alecto torvam faciem et furialia membra
    Exuit: in vultus sese transformat aniles . . . .
        [*Aen.* 7. 415-16]

[Alecto doffs her savage look and hellish members: she transforms herself in countenance into an old woman.]

Both figures, as Schwen notes, cover their heads with white, Alecto
with hair ("albos crines") and Avaritia with a mantle ("candida
palla"). Prudentius informs us that Bellona, the Roman goddess of
war, also puts on the likeness of Frugi; Bellona is "pronuba" (brides-
maid) to Alecto in Virgil (*Psych.* 557; *Aen.* 7. 319).
    Discordia appears in Virgil as a figure on Aeneas's shield, in
connection with the Furies and Bellona:

    . . . tristesque ex aethere Dirae;
    Et scissa gaudens vadit Discordia palla,
    Quam cum sanguineo sequitur Bellona flagello.
        [8. 701-703]

[. . . and the grim Furies from the air; and Discord comes
rejoicing in her rent cloak, whom Bellona follows with her bloody
whip.]

The lines are imitated by Prudentius, describing Discord: "scissa
procul palla structum et serpente flagellum / multiplici . . . iacebant"
(her rent cloak and whip made of many snakes lay far off—*Psych.*
685-86). Prudentius's Discord bears attributes of both Discordia
and Bellona in Virgil. The shield of Aeneas depicts future Italian
history ("res Italas"—8. 626), beyond the hero's comprehension.
This constitutes a radical departure from the description's model,
the shield of Achilles, which represents cities and country in activities

75

so constant and ever recurring—lawsuits, battle, agriculture, dance
—as to seem timeless, at least *sub specie humanitatis* (*Iliad* 18). Surely
Prudentius had no thought for the once-removed source of his line
(Homer does refer to Strife, Panic, and "the dreadful Spirit of
Death"); what we might grasp, nevertheless, is the intensely his-
torical, linear timefulness of Prudentius's second source, Virgil.

Why Prudentius should have specifically alluded to Virgil's Alecto,
Furies, Bellona, and Discord in handling his Avaritia and Discordia
is not far to seek. These Virgilian figures are nearly the same as
Prudentius's in function: they serve the artists (Prudentius and
Vulcan, the artificer of Aeneas's shield) as schematic representations
—somewhere between godhead and personification, in the classical
Roman way—of the agents of war. For both poets the figures are
used in a context of imaginative projection of significant history. One
of the other places in Virgil where the imaginative powers seem
dominant is the description of Aeneas's journey to the underworld.
There, too, we find "in the jaws of Orcus" at the entrance a group of
monstrous figures, among whom are Bellum, the Eumenides, and
"Discordia demens" (*Aen.* 6. 279–80). The Fury whom Virgil
singles out, Alecto, surely performs the worst and cruelest deeds of
any recounted in the *Aeneid*, and doubtless Prudentius alluded to her
for that reason. These are the demonic creatures, the shape-shifters
and deceivers and war-makers, who figure forth in Roman history
the basest vices—greed and discord—the public vices in man. Their
parentage is wretched; they come from hell.

Prudentius was not alone in drawing from this Virgilian fount;
Claudian, in his epic *In Rufinum*, perhaps written (395–97 A.D.)
shortly before the *Psychomachia*, likewise reactivates the Virgilian
furies, especially Alecto, in the manner of Prudentius. The influential
successor of Claudian's poem, the *Anticlaudianus* of Alain de Lille,
continued the near-allegorical use of Alecto in the high Middle Ages.
Fulgentius had interpreted the name Alecto as *inpausabilis* ("un-
ceasing"—*Myth.* I.6), and Boccaccio takes her as inquietude of
mind (*Gen. deorum* 3.7). In Virgil, Prudentius found both a model
for Latin epic strife and a source for a narrated progress in history as
well as the demonic forces which oppose the progress. The dark
creatures, personified abstractions, are as old as Hesiod and Homer,
but in Virgil they are subsumed in the magnificent enterprise of
Roman peace. When Concord and her cohorts return to the citadel

at the end of the *Psychomachia*, we are to think of the *pax Romana* and the Virgilian victory of the progressively human over the timelessly demonic.

THE NEW CITY

The counterpart of the infernal war of the *Psychomachia* is the reign of Christian peace. The war is fought on a bare *campus*; but in peace, in the final translocation of the geography of the poem, the virtues retire to a "sancta urbs" (753). We learn at last that they are citizens of this city, and that the whole battle has been an extramural, neo-Trojan siege. Faith and Concord lead the virtues, and their next project is to take up the task which Solomon instituted, to found a temple as a home for Christ. For, Faith says, Jerusalem was illustrious ("inlustrata"—811). This new temple will sanctify "purgati corporis urbem" (the city of the cleansed body—818) and make it pleasing to Christ.

So there will be no mistake, Prudentius is careful to describe the temple and its dimensions, its gates, its twelve jewels, in precisely the terms used for the New Jerusalem in Revelation 21. There are two differences between this temple in the heart and the heavenly city of the Apocalypse. First, St. John specifies that "I saw no temple therein. For the Lord God Almighty is the temple thereof, and the Lamb" (Rev. 21:22—Douay-Rheims trans.). Concordia is equally specific in her opposite mandate to adorn the city and welcome Christ with a temple (816–19). This is difficult to reconcile. Prudentius surely saw the logic of having the city represent the cleansed body and its temple the heart, the seat (as we learn) of the "interior home," the court of Wisdom (868–77). The allegory of the Lord's temple in the heart, Gnilka has shown, was commonplace (see Prudentius's *Apoth.* 518 ff., etc.). Perhaps this is enough explanation.

The other difference is the presence, at the threshold of the city but before the temple is built, of Discordia. Prudentius again is specific: Discord attacks Concord "dum . . . iam" (just as) she steps within the ramparts ("moenibus"—671). The vice, as we have seen, is a shape-shifter, and we are told that "Discordia nostros / intrarat cuneos sociam mentita figuram" (Discordia entered our lines counterfeiting the figure of an ally—683–84). The last verse of the

77

chapter in the Apocalypse uses a word from the same root, "mentiri," to lie: "Non intrabit in eam [urbem] aliquod coinquinatum, aut abominationem faciens et mendacium, nisi qui scripti sunt in libro vitae Agni" (Nor shall there enter into it [the city] anything defiled, nor working abomination and a lie, but those who are written in the book of Life of the Lamb—Rev. 21:27).

Prudentius may have meant nothing by admitting a temple (constructed like the city of Revelation itself) into the holy city of the heart, and by likewise admitting (briefly at the threshold of the city, not the temple) a liar. But I would conclude that Prudentius has deliberately distinguished the psychological and corporeal apocalypse in the *Psychomachia* from the cosmic Apocalypse of John of Patmos, on the evidence of the conclusion of the poem. There, in the present tense, Prudentius laments the strife now raging in our members: we are still "duplex substantia" (909) and always at variance within ourselves.

The vision of Faith and Concord on high, and Sapience holding court, is very much of the when and if; I think Prudentius meant to emphasize its unreal, potential nature when he compared it to the vision of John yet specified the differences. Even in our age of grace, the combat of virtue and vice goes on. In any case the format—a vision of a holy city into which a fraudulent Discord penetrates—persists throughout the Middle Ages. We see it in the character of Faus-Semblant, who slips into the castle of the Rose as a Dominican friar (*The Romance of the Rose*, 12,015–540); we see it in the little premonition of the earthly paradise Dante gives us in the eighth canto of *Purgatorio*, in which a serpent glides "forse qual diede ad Eva il cibo amaro" (perhaps like that which gave bitter food to Eve—8.99), recalling to us the archetype of the motif in Genesis. We shall see that this pattern recurs in *Piers Plowman* and Book I of *The Faerie Queene* and *The Confidence-Man*. The city of the apocalypse is the new shape of the Garden of Eden: neither can be present in this world and time: both now contain heresy and fraud.

The virtue of the *Psychomachia* is its fundamental historicity. Prudentius draws from the Bible the type of salvation, and from the *Aeneid* the type of salvation's rival, the discordant fury. It can be argued that the poem is not satisfying: the complete expression of interior human conflicts, paradoxically, rids the poem of an engaging sense of human conflict—a personification cannot have a tragic flaw. The successive descriptions of battles, after all, are not interesting. But by the crucial criterion in the Middle Ages, ecclesiastical favor (the Church preserved books), the poem was a success. I said at the outset that the poem had more literary than moral use—the trope of personification and the form of typology, adopted by later poets, became powerful instruments of analysis of history and personality. Although the *Psychomachia* is a great technical achievement, we look elsewhere in Prudentius for his best poetry.

At the heart of Prudentius is a distrust of the worth of man in the face of divinity. His response is orthodox and Christian: he perceives the vanity of history, and likewise its redeeming power in the shape of the novus and verus, the Incarnation. These lines, which Virgil would doubtless think precious, abstract, and decadent, give us Prudentius at his best, as the poet of figural lyric. They are about man, history, and Christ.

restat ut aëriam fingas ab origine gentem,
aërios proceres, Levi, Iudam, Simeonem,
aërium David, magnorum corpora regum
aëria, atque ipsam fecundae virginis alvum
aëre fallaci nebulisque et nube tumentum;
vanescat sanguis perflabilis, ossa liquescant
mollia, nervorum pereat textura volantum;
omne quod est gestum notus auferat inritus, aurae
dispergant tenues, sit fabula quod sumus omnes.
et quid agit Christus si me non suscipit? aut quem
liberat infirmum si dedignatur adire
carnis onus manuumque horret monumenta suarum?
[*Apotheosis*, 1010–21]

Imagine now how man is from the start
But air, and Judah, Levi, Simeon, all
The princes air, how air is David, air
The frames of our great potentates, the wombs
Themselves of fertile maidens swelling out
With mists and cloudy shades, deceptive air.
The blood is puffed and emptied; bones dissolve
Unstrung; the weaving of swift sinews ravels;
All our deeds the unfixed wind bears off

And gentle breezes scatter: we are fable.
And if He take me not, then what is Christ?
How free the sick if He disdain to enter
The burden of my flesh, if He abhor
The monuments He wrought with His own hands?

Bibliographical Note

The writings of two men were in my mind as I wrote this chapter: C. S. Lewis, who introduced many readers to the *Psychomachia* in *The Allegory of Love* (Oxford, 1936), and Frank Kermode, *The Sense of an Ending* (New York and London, 1966), who writes of time, history, apocalyptic, and literature. Macklin Smith's helpful *Prudentius' "Psychomachia": A Reexamination* (Princeton, 1976) appeared after I wrote. We differ, I hope fruitfully, on the matter of Prudentius's response to Virgil.

The newest edition of the *Psychomachia* is in Prudentius's *Carmina*, ed. Maurice P. Cunningham, Corpus Christ., Ser. Lat., 126 (Turnhout, 1966). Older fine editions are those of Johannes Bergman—a separate edition of the *Psychomachia* (Uppsala, 1897), and an edition of the *Carmina*, Corpus Script. Eccl. Lat., 61 (Leipzig, 1926). The fullest notes and commentary are found in Maurice Lavarenne, *Prudence: Psychomachia* (Paris, 1933) with Fr. trans. The Loeb edition is convenient and presents a facing English translation.

Studies of the *Psychomachia* which I have found useful are those of Laura Cotogni, "Sovrapposizione di visioni e di allegorie nella *Psychomachia* di Prudenzio," *ANLMSF*, ser. 6, 12 (1936): 441–61; Christian Gnilka, *Studien der Psychomachie des Prudentius*, Klass.-philol. Studien hgbn. Hans Herter und W. Schmid, 27 (Bonn diss.) (Wiesbaden, 1963); Reinhart Herzog, *Die allegorische Dichtkunst des Prudentius*, Zetemata. Monographia zur klass. Altertumswiss., 42 (Munich, 1966); Marc-René Jung, *Etudes sur le poème allégorique en France au moyen âge* (Bern, 1971), chap. 2. Jung notes the later success of Prudentius's "counterfeit" vice, the figure whom I call the *mendax*. I referred to the commentary cited in Hubert Silvestre, "Aperçu sur les commentaires carolingiens de Prudence," *SacE* 9 (1957): 50–74.

Christian Schwen has the fullest account of the borrowings from the *Aeneid*, in *Vergil bei Prudentius* (Leipzig diss., 1937); see also Albertus Mahoney,

Virgil in the Works of Prudentius (Washington, D.C., diss., 1934) and Pierre Courcelle, "Les Pères de l'église devant les enfers virgiliens," *AHDLMA* 30 (1955): 5-74 with full bibliography. More recent bibliographical notes are abundant in Cesare Magazzù, "L'Utilizzazione allegorica di Virgilio nella *Psychomachia* di Prudenzio," *Bollettino di Studi Latini* 5 (1975): 13-23. I have not seen P. F. Beatrice, "L'Allegoria nella *Psychomachia* di Prudenzio," *SPat* 18 (1971): 25-73. The quotations from Charles Muscatine are from "Locus of Action in Medieval Narrative," *RPH* 17 (1963): 115-22. If I am not mistaken, my remarks about Alecto correspond to the things Paul Piehler says about the *Thebaid*'s Tisiphone, in his *The Visionary Landscape: A Study in Medieval Allegory* (London, 1971), pp. 22-25. On the sources of Virgil's Alecto and Discordia see Eduard Norden, *Ennius und Vergilius: Kriegsbilder aus Roms grosser Zeit* (Darmstadt, 1966), pp. 18-33.

On medieval genres consult M. W. Bloomfield, *Piers Plowman as a Fourteenth-Century Apocalypse* (New Brunswick, N.J., 1961), chap. 1; here also is a good treatment of monastic *Denkform*. The locale of the action is treated in the excursus on the *Psychomachia* in Gerhard Bauer, *Claustrum Animae: Untersuchungen zur Geschichte der Metapher vom Herzen als Kloster*, vol. 1 (Munich, 1973), pp. 336-49. The influence of the *Psychomachia* has been studied most fully by Lavarenne, in his edition, and by Hans Robert Jauss, in "Form und Auffassung der Allegorie in der Tradition der *Psychomachia* (von Prudentius zum ersten *Romanz de la Rose*)," *Medium Aevum Vivum. Festsch. f. Walther Bulst*, ed. Jauss and D. Schaller (Heidelberg, 1960), and in other works by Jauss mentioned elsewhere in this book (see Index).

CHAPTER THREE

The Dream of History

Langland's *Piers Plowman*

And through Isaiah the Lord himself spoke, saying: "A vineyard was made for my beloved on a hill in a fertile place, and I put a fence around it and dug around the vine of Sorech and I built a tower in the middle of it" (cf. Isa. 5:1–2). He fenced it with a wall as it were of celestial precepts and a watch of angels. "For the angel of the Lord will encamp round about those fearing him" (Ps. 33:8). He puts in the Church as it were a tower of apostles, prophets, and doctors, whose duty is to keep peace for the Church. He dug around it, when he relieved it of the burden of earthly cares; for nothing burdens the mind more than solicitude for this world and desire for riches or power. . . . But this vine, when it has been dug about, is raised up and tied, so it will not droop back to the earth. Some shoots are pruned, others grow on: these are pruned which luxuriate in empty profusion; those grow on, which the good farmer has judged to be fruitful. . . . So the tower stands in the middle, to spread the example of those rustics, of those fishermen, who deserved to hold the citadel of virtues.

St. Ambrose, *Hexameron*, 3.12.50–51

"Wyte god," quath a wafrestre, "wist ich the sothe,
Ich wolde no forther a fot for no freres prechinge."

Piers Plowman, C 8.285–86

DIFFICULTIES OF FORM

Piers Plowman is so difficult a poem that its students have had to spend most of their energies describing what kind of poem it is and solving problems in it, not the least of which has been the still unfinished business of establishing a good text. An attempt to characterize the whole must be tentative. Reading *Piers* is like what reading *Paradise Lost* would be if our culture had preserved the Bible but lost the Greek and Latin classics altogether; there seem to be great ranges of knowledge and sensibility to which the poem appeals and to which we can respond only with humility and learning.

Langland adopts three conventions which hinder our grasp of the poem. The first is the convention of the naive narrator. From the beginning Will, the narrator, seems to know such things as that Christ is the savior, yet the meaning of this knowledge only slowly comes home to him. His progress is that of the hyperliterate who knows much and who is continually shocked when he experiences, as if it were new, something about which he has read. The classical case is that of St. Augustine, who knew Christianity at the outset but whose *Confessions* reveal the long struggle to comprehend and make vital what he knew.

The *Confessions* is a model for the kind of poem *Piers* is, an intellectual serial which reports a narrator's progressively more intimate and powerful understanding of man and God. But Augustine constantly judges and arranges his past in accordance with his present understanding as he writes, whereas Langland follows Will's vision contemporaneously, giving the reader greater knowledge through various ironies, allusions, and symbols which the reader can understand and Will cannot. The convention probably springs from the naive Socrates. Its classical manifestation for the Middle Ages is Boethius's *Consolation of Philosophy*, and the literary uses extend from romance inepts like Perceval to Christian progressors like the protagonist Mankind in the fifteenth-century play, *The Castle of Perseverance*, which closely resembles *Piers*.

This convention requires that the reader see through events which the narrator fails to understand. The reader's task can be difficult, and criticism of *Piers* is full of arguments as to which might be the good character in a given episode. Langland's clues as to how we should evaluate some situations and doctrines are not always clear.

83

The outstanding example of confusion on this point is the popularity of the poem in the Reformation, when Langland was taken for a Wycliffite proto-Protestant. The dream vision form of the poem only adds to this difficulty, for it is one of many devices which allow Langland to be unusually free to follow his inclinations in spite of mimetic norms, and which lead to surreal and often confusing shifts of narrative action. Langland exploits this freedom not only to consider and juxtapose, like Dante, an encyclopedic array of traditional and contemporary topics, but also, very unlike Dante, to take up and drop various fictional structures as his spirit moves him. Since the dreaming narrator, as both teller and creator of his vision, is especially close to the content of his narration, in *Piers*, the conventions of naive narrator and dreaming narrator in combination can be almost overwhelmingly hard to follow, as they sometimes are in Chaucer.

The second obstacle to an easy reading of *Piers* is the convention of encyclopedic satire. The landmarks of the genre are Roman and late Latin satire, called "Menippean" by Dryden and Northrop Frye, and the *specula* or fictional manuals of the late Middle Ages of which the *Romance of the Rose* is the great example. The Juvenalian term "farrago," "mixed grains" (grab bag) best describes the genre. Langland's propensity for the darting, diffuse attack and his allowance for extensive digression, in debates which develop into monologues, are characteristic of this mode: these hinder any attempt to perceive the basic lines of the poem. Further, as Morton Bloomfield cautiously proposed, *Piers Plowman* is similar in many ways to apocalypses, insofar as these constitute a genre: like them it is stuffed with flamboyant, half-articulated imagery, with a rage for prophecy, and of course with eschatological premonitions. Hence *Piers* has presented a problem for those who have attempted to make out its structure in any but the most general terms. The advantages of the satiric convention are freedom for Langland to go wherever he will, to display what Beckett's Molloy called "a passion for truth," and to render with vitality the chaotic and shifting state of phenomenal experience. These are qualities conspicuously absent in the *Psychomachia*.

The third convention is the most serious obstacle to our understanding *Piers*: the multiple techniques of allegory and the complicated interrelations among them. By this I do not mean the use of the "four-fold method" of allegoresis. We saw in the introduction that the whole range of allegorical fiction may be dissected in various ways. For medieval literature especially, it may suffice for now to distinguish broadly three kinds: personification, "analysis and categorization" (as defined in the introduction), and typology. The first two of these are kindred subclasses of the more general kind of allegory, reification.

One way of criticizing an allegorical fiction is to observe the weight it gives each of these three kinds of allegory. The *Psychomachia* predominantly personifies, although typology plays an important role. The *Commedia* is predominantly typological. Since typological forms are less familiar and inherently more difficult themes of literary analysis, their presence in a work is often unnoticed or rejected by modern students; hence I have found myself arguing with students that Dante's poem is, indeed, an allegory, in spite of the fact that its anagogical "level" is nearly identical with its "literal level." Secondary in Dante is analysis and categorization: the vision of the Church at the end of *Purgatory* is a good example (the scheme of geography of the whole poem is a better example). *The Romance of the Rose* is mainly personification allegory, with considerable analysis and categorization: its typological aspect seems limited.

Piers Plowman blends these three kinds of allegory in more equal proportions. Personifications are everywhere; even the narrator's name (Will), it has been suggested, alludes to the faculty *voluntas*. A prominent feature of the poem is the profusion of topics of analysis and categorization: the meaning of field, hill, and dale at the beginning; the kingly and legal courts of the Lady Meed episode; Piers's directions to the dwelling of Truth (passus 8);* the castle of Kynde (passus 11); the banquet of the friar (passus 16); the Tree of Charity (passus 19); the debate of the Four Daughters of God (passus 21); the founding of Holy Church (passus 22), and others. These topics, most of them traditional, act as centers of meaning for the poem, and focus masses of material into manageable visions. In this respect,

---

* References are to Langland's final version, called the C-Text, as edited by Walter W. Skeat, *The Vision of William Concerning Piers the Plowman* (London, 1886, 1954). Because it is thought that Langland did not revise the last two passus of the poem, which are my main interest here, I have been able to cite the new edition of the B-Text, passus 19 and 20, for C 22 and 23: George Kane and E. Talbot Donaldson, ed., *"Piers Plowman": The B Version* (London, 1975). Other references are found in the note at the end of this chapter.

THE DREAM OF HISTORY

Langland's kind of poetry is close to Spenser's. Finally, typology works as an essential mode of structure, increasing in importance as the poem proceeds, and finally becoming the crucial vehicle of the poem's meaning. This last kind of allegory is our subject here, because in the Middle Ages typology was both the theological response to the meaning of history and the chief literary response to the need for form.

From all I have said about the difficulties and complexities of *Piers*, it should come as no surprise that what follows is selective in a way that the essay on the *Psychomachia* was not. I will have to subordinate much of what goes in *Piers* in order to describe what I think are some of its essential features, features which are relevant to the general topic of allegory and history.

THE PROGRESS OF THE POEM

A brief account of the difference between the first version (A-Text) of the poem and the later versions will indicate the direction we should take. In A, the visions are primarily satirical. Will sees and criticizes the estates of society, and his theme is, as Father Dunning says, the right use of temporal goods. The dreamer first views the field of folk and their corruptions. The authoritative figure of Holy Church instructs him, as if he were a catechumen, in correct doctrine. Will then sees Lady Meed and the evils wrought by covetise in governance. The "folk" confess their sins, in the beginning of a penitential sequence, but the confession springs at best from an ambiguous contrition. The folk set out on a pilgrimage to Truth and, lacking a leader, are provided with Piers Plowman, who tells them the way. They are set to work in their vocations, and begin to refuse to labor. A personified Hunger, who looks very much like Ovid's "Fames" (*Met.* 8. 784 ff.), is only temporarily successful. Truth finally sends a "pardon," which says that if one does well, he will be saved. Will goes off in pursuit of Do Well, conversing with various personifications, and the poem breaks off.

The A-Text is a study in frustration and critical exploration. Perhaps the clearest line of movement is inward: Will changes slowly from observer to chief actor, and the things he sees become the things he thinks: his last discourses are with Thought (Will describes him

as "much like myself"), Wit, Study, Scripture, and Clergy (Learning). The climactic point of the A-Text is the entrance of Piers, who
shows that Truth's dwelling is in the heart, and who is the medium
through which we learn, for the time being, that salvation comes from
good works (that is, from the practice of charity). The almost hopeless corruption of the world forces on Will the need to look to himself,
and specifically (as the C-Text makes more clear) to judge his own
vocation, as minor cleric and religious poet, in the world.

Up to this point the poem is densely allusive. Biblical quotations
occur every few lines—Bloomfield says Langland "speaks Bible"
like St. Bernard. Lady Holy Church recounts the ancient foundations
of doctrine as well as the first breach of sin, the fall of Lucifer. It is
often noticed that Piers, the guide of the people, the man who
describes for the folk the Ten Commandments, the receiver of
something like the tables of the Old Law in the outward, paper
symbol of the pardon, is an antitype of Moses. His angry tearing the
pardon in two may refer to Moses' breaking the tablets, as well as
the New Testament antitype of the rending of the veil in the temple
at the moment of the Crucifixion when the New Law took effect.

These and other allusions are numerous in the A-Text, but they
seem inchoate fumblings when compared with the later (B- and C-
Text) versions of the poem. The A-Text is revised in detail, but the
main change is the addition of new material at the end: the B-Text
adds almost twice as many lines again as were in A, and C revises the
whole text up to the last two passus. The action of the added part is
simple. Will's quest for Do Well among various personifications
continues: Patience, Imaginatyf, and *Liberum-arbitrium* (Anima in
B) instruct him. Will has a vision of the Tree of Charity, which is
immediately followed by an account of the life of Christ, including
the Harrowing of Hell and a debate among the Four Daughters of
God. A vision of Pentecost returns the poem to the folk, as Holy
Church, a farm house named "Unity," is built. Antichrist (or Pride)
attacks; Conscience attempts to defend Unity, and the poem ends
with Conscience searching after Piers Plowman and Grace.

In many ways the poem seems to end where it began. We return
to a vision of folk, corrupt as ever, in an allegorical setting—in the
first passus a "field" (this world), in the last two passus a farmhouse
(the Church, emphatically Militant). The same personification who
first characterizes the folk, Conscience, is their moral leader (and

seems to fail as badly) at the end. The first instructions Will receives are from Holy Church: in sum she tells him to love if he would be saved. His last advice is from Nature, who tells him to "lerne to loue" (C 23.208). We should ask what movements have taken place between these two points.

One of the most striking visions of *Piers Plowman* is Will's glimpse of nature in "the myrour of Myddel-erde" (14.132 ff.). Will is amazed at the habits of animals, and, like Gulliver, asks Reason why men are not governed by orderly reason in their affairs, like beasts, instead of living viciously. This can be taken as a central problem of the poem; Jean de Meun would call it the complaint of Nature. Creation is good, and the world was in harmony until the fall. Christ saved men, and the age of grace has come upon us. Grace rights the imbalance of nature caused by man's sin. We are left with an odd situation, familiar to us from the *Psychomachia*: the world is saved, but neither individuals nor society seems to be saved. These are the ideas Langland sets out to resolve. His method is, while keeping his vision steadily in touch with the observable state of corruption in the folk, to see the world from larger and larger perspectives.

A result of this double focus is a cyclical, rhythmic form: Will recapitulates certain motifs again and again. The encyclopedism of the poem is motivated in part by Langland's desire to stay in contact with present reality by running critically over the estates of the world, and at the same time to encompass sacred history and theological doctrine so as to comprehend present reality in truth. As Mensendieck suggested over seventy years ago, the name "Piers Plowman" hints of both the long historical dimension of the poem (Piers alluding to St. Peter) and the short view of the people of this world in their occupations (plowman).

Along with the large sweep from the beginning of *Piers* to its apocalyptic recapitulation at the end, there are many smaller circular movements within the poem. Often they take the form of graded progressions which recur in the poem (or in Christian history). The goal of Will's quest, at least for a time, the answer to the question how to do well, is personified as Do Well and then split into a triad, Do Well, Do Bet, and Do Best. One personified abstraction after another defines these three to Will, who becomes more and more perplexed, and returns to the beginning of the question, asking who is Do Well, over and over. The meaning of the cycle of the second part of the poem, titled in the manuscripts the Lives of Do Well, Do Bet, and Do Best, has not been agreed upon: there may be reference to the three lives or states of mental life in medieval theory, to the three persons of the Trinity, the three ages of the world in Joachim of Flora's scheme, the three theological virtues, to some mixture of these, or to none of them. This state of uncertainty makes use of the triad in criticism difficult.

In a different kind of cycle, Will grows old. We find allusions to Will's baptism and wasted youth in the speech of Holy Church near the beginning; he worries about his advancing age in passus 16; we see him as elderly at the end. The cycle of Will's life constitutes a submerged structure of the poem. Another cycle is the plot of the Church year: in the last few passus Will meets Abraham in mid-Lent, dreams of Jesus' riding like a knight to Jerusalem on Palm Sunday, goes to mass on Easter Sunday, and finally has a vision of Pentecost. Will seems to embody both the biological and the institutional progress of his race: ontogeny recapitulates phylogeny. We will touch on other instances of recapitulated motifs below.

In general, the expanded portions of the B and C versions of *Piers* preserve both the attentiveness to social problems and the inwardness of Will's vision found in the A-Text. What is new is the direct introduction of Christian history into the poem. Langland joins a critique of society, an exploration of individual consciousness, and a view of sacred history. To discern the way these three angles of vision behave in combination is the chief business of criticism of *Piers*. It is to reconcile the vitally present with the memory of the past and the hope of the world to come.

THE "VISION OF DO BEST"

I will concentrate on the place where studies of many allegories should begin, at the end of the poem. The last two passus of the poem, the "Vision of Do Best," are no more involved than usual. In the following summary of their contents, I must remind the reader that they are nearly nine hundred lines of vigorous English alliterative verse. They begin with Will waking and writing down his last dream, the story of the Passion, Harrowing of Hell, and Resurrection. Will goes to mass, and "sodeynliche" dreams. He dreams of a figure bearing a cross before the people, Piers Plowman and at the same time Christ, probably carrying the slender "Resurrection Cross" familiar in Christian art. Will asks Conscience about the figure, and Conscience explains, looking back to the martial imagery of the Harrowing, why Jesus is called Christ, "conquerour." Conscience goes on to show Will how the life of Jesus—the epiphanies, the miracles, the Resurrection and the institution of the Church—is a paradigm of Do Well, Do Bet, and Do Best. We learn that Christ gave Piers the power to absolve men of sins if they do well. Piers here is associated with St. Peter and the Petrine power of binding and unbinding.

Will then dreams of the descent of the Paraclete on "Piers and to hise felawes," and the events of Pentecost. Conscience explains to Will that the Paraclete is God's messenger, Grace. Grace, in the dream, parcels out talents or "graces" to the divisions of men in their several estates: preachers, craftsmen, laborers, scientists, knights, and the orders of poverty. He makes Piers his "procurator" and "reeve," and invests him with an allegorical farmstead. The four oxen are the evangelists; the four bullocks are the chief Latin Fathers of the Church; the two harrows are the two testaments; the seeds are the cardinal virtues; the farmhouse, called Unity, is built from materials made of Christ's cross, baptism, and blood, Mercy (as mortar) and Scripture (as roof); a cart is called Christendom; the draft horses who pull it are Contrition and Confession; Priesthood is hayward. This is an example of allegorical analysis and categorization. Grace, with Piers, leaves the farm to "till truth" in missionary activity throughout the world.

Unfortunately, Pride sees all this activity, and gathers a host of vices to attack the farm. Conscience gathers the Christians into Unity for protection, since Grace is not present to defend them. They dig a moat which seems to be (it is not made explicit) repentance, except that the prostitute and a pair of perjured court officers ("a sisour and a somonour") do not join in the work. The moat is filled with the Christians' penitential tears. Conscience offers them the Eucharist, if they pay their debts properly. A brewer refuses to be ruled by "Spiritus Iusticie." Conscience laments, and an "ignorant vicar," a man perhaps like Will himself, joins him, regretting the sinfulness of the people, even the pope's cardinals. The vicar wishes cardinals would stay at Avignon (a papal seat at this time) where they belong, and that Conscience would stay in the king's court. He further wishes that Grace were the leader of the clergy, and Piers (here sharply distinguished from the pope) were "Emperour of al the worlde." A "lord" persists in tampering with his estate accounts. A king urges the right to tax the people, but Conscience asserts that his right is contingent on his ruling well. The vicar leaves for home, and Will wakes and writes.

The final passus opens with Will, awake and hungry, meeting Need about noon. Need berates Will for not arguing that he had a right to sustenance, too, because he teaches *Spiritus temperancie*. Need insists that no law governs a man in need, and need is next to temperance in virtue. Will sleeps, and dreams that Antichrist comes, turning upside down the "crop" of truth. Friars and monks follow him; only fools resist. Pride bears the banner, and a lecherous lord joins the attack on Conscience and his forces, the fools of Christ. Conscience again (and in nearly the same words as before), gathers his people into Unity. He cries out to Nature ("Kynde") for help, and nature sends diseases from the planets and brings Death. Old Age accompanies death, and in some lines doubtless inspired by the plague,

> Deeþ cam dryuynge after and al to duste passhed
> Kynges and knyghtes, kaysers and popes.
> Lered ne lewed he leet no man stonde,
> That he hitte euene, þat euere stircd after.
> Many a louely lady and hir lemmans knyȝtes
> Swowned and swelted for sorwe of deþes dyntes.

Conscience convinces Nature to cease his ravages, to see whether Christians would amend themselves. Then Fortune begins to flatter them, and sends Lechery to the few still alive. Covetise follows, then Simony, and they recapitulate in brief the Lady Meed episode early in the poem. Life, a figure of the pride of life, rides recklessly forth and takes a lover, Fortune: the lovers beget Sloth, who marries Despair. Conscience desperately sends Old Age against Despair and Life. Life seeks a physician, but Old Age kills the doctor himself. Life rides to Revel, a place of comfort. Old Age hastens after life, and with a sudden shift of reference rides over Will's head. Will becomes bald, deaf, toothless, gouty, and impotent, to his wife's disgust.

Will cries out to Nature to avenge him on Old Age, and Nature gives him some advice: go to Unity (the Church) and learn a craft. What craft? "Lerne to loue": love truly and the necessities of life will take care of themselves. Will takes the advice, perhaps the only time in the poem we find him doing what he is told to do, and finds Unity beseiged by seven giants (the deadly sins) and Antichrist. Conscience calls on "Clergie" (Learning) for help against the wicked priests. Friars (known for learning) come to help, but fail in covetise. Conscience invites the friars in, and urges them to love as the founders of their orders had. The population of friars is too great, and their begging and search for livings is too much a burden on the people. Conscience says they should be numbered and registered.

Envy sends the friars to school to learn communistic economics in self-defense. The people go to the friars out of shame to confess to their parish priests. Conscience makes Peace the porter of Unity, and Hypocrisy attacks and wounds many wise teachers. Conscience sends for a physician, Shrift (confession), who prescribes strong penance, which some refuse to accept. They ask for a more lenient doctor: Sir-Let-live-in-lechery groans about having to fast on Friday. Contrition tells Conscience of an eager physician, one Friar Flatterer. Conscience says only Piers is a better doctor than the secular (non-fraternal) orders of clergy, but he will let the friars in anyway, presumably in acknowledgement of the fact that friars did administer penance. The friar manages to get a letter from a lord giving him permission to "cure" (administer penance) as if he were a curator (secular priest). The friar arrives at Unity, and tells the porter Peace that his name is "sire *Penetrans domos*," alluding to the warning against hypocritical heretics in II Timothy 3:6. Peace rejects the friar, having known a similar one who was his lord's physician, who begot children on the household women. Courteous Speech, however, lets the friar in.

Conscience greets Friar Flatterer and asks if he can heal the wounded Contrition. The parson's medical plasters are too painful. The friar gives him a comfortable plaster, which is secret payment in return for prayers of remission. Contrition leaves, oddly enough, Contrition; that is, the state of contrition for sins is abolished by the Flatterer, and the figure who represented the state absents himself from himself.

Sloth and Pride, seeing this, assail Conscience again. Conscience once more cries out, for Clergy and Contrition. Peace says Contrition is drowned, enchanted, drugged with Flattery. Conscience resolves to become a pilgrim (recapitulating earlier incidents in the poem), to seek Piers Plowman, who can destroy Pride, and provide a living for friars who flatter because of need. He begs Nature to avenge him, and cries out for Grace. Will wakes up, and the poem ends.

Even this selective summary makes the head reel, and, as I have said, it is not untypical of the poem. The poet shows little concern for continuity of action. The levels of reality embodied in the characters are various and sometimes incongruous. The causation of events is sometimes purely fictional, that is, arbitrary and coincidental, and sometimes consists of rational consequences of the states which are personified. The narrator variously acts and observes. Motifs are repeated apparently with random succession. Some figures are not adequately identified; some seem to be handled with a relish for detail inappropriate to their importance. The relations among such presumably essential actors as Will, Conscience, Piers, and Grace are not clear (nor does the rest of the poem shed much light here). The environment in space and time inexplicably alters. Literary anticipation and suspense are absent. Topics of social, theological, or philosophical moment are eagerly developed only to be dropped, apparently at random. On the face of it, we are dealing with a confused mess whose redeeming virtues, if any, are local rhythmic power and the expression of passionate concern—the voice of an unintelligent but gifted singer.

I think this is a fair first impression of the poem. Yet I think a failure to come to terms with *Piers* is a failure to come to terms with allegory. *Piers Plowman* is a radical presence, and it is right that visionary urgency take precedence over cool intellection. It would surely be wrong to suggest that Langland is imitating actual dream experience (the suggestion has been made). It seems likely that the interpretation of dreams in any culture is a matter of convention; it is certain that Langland is at his most conventional when he chooses the dream vision frame. On the other hand, to dismiss the problems which *Piers* raises—of structure, characterization, causality, continuity, and general clarity—as problems only for the modern sensibility with its conventional demand for literary unity, is likewise wrong. One can allow for changes in an age's favorite forms and approach, as Northrop Frye especially urges us to do, a genre in terms of its generic qualities and not the qualities of the form of the novel. One can apprehend *Piers* as an encyclopedic, satiric, apocalyptic, homiletic dream vision, or whatever, and accept its lack of overt and continuously present narrative structure. Even allowance for sui-generic freedoms and restraints does not satisfy our desire for proper relations between elements of the poem. There is a kind of supergrammar in our literature, a set of presumptions about sequences, ontological states of fictional characters, narrator / narrative interactions, which *Piers* seems to disregard, and the poem is as unintelligible or offensive to some readers as bad grammar.

It is best to respond to these considerations by choosing a middle course. While one can say that the local force of small parts of the poem probably had sufficient impact on a contemporary audience immersed in the problems which the poem analyzes and satirizes, this does not compensate for a reflective critic's duty to discern whatever pattern may be discerned, however deeply it may be buried. Radically diffuse poems of prominent rhetorical impact are like happy families: they are all alike. If this is all the poem is, the reader interested in poetry for reasons other than historical documentation could better spend his time on a modern poem of radical diffuseness than on *Piers*, and not waste effort with the historical and philological matter of the fourteenth century. On the other hand, it does not suffice to decide that the recognition of literary conventions such as dream vision or encyclopedic form resolves the critic's problem. This is like saying of most modern poetry that it is "surreal"; the adjective, too inclusive, abolishes discernment. A right criticism of *Piers* must take into account both what is conventional and determinate in structure and technique, and also what is radical, existential, energetic, and making for chaos. This ideal criticism presupposes a knowledge of both literary convention and fourteenth-century English issues which we do not possess; but the effort is worth making.

The most prominent motifs in the last two passus of *Piers* are the paired actions of psychomachia and defense of a fortification, the motifs found in Prudentius's poem. And as in the *Psychomachia* a wicked character, Discordia, penetrates the ramparts of the camp, so in *Piers* the friar Flatterer slips within the barn Holy Church. So in Ariosto's *Orlando Furioso*, Michael discovers Discord and Fraud living in a monastery (14. 78–91). Henceforth we may call this figure the *mendax*, the liar. We have seen that his sources are the Fury Alecto and the liar, based on the Jewish idea of the false prophet,

94

who will not be allowed into the New Jerusalem. The attack on the new man by Alecto and the vices she assembles in the *Anticlaudianus* is one of the sources of the Old French psychomachias which are sources of *Piers*; the Fury lies behind both Langland's Pride (and Antichrist) and his Friar Flatterer in the last passus. Prudentius confirms the relationship of his action to the Apocalypse by describing his city in the terms used of the New Jerusalem; Langland, if confirmation were needed, shows us Antichrist himself. Mary Carruthers argues persuasively that Antichrist and Friar Flatterer recapitulate some actions of the figure False of the Lady Meed section of the poem, as we would expect, since all are coheirs of Alecto and the tradition of the *mendax*. These similarities between *Piers* and the *Psychomachia* are fundamental, and by no means surprising: the psychomachia with a lowercase *p* had become a common topic in medieval literature. But the difference in quality between the two poems, written nearly a millenium apart, is great. Langland has used the simple plot of Prudentius as a historical frame—just barely sufficient to orient the reader—while he explores his varied terrain.

RECONSIDERATIONS

Langland's version of the psychomachia is more diffuse and idiosyncratic than Prudentius's, and yet in some ways more controlled and resonant. In what follows I shall take up these two general qualities in more detail.

In Langland's visions a crowd of nearly undifferentiated people seems always to be nearby, apt to break upon the scene with gusto at any moment. In accordance with intellectual consistency they do not belong in the same fictional world as personifications like Conscience and Peace, but they return so often in *Piers* that we grow to tolerate their presence and even to take pleasure in their bustling, often bawdy intrusions. They are the "field full of folk" whom Will sees in his first vision. The "full" should be emphasized, as they add to the poem's quality of plenitude and richness—every crevice is stuffed with an irascible human being. Old French allegory seems to be the source of this quality; English critics are apt to characterize it as particularly English.

The folk enter the poem at rhythmic intervals. Their prominent appearances are at the beginning, at the confessions of the deadly sins, throughout the passus with Piers at the half-acre, in the meeting with Activa-Vita, who seems to personify the folk, and finally at the end. In each of these places some details recall the other appearances of the folk in the poem, and they are deliberately arranged according to some set of categories: their vocations, sins, or estates. The arrangement according to sins is utterly commonplace, and in fact in these cases the folk fill out the scheme, rather than the scheme's serving to analyze the phenomenon of the folk.

The other divisions are less usual. The issue of the proper vocation for a man seems to have caught on in fourteenth-century letters (we find versions of the question in Dante's *Paradiso* and the English poem *Pearl*) and is a dominant theme in *Piers*. The introspective passage added to passus 6 draws attention to Will's kind of work and his more or less feeble rationale for it. The opening scene of the poem satirizes the whole world by probing the occupations and laying open their flaws. In the scene of the folk in passus 9, Piers instructs several groups as to their proper work in society: laborers, women in various stations, and knights.

Judging Langland's motives from hindsight is perilous, but a deliberate sequence seems intended here. Will dreams of the folk, and sees their corruption. Many of these dreams are followed by an extended allegorical conversation, all of them by some culminating allegorical vision. The first view of the field full of folk is followed by Will's conversation with Holy Church, and the vision of Lady Meed. Then the vision of the folk (as the deadly sins) is followed by the appearance of Piers Plowman, who undertakes to guide them on a penitential pilgrimage. The folk stay on the stage during this vision, and become a problem when they refuse to help Piers with his plowing. The vision of the pardon culminates this sequence. Will goes off on his extended conversations about the way to do well, and meets the folk symbolized (more clearly in the B-Text) in the person of Haukyn the Active Man. There follows Will's discourse with Anima (*Liberum-arbitrium*), which culminates in the visions of the Tree of Charity and the deeds of Christ, which are the climax of the poem. Finally the folk reappear, as we have seen, in the episode of the "division of graces," the parceling out of vocations to mankind. The folk remain, in this succession, obstreperously and cantankerously the same, but Will's visions become deeper, more general, and more historical as the poem progresses. There is a steady movement from the rationally analytical to the numinous, as the workings of God in history are revealed. The motif of grace divided among men in a Pentecost vision makes sense of the initial business of the field full of folk, in much the same way that the theory of "natural man" might make sense, for a political philosopher, of the idea of the social contract. The myth of origins (or the myth of the end) underpins the vision of things as they are. The type of Pentecost is the Mosaic Piers delivering instructions. This is typology at work.

In this one instance, the treatment of the folk who generate much of the energy and many of the problems of the poem, we can see how one filament of the allegory which from close up looks tangled and unconnected is actually handled with some order in the poem as a whole. The locally chaotic can, given perspective, conform to an integrated whole. This phenomenon is characteristic of *Piers*. One need not surmise that Langland had clearly articulated a methodology along these lines. In part the movement of the poem may come from Langland's temperament, bodied forth in Will, as a poet unusually concerned about the righteousness of what he does and believes, in the face of the world which he sees around him; in part it may come from the nature of the poem—quest, encyclopedic satire, dream vision.

A second chaotic element in the last two passus of the poem is the figure of Conscience: his actions, on the face of it, make no sense. He is the first significant personification to appear at the opening of the poem: his first speech is an attack on the corrupt prelacy. Conscience and Reason are important advisors to the king throughout the Lady Meed episode, they lead the folk in penance in passus 6, they join in the friar's banquet in passus 16. Conscience, with Patience, meets *Activa-vita*. *Liberum-arbitrium* (Anima) defines conscience as the faculty which denies or consents. Conscience behaves in *Piers* as both a faculty of a single man's mind—Will's Conscience—and also as a faculty of discernment in general, as the conscience of a society, or the Church. Grace, one of the few figures in the poem whose statements are unambiguously correct, tells the community to crown Conscience king: it is as such that he directs the stage in the last two passus.

Conscience's poetic function is to move the action. He performs this function by considering it his responsibility to protect Unity, and by calling upon one personification after another to aid in the defense. As Conscience had said of Christ, "It bi-comeþ to a kyng to kepe and to defende" (C 22.42). The process begins with Will crying "wiþ Conscience" for help from Grace (22.212). When Antichrist attacks, Conscience gathers the folk into Unity, and with Kynde Wit (Natural Understanding) as his teacher, fortifies the Church. When the people rebel, and Antichrist attacks again, Conscience cries to Kynde (Nature) for help. Nature failing, Conscience cries again, this time for Clergie (Learning), whom Conscience had rejected earlier in the poem. Rather grudgingly, on Contrition's advice, Conscience admits Friar Flatterer into Unity. Near the end, Conscience cries again for Clergy, and in the last lines of the poem, he cries finally for Grace.

The folk are not so much truly mimetic presentations as a consistent and recurring entity which might have been personified by a title like Commune, and they are in effect personified, as Stella Maguire pointed out, by Haukyn, *Activa-vita*. Priscilla Jenkins has urged that Conscience needs to be understood in the opposite way: what is apparently a personification seems to be modified into a nearly mimetic character, capable of human emotions and human errors. Skeat tells us that Whitaker, in his 1813 edition of *Piers*, pointed out an inconsistency in the figure of Conscience: he complains to Flatterer that the parson's medication (penance) is too severe. Jenkins persuasively argues that Conscience typifies a "frustration of allegory," that the faculty of conscience as such cannot be quite true to itself in the face of the facts of corruption in the world. The pressures of need, the sophistical chopping of learned friars, the great strength of covetise can actually alter Conscience's knowledge of truth. This paradox is caused by the portmanteau reference of the word conscience.

The paradox of Conscience apparently acting inconscientiously rises from the larger paradox that the Holy Spirit has come, and grace has operated, and yet men do wrong. We live in a new dispensation, yet we are imperfect. As in the *Psychomachia*, we are in the presence of an unrealized apocalypse, an age of grace in which men are not gracious. This predicament seems all the sharper at the end of *Piers*, for the poet has shown us the action of redemption itself. The figure of Conscience, who seems best able to grasp the meaning of Christ, is most apt to come into conflict with himself. Conscience is both the cutting edge of Will's social and introspective criticism, and the instrument of reaching out for divine help in history, in grace, in Piers Plowman. This mental faculty resides at the meeting point of temporality and eternity, living in a corrupt world in the age of grace, and it shows the strain by succumbing to logical disintegration. Conscience is an alter (or super) ego of Will himself, and enables the dreamer, just barely, and temporarily, to stand back and see.

A third radical, chaotic aspect of the last two passus is the sequence of action. After the vision of Pentecost and the allegorical founding of the Church, there seems no reason for events to occur in the order they do. The outstanding case of apparently confused arrangement is the double account of the attack on Unity. When Pride and his forces first attack, Langland writes: "Quod Conscience, to alle cristene þo, 'my counseil is to wende / Hastiliche into vnitee and holde we vs þere'" (22.355–56). In the second attack, by Antichrist, in the next and last of Will's dreams, we have: "'I conseille,' quod Conscience þo, 'comeþ wiþ me, ye fooles, / Into vnite holy chirche and holde we vs þere'" (23.74–75). We feel déjà lu: either Langland intends for us to see that he is circling back to a former point in the plot, or he wrote the section between these two passages late and inserted it, or, perhaps most likely, both.

We have seen this kind of circling back before. Other examples are the recurrence of a document very like the pardon of passus 10, the Law of Love on "a pece of an harde roche," a Mosaic *petra*, in passus 20; or, even closer to the present case, the repetition of part of a line (surely not a formula) in two accounts of the Passion— "'*Aue, rabbi*,' quath that ribaud . . ." (19.170; 21.50). In all these cases the point is to see what comes between the repeated occurrences. After Conscience's gathering of the folk in passus 22, the poet depicts the breakdown of the system of morality within Unity. Will wakes and meets Need, who argues that he is next in rank to temperance among the virtues. Will falls to sleep again, and dreams, and this time Antichrist resumes the attack (as Pride becomes the banner bearer), and friars and monks join with the vices.

The reappearance of the folk, the introduction of Need, the introduction of Antichrist, the special attack on the irreligious religious— Langland stops the action to present us with this apparently diffuse material. Again, there is discernible method. The action here echoes the action in the half-acre episodes of passus 6 to 9. In passus 6 we see Reason preaching to the field full of folk. His message is that "for pride" plagues and tempests have come upon the people. This corresponds to the attack of Pride on Unity: the image of crops being blown down is common to both places. Reason urges the people to work, just as Grace set men to work in their crafts. Repentence makes Will weep, and the confession of the deadly sins follows, just as the Christians dig and fill a moat with tears of penitence. The people set out on a pilgrimage, and find Piers for a guide, just as Conscience offers the Christians in Unity the eucharist if they will repent and give satisfaction for their sins, and "pay" Piers's pardon.

The people balk against their tasks in passus 9, just as they do in passus 22. At the beginning of passus 23, Will meets Need, who performs a function very much like that of Hunger in passus 9. (I should confess here that no one yet has explained the figure of Need satisfactorily.) The ninth passus, just before the pardon episode, concludes with a mysterious, Saturnian prophecy, which says among other things, echoing Reason's sermon, that "Thorwe flodes and foule wederes frutes shullen faile; / Pruyde and pestilences shal muche puple fecche." Immediately after Need leaves, at the beginning of the last vision of the poem, we read that "Antecrist cam þanne, and al þe crop of truþe / Torned it tid vp so doun and ouertilte þe roote ..." (23. 53–54). Antichrist acts like an anti-Piers Plowman, disrupting the harvest of the Church.

The correspondences between these two actions are by no means exact, but the relative clarity of action of the earlier vision helps to give us purchase on the meaning of the last passus. The earlier action is lucid: it represents what John Burrow called "the arc of penitential action"—moving from sermon to confession to pilgrimage to pardon. The recapitulation of the motifs of the penitential arc in the last visions expands the meaning of the motifs at the same time that it disorients the reader. What had been seen is now understood. The *signs* of vice—plague and ruined crops—become the vices themselves; the need for penitence becomes a martial defense of the soul; the vocations of men are divinely ordained; the principle of sin is embodied in Antichrist; the idea of hunger as the goad to work is generalized in the idea of necessity as the invariable law of the economy of this world; this necessity is applied especially to the dreamer; and friars, the treasonous clerks, are singled out as disturbers of the economy.

Langland has pressed many of the main issues of the poem to their end, has more fully and abstractly allegorized them, and now presents those issues overtly in his fiction, apparently heedless of making confusion. What had earlier in *Piers* represented the sacrament of penance is now seen more abstractly yet equally vividly as the last ditch struggle for survival. Even within the struggle of the last two passus, we see the vice pride rendered into the ultimate historical figure, Antichrist, as typology replaces personification. Carruthers argues that slippery and confused, overliteral personification allegory, characteristic especially of the Lady Meed episode and of the final penetration of Unity by a company of vices, runs counter to the "redeemed language" of typological allegory, which had seemed to replace false personifications until these last actions of the poem. The pattern is nearly the same as that of the *Psychomachia*, which emphasizes personification in its main body, and typology at the end. In these allegories, the truth of Christian history rivals the truth of psychological allegory: phylogeny rivals ontogeny. I suggested in the last chapter that the *Psychomachia* is most valuable because it was useful, and the last passus are an example: the fiction of warfare has freed the poet to sustain his narrative at this most general level, in a sort of remythologizing of his own text.

THE PRECURSOR OF "PIERS PLOWMAN"

I cannot pretend to have solved the problems of the last two passus of *Piers Plowman* here, but perhaps the critical problem of how to cope with the farrago of confused material can be handled along the lines I have suggested. A commonly noted characteristic of late medieval literature is the ease with which an author turns his view from this world to that, from profane to sacred, from his interior to the exterior of the visible plain and the larger field of sacred history and redeeming fiction. With Langland this tendency comes near to the breaking point. He writes of a man who is wholly and variously a man, and at the same time Voluntas, or a man about to die, or a man engaging in the sacraments of the Church or the liturgical year, or a man with visions of his own time and of all time.

Allegories have a common purpose, to make sense of things: we do not make this demand of other modes of fiction. Langland refuses to ignore experience and the observed state of things in order to obtain sense. He carries friars and brewers and financial worries and common hypocrisy with him up the anagogical ladder of his vision.

Finally, a distinction needs to be made. I spoke in the last chapter of allegory as a reductive mode of literature in that it distills—from the spray of phenomena and the inarticulable mass of mental concepts—images and actions which are organized, manipulable, and comprehensible. With *Piers* we meet an apparent contradiction: these adjectives do not describe the poem, as they do the *Psychomachia*.

Piers does reduce experience and thought into the kinds of abstractions and patterns which we call allegory, but it does so in a complicated way. Where the *Psychomachia* has a simple, double action— battle and reestablishment of a city—*Piers* has a complex, single series of actions—a set of dream visions of great variety. Where the *Psychomachia* develops a couple of allegorical techniques of narration —personification and simple typology—*Piers* explores a bewildering panoply of techniques which are intricately overlapping and interwoven. Where the narrative stance of the *Psychomachia* is lucid—a removed narrator inspired by Christ generates a coherent set of abstractions, with a few "literal" absurdities—*Piers Plowman* poses an involved naive narrator, wholly human, who generates abstractions from his interior, meets enigmatic figures, moves, debates, alters in mood, sees and fails to see, becomes exasperated, swoons with delight, and ponders. The poem is reductive in that it penetrates to the simplest lineaments of man's understanding of the world; but it is complicated in that its techniques, material, and modes of presentation are elaborate and perplexing.

The narrative form of dream vision gives Langland the freedom to depict man's interior and his place in history at the same time. The *Psychomachia* possessed the same freedom, by means of the device of personification, but it is the lesser poem because it risks less: there is no human center to feel or reject the vision, and therefore no means of conveying human passion. Langland's solution lets him go, perhaps, too far in the other direction: there is so much a sense of perplexed suffering in *Piers Plowman* that the reader can miss the poem's underlying integrity. Spenser has another solution which, as we shall see, avoids the problems of both Langland and Prudentius: his adoption of the romance mode.

Bibliographical Note

Morton W. Bloomfield's article, "The Present State of *Piers Plowman* Studies," *Speculum* 14 (1939): 215–32, repr. in Blanch (see below), pp. 3–25, refers to most studies to 1939. The bibliographies in Knott and Fowler's edition of the A-Text (Baltimore, 1952) and in Vasta's anthology (see below) are full.

The text is being reedited: so far the A-Text and B-Text have appeared, ed. George Kane (London, 1960), and Kane and E. Talbot Donaldson (London, 1975). The best full-length treatments of *Piers* are those of Bloomfield, *"Piers Plowman" as a Fourteenth-Century Apocalypse* (New Brunswick, N.J., 1961); Robert Worth Frank, Jr., *"Piers Plowman" and the Scheme of Salvation*, Yale Studies in English, 136 (New Haven, 1957); E. Talbot Donaldson, *"Piers Plowman": The C-Text and its Poet*, Yale Studies in English, 113 (New Haven, 1949); D. W. Robertson, Jr., and Bernard F. Huppé, *"Piers Plowman" and Scriptural Tradition* (Princeton, 1951); Elizabeth D. Kirk, *The Dream Thought of "Piers Plowman"* (New Haven, 1972); and Mary Carruthers, *The Search for St. Truth: A Study of Meaning in "Piers Plowman"* (Evanston, Ill., 1973).

Three collections of essays on *Piers* are edited by Edward Vasta, *Interpretations of "Piers Plowman"* (Notre Dame and London, 1968); Robert J. Blanch, *Style and Symbolism in "Piers Plowman"* (Knoxville, Tenn. 1969); and with all new essays, S. S. Hussey, *"Piers Plowman": Critical Approaches* (London, 1969).

I referred in this essay to works by Northrop Frye, *Anatomy of Criticism* (Princeton, 1957); Stella Maguire, "The Significance of Haukyn, *Activa Vita*, in *Piers Plowman*," *RES* 25 (1949): 97 109, repr. in Blanch, pp. 194–208; Priscilla Jenkins, "Conscience: the Frustration of Allegory," in Hussey, pp. 125–42; the excellent article by John Burrow, "The Action of Langland's Second Vision," *EIC* 15 (1965): 247–68, repr. in Blanch, pp. 209–27; and Otto Mensendieck, *Charakterentwicklung und ethisch-theologische Anschauungen des Verfassers von "Piers the Plowman"* (Hamburg diss.) (Leipzig, 1900).

John Lawlor has traced Will's transition from sterile to experienced knowledge in a fine article, "The Imaginative Unity of *Piers Plowman*,"

RES, n.s. 8 (1957): 113–26, repr. in Blanch, pp. 101–16. On medieval genres, besides Bloomfield, *Apocalypse*, chap. 1, see Jay Martin, "Wil as Fool and Wanderer in *Piers Plowman*," *TSLL* 3 (1962): 535–48.

A survey of the various allegorical techniques in *Piers* may be found in the introduction to selections of the poem ed. Elizabeth Salter and Derek Pearsall (Evanston, Ill., 1967), pp. 3–28. Salter argues for the typological reading of *Piers* in "Medieval Poetry and the Figural View of Reality," *PBA* 54 (1968): 73–92.

I think Robertson and Huppé were the first to suggest that "Will" may signify *voluntas*. Five works treat the uses of history in *Piers*: Helmut Maisack, *William Langlands Verhältnis zum zisterziensischen Mönchtum: Eine Untersuchung der Vita im "Piers Plowman"* (Tübingen diss.) (Balingen, 1953), esp. pp. 25–26; Donald Wesling, "Eschatology and the Language of Satire in *Piers Plowman*," *Criticism* 10 (1968): 277–89; Bloomfield, *Apocalypse*; Bloomfield, "*Piers Plowman* as a Fourteenth-Century Apocalypse," *CentR* 5 (1961): 281–95, repr. Vasta, pp. 339–54; Bloomfield, "*Piers Plowman* and the Three Grades of Chastity," *Anglia* 76 (1958): 227–53.

On the three lives, Do Well and so forth, see John F. Adams, "*Piers Plowman* and the Three Ages of Man," *JEGP* 61 (1962): 23–41, and the earlier articles by Hussey, Dunning, and Coghill referred to there; also Bloomfield, *Apocalypse*, pp. 116–21, and Frank, *Scheme*. On the general topic of the false prophet, a source of the *mendax*, see James Nohrnberg, *The Analogy of "The Faerie Queene"* (Princeton, 1976), index, s.v., and the references cited there. On the connection of the friars to the idea of the false prophet see the excellent articles by Penn R. Szittya, "The Friar as False Apostle: Antifraternal Exegesis and the *Summoner's Tale*," *SP* 71 (1974): 19–46, and "The Antifraternal Tradition in Middle English Literature," *Speculum* 52 (1977): 287–313.

Howard Meroney, "The Life and Death of Longe Wille," *ELH* 17 (1950): 1–35, and Mary Carruthers Schroeder, "*Piers Plowman*: The Tearing of the Pardon," *PQ* 49 (1970): 8–18, both connect Piers with Moses. Carruthers wrote persuasively about Conscience in "The Character of Conscience in *Piers Plowman*," *SP* 67 (1970): 13–30. These articles appear revised now in her book. The comparison of the Do Best part of the poem to the half-acre episode was made by Henry W. Wells, "The Construction of *Piers Plowman*," *PMLA* 44 (1929): 123–40, repr. Vasta, pp. 1–21, and more elaborately by Kirk, *Dream Thought*, pp. 190–205, and Carruthers, pp. 152–73. The last two comparisons were made independently of one another, and of mine; my own version is closest to Carruthers's, but different enough, I think, to present. I say almost nothing about Piers himself here because I have treated him exclusively in another essay, "The Plowshare of the Tongue: The Progress of a Symbol from the Bible to *Piers Plowman*," *MS* 35 (1973): 261–93.

CHAPTER FOUR

The Knight at One

The Faerie Queene, BOOK ONE

But now in Christ Jesus, ye which sometimes were farre of, are made nere by the blood of Christ. For he is our peace, which hathe made of bothe one, and hath broken the stoppe of the particion wall, . . .

EPHESIANS 2 : 13–14 (Geneva)

If redemption is conceived of as a renovation of the *form* of man and the world, i.e., as a true *reformation*, then the focal point of intellectual life must lie in the place where the "idea" is embodied, i.e., where the non-sensible form present in the mind of the artist breaks forth into the world of the visible and becomes realized in it.

ERNST CASSIRER, *The Individual and the Cosmos in Renaissance Philosophy*

ARCHIMAGO UNVEILED

In the last canto of Book One of *The Faerie Queene*, the happy events of Redcrosse's bethrothal to Una are interrupted:

> With flying speede, and seeming great pretence,
> Came running in, much like a man dismaid,
> A Messenger with letters, which his message said.

All in the open hall amazed stood,
At suddeinnesse of that vnwarie sight. . . . *

The message is Duessa's assertion, in her assumed name of Fidessa, of a prior claim on Redcrosse's affections: "To me . . . / He was affiaunced long time before. . . ." When the messenger finishes reading, Una's father "sate long time astonished / As in great muse, ne word to creature spake."

For a moment the action is frozen, the merry sounds cease, and speech fails. If this had taken place early in the poem, before Redcrosse had learned what he knows at Una's home, the consequence of the intrusion would have been a fortuitous ("it chaunst") event, a providential salvation in the nick of time, or more likely a calamitous defeat for Redcrosse. We, as readers, have all along had access to privy intelligence which Redcrosse has not shared, because we have been reading, and receiving from the language of the poem, signals which only exist, in the fictional world which Redcrosse can see, for those who have the grace to know. The reader can take note that the messenger "flies," a sign of perplexity and weakness in the moral vocabulary of this book. The reader can recognize the ambiguity of "seeming great pretence"—looking as if he were important, or doubly pretending. The reader, perhaps aware of Dante's usage of *disfatto*, can even snatch a pun from "dismaid" (uncreated)— Hamilton notes that Redcrosse himself is twice emphatically so: "Disarmd, disgrast, and inwardly dismayde," and "disarmed, dissolute, dismaid." The reader can see in the retarded subject of the sentence, "A Messenger," a little period which recalls all the retarded bits of knowledge which he has experienced. Finally the reader can sympathize, as in this poem he so often does, with the amazement, the bewilderment—the entanglement in a maze or a wilderness—which characterizes innocent persons as they confront the machinery of evil. At any place in the poem, the reader could have unfolded the meaning of messenger and message in this way, but earlier on he

---

* I.12.24–25. Quotations are from *The Works of Edmund Spenser: A Variorum Edition*, ed. Edwin Greenlaw et al., *Book One*, spec. ed. Frederick M. Padelford (Baltimore and London, 1932). References to Book One cite only canto and stanza numbers; references to other Books cite book, canto, and stanza. For documentation and further bibliography see the note at the end of this chapter.

would watch Redcrosse succumb in delusion, blind to the truth of the matter which we can read out from the verbal surface of the poem.

Redcrosse has not had the advantage of perspective which we have. For us a thing "seems"—we see the words on the page and is untrustworthy on the face of it; for him a thing *is seen*, and he has none but visual access to the truth. Here, at last, at the end of the poem, his knowledge joins with ours. The message is signed—extra-metrically (that is, without the poem's consent) in stanza 28— "*Fidessa*." Redcrosse uncovers her name to the king: "*Fidessa* hight the falsest Dame on ground, / Most false *Duessa*," and Una identifies the messenger: "to discouer plaine, / Ye shall him *Archimago* find. . . ." Nothing in the text suggests that Archimago is disguised. Redcrosse and Una do not discover him for themselves, but for the royal company in Eden. At the end of the book they have acquired enough experience of the working of evil to perform the interpretations which the reader performs at the beginning with sheer literary intelligence.

The disjunction between the reader's rhetorical world—what we read—and the romance world which that rhetoric bodies forth— what Redcrosse sees—finally collapses. The other books of *The Faerie Queene* are about such themes as human power and relations, and the aesthetics of these, but Book One is conservative—Berger has called it "archaic." It represents the progress of a knight attaining the knowledge which we already have, a romance version of the original experience of Eden. I will argue that the main theme of Book I is the portrayal of sin as ignorance and knowledge as health. The philosophical assumption of the book is that the fictive portrayal of the health of knowledge as a genetic process, as a graded, unfolding movement, can best account for the sense we have of what we know. We are privileged to watch a romance knight, an image of ourselves as fallen man, lose his innocence and learn to distinguish good from evil, while we simultaneously understand—as readers—his ex-perience and sympathize—as humans—with his delusions and failures. We know at the outset, and experience learning; Redcrosse learns, and finally experiences knowledge.

A precedent for the poetics of this backward-looking, this archaism, this disjunction between innocent knight and sophisticated rhetoric, is the Bible in its historical dimension. The race of men in the Bible is blind, but the author of their history, its best reader, is God himself. The last book of the Bible is the book of the last prophet, the only one who could see the whole truth, who wrote the Unveiling. Those who know, John of Patmos or the reader of *The Faerie Queene*, who is compelled to know if he is to read at all, are as it were betrothed to the author, and will marry him at the end of history, "when iust time expired should appeare" (9.14), when Arthur will meet the Faerie Queene. We mark time.

Redcrosse moves from the world of pure fiction, the world of romance, in which the human state is manifest only in analogy and potentiality, just barely into the world of fallen Eden—our historical world. He discovers what Adam discovered, what is good and what is evil. We are aware that Redcrosse recapitulates the deeds of Christ, but he is not aware of any such typology—he is mostly amazed.

Spenser avoids direct observation of his hero's mental state, but we can get it through the way he talks, even though Spenser gives him little direct discourse. His access to knowledge can be determined by a simple comparison of his earlier to his later diction. His first speeches are loaded with terms like "shame," "virtue," "reward," "knighthood," "disgrace," "fear" and "afraid," and very frequently "rue." As the third stanza of the poem indicates, he is all caught up in the values of chivalry. When Archimago assumes Redcrosse's identity for a while, to deceive Una, he makes a good imitation of Redcrosse's style of speech, referring in "louely words" to "knighthood," "shame," "my liefe," "aduenture," "felon," "disgrace," "faithfull seruice" (3.28–29). But Redcrosse's final speech, revealing Duessa, sets forth the language of a man whose optic nerve has been cleansed: he speaks of "breach of loue, and loyalty betrayed," "I strayd," "faile," "false . . . falsest . . . false . . . false," "wicked arts and wylie skill," "Vnwares," "betrayed." Redcrosse presumably looks as usual, and he intends for six years to perform the usual sort of adventure "in warlike wize," but in his speech he shows that he is transformed.

Since Hankins demonstrated that Spenser drew many of the characters and events of Book One from the Book of Revelation, most critics have observed the apocalyptic structure of the book, that is, the relation of the chivalric quest to the beginning and end of Christian history. Frye says, "In the first book he uses up so much of the structure of Biblical typology that he could hardly have written a second book in the area of Revelation." The preceding chapters on the *Psychomachia* and *Piers Plowman*, having indicated a tradition, may encourage interpretation of this sort—Hamilton and Anderson have in fact argued that Spenser drew on *Piers* in constructing Book One. In these terms the three poems significantly differ in their endings, beginnings, and middles.

The *Psychomachia* ends with the establishment of the New Jerusalem itself, the city of Concord, which allegorically represents the human heart. The only trouble is the tentative entry into the city of the *mendax* figure, Discord. In *Piers*, the ending is less firm. The institution echoes, but is not, the New Jerusalem; it is the barn Unitas or Holy Church. The *mendax* here, the mendacious mendicant Friar Flatterer, prevails, and the temporary protagonist, Conscience, is exiled. If Unitas represents the heart, it is a secondary meaning of the allegory: first of all it is *una ecclesia. The Faerie Queene's* first book ends in the land of Eden, in a palace presumably near but other than the brazen tower in which Una's parents are besieged. (We first hear that Una's parents were exiled from Eden, then that they are within brazen walls, then in a brazen castle, and finally in this donjonlike tower; Spenser slightly redefines the image as we approach the place. He wants the bronze to suggest hell's harrowed gates.) Redcrosse had already had his Pisgah vision of the New Jerusalem from the Mount of Contemplation, and had been told that its peace (-salem) is not yet available to him; he must first complete his quest. The Eden of the end of the poem is not the heart, and is not the Church, but is a temporal and a mental state—by no means an end.

Spenser told his readers, in the letter to Raleigh, that "a Poet thrusteth into the middest, euen where it most concerneth him, and there recoursing to the thinges forepaste, and diuining of things to come, maketh a pleasing Analysis of all." I take this literally: Spenser will analyze good and evil, but will not depict the beginning or the end in his fiction except by recourse and divination, by the memories and visions of the protagonists. Spenser moves toward Eden in the imagery of Apocalypse, and analyzes the middle.

Redcrosse and Una, who is appropriately at one with Redcrosse at the poem's *termini*, are the alpha and omega of Book One, but Archimago, *The Faerie Queene's mendax* figure, slips into their lives near the beginning and is chained near the end. Prudentius's Discord personifies a relation within the soul, and is grounded on a Virgilian demon, the Fury Alecto. Langland's Friar Flatterer, halfway between a satiric vocational type and a personification, figures forth a social relation within the Church, and is grounded on a contemporary opinion of the fraternal orders. Archimago is neither type nor personification, but a very demon, with access to hell.

He is the arch-magician and the arch image-maker, as Berger points out, the "cunning Architect of cancred guile" (2.1.1), called "Hypocrisie" in the lemma of the first canto, and connected, as Nohrnberg has shown, with Simon Magus, the man-making (gentle-man-fashioning) arch-heretic. He appears early in the book because he bears part of the responsibility for moving the plot—he colludes with the author. One of his first actions is to send a sprite as messenger to the house of Morpheus; his last action is as a messenger to interrupt the banquet at the end. He is a mercurial go-between, a pimp of the imagination. He casts images before Redcrosse as Spenser casts them before us; he drives and frames Redcrosse's experience as Spenser does ours. He has a shadowy being, in Redcrosse's romance world, as Redcrosse has a shadowy being in our world. Archimago is an allegorist of evil.

The differences between Archimago and his forebears may help us distinguish between the mode of allegory employed by Spenser and the technique of Prudentius and Langland. The openings of the poems characterize these differences: Prudentius addresses Christ as muse and is thereby fully authorized to shape that complex spatial fiction of the battlefield which supports his warring personifications. Except for the valuable inconsistencies which I treated in the first chapter, the *Psychomachia* poses no human figure, but a series of fragments which may be composed in the reader's mind (as they were discomposed in Prudentius's) into a single psyche. The poem presents all object, no subject. Langland introduces an "I" and the mechanism of dreaming. No divine numen need authorize the contents of a dream: it is all subject. The personifications which occur in the poem blissfully ignore consistency of relation to the narrator: they are neither inside nor outside, and to ask them to stand still is to make a critical demand which *Piers* cannot bear. The emblem of *Piers*'s complexity is Piers Plowman, who is not exactly a personification, a social type, an antitype of Moses, Christ, and Peter, or a demonic potency, and who is humanoid and presents his own internal divisions, who changes, who moves and is moved by the plot. Prudentius's fiction is monotonously simple, and Langland wields his freedom so stoutly that he nearly overwhelms and bewilders the reader.

Spenser avails himself of the freedom implicit in fiction, that a poem can say wholly what it wants, without authority or verisimilitude, as randomly, chaotically, disintegrally, inconsistently, eclectically, madly as it will. In the term used in the last chapter, a poem can be radically diffuse. Spenser does not restrict himself by limiting the shape of the action (battle) as Prudentius had, or by exploiting the modality of narration (dream) as Langland had. He does make one crucial concession to intelligibility, which he explains in the stanzas prefatory to the poem, when he asks his muse to "Lay forth out of thine euerlasting scryne / The antique rolles, which there lye hidden still, / Of Faerie knights. . . ." He adopts the genre of romance. Fictions can say anything; romances say certain strange things, and the Spenserian sort of allegory makes romance tell the truth.

Spenser saw that romance could connect anything with anything, and seized upon that capability to provide a form for his fiction of the analogous universe. Probably from the "beginning" (or perhaps the first principle) of romance, and surely from the time of Chrétien, the structural pleasure of romance seems to be the acknowledgement of the one in the many, or in poetic terms, of rhythm in invention. The conspicuous feature of romance plots is *entrelacement*, and the logic or *ratio* of intertwined adventures is their significant redundancy: the various strands of plot allegorize each other.

The brief step from the idea of romance—pure invention of variations on a few themes—to allegorized romance can be looked at from two complementary points of view. One can look at Book One of *The Faerie Queene* as a rationalized romance, in which the plot bears a genetic relation to older romances, but which fills each element of the romance world with meaning by narrative comment, morally weighted rhetoric, and especially by the use of proper names—in extreme form personification. Sansfoy is the Bad Knight of "primitive" romance, sophisticated by his name and hence implicitly a judgment of Redcrosse's interior. Or, in the manner articulated

especially by Angus Fletcher and Harry Berger, Jr., one can look at
the poem as a schizoid or projective rationalization of Redcrosse's
interior, by which the simpler personifications in the poem (like
Sansfoy) are generated out of Redcrosse's disintegrating psyche—
the knight encounters fragments of himself as fictional entities,
reifications. He meets faithlessness because he is faithless. In this
second view, the encounters resemble romance events because
Spenser chooses this form to manifest interior psychic experience.
Both of these views are correct, opposite sides of the same coin; both
are genetic theories, the one taking romance conventions and the
other the demonic psyche as the generating powers.

Like Chrétien de Troyes, Spenser handles material which looks
prehistorical and prerational (Celtic), dark, anarchic, potent, richly
suggestive, a little frightening, and drags it struggling into the light.
These poets have it both ways: they narrate what seems Early and
hence deeper and more essential, yet their mode of presentation is
Late, sophisticated, gay, and persuasive of the control and confidence
which were available to poets in those days. Spenser anatomizes
romance, deliberates upon his analyzed material, and recombines it
in sequences which, by the formal principle of repetition, generate
intelligibility. Unlike medieval friars, romance motifs are limited in
number, but *The Faerie Queene* seems encyclopedic in its range because
Spenser cuts his stuff fine and rings changes upon it—the permuta-
tions seem numberless. The very poverty of romance plots works to
Spenser's advantage.

One can almost imagine Spenser following a certain method of
composition: the large plot of Book One—to kill a dragon and free a
maiden—is divided into the several events—slaying Error, meeting
Archimago, slaying Sansfoy, meeting Duessa, and so on. The events
are divided into their elements—locale, state of mind, emblematic
attributes, sensory perceptions, gesture, direction, speeches, time of
day, and so on. The elements of the events of the plot are divided
into their linguistic components—names, phrases, rhetorical stances,
loaded diction, and so on. This surely was not Spenser's actual
method, but Spenser's product looks this way more than the products
of Shakespeare or Chaucer or Dickens. Not, I think, that Spenser
especially "imposes meaning" on his poem, that is, renders it allegorical (by whatever technique), but that he discovers the connec-

tions—Foucault would say he divines the resemblances—among things by framing things in a certain pattern, by constructing a rhythmic system. Spenser does not so much create allegory, like Prudentius, as he finds it in the old stories and the inevitable structures of the world.

Murrin, making use of the insights to be gained from Frances Yates's *The Art of Memory*, has called *The Faerie Queene* "a kind of memory bank," a form which recollects and presents the relations, shapes, potencies, and attributes of certain moral and human constants, such as the balance of impulses in the soul or the path to perfection. These memorable forms of our moral culture are presented in a way analogous to the presentation of the narrative itself: Spenser knows large and general principles of truth which he disposes, in the manner of a romance plot, into fictional forms. The reader's job is to resynthesize by induction, to reconstruct the disposed and profuse rhetorical surface of the poem into articulate, cogent, synthetic principles. The chain of events of *The Faerie Queene* is notoriously hard to remember, but it becomes memorable when the principles of the system which generates it are understood—we can remember how Pyrochles and Cymochles behave if we grasp, with the aid of the etymology of their names, their significance as representatives of the irascible and concupiscent passions of the soul. It is like learning mathematics by induction instead of by rote—the former method is the firmer because it depends on what one knows already, on something as familiar as language.

C. S. Lewis, following some Romantic critics, has called upon us to strip away our sophisticated criticism of the allegorical burden of the poem and to respond to the monsters and battles with childlike wonder. This is well-meant advice, but impossible: the difficult thing is to respond to the poem simply. The reader *moyen intellectuel* must reconstruct the systematic underpinnings of the surface of the fiction if he is not to experience chaos, to misread, and to misremember. The dialectic of enchantment and rationality is like the conventional dialectic in medieval romance of Early event and Late redaction— it is for Redcrosse to wonder, and for us to recall his wondering as best we can. I think Spenser is not so much concerned to fix the border of mystery and reason as to tell the truth. The economy of the poem is that it is a paradigm of human life, presented paradigmatically, and an exploration of man's access to knowledge, presented knowingly.

STATICS: THE ARCH-MAGIC

Many Spenserians, chief among them Hamilton, Nohrnberg, Cheney, Berger, Anderson, and Hankins, have gathered and presented instances of the poet's repetitiousness and systematic use of correspondence. What follows depends on their labors, although I have added some. I have argued that allegory is communicated largely by allusion; and here I need to extend that principle, to observe that Book One of *The Faerie Queene* renders and controls its meaning by allusion not only to events, literary works, and institutions outside itself, but also by internal allusion or cross-reference. This is not an uncommon feature of poetry, but it charges the field of significance of Book One to a greater degree than of any other poem I know. We need to examine the systematics of the poem, and to consider their purpose, before we can get at the use of history in the allegory. The kind of criticism which is performed in this section is analysis, literally "splitting up," taken as far as seems worthwhile.

The most striking redundancies are the largest, the repetitions of episodes. (The largest redundancy of all, the parallelism of Book One and Two, has been much discussed and is beyond my scope.) What is clearest about the sequence of episodes is that it is not a matter of chance: the romance rhetoric of the accidental ("it chaunst") counters the increasingly visible design of the poem. The question, Why does this happen now? is always a fair one for a reader of Spenser. The evidence is not complete—some episodes in *The Faerie Queene* have yet to yield their secret—but it points toward perfection, so much so that if an episode were demonstrably inconsequential I think Spenser could be said to have nodded.

Una watches Redcrosse defeat a draconic figure in the first and penultimate episodes of the poem. The distance between these events is the measure of Spenser's voyage. The path may be seen as from Catholic ignorance, narrowness, and illusion to Protestant confidence, enlightenment, and power, or as Berger puts it, from romance

to Revelation, from carnal visions to redeemed fictions. The first
fight leaves Redcrosse and reader clotted and confused, but the last
fight is so transparent in significance and effect as to seem scarcely
fiction at all. Cheney observes that the poem ends with the situation
of the opening tableau, but *quantum mutatus* is Redcrosse. Between his
dragon-slayings he becomes St. George.

Judith Anderson has shown how many parallels there are between
the action of canto 1 and canto 5, in which Redcrosse defeats Sansjoy,
and Duessa with the aid of Night brings Sansjoy to Aesculapius to be
healed. In both cantos the battling knight is urged on by his lady;
Redcrosse is brought to bed; an elaborate Nile simile recurs; the figure
in the cave (Error, Night) is aroused by the sight of light; a body is
concealed from sight; a kind of underworld is visited. The notion of
health is explicit in canto 5; we shall see below how this theme is
introduced early. Redcrosse flies in secret haste from both locales. As
one of Archimago's messengers harrows Morpheus, and as Duessa
harrows the cave of Night, so does Arthur harrow Orgoglio's dungeon
(Duessa urged Orgoglio on), and Redcrosse harrows the similarly
bleak, desert, owl-haunted, corpse-bestrewn cave of Despair: Redcrosse, Arthur, and, ironically, Duessa, are like carbuncles that glow
in dark places. The general meaning of these episodes seems to be
that carelessness in its largest sense—imagined as sleep, joylessness,
near death, being one "that would not liue" (10.27)—precedes
disintegration. In his essay on Spenser's imagery, Frye shows that
Spenser connects sleep, death, and hell. Disintegration precedes
either, in the early part of the poem, flight and false restoration or
false harrowing, or, later, true harrowing, penance, and health, the
House of Holiness. I say "precedes," but I do not mean necessarily
in temporal sequence; as Berger says, in some sense the House of
Pride is a surface of which the cave of Night is the reality. The
sequence is easily grasped: Redcrosse's enemies—false Una, Sansjoy,
Orgoglio, and Despair—are progressively more overt in their
meaning—to Redcrosse.

The House of Holiness, every reader knows, resembles *in bono* the
House of Pride. The chief form of the latter is triumph, a rhetorical
and ceremonial celebration of a recognized order, here a law of vice,
to which the public assents; the form of Holiness is a private school,
an institution for discovering truth. Between these houses is the wild
outdoors, where Satyrane drives his version of the triumphal car,

yoking Panther, Bore, Pardale, Tigre, Antelope, and Wolfe which he constrains "in equall teme to draw" (6.26); these should be compared to Lucifera's "six vnequall beasts" (4.18). Satyrane's pleasure is like "a tyrans law," but Una educates him to "her discipline of faith and veritie" (6.31). Satyrane is halfway to Holiness, between triumph and school. The last triumph is the real one, with people instead of beasts, in Eden (12.3–8). All these earthly triumphs are beheld by the "Northerne wagoner" who drives his sevenfold team, the constellation Ursa Major (2.1).

Another rhythmic system, not properly of episodes, is the series of "epic" narrations of previous events. Una tells her "storie sad" (7.43–51) to Arthur, and he requites her with his story of what he knows of his own past (9.3–15); their exchange of stories is paralleled in this friendship canto with Arthur's and Redcrosse's exchange of gifts. We have seen that Redcrosse tells Una's parents his adventures. To these stories we should add Fradubio's account of his woody state (2.34–43); the Dwarf's single stanza "wofull Tragedie" of Redcrosse's adventures separated from Una (7.26); and the narrator's tale of Satyrane's youth (6.21–30). The most important tale is, of course, the one Contemplation tells Redcrosse about his own origins (10.65–66). These brief accounts of origins and experiences have their wicked counterparts: the false Una's tale, which shrewdly breaks off in tears when her lies become too obvious (1.52); Duessa's confused and lying account of her origins (2.22–26); and the tales of saints and popes with which, we are told, Archimago regales Redcrosse and Una in his hospitable way at their first little symposium (1.35). The good characters have pasts, and their origins are of interest to them: the *curricula vitae* are images of humanity and civility, naive and wholly mimetic examples of narration, of some poetic capacity. The stories fabricated by the wicked are bad poems, lies; Satyrane could scarcely tell his own tale, and Archimago or Sansjoy or Ignaro would have little to say, since their allegorical genesis is the last word on their present character. They do not develop and learn through experience; they have no pasts—they are simply named.

The settings of the various actions likewise acquire meaning through systematic redundancy. Cleopolis and the New Jerusalem are named or envisioned, but no action takes place in towns of the sort which we meet in medieval romance. All happens in castles, caves, or the forest. The forests are fully moralized, beginning with the "shadie groue" of Error "yclad with sommers pride": they are erotic, labyrinthine, primeval, chaotic, careless, godless. Redcrosse and Duessa enter the shade to escape not the rain but the sun, because Redcrosse's "new Lady it endured not" (2.29)—she might melt like snowy Florimell (5.3.24). The shepherd who appears in a simile in the wood of Error shuns the ground here: the trees are Fradubio and Fraelissa. When Una is forlorn, she too rests in a shady place, but her unveiled beauty "made a sunshine in the shadie place" (3.4). The satyrs' wood in canto 6 is a "forrest wild" in which Sansjoy attempts to ravish Una. Its center is the "shady arber" in which Sylvanus sleeps. Finally the meaning of the "ioyous shade" becomes overt, at the beginning of canto 7, where the developed *locus amoenus* acquires its full sense of unredeemed carelessness, and Redcrosse, poured out in looseness, is severely winded by Orgoglio. In contrast to these relaxed places are the wildernesses: the one where Una is tested (3.3), like Magdalene in the legend; the sterile plain of the unburied surrounding the cave of Despair (9.33–34); the "breathing fields" of corpses around the House of Pride, in which the courtiers take their solace (4.37–38); and the "wastfull wildernesse" where Duessa attempts to hide her shame (8.50). The final hell-mouth, the Dragon's, is likewise strewn with corpses (9.13).

Despite some of the narrator's fatalistic rhetoric, we know that in this poem the characters cause events and generate landscapes out of themselves. The most elaborate system of correspondences within Book One connects characters with each other in significant relations.

Redcrosse resembles in some way most of the major characters of the book. Beginning with the first canto, we see that both Redcrosse and Error are enraged, both described as "fierce" in one stanza (1.17). Like Redcrosse, Archimago is "deluded" and thereby enraged (2.2); both Redcrosse and Archimago fly, as it were, from themselves (2.10, 12); Anderson observes that Una's mistaking the impersonating Archimago for Redcrosse is a comment on Redcrosse (2.11, 3.24–32). The same critic, seconded by Cheney, connects Redcrosse with Morpheus: both are drowned in deadly sleep, with emphasis on the liquid humour (1.36, 40–41); both are careless; both are associated with murmuring insects (as is Archimago himself—1.22–23, 38, 41); both are rudely awakened (1.42–43, 2.4). Redcrosse is connected with Gorgon (1.37) by his real name, George, which Berger observes is scrambled in the name Orgoglio. Of course the sprite Squire who couples with false Una (2.5) is Redcrosse's double, for Redcrosse himself "Bathed in wanton blis and wicked ioy" in his dream (1.47). The knight's rage springs from this forced and premature acknowledgement of what love involves—the theme of Book Three foreshadowed. The Squire embodies the "secret ill, or hidden foe of his" (1.49), himself.

Redcrosse's bad company shadows his own problems: his garden variety sexuality, hurt feelings, fatigue, burst out as monstrous forms of Lust and Wrath, Envy and Slothful carelessness. His relation to the Sans brothers is transparent. When Redcrosse meets Sansfoy (having betrayed Una) the characteristic ambiguous pronouns (who is whose foe? which one is "prickt with pride"?) finally give way to the inclusive "they" (2.14–15) and the famous simile of the rams lustfully butting, "Astonied both." Redcrosse slams into a mirror.

Redcrosse is snubbed at Lucifera's party, so he meets Sansjoy, another knight who has trouble sleeping (4.45). The knights eye each other. Sansjoy "chaunst to cast his eye, / His suddein eye, flaming with wrathfull fyre" on his brother's shield, and Redcrosse seeks the veiled Sansjoy "with greedie eye" (5.10, 15). Duessa rejoices to see, in Sansjoy, Sansfoy's "ymage in mine eye" (4.45), and perhaps puns while confusing Redcrosse with her offer, "Thine the shield, and I, and all" (5.11)—eye, I, foy, loy, and joy all rhyme. Redcrosse sneaks out of the House of Pride to avoid "enuious eyes" (5.52), but he probably sees those eyes when he drinks from the fountain (7.6). Hamilton and Shroeder note that both Redcrosse and Sansloy, worn out by their activities, are found (by Orgoglio and Satyrane) in a shady place by a fountain (6.40, 7.2–7). Like Archimago and Redcrosse, Sansloy flies in fear (6.8). Spenser does not trouble to have him meet Redcrosse.

The Sans brothers, like the triplets whom Roche calls the Telamond brothers of Book Four, seem to pass on their animus with their oyes as they are defeated. Perhaps Orgoglio's stature which "did exceed / The hight of three the tallest sonnes of mortall seed" (7.8) symbolizes their accumulated powers. The counter-image *in bono* is Redcrosse's double revival in the Dragon combat. Besides the letters of their names and the lady, which Redcrosse and Orgoglio hold in common, they both are startled by a loud noise, it seems, *flagrante delicto*, as Shroeder observes (7.7, 8.5).

These gloomier correspondences can be summed up under the rubric "sad." Spenser uses the epithet for Redcrosse, Proserpine, Aesculapius, the House of Pride, Archimago, Duessa, and Abessa, as well as Una, her lion, and Repentance. Chency adds Hippolytus, and Berger adds Cyparisse, to the list of reflections of Redcrosse's sad psyche. They are all too narrow and exclusive in their desires, uptight, too closely aimed at an object which requires a broader vision, especially too fearful of love, too prone to frustrated wrath— the sadness of Milton's Moloch. A difference between Redcrosse and Arthur illustrates this: when Sansfoy curses the cross and attacks Redcrosse, we learn that "the sleeping spark/Of natiue vertue gan eftsoones reuiue" in him (2.19; cf. 3.3.45); when Una presses Arthur to name his "secret wound," the knight replies that "you sleeping sparkes awake" (9.8)—the memory of his love for Gloriana. Red-crosse's ire supplants Arthur's love. Another aspect of Redcrosse's improper loving is signified by Fradubio's story. Both Redcrosse and Fradubio offer garlands, symbols of marriage, to Duessa (2.30, 37); both are enchanted in sleep; neither is a true lover—here they are not sad enough, sad in the sense of "steadfast." Inclusiveness is proper love in its individual aspect; allegiance is proper love in the social sphere; grace underpins both virtues, and refers to the divine.

Other terms which yoke sets of characters with Redcrosse are "old" and "new." Archimago and Sylvanus are called "old" so often the adjective serves as their epithet, the one old in evil, like the "old Dragon" named in the lemma of canto 11, the other phylogenetically old, the emblem of early mythical consciousness and its pastoral version of outdated Edenic innocence. Along with Archimago, we may group old Ignaro, Sansfoy (who is likened to the "old ruines of a broken towre"), Corceca, the "ruinous and Old" hinder parts of the House of Pride (4.5), Night, "more old then *Ioue*" (5.22), and the revealed Duessa (8.46). These are old like St. Paul's Old Man, old in the law. With Sylvanus we may group those figures who are old in nature: Arthur's foster father "old Timon" and old father Nilus. Finally, Humiltá, in the House of Holiness, is old in grace. A fourth sense of old, of which Archimago is the parody, is the agedness of true wisdom, that of Contemplation and Una's parents, whose knowledge came from the "old dints of deepe wounds" in Redcrosse's armor, mentioned in the first stanza of the poem.

Many of Redcrosse's emotional responses coincide with a typical view of adolescence: he is a Perceval figure. He wants to learn his "new force" (1.3), and he is eager for new adventures; Una has to remind him to rest, "And with new day new worke at once begin" (1.33). In this vigor he most resembles Satyrane (6.36). When Archimago wakes Redcrosse after his unrefreshing night, he warns him that he "here wex old in sleep" (2.4). The young knight has come closer, in his dreams and delusions, to that old part of himself which the mage represents. We learn at the House of Holiness that aging and the individuation accompanying it are in the purview of Charity, as Charissa feeds her young babes, "But thrust them forth still, as they wexed old" (10.31). Although we might expect Redcrosse himself to be made new at the House of Holiness—new in a kinder sense than false Una, "that new creature borne without her dew" (1.46)—the purging and instruction there do not suffice. Only the Well of Life could "Renew, as one were borne that very day" (11.30), and like the fresh eagle Redcrosse emerges from it: "So new this new-borne knight to battell new did rise" (11.34). Compare the closing lines of Dante's *Purgatorio*. The Dragon adventure is the good news.

The chief agent, in romance terms, of Redcrosse's fortunate regress from old to new is Arthur, who resembles the hero, but differs from him in instructive ways. We have noticed that Arthur is one of the light-bearing harrowers like Duessa and Redcrosse; his shield withstands "magicke arts," disqualifying Archimago's bookish power, and reflecting power like the shield wielded by George's prototype Perseus. Like Redcrosse, Arthur dreams of bliss with a lady; both knights may be contrasted with the scorned Sir Terwin (9.27). Redcrosse woke to find false Una, and Arthur woke to find the "pressed gras" where Gloriana had lain. Cheney observes that the description of Arthur contains details "which earlier seemed to be indices of evil" —the dragon crest on his helmet, on which the "bunch of haires discolourd diuersly" recalls the "bounch of haires discolourd diuersly" in Archimago's helmet when he impersonates Redcrosse (7.32, 2.11). The parentage of the two heroes is similarly shrouded, as it should be in romance, but Redcrosse learns his from Contemplation —this is his book. A sharp moral contrast may be found in the heroes' connection with their tutors: Archimago serves as Redcrosse's Merlin. In fact, of course, experience displaces the mage as Redcrosse's tutor—Arthur's education is slightly more mythic.

In these correspondences Redcrosse's "character"—I think the use of this term is justified—is fully displayed. He is sexual, self-conscious, fatigable, sad, old, and renewed; he is careless, but narrow, and adolescent, but potentially heroic. He is, in short, a human being, whose chief flaw is that knowing ignorance which man acquired by eating the apple, and whose chief need is the enlightenment of grace. Opposing him are the evil forces of the world in which he finds himself.

The wicked of Book One likewise share traits. They correspond in their genesis, their serpentinism, their underneathness, and their backwardness.

Following medieval tradition, Spenser gives many of his allegorical characters a genealogy to be compared with the "real" backgrounds of Redcrosse, Arthur, and Una. The prominent examples are Lucifera, Orgoglio, and Duessa. Lucifera's parents are Pluto and Proserpina, but she thinks her "worth" surpasses them, and even Jove, and even any who should claim more height than Jove (4.11). Like Mutability at the end of *The Faerie Queene*, she cannot acknowledge her proper place, even her birth; she usurps a throne (4.12), and becomes a "mayden Queene" because she "made her selfe a Queene" in parody of Una, Gloriana, and Elizabeth I. Orgoglio's parents are Earth and Aeolus (7.9). Hamilton suggests that the elements parody the clay and spirit of Adam's genesis, and hence of Redcrosse's, the "man of earth" (10.52). Heninger, Shroeder, and Nohrnberg treat at length the meaning of Orgoglio's origins and make it clear that he more than any of the figures of Book One presents what Renaissance scholars called "physical" allegory. Duessa's dugs "like bladders lacking wind" (8.47) resemble Orgoglio's composition.

Duessa gives a false and a true genealogy. The false one is the parody of Una's ancestry which we have already noticed (2.22); her real parents, she tells her first ancestor Night, are Deceipt and Shame (5.26–27). Duessa flatters Night for her antiquity, as the "most auncient Grandmother of all" (5.22), and joins the Sans brothers into the family, children of Night's son Aveugle. These three sets of parents—drawn from classical myth, theory of elements, and psychological personification allegory—are similar: they are immortal, inhuman, and expressions of their children's characters, highly determining, perfect parents whose children need no adolescence. The children are more wrought or composed than born. Night is not really as original as Duessa makes her out to be, but perhaps Archimago and the old Dragon, who are given no ancestors, are original principles, this side of Manicheanism, of diabolic creation and destruction. The wicked characters' families have not provided for their nurture and development, but have merely stabilized them as types, much in the way a married person, at times, sees his in-laws as moral types who have determined the character of his spouse ("That's just like your mother"). No room is left for learning and grace.

Error and the Dragon are serpentine in contrast to the leonine Redcrosse (1.17, 3.7). Error has her brood; the Dragon appears to be female, in the sense that one wise man thinks he (the Dragon) may have a womb containing Dragonets (12.10). Duessa and Fidelia bear venom in their cups (8.14, 10.13), and Hamilton noticed that false Una, "fed with words," goes "slyding softly forth" (1.54). Steadman showed how Error is linked to her setting, the labyrinthine wood, by the ambiguous term "traine"; both figures were emblems of sophisticated rhetoric in some Renaissance symbolism. Despair is compared to a "Snake in hidden weedes," his tongue is "subtill," and Trevisan warns Redcrosse not to "try his guilefull traine" (9.28, 31), the train of his discourse. Archimago is likewise "subtill" and a user of "traynes" (3.24). Archimago hated Una "as the hissing snake" (2.9): either he or she is compared to the snake in the ambiguous line. Under Lucifera's feet lies a dragon "with an hideous trayne" (4.10), and Duessa rides on a monster compared with the Lernean hydra (7.17), another Echidna type.

The serpent *in bono* appears on Arthur's helmet. When evil is concealed it works maliciously, but Arthur's overt terror serves the good, just as his shield and Una's face scatter darkness when they are unveiled. Motifs involving the distinction of surface and underneath run through *The Faerie Queene*; the boar in the cave under the Garden of Adonis is an important example (3.6.48). This distinction informs the architecture of the House of Pride, whose cunningly painted "priuie Posterne," an anal exit which leads over the "donghill" of corpses (5.52–53), prefigures the Castle of Alma in Book Two. The largest member of this systematic distinction is the cosmos itself,

described in the famous first stanza of canto 2 as the firm and steadfast heaven which arches over us "that in the wide deepe wandering
arre." The "Northerne wagoner" has his own celestial version of the
sevenfold triumph which rides, like Lucifera's triumph, over a
troubled region underneath.

The diction of canto 1 points to another moral system in the poem
based on the terms up, forward, backward, forth, back. Redcrosse
is constantly associated with the sun, in the old Christological
metaphor, and the phrase "up rose . . ." frequently connects character with sun. Upton noted that the line "Vp *Una* rose, vp rose the
Lyon eke" (3.21) recalls the striking line from Chaucer's Knight's
Tale, "Up roos the sonne, and up roos Emelye" (2273). Spenser uses
the sun (Phoebus) as a sign of fresh activity and progress as well as
of light, so that Fidelia's ability to stay it or turn it backward (10.20)
seems particularly formidable. In the Error episode the words forward, forth, stay, back, backward, pile up and suggest resemblances
between the two combatants. Una warns Redcrosse to stay his step,
and when he refuses he is forced backward. Moral confusion and
ignorance cause this regress; the redeemed counter-images are Redcrosse's healing retreats into the Well and Tree of Life in the Dragon
fight. Redcrosse reaches that Augustinian rock bottom which is
preliminary to salvation. Trevisan and Ignaro are the backward-
lookers in the poem (9.21, 8.31): not too dangerous, not too evil,
they project an intellectual sloth or carelessness to which Redcrosse
is liable, a regression neatly symbolized by the backward-bent knees
of the idolatrous satyrs (6.11).

Berger describes the sequence of Redcrosse's visions during his
first adventures, from the dream figure of Una to the apparition, the
false Una concocted by Archimago, to Duessa, as "the gradual
objectification of the Morphean dream-world in which Redcrosse is
placed by Archimago. . . ." The wicked characters bear so many
resemblances to each other (Nohrnberg suggests that Duessa *is* false
Una), and so many to Redcrosse, that they do seem generated out
of a single pattern. They form in their totality a spectrum of being,
from divinities like Pluto, Gorgon, and Night to sprites to monsters
to beasts to the inhuman humans themselves, the hellish elves like
the Sans brothers. The range of shapes of evil suggests its power; the
systematic correspondences among the shapes suggest that one or
two keys (knowledge, say, and grace) will open up and collapse the

whole array like Orgoglio deflated. The major evil figures who confront Redcrosse—Archimago, Duessa, Orgoglio, the Dragon—
become progressively more visible as bad, more fixed in shape, and
easier to defeat. That Archimago cannot quite be fit into the array,
that his ontological status is not quite clear (is he a fairy? a devil?
a human? a sprite?), reinforces the view that he is best considered
as the dark shadow of the poet himself, and that to chain him would
be to end falsehood, and fiction, altogether.

There is little need to dwell upon some of the more obvious kinds
of system in the poem, repetitions which are subliminally received
by every reader even if seldom commented upon. The repetition of
phrases, names, ways of speaking, and the like, one of the hardest
things for a new reader of Spenser to respect, is virtually the signature
of the harmonious system itself. Spenser's moral vocabulary, the
grating gall, fierce despight, treacherous trains, secret wounds, foully
dight, lovely blandishments, sagely sad, and greedy hardiment,
repeats itself like the flies, garlands, and mythological sunrises through
the poem. Simple associations like fire with wrath or water with
concupiscence (Sansloy turned his "wrathfull fire to lustfull heat"—
6.3; Duessa's horse trappings are "wouen like a waue"—2.13) depict
Redcrosse's reciprocating passions in symbols which are hidden from
him but open to us. The four elements and the five senses provide
on occasion tiny systems of analysis, as in the description of Error
(see 2.10, 7.13, 11.21, 11.54, 12.1–2). Whole repeated phrases like
"so th'one for wrong, the other striues for right" (5.8–9), "he could
not tell" (8.32–34), or "So downe he fell" (9.54) force us to make
connections and synthesize meaning. The proverb-ridden, excessively
courtly language of several of the characters, especially Redcrosse,
reveals in its repetitiveness some of the dangers of common tradition—
I develop this notion in later chapters. A recurrent pattern underlies
Spenser's recalcitrance in giving names; he delays this information,
and seems to use names as little as possible, as if to keep the reader
nearly as much in the dark as his characters. (Anderson observes that
he inverts this practice later in the poem.) Closest of all to the surface of the work is that which makes it a poem, the repetitions of
sounds which make rhymed stanzas, and the divisions of the book
into cantos. Except for the division of the book into two groups of

six cantos, signaled by the phrase "in middest of the race" near the beginning of the second half (7.5), few of the numerological systems discovered by various hands (especially Fowler) can be found; but the obvious numberings of cantos and stanzas sufficiently demonstrates the poem's poeticalness, its made harmonies.

Systematic redundancy is a major, deliberate part of Spenser's design, and our recognition of parallelisms of event, setting, character, and language accounts for much of the matter of the poem. It might be objected that the repetitions derive from Spenser's use of sources which have limited sets of images and actions, or, from another side, that the redundancies are generated by structures in the human or Renaissance mind, rather than by any conscious deliberation. Both of these objections, which rise from some modern hermeneutic theory, tend to blur and diminish the poet's accomplishment. I would argue that Spenser chose romance forms in order to exploit their special idiom. He discovers, as if accidentally, the significant resemblances among things which fall into his systems of redundancy, but he establishes the system itself.

The evidence for these contentions may be found in Spenser's allusions in a more familiar sense of the word, the play with former literature. These allusions surround the poem with its own critical texts, what Berger and Fletcher have called "matrices." Spenser's implicit criticism of the writings to which he alludes gives authority to his own work and establishes a deliberate frame of reference for interpretation; an allusion is as orientating as a symbolic name like Duessa.

The hero's name links him to medieval legend, and his trade, dragon-killer, links him to medieval romance. Various trappings of the poem—extended similes, epic themes, heightened rhetoric, classical allusion—announce a claim of epic grandeur, although the epic invocation (if we exclude the prefatory stanzas) is delayed until canto 11, just before the Dragon combat. Even there the epic pitch is lowered to its "second tenor" so that "I this man of God his godly armes may blaze" (10.7); Hamilton observes that this line is a Spenserian version of the opening of the *Aeneid*. The ingredients of legend, romance, and epic genres were mixed before Spenser by his acknowledged sources Ariosto and Tasso. To them, as we have noted,

Spenser adds materials from the Bible, as well as important topics from English literature. From the point of view of literary tradition, one of Spenser's main tasks was to synthesize, what an exegete would call harmonize, these diverse kinds of fiction. Since this ground has often been covered, I will touch upon only a few cases of allusion which especially serve my purposes.

The allusions may be classified as overt or covert. Overt references to classical myth, found mainly in the descriptions of dawn and sunset, look at first like mere coloring, but the association of the hero with the sun allows some of these passages to yield meaning: the figure Morning (Aurora), connected with Una, rises first weary of Tithon's bed (2.7), and later blushes when she leaves the god (11.51), as if the moral progress of the action had brought innocence back. The two references to Hercules, a favourite type of Christ in the Renaissance, link his labors to Redcrosse's (7.17, 11.27); in the usual manner, familiar to us from Milton, Spenser claims that Redcrosse's torments were worse than Hercules'. More important than these allusions are the two places where the syncretizing tendency of Renaissance thought, recently outlined by D. C. Allen, are manifest: the Mount of Contemplation, likened to Sinai, the Mount of Olives, and Parnassus (10.53–54); and the Well of Life, which excels Silo, Jordan, Bath, Spau, Cephise, and Hebrus (11.30). The narrator becomes more knowing than usual at these moments and reveals the link between the landscape of fiction and the sacred places of Hebrew and Greek culture.

The resemblance of Redcrosse and Una to Adam and Eve is so striking that we hardly notice when we first learn, from Duessa's letter (12.26), that her parents are in Eden. The wood of Error resembles Dante's *selva oscura* as well as paradise lost. Error herself combines Satan's snakiness with Eve's femininity, and her bookishness recalls the knowledge which Adam acquired. The creation of false Una parodies Eve's creation from sleeping Adam: Nohrnberg documents her connection with Adam's other wife Lilith, a kind of Hebrew counterpart to the false Helen, of Greek legend, who lies behind snowy Florimell.

Spenser was able to cast the myth of Adam in romance terms through the mediation of the George legend. His use of classical epic is subtler. The *Aeneid*, the central epic of European culture, gave

Spenser the stories (as mediated by Ariosto, perhaps Dante, and others) of the speaking tree (Fradubio) and the descent to the underworld (Night); neither allusion is made overt. Both stories represent the more romantic, magical side of Virgil; both were taken up by Dante (*Inf.* 13, and *passim*), who may have lent Spenser the shapes of Duessa in his Geryon (*Inf.* 17) and of Ignaro in his false diviners (*Inf.* 20). Spenser chose motifs from classical epic which were apt for Christianization, and Hamilton observes that both these episodes have counterparts later in the poem in clearly Christian contexts, as the Tree of Life and Arthur's harrowing of Orgoglio's castle.

The poet whom Spenser especially honors in *The Faerie Queene* is "Dan Chaucer, well of English vndefyled" (4.2.32), whose description of Nature in his "Foules parley" is singled out as a source near the end of what survives of *The Faerie Queene* (*Mut.*7.9). The mention of "Chauntclere" in canto 2 of Book One is the most literary of the allusions in the book, and may be a signal to us that Chaucerian themes are about. It is fitting that the beginning and end of the poem recall Spenser's English master.

The first canto alludes covertly to Chaucer's dream vision poetry, three poems which are themselves markedly repetitious in theme. Spenser doffs his literary hat in the catalogue of trees, a *topos* which Sehrt has found everywhere in classical and medieval literature, but which certainly is meant to recall the similar catalogue in *The Parliament of Fowls*. That poem mingles Dantesque places with dream lore, enclosed garden with plain and hill, Venereal passion and Natural generation, common profit and courtly rhetoric, in the graceful, mock ignorant, plenitudinous manner which is quintessentially Chaucerian.

In both poems the multiple species of trees suggest the pleasures and dangers of plenitude itself, and Spenser seems to be going Chaucer one better when he moralizes the consequences of this kind of wood; Redcrosse and Una are "led with delight, and thus beguile the way" so that "in diuerse doubt they been" (1.10) and passively "fare" to the den of Error. The paths go "leading inward farre" (1.7), into that middle space which is Spenser's territory. Nohrnberg and Cheney in complementary readings have pinned down Spenser's use of the catalogue, as "the ambiguous variety of the world, as yet a world of only potential significances" (Nohrnberg) and "suggestive of a naive and disjunctive reading of nature," reflecting "man's confident moral dissection of the universe" (Cheney). The trees are described either in terms suggestive of moral properties—"proud," "neuer dry," "funerall," "weepeth," "forlorne," "sweete bleeding in the bitter wound," "warlike," "for nothing ill," "fruitful," "the Maple seeldom inward sound"—or of their uses in a civilization of ships, vineyards, wooden buildings, barrels, conquerors, poets, archery, and carving, a civilization which does not appear elsewhere in Book One. Redcrosse and Una make choices along the wide alleys, although they are hardly aware of the meaning of the woods they traverse, and Spenser, as it were, deliberately chooses to present the moral and symbolic, the mode of romance, rather than the urbane and mimetic.

The Parliament of Fowls, too, presents a choice to the dreamer of which he is scarcely aware, as to how he should evaluate love. This theme is symbolized by the Virgilian and Dantesque gates through which the dreamer passes into the love garden, labelled in gold and black with inscriptions representing love as either fruitful, healing, and happy, or deadly and sterile. Chaucer's narrator emphasizes his "errour" (meaning "doubt"—PF 146, 156), and the whole poem seems composed of a consciously conceived dialectical response to love. Where Chaucer holds everything in balance, Redcrosse of course falls, first to sleep, then to wrath and pride. The dripping hellish stone lair of Morpheus, and the difficulty of waking the god, come from Chaucer's other dream visions, The House of Fame and The Book of the Duchess, but the gates of ivory and silver which enclose Spenser's Morpheus's house come from the Parliament (ultimately, of course, from Homer and Virgil). From the same poem, I suspect, came Redcrosse's dreaming vision of Venus as a lustful mediatrix (1.48); and false Una's damnably courtly rhetoric (1.51–53) may come from the first and third tercel eagles' fashionably moribund diatribes. Finally the dream figure of Una, called by Archimago's messenger from Morpheus, recollects the dead body of Seys which Juno's messenger had Morpheus animate in order to speak to Alcyone in a night vision.

All of these motifs are literary commonplaces, but the combination of tree catalogue, locus amoenus, bad Venus, Morpheus, choice gates, courtly love jargon, and the Hectorean bedside messenger called by a spiritual messenger, convinces me that Spenser had his master in mind as he wrote his first canto. That he alludes in the first canto chiefly to Chaucer's dream visions makes sense; in these poems Chaucer is most erudite and bookish (excepting a few of the *Tales* and *The Legend of Good Women*), and here most overtly he examines the human interior. Hough and Anderson both treat the possibility that Spenser meant his poem to seem to open like a dream vision, as if to acquire fictional possibilities not available to a waking world, and, as Nohrnberg says, "It is the pre-allegorical character of a deepening *double-entendre* which makes the dream vision a useful starting-point for the allegorist." Many writers since Spenser have begun a narrative by hinting that it might be a dream: Hawthorne in "Young Goodman Brown," Kafka in *The Castle*. Spenser needs only to hint at a dreamer, as I have observed, because the genre of romance itself provides him with another world.

Spenser's allusions to his Italian forebears and Chaucer are not systematic in the way we have described his use of his own material, but they work in the same way. Redcrosse, for example, to a learned reader, can be defined in reference to the figures of Aeneas, Dante, Geffrey (Chaucer's speaker), Adam, and the heroes of Ariosto and Tasso, yet he is not like them in as many ways as they are unlike each other. Spenser deliberately sets his poem into the Western epic tradition, and makes use of that tradition as do all the "sentimental" epic poets—all except Homer—to secure his own place, redefining, rivaling, and controverting where he must, so as to achieve both authentication, from the power of the tradition itself, as a man gets authentication from his neighbors and his ancestors, and originality (in both senses: novelty and rootedness), as the tradition's most recent critic.

When we take in the details of Spenser's poem, and discover more or less completely the repetitions and resemblances which link its parts together and connect it with the poetic tradition, we perform a kind of abstraction from the raw events which the poem recounts. We are led to construct a system of correspondences which reveals, in much the same way nature can be understood to reveal, the relations between things and the meaning of things. We are able to push aside superficial appearances and allurements—in fiction, the rhetoric; in nature, the objects of perception—and learn the truth. Evil language and evil objects come out of hiding in spite of themselves. The reader's process of abstraction and connection is his counterpart to the poet's process of disposition; both processes may be called allegorical.

DYNAMICS: THE HEALING WORD

Allusions and systematic references within Book One must be grasped if we are to construe it properly, but too exclusive a view of these can blind us to other essential properties of the poem. On the one hand, the narrator's response to his own story, and on the other, our response to the process of reading it, are more immediate phenomena than the edifice of planned repetition. These direct relations between speaker and listener supplement—at times even appear to controvert—the heavier and more distant mechanics of resemblance.

A recent body of Spenser criticism, represented by Alpers, Rose, Sale, and Berger, reminds us to attend to the tone of the poem, particularly to note that the speaker is not "sad" in Redcrosse's sense of overly narrow, too sage and serious. Spenser is not utterly unlike Ariosto. The great Romantic critics seem to have responded easily to the delight of Spenser; but, it appears, at the expense of what they called "allegory," that elaborate scheme of generating meaning which we have been exploring.

To characterize the tone of a long poem among the fragments of lines and paraphrases necessary for other kinds of criticism is difficult. A narrator's attitude need not be consistent, except perhaps at some deep level of response. It is helpful to begin a description of Spenser's narrator's special range of feeling by examining a poem of manageable length, before returning to Book One. Here is a whole poem, my favorite sonnet from the *Amoretti* (no. 67):

> Lyke as a huntsman after weary chace,
>   Seeing the game from him escapt away,
>   sits downe to rest him in some shady place,
>   with panting hounds beguiled of their pray:
> So after long pursuit and vaine assay,
>   when I all weary had the chace forsooke,
>   the gentle deare returned the selfe-same way,
>   thinking to quench her thirst at the next brooke.
> There she beholding me with mylder looke,

sought not to fly, but fearlesse still did bide:
till I in hand her yet halfe trembling tooke,
and with her owne goodwill hir fyrmely tyde.
Strange thing me seemed to see a beast so wyld,
so goodly wonne with her owne will beguyld.

The implications and literary references of this poem are nearly as dense as of the best stanzas of *The Faerie Queene*, but I will not stop here to consider the collapse of the simile, the interesting locale, the metaphor of the hunt, the incapacity of a sonneteer to get inside his beloved's head, the fear and fearlessness of the "deare" which reminds me of Book Three, the implications of "game," "fly," "goodwill," or the active/passive resonances of "beguiled" which remind me of Book One. These are legitimate topics for criticism, but the first thing to notice is the speaker's tone of voice, which is not located in any one turn or piece of diction in the sonnet, but seems to be generated by the whole.

It is a tone of wonder and joyous surprise following perplexed frustration; even more, it is a tone distant from itself, as if it were written by a middle-aged man, like Chaucer's Knight, or the Knight's Theseus, recalling the twisting feeling of youthful love. It is whimsical, and clearly in complete control, so that all the ironic, but after all innocuous, implication of the final "beguyld" is fully expressed, without danger to the delicacy of sentiment. We find this tone everywhere in Spenser, in gestures of mock alarm at the action he presents, in serene verse which depicts horrors and confusions, in self-effacing but ready wit, in whimsical "sympathy," sometimes playful, sometimes paternal, for the often ridiculous stories he tells: a tone of wisdom, poise, confidence, and charm—incompatible with neither martial nor amatory themes—the tone of Virgil. Spenser's tone wavers on the borderline between the social and the theological meanings of "grace."

When this tone resides in the matter of Book One, the result is a comic degradation of evil and an acceptance of innocent simplicity, the pastoral form of the unity which is truth. Spenser may have derived from Chaucer the literary joke which has the poet so involved in his action that he forgets that he is its arbiter. The excessive personal sympathy the narrator shows for Una (3.1-2, 6.6) recalls Chaucer's narrator's devotion to Criseyde, and when Spenser asks,

"What wit of mortal wight" can free Una from Sansloy, we nearly forget that the poet has just this wit. The poet is the unnamed artist-judge who sits in the middle chamber of the turret in Alma's castle. Berger observes that the "world . . . [is] run by Spenser's, not God's providence," and gives a list of places where wicked forces, especially Archimago, receive comic, Braggadochian attention (1.29–30, 1.36–37, 2.10, 2.26–30). Monsters are funny, and passages like Redcrosse's exit from that whited sepulcher the House of Pride or the townsfolks' response to the defeated Dragon render this side of evil.

Book One has little of the broad bedroom farce of Book Three, scenes which might have been done by a Fielding or Dickens, but enough legerdemain to deflate puffed-up figures like Orgoglio. Redcrosse does not see the joke, nor does the "local" narrator whose rhetoric we read; but there is a more distant narrator, whose Olympian perspective the reader is led to attain, who smiles upon all. It is helpful to imagine as we read that one continuously changing voice is directly telling us the story—a naive and involved voice—and that another, more steadfast voice lies behind it, to arrange, understand, and smile with us.

Passages revealing the multiple consciousness of the narrator are among the best in the poem; two examples need brief comment. They are pastoral interludes: the shepherd simile in canto 1, and the memory of Sylvanus in canto 6.

> As gentle Shepheard in sweete euen-tide,
>   When ruddy *Phoebus* gins to welke in west,
>   High on a hill, his flocke to vewen wide,
>   Markes which do byte their hasty supper best;
>   A cloud of cumbrous gnattes do him molest,
>   All striuing to infixe their feeble stings,
>   That from their noyance he no where can rest,
>   But with his clownish hands their tender wings
> He brusheth oft, and oft doth mar their murmurings.
>
> [1.23]

This simile occurs in shocking juxtaposition to the gruesome descriptions of vomiting Error. The Nile simile is paired with it, two stanzas before; and the two, so different in tone from the horrors nearby, are likewise antithetical to each other; the Nile simile is mythological, exotic, and moralized by its diction to point to sexual pride, whereas this stanza is pure pastoral. In similes the poet is as free as anywhere in a narrative to express himself, and here the poet's mood seems as distant from the action as possible. The result is a leavening of our feeling, and we gratefully submit to the charm of the evening. In the simile the gnats are the counterparts to Error's disgusting brood, but these gnats have "tender wings," and the shepherd, in the role of Redcrosse, "doth mar their murmurings"— that graceful consonance, that easy metonymy, and that sudden access of solicitude preempts what had begun as judgment. The very sounds of the end of the stanza tease us out of thought like the flies in Phantastes's cell. The stanza is a *tour de force*, a demonstration early in the poem of how certainly this poet controls the meanings and values of his fiction.

In another piece of pastoral virtuoso, Sylvanus is stirred by the sight of Una:

> By vew of her he ginneth to reuiue
>   His ancient loue, and dearest *Cyparisse*,
>   And calles to mind his pourtraiture aliue,
>   How faire he was, and yet not faire to this,
>   And how he slew with glauncing dart amisse
>   A gentle Hynd, the which the louely boy
>   Did loue as life, aboue all worldly blisse;
>   For griefe whereof the lad n'ould after ioy,
> But pynd away in anguish and selfe-wild annoy.

[6.17]

Berger's reading connects Cyparisse to the special sadness of narrow love, and along these lines I would add that the love is "ancient" and hence questionable in terms of this book, of a piece with pagan idolatry. The end of the metamorphosis, spelled out in Ovid (*Met.* 10, 106 ff.; Natalis Comes altered the myth to a form closer to Spenser's), turns the boy into a cypress, the "funerall" tree, on a staff of which Sylvanus leans. In Ovid the god encourages the boy to grieve more lightly ("leviter ... doloret"), and the metamorphosis takes the sting out of the tale. Kent van den Berg pointed out to me the woody pun in "pynd." Cyparisse's grief here is "selfe-wild" (with a possible sight pun "willed / wild") and his love for the hind is inappropriate in either pagan or Christian ethics. Sylvanus's memory is as powerful as Aesculapius's art "to reuiue." Spenser probably remembered Virgil's story of Sylvia (*Aen.* 7), which Marvell recollects in the "Nymph Complaining": in that story the shot deer causes a war, and innocent pastoral yields to martial epic— shades of Alecto.

In spite of the moral atmosphere of the stanza, its first effect is of a sudden beauty which replaces the stern and systematic judgments of the rest of the book and appeals immediately to us. Again the last line's sound effect, the harmony of "pynd away" and "wild annoy," seems a sign of ecstasy; the harmony of the vowels and the unobtrusive consonants, in the special metrical position of the alexandrine, imply a deeper harmony which seems beyond the ordinary, referential power of language, a harmony as it were accidental, out of the poet's control, magically conferring value on the utterance. Both passages elicit our nostalgia for the youthful, the pastoral, the innocent, the bygone—a time that never was, but would that it were. Such sweet places—I would add Arthur's tactful cover for the embarrassed Redcrosse (8.44–45) and the narrator's fear of dishonorable burial—do not destroy the rest of the poem, but fulfill it. Poets like Guillaume de Deguileville, Lydgate, and Phineas Fletcher have written extended, systematic allegories, too, but we do not read them; they are not up to this kind of poetry.

What happens to the reader of Book One doubtless cannot be put in words, but these remarks about the narrator's special consciousness, at once innocently involved and knowingly distant from his own story, suggest a way of describing our response to the poem, for this is our position too. The poet knows everything, and makes both the action and its narrator; we see everything because we can unfold the poem's double meaning (the systematic rhetoric of moral value and the narrator's rhetoric of innocent response), so that at the end of the poem we know as much as the poet knows; Redcrosse learns everything, so that at the end, as I said in the first section of this chapter, all is unveiled to him. In her book on allegory, Gay Clifford quotes Baudelaire: "Un système est une espèce de damnation. . . ." In the dynamics of his poem, Spenser discharges and renders benevolent the effects of systems. He disarms Archimago.

BEING AND TIME

It is comfortable for us to speak, as nearly all recent critics of Spenser do, of Redcrosse's progress as his becoming one, his atonement with Una, an achievement of wholeness which is holiness (the Old English root "hāl" gave us "hale," "health," "whole," and "holy"). Perhaps in response to a feeling (which Freud shared) that Freud's psychology was too pathological for normative description, humanist psychology of the second third of this century, from Jung to Erikson to Piaget, has concerned itself with human development, and the processes of accommodation and individuation which accompany growth. The result of proper human growth is, of course, a man like the psychologists who are writing, with a certain balance of selfhood and otherness, a certain capacity for accommodation to the environment, a man who recovers his humanity, whatever that is, wherever it has been hiding. The currency of this image of man makes one suspicious of its eternal validity—there are rival schools— but it is hard for me to avoid considering Redcrosse finally as the patron of this holy state. The static properties of the systems described in the second section of this chapter are vitalized by the knight's progress through them, as he is healed and educated to become himself.

If the poem is working properly, then, what happens to Redcrosse happens to us readers: we are fashioned gentlemen. Nohrnberg points out that the image of the word itself in various forms in Book One, as speech and book, corresponds to the wordy phenomenon in which readers are engaged. (These next paragraphs are indebted to Nohrnberg's work.) The phenomenology of readership is one of Spenser's topics, so we turn back to the poem for answers.

Like Satan fixed in the bottom of the *Inferno*, Redcrosse in the dungeon of Orgoglio is at his lowest point. Spenser describes him in a harsh, inverted parody of a Petrarchan blazon of a fair lady:

Whose feeble thighes, vnhable to vphold
His pined corse, him scarse to light could beare,
A ruefull spectacle of death and ghastly drere.

His sad dull eyes deepe sunck in hollow pits,
   Could not endure th'vnwonted sunne to view;
   His bare thin cheekes for want of better bits,
   And empty sides deceiued of their dew,
   Could make a stony hart his hap to rew;
   His rawbone armes, whose mighty brawned bowrs
   Were wont to riue steele plates, and helmets hew,
   Were cleane consum'd, and all his vitall powres
Decayd, and all his flesh shronk vp like withered flowres.

[8.40–41]

Redcrosse's physical person is nearly emptied out, he is deathly, his eyes cannot even look at the sun to which he had been compared. He has almost been scratched out. All he wants, and all he wishes for (8.38), is death itself. He inhabits the temple of idolatry, whose altars cry out with the blood of innocents and martyrs. When he is rescued, he becomes for the second time in the poem (the first was in rage at Sansjoy—4.42) speechless.

Ignaro is the figure closest to Redcrosse at this point. He is old, blind, backward, and has the keys to the chambers in Orgoglio's castle. Arthur puts four questions to him, and he answers each time, "he could not tell": he is wordless. Arthur uses the keys (Nohrnberg suggests they derive from the key of knowledge of Luke 11:52) to make his way through the rooms, but when he comes to Redcrosse's cell no key fits, so he puts on his power with his knowledge and like Christ in hell, rends the door. We need now to examine Spenser's image of man most unlike man: Redcrosse as sick, wordless, and nearly empty and dead.

He is sick. The medical imagery, which begins with the deep wound on Redcrosse's armor in the first stanza, climaxes *in malo* at the House of Pride—proud flesh is either lustful or cancerous. There the wine and spices which Redcrosse and Sansjoy consume as martial aphrodisiacs "to kindle heat of corage" (5.4) before their fight make a mockery of the wine and oil which the leeches pour on Redcrosse's wounds (in imitation, Upton notes, of the Good Samaritan). The supposedly healing music at the bedside "did diuide" (5.17). We saw in *Piers Plowman* the commonplace metaphor of soul-healing; in early Christian thought Aesculapius was often contrasted with Christ. Aesculapius is "in chaines remediless" (5.36). His art is too mechanical and external, as he merely joins parts: the physician should heal himself. Anderson calls the Hippolytus story "a parody of wholeness." Redcrosse leaves the house "Not throughly heald" and soon after, with Duessa, is "Both careless of his health, and of his fame" (7.7). Then Orgoglio attacks.

The proper art of healing involves education. Una is the teacher who instructs the satyrs and Satyrane in formal lessons; like a good teacher, she herself can learn (6.12). As rhetorical education is humanist man-making, the sacraments, which Aquinas calls *remedia*, are the Christian liberal arts, especially that enduring process of inward scrutiny, medicinal penance. We first see Archimago beating his breast "as one that did repent" (1.9); Corceca performs grisly forms of penance in her blindness (3.13–14); and Aesculapius tells Night "endlesse penance for one fault I pay" (v.42).

Redcrosse's wordlessness must be painful, since he had told Fradubio that "He oft finds med'cine, who his griefe imparts" (2.34). We have seen how telling stories can expose human civility or some corrupt parody of it. Both wicked figures in the first canto are bookish. Error vomits books and papers—perhaps because they are lukewarm like the works of the Laodiceans (Apoc. 3:16)—in parody of the book of prophecy which the angel gave John of Patmos to eat, which was bitter in his belly (Apoc. 10:10). Nohrnberg links Error with the spitting Blatant Beast at the end of Book Six, the unchained antipoet. Archimago's book looks like a hermit's gospel hanging from his belt (1.29), but at night he uses magic books (1.36)—Hankins connects him with the False Prophet of the Apocalypse, another version of the Prudentian *mendax*, and Waters connects him with a Protestant image of a corrupt Catholic teacher.

Una tells Arthur that Redcrosse, in Orgoglio's dungeon, is "remedilesse" (7.51). In fact, of course, the House of Holiness, as school, hospital (10.36), and place of penance (in short, a Protestant monastery), "did to health restore / The man that would not liue" (10.27): "so perfect he became" (10.45, cf. 10.51). Upton and Fowler, in the *Variorum*, find sources for Dame Caelia, the lady of the house, in "Erudition" of *The Table of Cebes* and "Dame Doctrine" of Hawes's

Pastime of Pleasure; her lineage goes back through *Piers*'s to Boethius's and the Shepherd of Hermas's instructive ladies. The chief resident, Patience, who may be borrowed from *Piers*, uses "words of wondrous might" among his medicines to cure Redcrosse's "grieued conscience," and encloses Redcrosse "Downe in a darksome lowly place farre in" (10.25). The charmed words of Archimago, Duessa (2.42), and Despair (9.48), as well as Orgoglio's dungeon, have their counterpart in Patience's cure. Of course the worst mage is the vision-maker Archimago, an old hermit with a counterpart in Contemplation, who reveals the New Jerusalem and whose catechism controverts Despair's.

Despair insists that for all men "Their times in his eternall booke of fate / Are written sure" (9.42), but Una reminds Recrosse that he is chosen, and that grace "that accurst hand-writing doth deface" (9.53). Fidelia releases the power of the word, "her sacred Booke, with bloud ywrit": "For she was able, with her words to kill, / And raise againe to life the hart, that she did thrill" (10.19). The gift Redcrosse gave Arthur, a gold letter edition of the New Testament, is "able soules to saue" (9.19). The gift of a New Testament was part of the sacraments of Confirmation and Holy Orders. Redcrosse's healing education, begun in Penance, is completed with the baptismal water of the Well of Life, the unctionlike Eucharistic balm (sacramental chrism is oil and balsam) of the Tree of Life, and the betrothal to Una. The Word and the sacraments are the knight's medicine.

Redcrosse is healed to become himself. Una asks him, when he is freed from Orgoglio's dungeon, what evil star has frowned "That of your selfe ye thus berobbed arre . . . ?" (8.42). At the end of his soul-making at the House of Holiness, dazzled by the light Contemplation has shed, he comes to himself: "At last whenas himselfe he gan to find" (10.68). The grammar of "self" in English allows useful ambiguity: when Dante says "mi ritrovai" (*Inf.* 1, 2) we understand "mi" as a reflexive, as practically a segment of the verb; but "I came to my self" can indicate the self as an entity, separable from "I." Berger first grasped this because he first clearly explained the projective sense of Spenser's allegory. Berger's example is Archimago's gloating over Redcrosse and Una "diuided into double parts" (2.9); he takes the words literally—they are divided from one another, and divided each within himself. Redcrosse immediately meets the emblem of doubleness, Duessa, and tilts with a shadow of himself, Sansfoy. Not until he establishes atonement with himself and with Una can he escape the "other" world of projective allegory, "otherspeech."

Several versions of ontological displacement in the poem should be distinguished and compared. Archimago's composition of false Una from "liquid ayre" creates a humanoid entity, whereas "one Duessa," as Fradubio calls her, unmanned him. He will not return "to former kynd" until he bathes in a living well, and now he bides "time and suffised fates" (2.43). The two Ovidian metamorphoses to which Spenser alludes are never quite realized in the poem. Cyparisse pines, but no reference is made to his becoming a cypress; and the effeminating fountain of which Redcrosse drinks (7.5) does not literally make him "semivir," as the nymph Salmacis made Hermaphroditus. Spenser has no need for complete mythic change, although the case of Fradubio shows that he does not avoid it: his psychological allegory carries the same meaning for a different sort of consciousness. The allusions suggest how the allegory should be read (Redcrosse is weakened by lust) but they are demythologized.

We observed before that the evil figures in the book fill out a spectrum of being. The masculine and feminine bases, or principles, of the spectrum are the mage Archimago and his ally Duessa, who may be said to represent the coordinate universal evils of miscreation and duplicity. Both figures are themselves shape-shifters. Archimago is compared to Proteus near the beginning (2.10), when he "put on" the person of Redcrosse, and still "often semblaunce made" at the end, trying to escape (12.35). He can so divorce himself from himself that, like Trevisan (9.21), he fears himself (2.10)—compare Lucifera envying herself (4.8). Duessa tells Night that "I that do seeme not I, *Duessa* am" (5.26), in parody of God's ontological name (Exod. 3:14); when she is disarrayed, she appears "such as she was," old above and monstrous underneath (8.46).

Except for the figures in the House of Holiness, the ontological spectrum of the *good* people in the book is relatively narrow. Satyrane is almost satyrean, and Arthur is almost divine, but both are human. Una's lion stands alone as a friendly agent who is not human, but he is relentlessly natural, and never pretends beyond himself. Redcrosse had thought himself an elf, but Contemplation explains that

he is really a human: "Such men do Chaungelings call, so chaungd
by Faeries theft" (10.65). He was raised "in ploughmans state to
byde," but inexplicably set off to win fame. In fact, of course, he
had not changed; his poem reveals him at once discovering and
enacting what he is—a knight. According to Frye, the Eden at the
end of the poem is "recovered human nature." In Eden even Una,
constant as she is to herself, can more freely radiate her being, she
"who in her selfe-resemblance well beseene, / Did seeme such, as she
was, a goodly maiden Queene" (12.8). Bad persons multiply, but
good persons only become themselves. As Nature judges, at the end
of what we have of *The Faerie Queene*:

> They are not changed from this their first estate;
> But by their change their being do dilate:
> And turning to themselves at length againe,
> Doe worke their owne perfection so by fate. . . .
>
> [*Mut.*7.58]

When Redcrosse achieves his oneness, the whole projective, mytho-
poeic allegoricalness of the fiction collapses, and at the end we are
left with a single powerful allusion to the marriage supper of the
Lamb.

At a certain time Arthur will see the Faerie Queene (9.14), and
Fradubio will be enlarged (2.43), and Despair will be able to die
(9.54). Charissa is married, but Fidelia and Spes, even though they
are the elder sisters, are "yet wanting wedlocks solemnize" (10.4).
Redcrosse wants to have contempt for the world, but Contemplation
tells him "ne maist thou yit / Forgo that royall maides bequeathed
care" (10.63); Redcrosse later recalls his vow to serve Gloriana for
six years (12.18–19). As Murrin suggests, "allegorical plots habitually
end inconclusively." The reason is not far to seek: what ends most
plots is marriage or death, but these are events in a fiction, and in
an allegory the powers which generate universality cannot be laid
to rest while the universe exists. Langland's character Will might die,
or Redcrosse might marry, but Conscience or Contemplation would
persist—it may be in recognition of this that Will does not die, nor
Redcrosse marry.

Book One inhabits, then, a middle time: its climaxes are the fatalistic, moony (8.38) three months while Redcrosse pines (8.40) in Orgoglio's dungeon, and the three days, "High time now gan it wex" (11.1), of his triumph over the old Dragon. In the second section of this chapter I tried to present the statics of the poem by observation of its allusions and cross-references. The statics constitute a poetic eternity, and are primarily (not exclusively) associated with evil, since fixity of correspondence may be seen to inhibit freedom and grace. Duessa bathes herself in "origane and thyme" on Walpurgisnacht (2.40), but she has no origin and operates out of time. In the third section we looked at the dynamics of the poem, the moving consciousness of the narrator and the edification of the hero, which find their analogue in the ecstasy, boredom, enjoyment, the inter-est, of the reader. In these movements is the salvation of the poem, which is all knowledge and faith, and which is summed up in the New Testament, Redcrosse's gift.

Redcrosse learns to cease to "covet in th'immortal booke of fame / To be eternized," even though Cleopolis is the fairest "for earthly frame" (10.59); that is, this fiction, which is the book of fairy fame, which is romance, is set beside the truth, which is divine—Redcrosse is enrolled in the Book of Life. William Nelson suggests that Book One is "a kind of Bildungsroman," but that its emphasis on human depravity and divine election "makes it impossible to interpret in any profound sense as the history of an education." In a way, this is right—there is as much systematic analysis as history. But the form is education, and the meaning of this form is that the poet and, by attraction, we, have been given the perspective of a being who sees history simply, as analysis, who stands time on end, who resides, if we can conceive it, in what Coleridge called "the true imaginative absence of all particular space or time," like a god.

Bibliographical Note

The best treatments of Book One, to which I continually refer, are those of Harry Berger, Jr., "Spenser's *Faerie Queene*, Book I: Prelude to Interpretation," *SoRA* 2 (1966): 18–48; James C. Nohrnberg, *The Analogy of "The Faerie Queene"* (Princeton, 1976), which I had the privilege of reading in typescript draft form; A. C. Hamilton, *The Structure of Allegory in "The Faerie Queene"* (Oxford, 1961); Donald Cheney, *Spenser's Image of Nature: Wild Man and Shepherd in "The Faerie Queene"*, Yale Studies in English, 161 (New Haven and London, 1966); and Mark Rose, *Spenser's Art: A Companion to Book One of "The Faerie Queene"* (Cambridge, Mass., 1975). The last decade has produced many books on Spenser; here I note only the works I found most useful and actually referred to. The *Variorum* notes are distinguished by inclusion of the researches of the great eighteenth-century Spenser editor, John Upton. Recent student editions of the poem which are very helpful are those of Robert Kellogg and Oliver Steele (New York, 1965) and Hugh Maclean (New York, 1968); I understand that a new edition by Hamilton is under way.

The classic studies which lie behind the typological view of Book One are by John Erskine Hankins, "Spenser and the Revelation of St. John," *PMLA* 60 (1945): 364–81, printed with few changes in his important *Source and Meaning in Spenser's Allegory* (Oxford, 1971); and Northrop Frye, "The Structure of Imagery in *The Faerie Queene*," *UTQ* 30 (1961): 109–27.

The epigraph from Cassirer is trans. from *Individuum und Kosmos in der Philosophie der Renaissance* (Leipzig and Berlin, 1927) by Mario Domandi (Oxford, 1963), p. 67. The following articles and books are listed roughly in the order in which I refer to them, except that I single out a compact and stimulating article which I used intensely, Judith H. Anderson, "Redcrosse and the Descent into Hell," *ELH* 36 (1969): 470–92, now included in part in her book, *The Growth of a Personal Voice: "Piers Plowman" and "The Faerie Queene"* (New Haven and London, 1976). Along with Anderson, Hamilton treated the possible relation of *Piers* and Book One in "The Visions of *Piers Plowman* and *The Faerie Queene*," in William A. Nelson, *Form and Convention in the Poetry of Edmund Spenser*, Sel. Papers from the Eng. Inst. (New York, 1961), pp. 1–34; the article reworks material which appeared in *SP* 55 (1958): 533–48. Berger spoke of Book One as archaic in "The Spenserian Dynamics," *SEL* 8 (1968): 1–18. Clifford treats system and change in allegory in *Transformations of Allegory*. On duplicity, Protean mutations, and wholeness, see A. Bartlett Giamatti, *Play of Double Senses: Spenser's "Faerie Queene"* (Englewood Cliffs, N.J., 1975).

Two brilliant studies of Renaissance thought to which I refer are Michel Foucault, *The Order of Things: An Archaeology of the Human Sciences*, trans.

from *Les Mots et les choses*, and Frances A. Yates, *The Art of Memory* (London, 1966). Both Michael Murrin, in *The Veil of Allegory: Some Notes toward a Theory of Allegorical Rhetoric in the English Renaissance* (Chicago, 1969), and Maurice Evans, *Spenser's Anatomy of Heroism: A Commentary on "The Faerie Queene"* (Cambridge, Eng., 1970) make good use of Yates.

William Nelson's book, *The Poetry of Edmund Spenser: A Study* (New York, 1963), is useful, and first explained what Spenser's woods mean. I refer to articles by John W. Shroeder, "Spenser's Erotic Drama: The Orgoglio Episode," *ELH* 29 (1962): 140–59; S. K. Heninger, Jr., "The Orgoglio Episode in *The Faerie Queene*," *ELH* 26 (1959): 171–87; John M. Steadman, "Spenser's *Errour* and the Renaissance Allegorical Tradition," *NM* 62 (1961): 22–38; and Ernst Th. Sehrt, "Der Wald des Irrtums: Zur allegorischen Funktion von Spensers *FQ* I.[i.] 7–9," *Anglia* 86 (1968): 463–91; and to D. C. Allen, *Mysteriously Meant* (Baltimore, 1971).

Other books on Spenser to which I refer are the fine and influential critique by Paul J. Alpers, with some of whose theory I disagree, *The Poetry of "The Faerie Queene"* (Princeton, 1967); Mark Rose's *Heroic Love: Studies in Sidney and Spenser* (Cambridge, Mass., 1968); Roger Sale, *Reading Spenser: An Introduction to "The Faerie Queene"* (New York, 1968); Thomas P. Roche, Jr., *The Kindly Flame: A Study of the Third and Fourth Books of Spenser's "Faerie Queene"* (Princeton, 1964); Graham Hough, *A Preface to "The Faerie Queene"* (New York, 1963); and A. D. S. Fowler, *Spenser and the Numbers of Time* (London, 1964). More recent noteworthy books are the compilation of surveys and full bibliography of *Faerie Queene* studies (1900–1970) ed. Richard C. Frushell and Bernard J. Vondersmith, *Contemporary Thought on Edmund Spenser*, with a provocative article (pp. 121–49) by Carol Kaske, "Spenser's Pluralistic Universe: The View from the Mount of Contemplation" (Carbondale, Ill., and London, 1975), and Isabel G. MacCaffrey, *Spenser's Allegory: The Anatomy of Imagination* (Princeton, 1976), which I have handled but not studied. I have not seen Douglas Brooks-Davies, *Spenser's "Faerie Queene": Critical Commentary on Books One and Two* (Manchester, 1977).

Aquinas on the sacraments may be found in the *Summa contra gentiles* 4. 56–58. On education and the self see Thomas Greene, "The Flexibility of the Self in Renaissance Literature," in Peter Demetz, Greene, and Lowry Nelson, Jr., ed., *The Disciplines of Criticism* (New Haven, 1968), pp. 241–64; on Spenserian process see the same author's chapter on Spenser in *The Descent from Heaven: A Study in Epic Continuity* (New Haven and London, 1963). I referred to D. Douglas Waters's article, "Errour's Den and Archimago's Hermitage: Symbolic Lust and Symbolic Witchcraft," *ELH* 33 (1966): 279–98. On Christ versus Aesculapius see Rudolph Arbesmann, "The Concept of 'Christus Medicus' in St. Augustine," *Traditio* 10 (1954): 1–28. Coleridge's words on Spenser are from his course of lectures, 1818.

CHAPTER FIVE

The Sun's a Thief

MELVILLE'S *The Confidence-Man*

The sun's a thief, and with his great attraction
Robs the vast sea; the moon's an arrant thief,
And her pale fire she snatches from the sun;
The sea's a thief, whose liquid surge resolves
The moon into salt tears; the earth's a thief
That feeds and breeds by a composture stol'n
From gen'ral excrement; each thing's a thief.

Timon of Athens 4.3.439–45

That was the true light, which lighteth every man that cometh into the world. He was in the world, and the world was made by him, and the world knew him not.

JOHN 1:9–10

The Confidence-Man: His Masquerade is a modern novel. It is modern in its skepticism of the authority of ancient models and morals, its black humor, its criticism of its own fictionality, its allusion to myth in the guise of mimesis. Like other novels, it is definitely located in space and time, it exploits social types and current topics of satire, it imitates probable everyday life in prose. But it is likewise a typological allegory. The uneasy fit of these two fictional modes constitutes not only Melville's manner, but his theme. This will be our subject in this chapter, an essay in the continuity of allegory into the post-Romantic era; the chapters on Hawthorne and Kafka are intended to complement what is said here.

ROMANTICISM AND ALLEGORY

Antique structures may be found underlying any good, extended fiction. What is wanted to make us call a fiction "allegory," we have observed, is not merely the discovery of the presence of such structures, but evidence of deliberation and of material which "distracts" the reader and draws his attention to a preconceived structure. A novel like *Ulysses* clearly does this. But we are not so willing to call *Ulysses* an allegory, probably both because its source, the *Odyssey*, does not have the sort of religious finality which the source of many great allegories (the Bible) has, and because the typology of structure of *Ulysses* is overwhelmed by those elements of naturalism—arbitrariness, circumstantial and accidental sequence, the detail of palpable life—which are an antithesis of allegory. *Ulysses* is not rational, any more than the *Odyssey*. Our sense is of Joyce's narrators' discovering resemblances of structure between Bloom's and Odysseus' histories, not making them. *The Confidence-Man*, however, in the midst of a mass of naturalistic description, admits of a Biblical structure so imposing as to make us feel that it essentially crosses the border into allegory; that the typological plot is made, and as it were prior to the incidental detail.

The beginning and end of *The Confidence-Man* establish its typological structure. In the beginning we have the "advent" of the "lamb-like" man, the Confidence Man, at sunrise, who imposes on his fellow passengers of the riverboat *Fidèle*, Melville's microcosm, his mute admonitions to practice charity—a Christianized Genesis. In the last chapter we have apocalyptic references to the Confidence Man as bridegroom and dispenser of morning, as the lights go out, and play upon the words "apocrypha" and "Apocalypse."* As in the

---

* Chapters 1 and 45. References are to Elizabeth S. Foster's excellent edition (New York, 1954) by chapter and page. Other documentation and bibliography may be found in the note appended to this chapter.

Psychomachia, Piers Plowman, and Book One of *The Faerie Queene,* we find a beginning which recalls *the* beginning, narrations of experiences, and an end which recalls the apocalypse. The linear journey of the boat down the Mississippi even recalls the pilgrimage-quest form favored by allegory—the passengers are called "that multiform pilgrim species," and the lamblike man goes "shield-like bearing his slate before him." The voyage is literally from St. Louis to a little below Cairo, but symbolically from Eden to the New Jerusalem, "from apple to orange" (2.7). The Mississippi acquires symbolic status as the fluid medium of the pilgrimage, the borderline between spiritual and geographical East and West, the frontier of civilization and the interior channel of the people. Likewise the duration of the novel's events, within one day and night, like *Ulysses,* implies meaning: the uniqueness of a single day inversely suggests that it is universal, that all days are alike. The action on the boat is unusually simple: a series of confidence games as repetitive in structure as the battles of the *Psychomachia.*

Nothing could be more allegorical: the allusions to Biblical structure, the repetitive and reduced series of actions, the significant locale and tempo. But if *The Confidence-Man* is allegory, it little resembles such classical allegory as the first book of *The Faerie Queene.* The day is April Fool's Day; at the midpoint of the novel the *Fidèle* reaches a place called the Devil's Joke (22.146); if there is a quest, no dragons are killed, no revelations occur, no marriage takes place. The allegorical form of the novel suggests more than anything else the lack of the usual allegorical content, the achievement of the heavenly city. In this as in many ways the novel resembles *Piers Plowman.* Whereas Book One of *The Faerie Queene* presents the paradigm of the human achievement of knowledge, *The Confidence-Man* puts in doubt the nature of knowledge itself. It is a negative allegory, a Romantic allegory.

After the seventeenth century, the principle of analogy—of the validity of representation by similitude, and of the validity of the correspondence of spirit and matter—perished. The metaphor of the cosmos as hierarchy lost its efficacy. Platonic realism, which conceived of material objects and rational propositions as underpinned by substantial spiritual entities, was replaced by a Romantic version of Platonism, which poses the primary reality and autonomy of the faculty of imagination. Attention shifted from the character of the cosmos to the character of the observer. Doubt was cast on the validity of perception, the righteousness of authority, the harmony of man in nature, the veracity of religion, and the usefulness of ancient literary types and visual forms. Between the Renaissance and the first age of the Romantic period—insofar as there is really any gap—allegory had little to recommend it; for the most part allegory was replaced by more or less slight personification fictions, whose form served as a slender mast on which to spread a mighty sail of satire. Typological and psychological allegory were nearly forgotten.

The Romantic idea of the imagination could admit again into literature the old demons, myths, and analogies which classical allegory depends on, and which the rational and empiricist spirit of the Enlightenment had dampened. But the intellectual apparatus which supports allegory had to restore itself under new conditions of subjectivity: nothing was given, all had to be imposed. Much of the finest work of the English Romantics is a poetry of assertion of the primacy of the imagination, or of anguished exploration of the basis of imagination: the role of the mind with respect to nature, what we half create and half perceive. The best literature, surely, of modern times both asserts the validity of imagination, which makes poets the legislators of the world, and questions that validity. Romantics, in brief, emphasized the hypothetical nature of nonhuman realities, which made serious allegory again possible for them.

The novel, with its emphasis on the irrational, topical, concrete forms of life, may be considered the medium *par excellence* of the Enlightenment's distance from classical allegory; but as Prudentius was able to exploit Virgilian epic, so Goethe (in *Elective Affinities*) and Hawthorne had used the novel for allegory before Melville wrote *The Confidence-Man*. Hawthorne was able to convince Melville of the "part-&-parcel allegoricalness of the whole" of his earlier masterpiece, *Moby-Dick*. Novels are considered intensely mimetic, approaching in form the unfiltered objectivity of chronicle. (I am speaking of a norm; of course there are exceptions.) Insofar as a novel controls its events, rather than (as modern novelists say) "letting the story run away with itself" in the direction of "pure" mimesis, it approaches the other modes of fiction—as Cervantes inverts romance, and Fielding writes a "comic epic poem in prose"— and admits the allusive rationality of structure which we call allegory. The formal tension between the novel's proximity to chronicle, epistolary exchange, diary, police record, "social notes," log, and its potential as epic, romance, satire, dream vision, is analogous to the tension between the Romantic doubt of the validity of the faculties of the mind and the Romantic assertion of the mind's priority. The novel, then, is an ideal testing ground for epistemological principles, or, as Melville's novel puts it, for the question of confidence.

THE POSER: HIS MASQUERADE

It is fitting that the protagonist of a post-Romantic allegorical novel should not be a romance knight who learns the meaning of the world and achieves victory. In *The Confidence-Man: His Masquerade*, the figure whom I have called the *mendax* in classical allegory, the False Seemer, the fraud, the Archimago type, becomes the protagonist. His relationship to the action is no longer adversary. The illusions he casts before the other characters are no longer dispelled. Archimago is not a personification but a mage and a demon; likewise the Confidence Man is not a personification but an impersonator. The imposer of meaning is an impostor. A problem which appears peripherally in classical allegory, the status of this figure, becomes central in Melville's novel. The novel wheels around him, to use its own image, like planets around a sun; like objects illuminated by a revolving Drummond light, "everything is lit by it, everything starts up to it" (44.271). We need to understand the Confidence Man to begin to understand the novel.

He appears in eight impersonations, as the lamblike deaf-mute (1–2); the cripple Black Guinea (3); the man with a widower's weed on his hat, John Ringman (4–5); the man in the gray coat, agent for the Seminole Widow and Orphan Asylum (6–8); the ruddy man in a tasseled traveling cap, John Truman, president of the Black Rapids Coal Company (9–15); the Herb-Doctor in his snuff-colored surtout (16–21); the Philosophical Intelligence Officer (22); and the Cosmopolitan, Frank Goodman, in rainbow, butterfly array (23–45). Articles of clothing appear as the signatures of the impersonations in the clothes philosophy of the book. All the characters of the novel are emblematized like allegorical icons with their attributes. If the Confidence Man has a name, it may include, if we put together

148

"Ringman," "Truman," and "Goodman," the name of a good man who rings true. John Shroeder asks us to compare these chiming names with those of Spenser's "Sans" brothers.

These eight impersonations may be grouped into three series, marked by the method of the games which the Confidence Man employs, and by sartorial color symbolism of the sort which we might expect from the author of "The Whiteness of the Whale" and *Mardi*.

The first two masks are studies in black and white, the lamb-like man and Black Guinea, who test and prove the cruelty and crabbed egotism of their fellow passengers. These first games are done in silence or enigmatical, dialectal speech. Melville reminds us that, however deceitful his protagonist may be, he is not slaughtering any innocents. That charity which is the necessary colleague of faith is not present on the *Fidèle*.

The second group of experiments is performed by the Confidence Man in shades of gray (4–22), taking us to the halfway point of the book. Here straightforward confidence games, mainly a matter of patter, expose greed for money and health. The climax of this sequence is the double attempt, finally successful, on the "Hard Case," the Missouri woodsman named Pitch, who turns out to be soft on the inside. He is duped as the *Fidèle* leaves the free states behind (the game with Pitch turns on the question of slavery) and reaches the feverish swamps of Cairo at twilight.

The third sequence is governed by a single, all-encompassing mask, which matches the "cosmopolitan and confident tide" of passengers (2.8) on the ship of fools. This is the Cosmopolitan, whose clothing is of all colors, in the styles of all the world, "a florid show" (24.150), the colorless all-color of Moby Dick split by the prism of the various eyes which perceive him. The second half of the book is the more interesting; the games become so elaborate and self-conscious as verbal fictions, under the Protean and Archimagean power of the Confidence Man, that the reader experiences the exhilaration of being himself meshed, as trickster and victim, in confidence ploys. The artificial light under which this half of the book takes place is finally snuffed out, color disappears, and all sleep. The reiterated movement of the games is imposture, exposure, and repose.

Hundreds of references in the novel help to fix the meaning of the Confidence Man in terms of tradition, both literary and popular. As is proper for a work which fuses the local color and topicality of the novel with the antique structures of typology, the Confidence Man has two lineages—one from popular American lore and one from antique and Christian myth. Elizabeth Foster, Shroeder, and Richard Chase call attention to the lore of Brother Jonathan, Jeremy Diddler, and the other confidence men of American tradition, John Murrell, the Harpe brothers, disguised Jesuit emissaries. Johannes D. Bergmann has shown that a man who went for a time under the name of William Thomson, in the years just before Melville wrote the novel, used tricks which earned him the label "the Confidence Man," in press accounts to which Melville had access; one New York editorial writer seized upon the theme for a satiric sketch which moves in the direction of the novel.

Nearly all students of the novel have pointed as well to the more exalted ancestry of the Confidence Man, which Melville hints at obtrusively: surely in ways he resembles Satan and Christ, and perhaps as well Proteus and the gods who deceive and expose, Asmodeus (mentioned in the text) or Hermes. In the shape of John Truman the Confidence Man harrows the inner cabin of the boat "like Orpheus in his gay descent to Tartarus," speaks in Christlike terms, and is told by the victim, "I confide, I confide; help, friend, my distrust" (15.81, 84; cf. Mark 9:24). The lamblike man, in his "advent" at the beginning, and the Cosmopolitan, the "bridegroom" at the end, likewise bear allusions to Christ. The old man at the end of the book is compared to Simeon, who was not to die until he saw Christ.

Most prominent are the hints that the Confidence Man is a devil, or Satan himself. He changes shape, speaks smokily, and writhes snakily, like the Father of Lies. Pitch sees through him, too late:

> Analogically, he couples the slanting cut of the equivocator's coat-tails with the sinister cast in his eye; he weighs slyboot's sleek speech in the light imparted by the oblique import of the smooth slope of his worn boot-heels; the insinuator's undulating flunkyisms dovetail into those of the flunky beast that windeth his way on his belly.
>
> From these uncordial reveries he is roused by a cordial slap on the shoulder, accompanied by a spicy volume of tobacco-smoke, out of which came a voice, sweet as a seraph's . . . . [23.148]

This clearest unmasking of the Confidence Man's serpentinism is immediately enveloped in smoke, a signature of the Cosmopolitan, which in this book sometimes suggests hellfire, but more often the miasmal cloud of doubt which surrounds every issue which Melville presents—we learn that smoke is anathema to a backwoodsman (26.164—compare the miasma in *Martin Chuzzlewit* or the fogs of *Lord Jim*).

The most interesting instance of the Confidence Man's Satanic snakiness occurs during the Cosmopolitan's conversation with Mark Winsome, a cold transcendentalist modeled on Emerson. The Cosmopolitan leaps at Winsome's suggestion that love and truth must accompany beauty (he might have been responding in an ironic way to a remark of Thoreau's: "I am particularly attracted by the motion of the serpent tribe") :

> "Yes, with you and Schiller, I am pleased to believe that beauty is at bottom incompatible with ill, and therefore am so eccentric as to have confidence in the latent benignity of that beautiful creature, the rattle-snake, whose lithe neck and burnished maze of tawny gold, as he sleekly curls aloft in the sun, who on the prairie can behold without wonder?"
>
> As he breathed these words he seemed to enter into their spirit—as some earnest descriptive speakers will—as unconsciously to wreathe his form and sidelong crest his head, till he all but seemed the creature described. [36.213]

The Cosmopolitan here "all but" undergoes a reification of his moral being, in physical parody of what he says. Hints that the Confidence Man is other than human are scattered through the book. When the boat's barber, dozing, takes the Confidence Man's voice for "a sort of spiritual manifestation," and is relieved to find when he turns around that "it is only a man, then," the Cosmopolitan replies,

> "*Only* a man? As if to be but man were nothing. But don't be too sure what I am. You call me *man*, just as the townsfolk called the angels who, in man's form, came to Lot's house; just as the Jew rustics called the devils who, in man's form,

haunted the tombs. You can conclude nothing absolute from the human form, barber." [42.254]

Elsewhere the Cosmopolitan implies that he has no human interior: he tells Charlie Noble that having "a heart of a certain sort" he cannot be resolute (28.180); and he twice tells his last victim, the Simeonlike old man, that he never uses anything like the "life-preserver," the commode chair, as if he were physically without insides. These hints load such remarks as Charlie Noble's question to the Cosmopolitan, "Are we not human?" (30.198). Redcrosse recovers his humanity, but the Confidence Man is alien to it.

At one point the power of the Confidence Man outstrips metaphor. In chapter 31, "A metamorphosis more surprising than any in Ovid," the Cosmopolitan's companion Charlie Noble changes from friend to enemy at the words, "in want of money." In chapter 32 this psychological metamorphosis is reified: "Out of old materials sprang a new creature. Cadmus glided into the snake." The Cosmopolitan makes a magic circle of gold coins (of course) around the new creature, and muttering "cabalistical words," binds Charlie with a spell. The magical underpinning of the allegory only this once erupts into the surface of the fiction.

In sum, the character of the Confidence Man derives from a traditional American type, and from classical and Christian tradition. He is a serpent, a worm who can transform himself into a butterfly, a mage, a consummate actor ("To do, is to act"—6.35), all things to all men. His associations are superhuman, but whether he particularly represents a good or a bad angel, Christ or Satan, seems not open to judgment. Melville believes, with Spenser, that the nature of the agent who exposes sin and ignorance scarcely matters; a man cannot be deceived or entrapped if he has faith and practices charity. Melville's Romantic character Pierre finally realizes that "if a man must wrestle, perhaps it is well that it should be on the nakedest possible plain" (*Pierre*, 22.1).

If the Confidence Man is the angel with whom Jacob must wrestle, he is also Jacob. His relentless games become moral and nearly heroic, while his antagonists prove more and more shallow as they become more and more sophisticated. The Inquisitor is Grand. The *mendax* plays the part of the questing knight by default: no one is left to take up the role. He is "in the extremest sense of the word, a stranger" (1.1), and, as Joel Porte observes, he is the figure of the artist. Classical allegory has undergone a change: it is the allegorist, now, who is the hero. He has to assume the array of shapes which properly corresponds to the array of moral types which he confronts. He is both a projector and a reflector, mirror and lamp.

This constitutes a problem. The *mendax*, now an angelic or demonic impostor, the figure of the artist, exists only putatively in the human world, as an artist exists only as a spirit from the point of view of his work. What has happened to humanity? In Melville, it is sliding off the edge of his canvas, the world. The lamblike man is compared with "Jacob dreaming at Luz" (2.6) as he sleeps at the foot of a ladder; the book is, as it were, his dream—"Speeds the daedal boat as a dream" (16.86). The last chapter recedes into a dreamy sleep. First the lamblike man is "like some enchanted man in his grave" (2.6); and finally the Cosmopolitan becomes "more and more grave" (45.283). Melville is capable, as his magnificent tales "Cock-A-Doodle-Doo!" and "Bartleby the Scrivener" reveal, of allowing his fictions to terminate in a kind of pure, meaningless death.

We need not depend wholly on intuition to arrive at the conclusion that, as a figure in allegory, the Confidence Man is consistent, real, and original. These are the points of the three critical digressions included in the novel, chapters 14, 33, and 44. In the first, we acquire a theoretical basis for understanding the Confidence Man both as radically inconsistent (an author can "exhibit but sections of character" like the masks of the masquerade) and yet as that "*rara avis*," a consistent character. The Confidence Man has the purity of heart to will one thing, namely the exposure of his victims, and his is a model of constancy. Fundamental consistency beneath a Protean variety of guises is characteristic of personifications, and Melville's irony suggests that the passengers on the *Fidèle*, too, are nothing but masks.

Chapter 33 argues that the romance form is "real": "It is with fiction as with religion: it should present another world, and yet one to which we feel the tie." In romance people can "act out themselves" without the hindrance of the accidental and contingent—moral being may be displayed in (fictional) life. Melville might have been defining allegory. The Cosmopolitan, of course, is in many ways a paragon of verisimilitude, down to his maroon slippers, yet he is fundamentally unreal. We see of the Confidence Man only his masks, but this is all we ever see of anyone. The very devil has more reality than the mean and selfish populace of the *Fidèle*. The refusal of "fidelity to real life" in his fiction gives Melville the freedom to be truly faithful to reality, and as H. Bruce Franklin notes, "fidelity" has a special charge of meaning in this book.

The third critical essay, chapter 44, is most important. Melville takes up a phrase dropped by the barber in the preceding chapter, that the Confidence Man is "QUITE AN ORIGINAL." Here he speaks of the original character in fiction, a Hamlet, a Don Quixote, a Satan, as being as prodigious in fiction as a "new law-giver, a revolutionizing philosopher, or the founder of a new religion" in the world.

> ... the original character, essentially such, is like a revolving Drummond light, raying away from itself all around it—everything is lit by it, everything starts up to it (mark how it is with Hamlet), so that, in certain minds, there follows upon the adequate conception of such a character, an effect, in its way, akin to that which in Genesis attends upon the beginning of things.

The Confidence Man, of course, constitutes just such a character, a sun god or solar lamp who illuminates the world, or at least a parhelion (29.188) or "hidden sun" (30.194).

But, as Milton's God is cloaked in his own radiance, the Confidence Man is light invisible. The sun's a thief. What exactly he is cannot be settled with confidence. We can only discern him in relation to others, molding himself to adapt to each new victim as if he were the chameleon spirit of metamorphosis come to be the land-surveyor of men's souls. He is determinate only insofar as reflections of a light explicate their source. The mirrors, in this metaphor, are the victims of the Confidence Man's masquerade.

THAT MULTIFORM PILGRIM SPECIES

In the last chapter I suggested that the landscape and the action of *The Faerie Queene* are an exposition and deposition into fictional forms of certain principles of the nature of good, of man, of knowledge, and so forth. *The Confidence-Man* also consists of an array of characters, not so finely articulated as in *The Faerie Queene*, who bustle into and out of the story like the "folk" of *Piers Plowman*. The passengers of the *Fidèle* share one governing characteristic: they are all confidence men themselves. They are doubles of the Confidence Man as Redcrosse's enemies are his doubles, and they define him and are defined by him.

The victims (only the wooden-legged man and the Titan are not victimized) as a group conform to the first general image of man in the book, which emphasizes the plenitude and brashness of their "visage and garb"; they serve the "dashing and all-fusing spirit of the West, whose type is the Mississippi" (2.8). Whether they act like philanthropists, misanthropes, or just thieves, none has any well-grounded charity or trust in man. All have their eyes on the main chance. Their dodges are as various as the Confidence Man's, and they possess a similar purity of desire. Their moral being is dissolved in metaphors of clothing—masks, cases, skins (animal and racial), theatrics, and smoke—which correspond to their duplicity, fiction, and deceit: all mask an obliquity of impersonation or representation of what is inside. The Confidence Man is the reification of their collective lack of interior value. They are empty.

One group of victims, the easy marks, are distinguished by self-delusions so complete that the Confidence Man scarcely troubles with them, as Satan concerns himself little with the already damned—the fat burghers, the "charitable lady" with her barely concealed sexuality, the Episcopal clergyman blinded with piety, and the old man at the end, made a fool by senility.

Then there is the swarm of professional thieves and confidence men: the pickpockets, possibly the Methodist minister (if Franklin's suggestion is right), and the Cosmopolitan's alter ego, the confidence man Charlie Noble. The alternating speeches of Charlie and the Cosmopolitan are difficult to attribute properly, as the Cosmopolitan acknowledges: "our sentiments agree so, that were they written in a book, whose was whose, few but the nicest critics might determine" (28.179). They are like Redcrosse and Sansjoy. Finally, the toughest opponents are the misanthropes—the sophomore and the backwoodsman Pitch—and those who think they transcend humanity, the cold philosophers Mark Winsome and Egbert. In his elaborate psycho-drama with Egbert, the Cosmopolitan and his victim take on new identities, and Egbert takes the name of the professional confidence

man, Charlie Noble. Melville is particularly savage with the egotisti-
cal "shrewdness and mythiness" of transcendentalist morality, which
he must have considered a *trahison des clercs* in the face of the world's
iniquity. The beauty of rattlesnakes! Only in this episode can
Melville's moral fervor be felt in its full force; Egbert and his master
are worse than the devil, and the Cosmopolitan leaves Egbert in
"grand scorn," *giving* him a shilling (41.253). Like all the allegorists
we have examined, Melville particularly condemns the bad clergy.

The two characters who cannot be victimized tell us most about
the nature of this voyage. In spite of the sympathy which the Confidence Man shows toward the old man as he leads him to his death at
the end, the book seems to me fundamentally dark because of the
character of the two who escape deception and exposure. Neither
prevails because he practices charity; both are protected by their
visions of humanity, dark as the Confidence Man's—they have
nothing to lose. The wooden-legged man, "it may be some discarded
custom-house officer," is surely modeled on Hawthorne, the Wordsworth to Melville's Coleridge. He makes as if to strip the Confidence
Man's second mask, Black Guinea, of his disguise, but he is stopped
by the crowd. It is he who calls the *Fidèle* a "ship of fools" (3.15).
In demonic imagery like Hawthorne's of, say, "The Celestial
Railroad," the wooden-legged man laughs like "a high-pressure
engine jeering off steam" (6.34). There are hints that even the
wooden-legged man's vision of the blackness of the heart is limited:
the Methodist minister (a dubious witness) suggests that his one leg
is "emblematic of his one-sided view of humanity" (3.15); and later
the wooden-legged man says that Black Guinea's sham is evident
"'To the discerning eye,' with a horrible screw of his gimlet one"
(6.35). The wooden-legged man is a fellow artist, who fails, if at all,
only because he is not black enough.

The Titan, who bears the punning epithet "invalid," confronts
the Confidence Man in his mask as Herb Doctor in chapter 17. He is
a gigantic, nearly mythological figure, who emerges from darker
woods than even Pitch's. His features suggest natural objects, and
his illness portends present tragedy, the rock bottom. He pronounces
that death is the only cure for some diseases, scorns the Herb Doctor,
and finally strikes him. His hatred is final and absolute; as a Titan, he
is on a par with the Confidence Man, connected more closely than
the Olympian gods to the flinty bedrock of nature (*Pierre* presents

some of this mythology). His approaching death makes him unavailable for the game. Hopelessness precludes faith.

If we asked of his victims what we ask of the Confidence Man, just what is inside you, we could answer for the Titan—nothing. Of the others we can have less confidence. Since persons present themselves most authentically by what they say, to answer the question we need a literary criticism which can judge and evaluate the truth of the fiction.

THE ORIGINAL STORYTELLER

Allegory is an oblique kind of fiction which requires, on occasion, strenuous interpretation by the reader. Stories are seldom purely stories, but allegories confront us with impurities of story so gross as to require explication if even the plot is to be grasped. The indirection (other-speech) characteristic of allegory has its analogue in the indirection of narration of sophisticated fiction. As we need to know what kind of being a figure in an allegory is, whether human, fairy, demon, magician, god, idol, or shade, so we need to know the slant of obliquity of a narration, the kind of reliability and judgment we can expect from its narrator, who is the lens of the story. With the increased attention paid, from the late eighteenth century on, to the operations of the mind, the narrator of a story began to supplant the story itself as the focus of interest—autobiography resumed its place as a major genre.

The principal devices by which a fiction expresses its narrative self-consciousness are digressive critical essays, fictions enclosed within the fiction, and comment upon those enclosed fictions. I hesitate to speak of these devices of indirect self-commentary as allegory, simply because the term has not been applied that way; but we can note that fictions which are highly involuted often contain the more usual features of allegory as well—I think especially of *A Tale of a Tub*—and seem especially modern. The inset stories themselves are often more obviously allegorical than their surrounding fictions. They may present personifications or reduced moral types; more interesting, they may reflect, in small, the larger narratives which enclose them, and thereby help to interpret them. This last kind of relationship we have called typology.

157

Since Melville's theme is consciousness, or the relation of human perception and reason to truth, he makes special use of indirect narration in *The Confidence-Man*. His acute concern with narratorial mediation can be seen in the cold Egbert's disclaimer of the sentimental style of the story of China Aster, which he is about to tell:

> I wish I could do so in my own words, but unhappily the original story-teller here has so tyrannized over me, that it is quite impossible for me to repeat his incidents without sliding into his style. I forewarn you of this, that you may not think me so maudlin as, in some parts, the story would seem to make its narrator. It is too bad that any intellect, especially in so small a matter, should have such power to impose itself upon another, against its best exerted will, too. However, it is satisfaction to know that the main moral, to which all tends, I fully approve. [39.233]

The problem may be set: who is the "original story-teller," who can "impose" (as an impostor) his will on his fiction forever after? In *Pierre* Melville writes that the only original author is God (18.1).

In some ten examples, from stories the reader is never allowed to read, to anecdotes, to full-blown short stories, from deliberate fables to putative autobiographies, Melville measures the distance from the Spenserian tale-tellings we examined in the last chapter, which are wholly truth or lies, and to which the responses are simple tears or joy. Four of the inserted tales are pages long: the story of the man with the weed, John Ringman, and his wife Goneril; the story of Colonel John Moredock, the Indian-hater; the story of Charlemont, the gentleman-madman; and the story of China Aster. The theme of all the tales is the folly of trust in man, and the rewarded virtue of no confidence. The Confidence Man himself is the principal literary critic of the tales, and his response to all, perhaps like our response to Melville's novels, is to exculpate, to gloss over, to take another point of view, to question whether Goneril "was, indeed, a Goneril" (13.73). He cringes, and wants to see evil as good. Pitch put his finger on it: "You are the moderate man, the invaluable understrapper of the wicked man" (21.127).

The tales of Goneril and of Moredock, the Indian-hater, are

fictions of opposite kinds which are linked together by the trains of the Confidence Man's criticism. The tale of Goneril is intensely fictional. Her name comes, of course, from *Lear*, but may suggest "gonorrhea"—she has an "evil touch." ("Touch" is also a cant term meaning to con, extort, or liquidate a man.) The story, doubtless made up in the first place, about a doll of a woman with a name from an old play, a name which nearly personifies her, told by, confirmed by, and told to various masks of the single Confidence Man, told to us in words pronouncedly not the teller's own (11.64), and immediately and wholly glossed and reinterpreted in sophistical chatter, inset into a novel which proclaims its fabling nature on every page and in many chapter titles, takes us about as far into the Chinese boxes of fictional reduction as literature has gone. We have no access at all to the "calm, clayey, cakey devil" of a woman about whom we read. The story demands a willing suspension of disbelief, a kind of confidence—and so, we may reflect, does any fiction. If it is real, its reality has its source in moral truth, as allegory, and not in historical event or its imitation. So with the novel as a whole. The story of Goneril is only obliquely about a bad woman, but principally about the relation of fiction to truth. There may be, Melville implies, a substance called moral being, but we have access to it only by way of allegory, through mirrors and in narrow perspectives. Truth is a "cold cave" and "will *not* be comforted" (13.74).

The story of the Indian-hater is told by the confidence man Charlie Noble to our Confidence Man in the mask of the Cosmopolitan. More than three chapters are given over to the account of Moredock and the issues of "the metaphysics of Indian-hating." Charlie claims to have heard the story repeatedly from his father's friend, James Hall, the judge. In fact much of the story comes directly from Hall's sketches, published in 1835; as Charlie says, the judge "seemed talking for the press" (25.161). The Cosmopolitan lends his ear to Charlie's narration at such an angle "that each word came through as little atmospheric intervention as possible" (25.162). We have, then, a story which we know from a source outside Melville's novel, a true story, told with unusual directness, "almost word for word," to an unusually attentive hearer. The situation is precisely opposite to the story of Goneril, except that the audience remains the Confidence Man.

An Indian-hater, we come to understand, is in acute form the kind of paranoid which the Confidence Man had described as resembling the wooden-legged man:

> "... it is one of the imbecilities of the suspicious person to fancy that every stranger, however absent-minded, he sees so much as smiling or gesturing to himself in any odd sort of way, is secretly making him his butt. In some moods, the movement of an entire street, as the suspicious man walks down it, will seem an express pantomimic jeer at him. In short, the suspicious man kicks himself with his own foot." [6.33]

The street becomes a theater of no confidence, in which the suspicious observer is a Drummond light who gives dark meaning to all. Charlie Noble, and his source Judge Hall, give themselves away as Indian-haters as well.

Moredock's story, then, is true in most of the ways that Goneril's is false, but the two fictions arrive at the same place. Goneril's evil is real, but lessens as it is refracted through the several narrators' consciousnesses, because her actual existence is dubious. Moredock is likewise evil, and he actually existed, but his evil lessens because the narrators (Judge Hall and Charlie) scarcely seem aware of it as evil, being "suspicious" men themselves. Again perspective and indirection obliterate the moral center of the character in the narration. We are given, however, what appears at first to be an unusually direct purchase on Moredock, an eye witness.

When he was a boy, Charlie saw Moredock's rifle in a cabin, and he stuck his head up into the loft where he had been told the great Indian-hater was sleeping after a "hunt."

> Not much light in the loft; but off, in the further corner, I saw what I took to be wolf-skins, and on them a bundle of something, like a drift of leaves; and at one end, what seemed a moss-ball; and over it, deer-antlers branched; and close by, a small squirrel sprang out from a maple-bowl of nuts, brushed the moss-ball with its tail, through a hold, and vanished, squeaking. That bit of woodland scene was all I saw. No Colonel Moredock there, unless that moss-ball was his curly head, seen in the back view. [25.160–61]

Here is the ocular proof, rendered, remember, by a petty confidence man. The Indian-hater, after all, is woodsy nature itself, no more human than Goneril: he amounts to a mental construction. Like Malbecco, Moredock, even though he is a historical person, vanishes into his own inhuman source, amoral nature. The story of Goneril begins with the question which the Cosmopolitan, we have seen, echoes much later in the book, "whether the human form be, in all cases, conclusive evidence of humanity." Apparently not: humanoids can be inhuman; and speciously human things can be taken for human.

These stories, and the others interpolated into the novel, so confuse fiction with life that the attentive reader should be helplessly perplexed. Antagonistic evaluations seem equally plausible. No final evidence as to which is which is available, as we are involved in the confidence game. We cannot get inside people, and we cannot distinguish a Drummond light of fraud from one of truth. Any author, even Shakespeare, "does not always seem reliable" (30.194) when he creates a character like Autolycus, the best-known of confidence-men. We need to examine more directly the epistemological problem which the inset stories arouse. The problem has to do with the claim of literature to tell the truth.

SUSPICION AND REVELATION

The pace of *The Confidence-Man* is jerky, as it pulsates with speedy encounters and even swifter partings. This choppy rhythm seems to imitate the mental contortions of a man trying to authenticate what he knows. Melville has done what the Herb Doctor, after St. Paul (I Thess. 5:21), recommends to a sick man: "Prove all the vials; trust those which are true" (16.93). None prove true.

One wants to know what is good and what is bad. How one knows involves the source of one's knowledge. We can roughly divide these sources into internal and external forms—if we remember that this will create artificial problems in the end—and treat first Melville's testing of man's interior resources. These consist of his capacity to experience, to cogitate, and to remember. I shall treat raw perception later, as an exceptional case. In general, Melville exposes as vanities all the efforts to know by means of these faculties.

Experience is a guide, but in his essay on consistency Melville reminds us that "as no one man can be coextensive with *what is*, it may be unwise in every case to rest upon [experience]" (14.77). The education of youth yields small results, as Pitch argues. The case of the education of certain backwoodsmen, detailed in "The metaphysics of Indian-hating," shows that nurture can be wrong. Of the more rational faculties, the Herb Doctor impugns mathematical intelligence with his faulty additions. Most of the conversations in the novel shed darkness on the science of logic: Pitch says analogical argument is a "pun with ideas," and "to the devil with your principles" (22.141, 130). The use of hypothesis is undermined by the psychodrama of Egbert and the Cosmopolitan as "Charlie" and "Frank." Scholarship, in the Emersonian pronouncements of Mark Winsome, amounts to obscurantist claptrap. Dialectical dispute and critical thought are ridiculed in the radically alternating responses to the lamblike man at the beginning of chapter 2, and the remarkable interpretation of the character of Polonius put forth by Charlie Noble. Pitch satirizes liberal tolerance, too.

Even that final retreat of a man who would know, his sense of humor, is challenged: "The bravadoing mischievousness of Autolycus is slid into the world on humor, as a pirate schooner, with colors flying, is launched into the sea on greased ways" (30.195–96). Beauty can be perceived, and the man with the weed identifies ugliness with wickedness, as Winsome claims that love and truth must accompany beauty, and easily praises the rattlesnake. We have seen how Melville entertains that beautiful creation, man's fiction: aesthetics and epistemology do not mix. All these ways of knowing depend on self-reliance, the existential thesis of Emerson which Melville considered simple egotism. The character who does create his own moral world, and hence knows it and may judge it, is the sunny Confidence Man; but there is question as to whether he has a "self" on which to rely.

A half step beyond man's mental faculties as an access to knowledge is his sense of his nature: a "symmetrical view of the universe" (the Cosmopolitan's term) implies that the way man is constructed coincides with the truth of things. The usual metaphors for this epistemological relationship are the doctrines of innate ideas, of health, and of the harmony of external nature. Melville explodes the idea of innate ideas by his references to Peter the Wild Boy and Casper

Hauser (21.121, and 2.6). The Platonic and Wordsworthian doctrines of recollection are satirized by "a small sort of handbill of anonymous poetry, rather wordily entitled:—'ODE / ON THE INTIMATIONS / OF / DISTRUST IN MAN . . .'" (10.57). On the question of health as truth, we have the Herb Doctor, and the sick man's reference to Jacob Bigelow's book (Boston, 1854), *Nature in Disease*, a title which in its ambiguity sums up Melville's attitude. In the manner of classical epistemology, Melville lays low the optimistic idea of the harmony of nature, first by presenting the Titan, and then by referring to the Lisbon earthquake, the favorite example of eighteenth-century sceptics. Neither human nature nor the perceived world generates truth.

Authority, the traditional source of truth, is represented by old literature, principally the Bible and Shakespeare. Shakespeare, who "has got to be a kind of deity" (30.195), is quoted profusely throughout *The Confidence-Man*, especially the dark *Timon*. Enough has been said about the contorted efforts to steer by his "hidden sun." The Bible, as source of quotation, appears chiefly in its most authoritative, because most traditional, part, in the wisdom literature; but much is made of the fact that many of the sapiential books were proclaimed apocryphal. Ecclesiasticus, the book being read in the last chapter, is apocryphal, a term which "implies something of uncertain credit" (45.275), and the "good news" is "too good to be true" (45.273). We have seen that Indian-hating, as well as fiction in general, is compared to religion, a comparison which tends to weaken the religious claim to knowledge. The press, the modern conveyor of public authority, can be apostolic or Satanic, or just a wine press. Melville is perhaps the most allusive of American writers before our generation, and the most critical of the authors to whom he alludes. The religious possibility, as Melville depicts it in its contemporary form, is at the opposite end of an inauthentic spectrum from the faith held by "mature man of the world" (24.150), the experienced Cosmopolitan.

Beyond authority, mysteries of various kinds offer their private gnosis. Winsome, the magian mystic, presides over belief in metempsychosis and a sort of Neo-Platonic transcendentalism. The merchant and Charlie Noble both espouse the doctrine *in vino veritas*, and the Confidence Man makes the analogy of smoky table talk to the wisdom revealed at the Last Supper (22.142). Pitch thinks of the Confidence

Man as "that seedy Rosicrucian" (23.148). The last word on epistemology is spoken by one of the unnamed commentators on the
unmasked Herb Doctor: "True knowledge comes but by suspicion
or revelation. That's my maxim" (18.104). This takes us the whole
way, from the most mysterious, purest source of knowledge, God
revealing himself directly, symbolized in this book by the advent of
the Confidence Man, to the least hopeful depth of knowledge in man's
interior, his refusal of faith.

The narrator shows us Pitch's interior monologue after he realizes
he has been duped by the Philosophical Intelligence Officer. He
wonders where he has gone wrong, and slips into a piece of archaic
allegory, Bunyanesque personification, of which the book has other
examples. He makes a little castle fable with personifications of the
medieval sort:

> Philosophy, knowledge, experience—were those trusty knights
> of the castle recreant? No, but unbeknown to them, the enemy
> stole on the castle's south side, its genial one, where Suspicion,
> the warder, parleyed. [23.148]

William Pommer in *Milton and Melville* noticed the relation of this
fable to the account in *Paradise Lost* of Satan's deception of Uriel, in
which Pitch corresponds to the sun angel, and the Confidence Man,
of course, to Satan:

> For neither man nor angel can discern
> Hypocrisy, the only evil that walks
> Invisible, except to God alone,
> By his permissive will, through heaven and earth:
> And oft though wisdom wake, suspicion sleeps
> At wisdom's gate, and to simplicity
> Resigns her charge, while goodness thinks no ill
> Where no ill seems: which now for once beguiled
> *Uriel*, though regent of the sun, and held
> The sharpest sighted spirit of all in heaven;
> Who to the fraudulent imposter foul
> In his uprightness answer thus returned.
>
> [3.682–93]

This is the classical view, Milton's brief essay on the *mendax* figure. Imposture is permitted and therefore contained by God's will. In Melville's version, in the Romantic paradox, suspicion alone can withstand untruth, but suspicion, a devilish power itself, can never see truth.

BEING AND TIME

Two possible ways out of these frustrating dead ends of human corruption and philosophical despair remain to Melville. The first is reliance on raw perception, and the second is the possible truth submerged in the temporality of the allegorical form of the book. Neither exit is completely opened in *The Confidence-Man*. It is possible to conceive of Melville's literary career as having two peaks corresponding to these two possible solutions. In *Moby-Dick* (1851), he relies upon the massive presentation of objects to secure our confidence— the book is appropriately subtitled, *The Whale*. Its collections of unpoeticized facts preclude distortion. The whales are possessed of an objectivity so inviolable that they domineer the fiction. In *The Confidence-Man* (1857), the way of allegory prevails (the subtitle is *His Masquerade*), and Melville relinquishes his grasp upon objects presented "pure," as it were for themselves, in favor of that typological form which brings the novel to our attention here. The latter way is less successful for Melville, and his second is his lesser peak. The valley is strewn with *Mardi*, with *Pierre (Or, the Ambiguities)*—the midpoint novel (1852) which presents both pure objects and allegory in uneasy suspension—and with the great tales.

In *Pierre* Melville alludes to Kant's terms, subject and object. In a description of an object, what arouses the reader's interest is the presentation of subjectivity, or the method of that presentation. In the first stone scene in *Pierre* (7.4–6) Melville mockingly shapes the stone like a phallus, and lets the reader see it if he will; whereas the rock Enceladus at the Mount of Titans (25.4–5) is openly described as humanoid, and surrounded with mythological interpretation. The latter rock loses much of its objectivity for the sake of allusiveness and literary resonance. I believe Melville as an author, like Langland, had so active a mind, was so self-critical and tormented, so painfully conscious of the way the world is, that he had to struggle to preserve self-integrated objects in his fictions, and that the story of his declining powers after *Moby-Dick* reflects his increasing sacrifice of the mysterious power to describe things transparently for the sake of attributing meaning in a medium of allusion and rhetorical innuendo, that is, for the sake of allegory. He lost faith in the universality of the concrete ("the whale"), split image from idea, and wrote reductive and sceptical allegory.

The few vestiges of transparent description in *The Confidence-Man* do not offset so much as set off the steady drive of verbally seductive meaning. The most pleasant are the pair of rural similes at the ends of chapters 1 and 7, both of which speak of morning, spring, sugar-snow, and thaw on a March farm. They have not the power of the pastoral interludes of Spenser to redeem the whole poem from time and the systematic devil; here they make the knife of truth stick deeper by recalling the American agrarian dream, and the universal hope of resurrection: Wadlington calls the novel a parody of the regeneration of life. We have looked already at the description of Moredock the Indian-hater as "a bit of woodland scene." Here the close association of human hatred with the forest impedes the objectification and prevents the easy expansion of the reader's imagination when faced with a pure object. Melville's earlier impulse was "lithic," desirous of retaining the rocklike integrity of things outside of intelligence and organic form. Melville was on his way to becoming a lyric poet, for whom the object recedes in favor of the presentation of the speaker's consciousness—at least in modern poetics. The pull of allegory toward the universal and of the satiric novel toward the topical mix unhappily with the lithic and lyric quality of his early masterpiece and his later poetry. The book's achievement is its moral passion, not its perfection of form.

On the level of style, in *The Confidence-Man* we have to deal with allegory's cousins, irony and satire. There is, as the Cosmopolitan says, "something Satanic about irony. God defend me from Irony, and Satire, his bosom friend" (24.155). As part of the novel's program of self-criticism, Melville uses the Satanic style, a style which squirms and looks embarrassed as a Yankee caught in the act of writing poems, an overwritten, sophomoric, pedantic, flunky style:

> Meditation over kindness received seemed to have softened him
> something, too, it may be, beyond what might, perhaps, have

been looked for from one whose unwonted self-respect in the hour of need, and in the act of being aided, might have appeared to some not wholly unlike pride out of place; and pride, in any place, is seldom very feeling. But the truth, perhaps, is. . . . [5.26]

This passage is not typical, but I think it is quintessential. The object of these remarks scarcely matters. We are so immersed in the deluge of over-qualified rhetoric that qualification itself becomes the object we see as well as the medium of our seeing. Foster's analysis of some pages of manuscript of *The Confidence-Man* shows Melville deliberately altering his style in this direction. The hyperactivity of the narrator, and the superfetation of consciousness which that involves, suppresses objects in favor of the faithless act of knowing; as a by-product the novel has the verbal density of a poem. This is the essential style of *The Confidence-Man*. The way of objects remains closed.

The immediate presentation of objects commands trust because so much human experience ratifies the authority of sense perception. In *The Confidence-Man* Melville gives us objects obscured in smoke, but makes instead a potentially trustworthy alternative, the allegorical form of the book. Melville might have begun to say with Blake that "Natural Objects always did & now do Weaken deaden & obliterate Imagination in me," but he was never able to put his whole trust in the power of the imagination. *The Confidence-Man* stands between the devil of objects and the deep blue sea of the imagination; Melville could not rely on the structure of Biblical typology, apocalyptic in intent; he would consider the idea of a personal apocalypse through the imagination simply a selfish lie in the face of the condition of the world. So his apocalypse becomes apocryphal, "something of uncertain credit."

Melville gives to a suspiciously transcendental character in *Pierre*, one Plotinus Plinlimmon, who much resembles Mark Winsome, an essay called "Chronometricals and Horologicals." The essay is fraught with irony, but we can sort out and attribute some of its ideas to Melville. It contends that the measure of absolute truth, from the divine point of view, is like a sea chronometer which keeps Greenwich Mean Time; as time zones change away from Greenwich, the chronometer will always "be contradicting the mere local standards and watch-maker's brains of the earth." From time to time a

chronometer appears personified on earth, keeping more or less perfect celestial time but out of phase with the customs of the world.
Bacon was a mere watch-maker, "but Christ was a chronometer."
"But why then does God now and then send a heavenly chronometer
(as a meteoric stone) into the world, uselessly as it would seem, to
give the lie to all the world's timekeepers?" As a reminder, that God
goes by a different time. Men abide by horological time, by the
practical ethics of this world. Anyone who sets out (as Pierre does)
to follow chronometric time commits "a sort of suicide"; he will be
reviled and sacrificed. For a man not to indulge in the venial sin of
following horological time, human ethics, "would be to be an angel,
a chronometer, whereas he is a man and a horologe." "A virtuous
expediency" is man's excellence; it is improper to "make a complete
unconditional sacrifice of himself on behalf of any other being, or any
cause, or any conceit." Billy Budd be damned.

This last sounds un-Christian, but Plinlimmon argues, "And yet
it follows not from this, that God's truth is one thing and man's
truth another; but—as above hinted, and this will be further eluci-
dated in later lectures—by their very contradictions they are made
to correspond." If chronometricals are understood, evil is acceptable,
"For he will then see, or seem to see, that this world's seeming
incompatibility with God, absolutely results from its meridian correspondence with Him." Seem to see. In fact, this lecture itself is
imcomplete—Pierre comes upon a pamphlet whose last pages are
missing—and we see nothing of the other 332 lectures which Plinlimmon promised, so the explanation for this correspondence in contradiction is lacking. It is as Kierkegaard said of Hegel's system, that
it was due to be completed next Sunday.

The narrator of *Pierre* tells us that Pierre does not understand this
essay, because it contradicts the action which he is undertaking, the
sacrifice of his comfortable life and love for the sake of fraternal duty
and a half-realized incestuous passion. Pierre behaves like a Romantic
Christian, abides by his vision of chronometrical time, and meets a
miserable death in suicide. The novel poses the question of whether
Pierre is like Christ, or a fool.

The Confidence-Man presents the horological world in its rich array
of expediency, corruption, and gracelessness, into which enters like
the angel of chronometric time the Confidence Man. He descends
on the *Fidèle* "as a meteoric stone," in a parody of the Incarnation,

to see how the watches of the passengers are set. He has the special capacity of an outsider to see and judge a society, to know the thoughts of men's hearts. Yet he offers us no way of knowing whether his standard "corresponds" to absolute time, or is merely a diabolic temptation to fall, in pride, into a false imitation of Christ. In fact what he offers of the absolute is not encouraging: either the horrible awareness that one is living a lie, or the final repose of death.

Melville's plot can be taken as presenting three schemes of time which uphold three different dynamics of meaning. The first and most obvious is the traditional plot of allegory which I have already discussed. This plot is linear, and the carefully detailed journey down the river at carefully detailed and symbolic times of day is the image of this plot. From it we expect a graded sequence symbolizing the genesis and development, on the model of the Bible and Book One of *The Faerie Queene*, of an individual human and of history. This aspect of plot should end with recollections of the Apocalypse. While this is the outer shape of *The Confidence-Man*, I hope that this essay has shown that Melville only uses this shape, and puts no confidence in it.

The second form of the plot could be diagrammed as a zigzag line representing the sudden dialectical confrontations of the Confidence Man with his victims and his equally sudden departures from the scene. This plot seemed to F. O. Matthiessen flawed because it avoids sustained development and lapses into gimmicks to keep things moving. But the shape-shifting of the Confidence Man and the hellish repetitions of his exposures of his victims are essential to the meaning of the novel. The dialectics of his entrances and exits mirrors the dialectical conversations which he elicits: both motions symbolize the presence of alternatives and the lack of a high road to truth. This plot resembles that of a morality play, or *Timon of Athens*, except that no conclusion can be reached. The novel is not dramatic, in the Romantic sense of staging an event in a man's interior, but it is thoroughly theatrical.

The third shape of the plot is least visible, that is, has least topographical symbolization, but is most inclusive: the circular form which Kernan, in *The Plot of Satire*, describes as an image of satiric desolation in which "the world goes round and round, and dullness never dies." The confidence games cease only because of a temporal accident, bedtime and death, and not because any resolution is attained. The states of repose which the victims reach are negative and open-ended; they will begin their active deceptions of themselves and others with the new day, unless they happen to die in the night. The characters in *The Confidence-Man* are condemned to act out themselves, like the demonic personifications in Spenser. The Confidence Man's obsessive desire to press his games, the victims' pathetic vulnerability, and the narrator's withdrawn and ironic style, all persist with tedious constancy. The action of the book wheels on a single circle of a Dantesque hell, and there is no trustworthy image, after the lamblike man's ladder, of vertical, redeeming movement across the circles, no Virgil or Beatrice to guide us out. Not only is the apocalypse unrealized, it would be meaningless if it occurred. The Confidence Man and the structures of doubt he provokes cannot be chained like Archimago, but will return eternally, marking time, so that something further must always follow of his masquerade.

Bibliographical Note

Elizabeth S. Foster's "Hendricks House" edition of *The Confidence-Man* (New York, 1954) is a labor of love whose commentaries and critical introduction have not been outdated. Two recent editions contain elaborate notes and other aids: H. Bruce Franklin (Indianapolis and New York, 1967) and Hershel Parker (New York, 1971), "A Norton Critical Edition." The latter has an annotated bibliography of all the "significant commentary" to 1971, and reprints pertinent material from Melville's writings, a source or two, and some recent criticism. I mention here only the works I found most useful.

The best general account is that of R. W. B. Lewis, in *Trials of the Word: Essays in American Literature and the Humanist Tradition* (New Haven, 1965), pp. 61–76. Brief remarks which I think consonant with my own are in Charles Feidelson, Jr., *Symbolism and American Literature* (Chicago and London, 1953). Other good criticisms are in Joel Porte, *The Romance in America: Studies in Cooper, Poe, Hawthorne, Melville, and James* (Middletown, Conn., 1969); Edgar A. Dryden, *Melville's Thematics of Form: The Great Art of Telling the Truth* (Baltimore, 1968); Daniel G. Hoffman, *Form and Fable in American*

Fiction (New York, 1961); Ernest Tuveson, "The Creed of the Confidence-Man," *ELH* 33 (1966): 247–70; Warwick Wadlington, "Hidden Suns and Phenomenal Man" in his *The Confidence-Game in American Literature* (Princeton, 1975), esp. pp. 137–70.

Of the numerous studies of the literary background of *The Confidence-Man*, the best are, besides Foster, John W. Shroeder, "Sources and Symbols for Melville's *Confidence-Man*," *PMLA* 66 (1951): 363–80, repr. in Parker's edition; Richard Chase, *Herman Melville: A Critical Study* (New York and London, 1949); Egbert S. Oliver, "Melville's Picture of Emerson and Thoreau in *The Confidence-Man*," *CE* 8 (1946): 61–72; Hershel Parker, "Melville's Satire of Emerson and Thoreau: An Evaluation of the Evidence," *ATQ* 7 (1970): 61–67; Johannes D. Bergmann, "The Original Confidence-Man," *AQ* 21 (1969): 560–77; H. Bruce Franklin, *The Wake of the Gods: Melville's Mythology* (Stanford, 1963); Paul Brodtkorb, Jr., "*The Confidence-Man*: The Con-Man as Hero," *SNNTS* 1 (1969): 421–35. On the three critical chapters in the novel see Allen Hayman, "The Real and the Original: Herman Melville's Theory of Prose Fiction," *MFS* 8 (1962): 211–51.

The quotation from Blake, which I owe to my colleague Barbara Packer, is found in an annotation he made on a copy of Wordsworth, printed by David V. Erdman, ed., *The Poetry and Prose of William Blake* (Garden City, N.Y., 4th printing rev., 1970), p. 655. F. O. Matthiessen's *American Renaissance* appeared in New York and London, 1941. In *Transformations of Allegory*, Gay Clifford has a good account of the change in allegory in the Enlightenment. Thoreau on snakes is quoted from James McIntosh, *Thoreau as Romantic Naturalist: His Shifting Stance toward Nature* (Ithaca, N.Y., 1974), p. 122.

PART TWO
The Reflex of the Heart

Allegories of Love

. . . he shall be compared to a man beholding his own countenance in a glass. For he beheld himself, and went his way, and presently forgot what manner of man he was.

JAMES 1:23 24

For now we see through a glass, darkly . . . .

I CORINTHIANS 13:12

. . . let the hour
Come, when thou must appear to be
That which thou art internally.

Prometheus Unbound 1.297–99

Proem to Part Two

THE works treated in part one focus on the history of salvation, and the process of an individual's salvation in terms of his ability to recognize and conform to the grace of Christian history. Emphasis falls as much on cosmic revelation as on individual character, and the works may be called impersonal. When elaborate attention is centered on an individual, as in Melville, the individual appears rather as a *persona* than as a human. The themes are grace, sin, and knowledge; the authors express little concern with the quality of a character's relations with himself, with others, and with the natural world. Except for the hieratic symbol of atonement, the marriage supper of the lamb, which concludes the first book of *The Faerie Queene*, the four allegories do not address the topic of love.

Part two examines allegories of love. The focus is on the individual and his experience in nature, as he discovers himself and his place in the world. Where the allegories of part one are primarily typologies, in which a form of history is expressed in the plot, these allegories are primarily reifications, in which the mental states and linguistic forms of the human interior are presented as physical, material entities. Being in love affects the experience of things, and allegories of love express that "affect" by controlling the nature of things presented. The allegories are pastoral, because it is in uncivilized landscapes, we feel, that brooks best can sing and trees quiver with our love. In a myth, the brook and the tree may turn out to be former nymphs or humans; similarly, in an allegory, the natural objects may turn out to be labeled reifications of states of mind: the Fountain Perilous or the Garden of Pleasure. Allegories of love bear an especially close relation to classical mythology, doubtless because of the influence of the grand mythographer of love, Ovid.

Two features of the allegory of love will command our attention in the next chapters. First, the initial process of love is depicted as a turning outward of a person's soul, first to consciousness of his self as a self, and then to consciousness of an other. As classical pastoral often invokes images of echoing and of natural response to human feelings, so do the allegories of love. The special image for the first step of love is the mirror—the image of the image—which reveals a person to himself, and reifies the responsive relation of a person to the natural world of objects. The Narcissus myth is the classical fiction of the first step toward love; as we shall see, the Pygmalion myth is its counterpart. Narcissism and pygmalionism characterize, in different stages of their development, the lovers whom we will consider. Love is a way of looking, and the beholding of objects will be one of our topics.

Secondly, all of these allegories, but especially *The Romance of the Rose* and the central books, the third and fourth, of *The Faerie Queene*, display a special consciousness of the language of love. It need scarcely be repeated here that the love lyric in its new form, which arose in Provence a century and more before Guillaume de Lorris began to write his part of *The Romance of the Rose*, was an intensely self-conscious, verbally artificial genre. The new language of love for several centuries fed upon itself, and its poetry developed in a complex process of self-criticism and retrenchment. A constant theme of medieval and Renaissance love poetry is its own mode of expression. Reification allegories, so capable of presenting language itself in the form of personifications and metaphors which are realized in· the fiction, engage extensively in the critique of the poetic language of love.

Our authors, except for Kafka, are Christians, and doubtless all would subscribe in some way to the truths presented in the first book of *The Faerie Queene*. But Christian doctrine has not much to say about nature and about human love; early Christianity tends to use these phenomena as mundane analogies to the more important realities with which it is concerned. None of the allegories we are to treat is anti-Christian, but all are relatively un-Christian. They attend to the holiness of the heart's affections. They may be felt to be incomplete in their limited concern with revelation's final things—Jean de Meun pointedly says as much—but they are not so much blasphemous and heretical as profane. Unlike the fictions treated in part one, these unfold not *sub specie aeternitatis*, but *saeculi*; if they are timeless, it is not because they transcend time, but because they are too short-sighted to see it, like a young lover unmindful of aging. They take place in enclosed gardens, protected and exclusive. They turn to the pagan world for their imagery, and the Biblical material which is included in them often serves the purpose of irony. None of these authors, I think, wishes to rival Christian love with his paganizing myths and pagan psychology, but each wishes to explore natural love as fully as he can within the limits of nature, and nature for us is the nature of the Greeks. The case of Spenser is instructive: by the time the reader comes to the books of love, he has already read Spenser's book of revelation.

Allegories of history "mark time" as they measure the distance from the revealed form of salvation and the not-present fact of salvation. Allegories of love, in analogous fashion, seek out the prelapsarian world for their setting. It is the property of a lover to be blind in the intensity of his seeing, and to imagine that he is in Eden. Without the *felix culpa* of the Fall, Christianity would not have been necessary, and we would inhabit a pagan and pastoral world. It is thought that "pagan" originally meant "rustic." The allegories of love pretend that the Fall has not taken place—in this way they are removed from time—and yet they reenact the Fall in their own process. They are archaic, the way the pastoral interludes in Langland, Spenser, and Melville are archaic; and the lover's paradise is as distant from the original, true Paradise as the knight's apocalypse is distant from the true Apocalypse. Allegories of love are allegories of the Fall, which in the natural world is the onset of seeing, the initiation of consciousness, and the knowlege of self which precipitates the knowledge of good and evil.

CHAPTER SIX

Adornment

The Romance of the Rose

In order that the structure of the cosmos (mundi . . . ornatus) be perpetual,
great care is taken by the providence of the gods that there should always be
the families of animals and trees and everything supported by stalks.

CICERO, *De natura deorum* 2.51

O blisful light, of which the bemes clere
Adorneth al the thridde heven faire!
O sonnes lief, O Joves doughter deere,
Plesance of love, O goodly debonaire,
In gentil hertes ay redy to repaire!
O veray cause of heele and of gladnesse,
Iheryed be thy myght and thi goodnesse!

In hevene and helle, in erthe and salte see
Is felt thi myght, if that I wel descerne;
As man, brid, best, fissh, herbe, and grene tree
Thee fele in tymes with vapour eterne.
God loveth, and to love wol nought werne;
And in this world no lyves creature
Withouten love is worth, or may endure.

Troilus 3.1–2

The Romance of the Rose rivals the Bible, the *Aeneid*, and the *Metamorphoses* as the most influential works of Western literature, yet it is at first a difficult task for the modern reader. We have lost some essential context for understanding it. Its most conspicious features are emphatic rhetoric, which becomes a theme of the poem, and presentation of the plenitude of the natural world. Rhetoric and plenitude are of a piece with love, and in this chapter I propose to examine the relations among these themes and their bearing on allegory. These are matters of special import in the thirteenth century, and the poem is a perfect exemplar of its time. We need to resurrect some of this context to see the life of the poem.

LOVE

The Romance of the Rose is all about love, and about all kinds of love, so we should begin this investigation of the allegory of love by recalling some of the meanings of the term in the Middle Ages. We must presume that sexual passion is the *sine qua non* of love; that if a desire or relationship bears no analogy to sexual passion it would fail to qualify as love. Medieval thought conceived of sexual passion entirely as an attraction toward an object, an intention.

Doubtless we can attribute to Augustine the Christian capacity to incorporate the idea of sexual passion into the most serious speculation, far beyond what Plato had managed in the *Symposium*. Christ had preached love; and the same faculty, the will, and the same quality of ecstatic experience, attended upon both sexual love and the love of God. The mystical tradition, culminating in Bernard of Clairvaux, and the tradition of religious poetry with its easy use of sexual language to describe religious passion, and the tradition of exegesis of the Song of Songs all contributed to this strain of medieval thought. Antisexual opinion in the Church—the monastic ideal, the praise of virginity, the rise of clerical celibacy, the vigorous condemnation of *luxuria*—should not obscure the erotic character of medieval Christianity. Avoidance of sexuality stands in a dialectical relationship with respect for sexuality.

Another meaning of love springs from early Greek conceptions of physics and cosmology. From Empedocles and Lucretius and Stoic thought derives the notion that Love and its contrary Strife (Concord and Discord) are the primal forces which join and separate the elemental matter of the world. From early on, before Plato wrote the *Symposium* and the *Timaeus*, this theory of elemental attraction, which is still with us, was attached to another theory of love in physics. This involved a concept of the primordial dissociation of masculine and feminine principles, considered as forces, as forms, as aspects of matter, as, perhaps originally, sky (sun) and earth (matter, chaos), and their occasional recombination, as the principle of generation of the world of becoming.

Associated with Neoplatonic speculation, especially with Plotinus and pseudo-Dionysius the Areopagite, is the elaboration of these physical conceptions into a cosmic theology, in which the starry spheres and other spiritual entities mediate the superabundant, emanating divine love to earth, filling out the graded universe in a dance of harmony. The sciences of astrology and demonology which are grounded in this scheme are not emphasized in the main line of orthodox theology from Augustine to Aquinas—astrology in particular was rejected as a denial of providence and free will—but the scheme itself appears in medieval literature from Boethius to Chaucer and Dante.

This speculative view of cosmic love bears special relevance to Jean de Meun's part of *The Romance of the Rose* because, as has long been recognized, he borrows from the twelfth-century poets associated with what now is known only loosely as the "School of Chartres": Bernard Silvestris, author of *De mundi universitate*, better called the *Cosmographia*, and Alain de Lille, author of the *Anticlaudianus* and *De planctu naturae*. Fired by the Neoplatonic tradition and by direct knowledge, in a Latin translation, of Plato's *Timaeus*, these philosopher-poets wrote cosmic allegories of the Creation or of such characters as Genius and Natura, who treat such topics as the harmony of the world in natural love and the problem of the existence of man. Postlapsarian human love can fail to harmonize with natural love; sexual desire is of a piece with nature, but man in his freedom can pervert his lust. This is a theme of the *Romance*.

Apparently far removed from this nearly cabalistic tradition, and more obviously associated with Guillaume de Lorris's part of the *Romance*, is the tradition of love poetry usually labeled "courtly love" or "Petrarchan," which was in full flower, and not to fade until the seventeenth century. In this tradition the masculine lyric voice expresses its love-longing and pain, its sense of how one behaves when one is in love, in terms of the natural progress of seasons, of Venus and her attendants, of the institutions of religion and chivalry, of hyperbolic similes (My love is sweeter than . . .), and, most characteristically, in the more purely grammatical terms of oxymoron, the conceit of felt contraries (freezing fire). From the very outset this tradition is more or less decadent, in the etymological sense of that word, in that the poetic language had fallen away from the objects, the women, it claimed to represent. A peculiar feature of the tradition is its willingness to deny its own mode of expression. ("My beautiful words cannot say how I burn.")

Perhaps the most striking characteristic of these notions of love, all of which influence *The Romance of the Rose*, is their inadequacy as descriptions of the nature of love itself. The genesis of love in a human, the etiquette and *savoir-faire* of a lover, the shape of the effects of love in the cosmos, the relations of secular and religious love, the mythological constructions of the etiology and progress of love, none of these topics actually attempts a description of what love is. Love is blind. Medieval writers on love seem always to find room for a response to what their predecessors, or they themselves, have said before about love, as if the former expressions were just so much rhetorical spinning about the real issue, and then to proceed on a higher level. This continual recognition of the failure of expression accounts, in part, for a typical medieval literary structure, the palinode or bipartite form. The response by no means implies outright rejection, nor is the process quite dialectical; more often the response involves a shift of point of view to a more inclusive perspective. Andreas Capellanus's *Art of Loving*, Chaucer's *Troilus*, and *The Romance of the Rose* display this form.

RHETORIC

I have suggested that the hyperboles and conceits of the lyrical tradition raised the question of the proper use of language in writing of love. A heightened awareness of the craft of writing flourished in the thirteenth century, as the multitude of rhetorical treatises attests. Some were written by men, like Matthew of Vendôme, associated with the poets of the "School of Chartres," with Paris, and with

Orleans—near where Jean and Guillaume were probably born. Alan M. F. Gunn has exhaustively studied the rhetorical topics and figures in *The Romance of the Rose*, but we need to look again at the poem, especially Guillaume's part, in order to get at the relation of the poem's rhetorical structure to the theme of love and to our topic of allegory.

Rhetoric is classically defined as the art of persuasion by speech, and it includes the idea that language, the manner of speaking, is separable from the subject of which one speaks. The grammar, prosody, structure, topics, and figures of speech of a discourse become autonomous entities which can be studied in themselves, and language can be adorned without reference to its content.

Guillaume emphasizes at every turn the standard topics of the schools, as if to support his claim to create by his rhetoric another world—a romance world—with only the slightest relation to ours. He opens the poem in a *locus amoenus*, with a Maytime *reverdie* in which his narrator, Amant, falls asleep and dreams. Amant, in the dream, wakes in another, similar pleasance, a springtime setting with birds and rippling water. He comes upon the wall on which are depicted the ten love vices, which he describes in detail. Oiseuse leads Amant within the wall to a third *locus amoenus*, Deduit, the garden of delight. Comparing the garden to Eden, he describes it in detail, and describes the figures he meets within it, the god Amors himself and the dancing company which includes personifications of ten love graces, attendants in the court of Amors, the "barons" of love.

Amant leaves the dancers to explore the garden, and describes it at greater length. Unaware that he is being followed by Amors, he finds the fountain of Narcissus, and tells the story from Ovid. Looking into the Mirror Perilous, the water and the two crystals, he views the reflected image of the whole garden. He sees the image of a rosebush in an enclosed plot which amounts to a fourth *locus amoenus*. The rose itself, like its garden setting, is symmetrical and enclosed. As he moves toward it, tempted by its sight and smell, Amors pierces his heart through his eye with five of his ten allegorical arrows.

Here, not quite a tenth of the way into a poem of over twenty-one thousand lines, not quite halfway through Guillaume's part, let us stop in recognition of the fact that Amant's falling in love marks the first turning point of the poem. Up to this point there have been only a few lines of direct discourse; after this the bulk of the poem is presented as conversation. The pace of the action has been, remarkably enough, relatively rapid so far, both in the under-meaning of the transparent allegory, the progress of Amant's love, and in the presented interaction of the personifications. But the bulk of the matter so far has been description, the principal concern of contemporary rhetoricians. Marc-René Jung calls this part of the poem "static" allegory.

The rhetoric of description may be approached in two ways. The first and more obvious is to consider the particular objects chosen to describe, and to explain the relations among them. First, Guillaume describes *loci amoeni*, a progression of four which enclose each other like Chinese boxes, from the May day in which he dreams to the hedged-in rosebush itself. This effect reinforces the autonomy and inwardness of the vision, just as the dream form frees the poet to say what he will. Then there are the personified qualities surrounding the incidence of love, the wall figures and the company of Amors. The three objects which bear the brunt of the description, vices, virtues, and pleasures, could not be more typical of the rhetorical tradition. The structure of the descriptions is simple concatenation, in a kind of *Voie* (to use the Old French technical term) or series of visions whose order is determined by the progress of the seer. The poem so far is absolutely, relentlessly artificial, and as we shall see, deliberately so. Guillaume's garden of Deduit is four-square.

The other approach to these descriptions is to consider their content individually. The description of the personifications draws from vices and virtues traditions which extend back through Prudentius, modified in accordance with the theme of love rather than Christian morality. Of course the moral implications of some of the descriptions lightly suggest lapses in the moral harmony of the garden, as do the references to Sirens, Eden, and Narcissus. Neither the details nor their order of presentation in these descriptions would have seemed strikingly new to a thirteenth-century reader. The comparison with the figures in Chaucer's *General Prologue* is inevitable: what is lacking in Guillaume's descriptions is that rare irony of apparently accidental juxtaposition of which Chaucer is master, and in general a critical sense; but what is present, as is appropriate for a scheme of allegorical personifications, is an almost mathematical orderliness of presentation. Guillaume keeps his eye steadily on the ideal. Like much of the rest of the poem, Guillaume's descriptions of

Amors's courtiers give his readers what they must have wanted, knowledge of how one looks and how one behaves in the best circles if one is in love; the appeal is partly to that desire for *savoir-senser* which Henry James's novels seem to satisfy for the modern reader. The medieval term for a work which summarizes knowledge of a topic and gives examples of proper behavior is "speculum," mirror. Following Gunn, we can call *The Romance of the Rose* a speculum; Jean himself calls it a "Mirror for Lovers" (10,651).*

The descriptions of the pleasances, especially the pair of descriptions of Deduit itself, contain all the elements—birds, mild breezes, flowing waters, grass, trees, flowers—singled out by Curtius in his influential study of this topic. The prolonged elaborations of these elements stands out, and it is to the method of these that I wish particularly to direct attention. The birds of Deduit are named, a dozen or so, in a catalogue. Some time later Amant catalogues the trees and spice bushes, naming some thirty-five: this list is among the sources of Chaucer's *Parliament of Fowls* and Book One of *The Faerie Queene*. Immediately after this the animals are named, deer, squirrel, and thirty (unenumerated) species of rabbits. Not until he comes to the flowers, and names two kinds, does Amant stop the process with the rhetorical gesture that he has said enough. These catalogues— we should add the catalogue of jewels in Richece's garments— represent the device of "amplification" or "polishing off" (*expolitio*), the essential device of narrative retardation in medieval rhetoric, and the fundamental artifice of the first part of the poem.

Gunn describes amplification as a branching out, and this image aptly describes the poet's progress. The method resembles the branch-and-twig structure of some scholastic philosophy and one school of medieval homiletics, of which The Parson's Tale is a familiar example. The two simple topics, description of a person and description of a pleasance, are divided into parts—the sets of love vices and love graces, or the elements of a *locus amoenus*. (The two topics are not divided according to the same principle). Then these parts are

---

*The edition of *Le Roman de la Rose* which I cite is edited by Ernest Langlois for the Société des Anciens Textes Français, 5 vols. (Paris, 1914–24). Further documentation and bibliography may be found in the note appended to this chapter. To obtain the line number of the Lecoy edition, subtract 30 from the number I give from Langlois (after line 4,000). Translations are my own. The word "Nature" capitalized refers to the lady of that name in the poem.

exhaustively described: in the personal descriptions by details of their array, and in the local descriptions by the catalogues of species present. The effect of the whole is of leisure and ideal symmetry, of immense variety curbed within careful order—the virtues, in short, of a formal garden. It is a rhetoric of plenitude, a stylistic expression of what is, as we shall see, a theme of the poem. In a mnemonic catalogue, a poet implies his Adamic power to name things, and his similarity to the divine power which creates things "a orne."

When Amant looks into the Mirror Perilous, he sees the elements of the garden: "i pert tot a orne" (all appeared there *a orne*—1,552). Langlois follows the standard dictionary translation of "a orne" as "in order," and the word is related to the Latin word from which comes our "ornament." Daniel Poirion, following E. Koehler and Jean Frappier, suggests that the phrase means "in its essential order" —that the essential nature of the garden is magically revealed in the mirror. What Amant sees, I think, is the garden disposed according to the rhetorical principles displayed heretofore in the poem. We need to remember that Amant is writing, according to the fiction, five years after he dreamed, so that like Dante's or Chaucer's visioners he can use the knowledge of the end to write the beginning. Just as Redcrosse learns late what the reader can see at the beginning, so Amant cannot see until he looks in the mirror of Narcissus the orderly anatomy of the garden which strikes the reader immediately because of the rhetoric of *expolitio*. The Mirror Perilous reveals the fictional genre of the speculum. When Amant grasps the nature of the place he is in, desire kindles within him to possess the rose. The perception of order, presented by Guillaume as magically induced, is associated in the time scheme of the poem with the inception of love.

ALLEGORY

The garden of Deduit is an image of Paradise, whose design is meant to elicit our deep longing for the happy and innocent past. Its rhetorical disposition aligns its elements with a philosophical conception of the just proportions, the *ratio* or Reason, of the cosmos. It is a garden of love as it might be, and hence the springboard of the rest of the poem, which treats the intelligence of natural, harmonious love as a problem in relation to fallen man. At the same time it is the locale of an allegorical narrative, in which twice already—in the early part of the poem which we have been considering—Guillaume has promised us an explanation of what is dark. Let us examine now the kinds of allegory we find in the poem, with a view to understanding the relation of its allegory to the mode of rhetoric and the theme of love.

First of all, the poem is full of personification allegory, primarily from the tradition of Prudentius, which by Guillaume's time had been supplemented by cosmic personification of the sort associated with the "School of Chartres" and by the personifications of the qualities of love, which may be found, in relatively abbreviated versions, in twelfth-century lyric and romance. The first set of personifications we meet, the plastic, emblematic group of love vices on Deduit's wall, represents a doffing of Guillaume's cap to Prudentius, and introduces us to the poem's allegorical form in the simplest way. Not until late in Jean's part (15,303 ff.) does a proper love psychomachia occur. The wall figures do not speak; but occasional frozen gestures—Hate's frown, Envy's slipping eye—imply that action of which Prudentius made an epic. The wall figures represent not mental faculties but states of mind—and in the cases of Poverty and Old Age, states of physical ill-being—which prohibit love. The dancers within the garden represent the contrary states, conducive to love. Although they are active and alive, their action contributes nothing to their meaning, except, as Hans Robert Jauss observes, to emphasize the vitality of the situation of loving and to sharpen its contrast with the love vices. That they dance before their love-making symbolizes the musical disposition of the world they inhabit, but the dance might as well have been painted. Oiseuse's admission of Amant to the garden initiates the basic allegorical scheme of the poem, the interaction of Amant with the various personifications.

Amant himself is not exactly a personification, but an impersonation of the author, a whole man capable of being divided within himself. Like Redcrosse, he is the "patron" of a state—Holiness, Loving—and not the reduced representative of it. At least one personification he meets later in the poem, Raison, represents in part a projection of his own faculty. The only other entire human in the poem, who represents neither an abstraction nor a generalization, is the lady. However, we never see her *in propria persona*, but only as a symbol—the rose—and as a bewildering set of personifications of supposed feminine qualities which war among themselves: Daungere and Bel Accueil, Shame and Pity, Fear and Franchise, and the rest. Her being is analyzed and reified.

Two other sets of personifications complete the scheme: the "types" or personified generalizations of Theophrastian characters—Ami, la Vieille, the Jealous Husband, Faus Semblant—and the personifications of cosmic forces and principles—Nature, Genius, Venus, and in her broader aspect, Raison. Two figures come from classical sources by way of medieval mythography: the god Amors represents the possibilities and limitations of love within the erotic tradition of French lyric—Gunn calls him a "culture deity"—whereas Venus represents the natural, flaming passion of love as it is, so to speak, outside of literary convention. Amors is Amant's knowledge of love poetry, and Venus is the lady's recognition of her body. In Jean's part, Venus and Genius play the role given to Amors in the first part.

Bel Accueil, Faus Semblant, Genius, Envy, and Venus derive from different spheres of intellectual concern. They are twigs of five different branchings, spliced into *The Romance of the Rose* without violence because of the freedom available to an allegorical poet. In a common medieval device, used with comic force in the Lady Meed episode of *Piers Plowman*, many of these personifications are linked by allegorical kinship. Shame is daughter of Raison and Ill-done; Bel Accueil is Courtesy's son; Badmouth is son of Irate, Raison is God's daughter; Gentility is Fortune's daughter and Misfortune's cousin; Poverty begat Theft; Deceit and Hypocrisy are parents of Faus Semblant, who is fathering Antichrist on Constrained Abstinence; Amors is Venus's son; and Shame is cousin of Fear. The logical conclusions, that Shame is God's granddaughter and Ill-done his son-in-law, are not perfectly consistent with a branching method of generation of these figures—a tree diagram would be difficult to construct—and should warn us not to attempt to piece together all the allegorical manifestations in a long poem. In Payen's terms, the poem has a semiology but not a semiotic. In fact *The Romance of the Rose* is no exception to the general rule that sets of personifications in extended fictions come in scattered clumps: perhaps our image should be, not a tree, but daffodils.

Personification allegory dominates *The Romance of the Rose*, but other kinds of allegory are present. Associated with the topographical and architectural features of the setting are examples of what I have called analysis and categorization, the allegorical rationalization of a divided image like the Tree of Charity scene in *Piers Plowman* or the great architectural pageants in Spenser. The garden's elements are not systematically interpreted after the fashion of Philo Judeus, but features of it are: the fountain, most obviously, and the wall, four square, of Deduit, contrasted with the more perfect circular wall of the *beau parc* described by Genius. Within Deduit we find the tower of Raison, the hedged plot of the rose garden, and the castle in which Jealousy immures Bel Accueil and the Rose. The last, especially, when compared with the mount on which Venus's dwelling is located (outside the garden), and with the sexual allegory of the end of the poem, is part of a body allegory. We are far from the systematic anatomy of Spenser's House of Alma or Fletcher's Purple Island, but the reflecting crystals, in which C. S. Lewis saw the lady's eyes, Raison's tower—derived from Isaiah 5, the *Shepherd of Hermas*, and apocryphal literature—and the rose's enclosure uphold the tradition that the garden is a body allegorized.

The idea of the whole space of the poem as a single body corresponds with the idea of personification: if the persons of the poem are primarily particles of states of mind, the topography on which they operate may easily be conceived as a giant body. We have seen this in the *Psychomachia*. This may be the reason why fairies and such, the supernatural but (assuming suspension of disbelief) real analogues of fictional personifications, are so small. The castle-prison itself is anatomized: personifications keep watch at its four gateways (as they do for Pitch in *The Confidence-Man*) and the defense materials are allegorized in the fashion later developed in the barn Holy Church scene in *Piers*.

While I do not intend to enumerate all the kinds of allegory in *The Romance of the Rose*, I should mention three more, of which I will treat the first two in another connection. First is typology, the kind of allegory which was the subject of the first part of this book. We find it only in subordinate, vestigial form in *The Romance of the Rose*. The garden of Deduit resembles Eden, and D. W. Robertson, Jr., and John V. Fleming have emphasized the potentiality of Guillaume's part of the poem as a type of the Fall. Another trace of Biblical typology is the figure of Faus Semblant, another *mendax* type. He compares himself with Proteus (11,181 ff.), is the child of Deceit and

Hypocrisy, is about to be the father of Antichrist, and is a friar like the *mendax* of *Piers Plowman*. He does not have the apocalyptic resonance of Prudentius's Discord—M.-R. Jung connects him with the earlier poet's Cupiditas disguised as Frugi—nor the poetic function of Archimago or the Confidence Man; still, as Langland does with Friar Flatterer, Jean singles him out for especially virulent attack which seems so personal that it probably is personal—the attack by a defender of religious culture on a pretender to that role. Fleming has tried to connect Faus Semblant to the central themes of the poem by explaining that Faus Semblant is a self-lover, a perversion of grace; Wetherbee suggests he expresses a materialism which is the inverse of the "lost allegorical harmony invoked by Raison." He is an intruder into the poem from another allegorical tradition; Nature rejects him as a false prophet (19,350), which puts him rather in Spenser's apocalyptic world than in the cosmos of love.

A second kind of allegory I shall only mention here, the allegorization of classical myth. Finally, there is the kind of allegory which almost escapes attention because it is so simple and so fundamental. It is, at last, the allegory which fits the classical definition of the term as "continued metaphor," our "reification." The rose represents the lady; or, to be more precise than Guillaume or Jean usually need to be, the lady's genitalia. The *tertium quid* of the metaphor—the sensual pleasure which rose and lady can give, their beauty—is suppressed, and hence the allegory is technically enigmatic. On this continued metaphor depends the connection of Amant's quest with the institutions of feudal chivalry, academe, and religion. Amors as lord, Raison as pedagogue, and Genius as priest are reified extensions into the fiction of what would be submerged metaphor in a nonfictional essay on love.

The enigma is not very dark, but both Guillaume and Jean, with tongues in cheek, avow that all will be explained in the end—of course Guillaume might have carried out his promise had he completed his poem. Jean's Genius, irrepressibly, borrowing from Alain and elsewhere, elaborates the masculine counterpart of the rose in spacious discourses on plows, pens, and hammers which cultivate, write, and forge in fields, paper, anvils. The humor of these sexual enigmas should not keep us from seeing that the instruments in the metaphors are both maintainers of civilization and procreators, which is Genius's point.

RHETORIC, ALLEGORY, AND LOVE

There is every reason to suppose that Jean de Meun thought of the term "allegory" as meaning a kind of interpretation of Scripture, and insofar as it might be applied to secular literature, as a term from rhetoric, a method of adornment and concealment (his terms might be *involucrum, integumentum*), according to classical and early Christian doctrine. Faus Semblant's comical interpretations of Peter and John and of the corporeal versus the spiritual hand (11,858–70; 11,479–82), the debate between Croesus and Phanie on the interpretation of his dream (6,601–19), and a rudimentary sense of personification, may well exhaust the particular express theory of allegory available to either author of the *Romance*. The connections I am about to draw out, for the rest of this essay, between allegory and rhetoric, and between these modes and the meaning of *The Romance of the Rose*, spring not from a fully articulated theory of allegory and reason in the thirteenth century, but from the merger, in the poem, of ideas and techniques which were inevitable, at least in the sense that major literature which expresses its age is inevitable.

In the essay on Book One of *The Faerie Queene* I tried to show how allegory may be viewed as the multiple disposition, into such fictional forms as projected characters, parallel episodes, and repeated motifs of all kinds, of one or a few underlying principles, such as deception, ignorance, wholeness, and grace. The principle can be man himself, as it were hypostatized, in a chastely simple form as in Spenser's House of Alma, or a more complex form as in the *Psychomachia*. Both the complete form of personification, in which a thing becomes an actor in a fiction, and the partial form in which a thing assumes some human feature such as a body or voice (like the wall vices in *The Romance of the Rose*), are apt vehicles for expressing the analysis of a principle. From this point of view, the formal connection between rhetoric and allegory becomes easy to state: allegory, especially in the form of the analysis of the human psyche by personification, is analogous to the branching *expolitio*, the multitude in unity, characteristic of high medieval rhetoric. As rhetorical topics split nature into catalogues of terms, so psychological personification allegory splits the soul into catalogues of terms.

Both historical and contemporaneous causes lie behind the efficacy of this analogy. M.-R. Jung, following Lewis, observes that personification allegory was originally an *ornatus*, a rhetorical elaboration, contained within nonallegorical fiction, like Ovid's Envy, Virgil's Fame, and the personifications in Statius, and that this local device developed into an autonomous form, controlling an entire fiction. The historical process can virtually be ascribed to the literary career of Prudentius himself. In the intellectual surge which began in the eleventh century and included the founding of the universities, the rediscovery of antique philosophy and science, and the rise of scholastic philosophy, the analytical method of thought achieved that dominance which was to last through the sixteenth century. The musical *organum*, the severely rhythmical analyses found everywhere in the plastic arts, the rhetorical form of *The Romance of the Rose* and the other works of its kind, as well as the incremental repetitiousness of Old French epic and the intricately woven, limited vocabulary of motifs of the new genre, chivalric romance, reveal the influence of the principle in the arts. The unique mixture of genres found in *The Romance of the Rose*—speculum, voie, romance, satire, dream vision— makes it an ideal expression of the high medieval solution of rhetorical craft and allegorical form.

I have emphasized the autonomy of the fiction of *The Romance of the Rose*—its self-consciously rhetorical, dream vision, allegorical mode—but now I wish to turn about and to examine how the form of the work engages outer reality; not, for the moment, the everyday, satiric reality from which Chaucer drew his Pardoner and Wife of Bath, a reality which Poirion observes is as conventional and derivative an aspect of *The Romance of the Rose* as any other, but the Neoplatonic reality of the "School of Chartres." The ordered sequences of objects and sets of qualities imitate the structure of the cosmos, as Jean explicitly, Guillaume perhaps only implicitly, conceived it. The Greek term "cosmos" means both "the world as rationally understood" and "ornament, jewel." Ornamented language corresponds to the world conceived Platonically, as "intelligible"—that is, composed of intelligible substances, invisible, mathematically harmonious—or as "rational," "logical"—that is, composed according to the principles of just proportion (*ratio*). Rhetoric may imitate reality—an idea not too distant in this age of Kant and the structuralists—and earthly plenitude and rhetorical analysis are two sides of the same coin. Rhetoric is nature cosmeticized in language.

This relation of rhetoric to the shape of the world, in a properly

Neoplatonic setting, appears in Bernard Silvestris's *Cosmographia*. The story goes that Nature had complained of the confusion of primal matter, "id est hyles," and Noys (the Greek *nous*, "mind") makes the world for her, a world which Bernard expressed in catalogues of the things of the world. Noys gives Nature her domain by drawing a decorous order out of chaos, because Nature "Artifices numeros et musica vincla requirit" ("seeks for artful numbers and musical bonds"—1.1.21). In the prefatory summary to this work called the "Breviarum," Bernard calls this creative ordering of the world *expolitio mundi*: we have seen that the *expolitio* is the rhetorician's technical term for their amplification device, "polishing off." As Wetherbee puts it, "Chartrian thought begins and ends in a kind of poetry, for its Platonic cosmos is itself a kind of work of art." The creation is God's ornament, the "ornatus mundi" of Cicero.

Gunn's study of the *Romance of the Rose*, making use of A. O. Lovejoy's classic, *The Great Chain of Being*, has traced the connection between the poem and the "Chartrian" idea of ordered nature. The crucial idea of plenitude has the world necessarily filled in every space with intelligibly graded species of being. Poirion speaks of Jean's "metaphysique de la plenitude," his almost mystical fervor, in enunciating the need for constant generation—the job of Genius who mediates between Nature and the world of becoming. The natural world would revert to chaos if Genius did not fill the hierarchy of being. I should note here that this is not Jean's final view of the world, but only of the natural world. Wetherbee observes that Alain de Lille's figure Natura has little sense of God's intervention for man, of the Incarnation, and that Jean refuses "to acquiesce in Alain's poetic sense of the natural order as the type and vehicle of the order of Grace." Jean's Nature carefully sets aside as beyond her ken the more Hebrew, Christian cosmology of original sin and grace (19,140–244).

The literary form which expresses the plenitude of the world is the catalogue of things which exist. In Judeo-Christian tradition, especially after St. Ambrose, such a catalogue often follows the order of the six days of Creation, according to Genesis, and we may call the form hexameron. The original hexameron, the Creation by the Word, is God's version of rhetorical description, whose counterpart is found in Guillaume and his catalogues. The *Cosmographia*, and Book Seven of *Paradise Lost*, Milton's most musical book, are hexameral poems; the bulk of Nature's speech in *The Romance of the Rose* (16,729–19,054) is a comic, meandering, self-consciously prolix version of a hexameron. Here most explicitly in the poem we find the theme of abundance concatenated, only implicit in Guillaume, asserting itself.

The will to multiply is love: its natural version is distaste for chaos and vacuum, and its human analogue is sexuality. Genius presides over natural generation, Venus over the physiology of sexuality, and Amors over the human culture of love, the erotic language of the lyric tradition. The human, or in Bernard's term, microcosmic version of the hexameron is the "gradus amoris," the sequence of the progress of love from look to intercourse which was formulated by medieval rhetoricians and followed in no programmatic way by Guillaume. Jean responds to Guillaume by going underneath—by presenting sexual affairs as they are (in the comic, antifeminist tradition) in the speeches of Ami, la Vieille, and the Jealous Husband —and by going over, by reference to love in its cosmic dimension. Jean's play of attitudes and levels of meanings resembles Langland's, who likewise brings the mundane, pragmatic, and sordid to bear on the anagogical and typological.

To summarize: Guillaume presents the traditional language surrounding love in an emphatically rhetorical form and rationalizes the rhetoric in allegorical form; Jean criticizes the view of love presented by his predecessor, both by demolishing the rhetorical structure which underpins it, and by presenting his own, parodic, hyperallegorical version of love in terms of cosmic theosophy. We should examine Jean's response to Guillaume more closely, as a necessary preliminary to grasping his meaning.

JEAN'S RESPONSE

The problem of *The Romance of the Rose*, as Jean sees it, is the disintegration of the three aspects of love, personified by Genius, Amor, and Venus, the General, Venereal, and Amorous, their failure to be in accord with one another and with the facts of the fallen world. The Golden, Saturnian Age is gone; men are corrupt and behave unnaturally; love jars with love. The signature of this decline—*The Romance of the Rose* follows ancient tradition in speaking of a perfect "then" and a decadent "now"—is the corruption of language, especially of grammar, that old art of exegesis and eloquence which was being overwhelmed, in the schools, by logic, the new science. The defense of humanism was not yet under way. Alain de Lille begins his *De planctu naturae* with puns on the perversion of grammatical cases and genders which correspond to sexual perversion, Nature's complaint. Examples of this medieval joke would be easy to multiply from the preserved corpus of schoolish Latin lyrics.

Amant's brazen interruption of Raison's speech, on the grounds that her use of the term "coilles" is ribald, indicates, as Wetherbee observes, his confused and fallen sense of the relation of language to things. Raison points out that she, after all, originally gave names to things. Jean opens his part of the poem with school terms of logic ("sillogime," "conclue") and has Genius, speaking of the *beau parc*, play on the grammatical tenses, the lack of preterite and future in paradise (20,016–26). Jean is going Guillaume one better, as usual, admitting not only the rhetorical forms but the very terminology of the schools into his poem. Elsewhere Jean says he will enumerate the barons of love "Briement . . . senz ordre" (Briefly, without order —10,447), parodying the epic theme, the catalogue of forces, and roughly asserting his poetic, which is both too self-consciously rhetorical and antirhetorical.

The point of Jean's play may be observed in a comparison of the uses of oxymorons by the two poets. Guillaume, describing the allegorical arrows with which Amors shot Amant, names the last Fair Seeming, which has the power to hurt, but is coated with a soothing balm which simultaneously relieves the pain. "Ceste floiche a fiere costume: / douçor i a et amertume" (This arrow has a strange manner: it has both sweetness and bitterness—1,873–74). Guillaume, typically, has rationalized in allegorical form a rhetorical device found everywhere in the love lyric (O pleasing pain!), giving a fantastic physiological explanation for the commonplace feeling. On the other hand, when Jean's Raison begins to teach Amant about love, she lists more than forty oxymorons:

> Amour ce est pais haïneuse,
> Amour, c'est haïnc amoureuse; . . .   [4,293–334]

> [Love, a hateful peace, a loving hate . . .]

195

This is not the delicate sensibility of a Provençal lyricist, but parody by excessive imitation; Jean undermines the art of rhetoric by singling out a feature of it and blowing it out of proportion. Zumthor calls Jean's work a "disaggregation of the pre-text" written in a "demystifying rage." La Vieille overworks the device of the exemplum (Chaucer's Wife of Bath, who likewise argues the virtue of experience over authority, is likewise pedantically excessive in her show of learning). She and Ami overdo the "how to do it' aspect of loving. Nature says "Bon fait prolixité foïr" (It is well to avoid prolixity— 18,298), but fails. It is only speculation, but I guess Guillaume would not have introduced a full-fledged psychomachia between Amors's barons and the defenders of the Rose; I am certain he would not have begun it with Faus Semblant's slitting out Badmouth's tongue. Jean is an allegorist himself, but he satirizes the casual, ornamental use of allegory so successfully that some readers of the poem, as if forgetting that Nature is not really nature, have felt that Jean's part is not allegory at all.

Jean's most formal response to Guillaume is of course the *beau parc* which Genius describes and overtly contrasts with the garden of Deduit. The *beau parc* likewise stands in contrast to one of Jean's other *loci amoeni*, Ami's description of the world of the Golden Age (8,355 ff.), whose decline to the Silver Age, the passage of dominion from Saturn to Jupiter, is narrated by Genius in the midst of his description of the *beau parc*. These three major pleasances symbolize not only the human wish for paradise, but also hexameral nature in little: the gardens are microcosms of rational nature just as according to Nature man is a "petiz mondes nouveaus" (new little world— 19,053). The comparisons of the *loci amoeni* which Genius makes exemplify the dialectical potential of allegory, here not as the battle among divisions of a soul, but as the conflict of worlds.

The fall of the quasi-timeless Golden Age, sustained by mythological divinities, is signalled by a new eschatological imperative to choose between heaven and hell, the *beau parc* or the abode of the devils without. In fact the consequences of this natural fall are not continually felt in *The Romance of the Rose*; in the dynamic temporal state of the poem, Adonis has not yet been gored—this event occurs "after" the action of the poem, but "before" it is narrated (15,659– 771). Jean presents the mythical and merely natural, which are mutually sustaining, as poetically contemporaneous with the fallen and historical, in a perplexing dialectic made possible by his freedom as an allegorist. I will return to this point.

The *beau parc* is the residence of those who follow Genius's commands (20,627–48), the alternatives to the rules of Amors (2,057 ff.). Just when a follower of the commandments may enter the *beau parc* remains unclear—not, we may be sure, in the state of idleness, beauty, wealth, and the rest who attend upon the entrance to Deduit. Of course it is at death after a good life, but this idea must be outside the imagination of the principle of generation himself. Genius's commandments are these: honor and serve Nature; repay what you owe; do not murder; be clean; be pitying; be loyal. This is the law of nature, a reasonable law such as a pagan might devise. It is a mandate of common sense which enters the poem like a breath of fresh air. A Christian would not reject it—unless "Nature" were defined in an unusual way—but would only say it is incomplete. Oddly enough, what the law of Genius and Nature leaves out is love—of neighbor and of God.

The *beau parc* is always in a spring day: it is essentially eternal, surpassing the quasi-spring of the Golden Age, sustained by Saturn, and the present but limited springtime of the garden of Deduit (winter, denatured, exists there too—1,402) which is the projection of a state of mind, and a brief time of physical existence—the delight of first love. Deduit, says Genius, "n'a chose qui seit estable, / Quanqu'il i vit est corrompable" (has nothing stable; whatever he saw there is corruptible—20,353–54). The wall of the *beau parc* is round—Platonically perfect—and not the square of human order in Deduit. On the walls of the final garden are depicted the devils of hell, and the whole world in its plenitude. The fall, or the decline from the Golden Age, has divided the world into three stories, and the lower two, in the world of becoming, are excluded from the *parc*. The fountain of the *beau parc* is a fountain of life, a thirst-slaker, and self-sufficient in its Three-in-One source, the Trinity; the fountain of Narcissus in Deduit is death-dealing, and dependent on an outside source. The two crystals of the Mirror Perilous, which reveal only one-half of Deduit at a time, are contrasted with the light-generating carbuncle of the *parc*'s fountain, whose facets are Three-in-One, and whose reflection gives complete knowledge of everything in the *parc*.

The differences between the garden of Deduit and the *beau parc* may be summed up: the *beau parc* is eternal; it is generated by the self-sufficient Trinity; it yields true knowledge and life, not vain knowledge and death. Genius gives us a pair of terms which epitomizes the difference: he asks the barons to choose between the gardens "E d'accidenz e de sustances" (With regard to both accidents and substances—20,600). He means with regard to the appearances and the inner meanings (that is, life and death, vanity and truth) of each of the gardens, but we may use the terms to distinguish the accidental garden of Deduit—all sensual vision, clothed in rhetoric—and the substantial *beau parc*—a Christianized Platonic ideal expressed in fantastic optics resembling what Dante called intellectual vision. The Mirror Perilous gave Amant a vision of the garden "a orne," but Genius gives us the real substance of the garden. Jean, through Genius, does not so much reject the garden of Deduit as see through it.

Jean criticizes Guillaume's garden first from the point of view of the natural fall, the decline of the Golden Age, and then from the point of view of a consequence of that fall, the *beau parc* which men must choose to enter, which is ideal and therefore—as Genius acknowledges—indescribable. But the vision of the *parc* is not the solution to the poem, even though it is its intellectual climax. Omitted are the Christian sense of original sin and the need for grace, and hence the commandments of Christ which supersede nature and law. Jean by no means makes this crucial omission clear; his method, the satirist's, is to run around a topic, leaving a gaping hole in the middle, emphasized by sharply contrasting juxtapositions within his material, a hole which the reader must fill, to his edification. The limitations of the *beau parc* are hinted at by the exclusion of the whole natural world outside its walls. What is omitted may best be seen by comparing small things with great, the vision of the Fountain of Life with the similarly inconceivable optics of Dante's final vision of the Trinity, in which appears a human face.

MUTABILITY

From these implications of Genius's comparison of the gardens we should not conclude that Jean is burdened with a message, to pose a moral imperative that we acknowledge sin and sue for grace—at least not immediately. Rather Jean points to the incompleteness of Amant's vision of love by drawing out its meaning to absurdity, so that the gap between the vision and the truth of things confronts us embarrassingly. We think of a skillful satirist not as telling us what to do, but as showing us the way things are so that what we should do becomes obvious. The way things are, as is implicit in Guillaume but not realized by Amant, includes the fact of the transitoriness of human affairs, and of mortality: the Golden Age is past; with man's knowledge in Eden came death; the *beau parc* is a thing of the future and the afterlife; the rose fades and time marches.

Jean's Raison, at her most Boethian, urges Amant to rise above his service to Amors, which she considers a vanity, a blindness equivalent to subservience to Fortune, that is, to the contingencies of the visible world. Her description of the isle of Fortune (5,921 ff.), drawn directly from Alain's *Anticlaudianus*, wonderfully encapsulates Jean's critique of the garden of Deduit. The isle is a *locus amoenus* like the others, but it displays on its surface, as it were, the deathliness which is latent in the other gardens, excepting the *beau parc*. The blooming flowers, plentiful trees, fresh waters, soft grass, balmy breezes, and chanting birds are here, but the elements of the pleasance are continually transforming themselves into their opposites—cold blasts, sterile trees, polluted waters and screeching owls. The island is a Proteus in the sea, an image of the mutability of the sublunar world, and a visible emblem of the dialectic of delight and death.

It may seem too strong to speak of death implicated in Deduit, but the fact emerges even in Guillaume, and Jean as usual spells it out. The first *locus amoenus* of the poem, the spring night on which Amant falls asleep to dream his dream, makes its show of foliage against the background of the recent winter. The sense of winter gives point to the spring; Genius cannot describe the delights of the *beau parc* because no winter comes there, and if one's element is perpetual spring one becomes insensible of it, unless one remembers. In a similar way the scattering of French place names through the first part of the poem emphasizes Deduit's unworldly space. Amant knows that the garden of Deduit is a temporary affair; and even, like Shakespeare's Troilus, with a self-serving sophistication which we must consider inappropriate for a young lover, is most drawn to his rose because it is a bud, not yet open and liable to rapid decay (1,644–48). Narcissus dies; I will return to this later. Koehler and Donald Stone, Jr., draw attention to the absence of time from Deduit, to its deliberate banishment as part of the description of Old Age, one of the figures depicted on the garden wall. The narrator's digression on time and mutability in this description stands out from the other descriptions in its level of abstraction: it is clearly there for a special purpose.

Stone speaks of the events of the garden as outside of time, and of the meaning of Guillaume's Raison's speech, with its references to active careers in the world and to the brevity of life, as urging Amant to reenter temporal affairs, to break out of the aesthetic impasse of his love which has become an art of waiting. In the digression on time, Amant particularly observes that time will do its work, and "nos envieillira" (it will age us—385). His tentative exit from time as he enters the garden in fact threatens his humanity, as he seems to know, making him for the time being a reduced allegorical figure. Whether Guillaume would have yanked him out of the garden, into a world where spring is not far behind because winter can come, we do not know; Jean certainly abolishes Amant's temporizing.

Jean's Raison describes the miserable gifts of old age for Amant, particularly dwelling on the connections between dissipated youth and the sense of waste which age brings—the moral consequences of time (4,421–544). She goes on, as we have seen, to describe the isle of Fortune. In the long "middle" of the poem, dominated by Ami, the Jealous Husband, Faus Semblant, and la Vieille, acknowledgement of mutability is repressed. The exception is la Vieille's grim recollection, at the end of her speech, of her advancing age, and her advice—parallel to Raison's, but with a difference—that one should get money while young (14,441–546), a poignant half-blind knowledge which inspired the creation of the Wife of Bath.

Jean abruptly introduces his figure Nature. We glimpse her forging new individuals, in order to save the various species from the attacks of Death, personified as a greedy huntsman who drives humans in fear to their various pursuits (15,891–16,012). In Nature's struggle with Death we see explicitly, from the cosmic point of view, what was only glimpsed before in terms of each man's sense of aging. In this context Genius exhorts the barons to reproduce in order to stave off death, now classicized as the Fates, Cerberus, and the Furies in hell mouth (19,753–864). The theme of mutability admits the Virgilian demons into the poem. Love and the passage of time are muted, ceremonialized, and static in Guillaume's part; in Jean these experiences are rewritten as reproduction and death, and filled with frantic, irascible energy. Jean sees through and transforms Guillaume's delicately mutual relationship of pleasant desire and mutability into the pitched battle of eros and thanatos.

MYTHS AND MIRRORS

Three stories drawn from classical legend summarize the themes of love and death—the tales from Ovid of Narcissus, Adonis, and Pygmalion. Each of the tales is inserted into the poem with that abruptness which Berger has called "conspicuous irrelevance," which teases the reader into allegorical interpretation. Although other tales from mythology appear in the poem, usually in the form of exempla, these three are distinguished as the only ones told directly by the narrator. Each story interrupts the action at a rare moment of suspense. Each tells of a man who loves a being which is not human— an image, a goddess, a statue. The Narcissus story particularly presents itself to our attention, coming as a relief after the descriptions of the first part of the poem; unlike the usual medieval exempla— even Chaucer's—which tempt the reader to skim, these tempt the reader to slow down and take note. And so readers have done; therefore I am particularly obliged in this section to acknowledge my debts to the fine recent articles on Narcissus and Pygmalion by Poirion, Koehler, Frederick Goldin, and Thomas Hill. That the stories are set up by formal means does not wholly account for their special interest, but some elusive quality in them suggests that they provide a key to the poem. In what follows, I attempt first to open out the meaning of these tales with the help of the recent interpreters, and then to articulate how myth cooperates with allegory in *The Romance of the Rose*.

We should observe that the Narcissus story, drawn from Ovid, was already popular in Guillaume's time. Langlois notes that Petrus Cantor refers to the tale as typical of a minstrel's repertory; Matthew of Vendôme uses the tale as an example of "enigma"; Alain de Lille cites Narcissus as a type of beauty. Goldin has studied Guillaume's version in comparison with an Old French lay, *Narcisus*, still extant, which Guillaume may have known. M.-R. Jung suggests the story may have been used as a school exercise. We have lost any precise sense of this literary context, but we can assume that Guillaume modified the tale to suit his purposes.

We can divide his Narcissus story into three constituents: its setting, its basic plot of love scorned and avenged, and its principal object, the mirroring water.

First, I will examine the setting. Amant has compared the garden of Deduit to Eden, and the great pine tree and Fount of Love are surely meant to recall the originals, the Trees of Knowledge and Life, and the Fountain of Life. Koehler argues that the crystals in the fount allude to both the magic gems of romance and the description of the River of Life in Revelation 22:1 as "splendidum tamquam crystallum." It would be misleading to press the point now, but the outlines of a simple typology are here as potential criteria for interpretation: Narcissus falls like Adam, and his knowledge is his death. Fleming reminds us of the medieval mythographers' condemnation of Narcissus: he is cupidinous (*Integumenta Ovidii*) and vainglorious (Alexander Neckham), and deceived by the "faulz miroirs de cest monde" (*Ovide moralisé*).

Another aspect of the setting of the Narcissus tale is the presence of Amant and his relationship to it. As Narcissus looked into a mirror, fell in love with an image reflected there, and experienced pain, so does Amant. Poirion has read this relationship acutely: the complacent self-admiration of Narcissus parallels Amant's hypermasculine, distant love of the rose; both lovers love love before they love its object; they typify the rhetorical love of the erotic lyric tradition; the beloved is apprehended as unfleshly and cold, like water, an image, an idol, a mere reflection of the lover's newly discovered self, an Echo. The contemporary scientific writer Robert Grosseteste associated mirror reflection with echoing. The Narcissus legend exposes Amant's psyche more deeply, by the powerful implications of the elements of the narrative and traditional interpretations of its meaning, than the relatively mechanical, if lively, analysis of the rose's character into personifications. We are dealing with two kinds of allegory—personification allegory and a mythographical typology with which any reader of Spenser is familiar.

The second constituent of the Narcissus story is the plot. Narcissus refused to love Echo. Both an anonymous commentator on the *Integumenta* and the *Ovide moralisé* interpret her as reputation or good fame; Poirion sees her as the impersonal projection of femininity characteristic of courtly love—the chanson d'amour is not a dialogue but an echo. These two ideas, the moral and the literary, are not essentially distinct, and both should be maintained. In either case Narcissus fails to love her because Echo as echo is invisible, and Narcissus needs to see to know and to know to love. Like Chaucer's Troilus and Spenser's Prince Arthur or Britomart, Narcissus appears as a youth before his first love, just barely able to love himself; unlike those others he stops there, forever, a figure in myth whose destiny is to exemplify premature loving. In Ovid he undergoes metamorphosis—to finish his story outside of death, to fix him forever in the tapestry of myth, and to leave his image everywhere in flowers—but as we have seen in Spenser, allegory is likely to suppress metamorphoses, because in allegory the end of a myth is usually not in itself but in the protagonist's mind. So in *The Romance of the Rose*, the stasis of Narcissus is transferred immediately to Amant, and metamorphosis becomes metanoia, conversion. Amant sees himself, too, in the Mirror Perilous, but the god of love does not condemn him to love his image—rather he confirms his love for the rose.

The final constituent is the mirror. Folk beliefs in Europe forbid children to look in a mirror until a certain age, on pain of death: in the mirror one sees the devil, or a Doppelgänger, or one's own soul—shadows lie down on the ground while men stand in the sun, so the dead are shades. Mirror-gazing is especially dangerous for children, who may become attached to what they see there. Children are said to divine with mirrors according to medieval scientists such as Michael Scot and William of Auvergne. How much of this lore was familiar to Guillaume de Lorris we do not know, but perhaps the sense of mirrors as powerful and dangerous, especially for the young, struck him. In his essay on the theme of the mirror, Frappier follows Guy Michaud, a critic of Mallarmé, in observing that the mirror is "the very symbol of symbolism," "the revealer of correspondences and hence the instrument par excellence of poets." In our terms, this means that the mirror is an object which works in the real world the way allegory works in literature, splitting up things, connecting images with realities, making the invisible visible.

Narcissus sees himself. Ovid hints that his image is like a work of art, a statue or wax figure, which Narcissus can improve by such natural artifice as beating his breast, so that the image flushes sensuously. Narcissus's grief makes the image more tantalizing: his image is projected in an illusory way. Goldin analyzes what happens to Narcissus: he scorns love but has, like all humans in the Augustinian view, unconscious self-love. The mirror externalizes his self-love, and at the same time, since he sees himself, splits him into a subject and an object. This division is called self-consciousness, which imitates the moral refinement which love induces—a man aware that he appears can care how he appears. Narcissus loves himself; and then, agonizingly, becomes aware that it is himself that he loves, his echo reified, and he dies. Amant undergoes the same process but goes further, projecting his echo onto the rose. The last step, the discovery of the rose as an other, takes place, if at all, in the ghost poem, Guillaume's unfulfilled intention to complete his work. The myth of Narcissus, in *The Romance of the Rose*, provides the terms for the allegory of Amant.

Jean's narrator briefly outlines the story of Venus and Adonis, and points the moral that men should listen to and believe in their beloveds' counsel, a moral as obtuse as the moral appended to the tale of Narcissus, that ladies should return men's love, or the men will die. Obtuse, but not wholly misleading: in the case of Narcissus, the moral suggests that there are certain consequences to the avoidance of love; in the case of Adonis, that there are consequences to behaving childishly when an adult's job, loving, is to be done. Adonis stands halfway between Narcissus and Pygmalion: he can love, and engage in active life in love, but his activity is a toy, the hunt. The divinely protected bower of Adonis' mythical love—our last *locus amoenus*—is half humanized, pulled halfway into time, by his energy, but his energy is misdirected. Jean withholds Adonis's metamorphosis as Guillaume withheld Narcissus's. The failed lovers from Ovid just die, but Amant learns.

Jean directly confronts the Narcissus story in two ways: by reconsidering the idea of the mirror, and by telling the story of Pygmalion.

Jean splits the idea of the mirror into two parts, which we may label scientific and Neoplatonic. In an active frontier of thirteenth-century science, directed by the new influx of Arabic learning, the optical principles of reflected and refracted light were being understood—developments chronicled for us in A. C. Crombie's book on Robert Grosseteste. In Nature's complaint, she refers to this new learning (16,855–80; 18,044–60; 18,153–298), dwelling on the mirror's power to deceive, to project "fantosmes" (18,181), and to make the ignorant think they have seen devils. Neoplatonic thought, and strictly Christian variants of it, use the figure of the mirror in a variety of ways, as described in Gunn's book and in articles by Sister Ritamary Bradley and Hans Leisegang. Mirrors can replace the metaphor of the chain as the image of the mediating powers, the reproductive agents, which reflect divine being downward through the hierarchies of the cosmos (neither mirror nor chain is wholly successful as an image for this: the image of the planetary spheres is best). Angels, then, are mirrors of God, and men mirrors of angels; Jesus is God's mirror. Men's minds or souls are mirrors—as can be seen by looking in the pupil of the eye—which receive images of the intelligibles. The sensible world is the reflection of the world of ideas, mediated by the Logos, the image of God. The Demiurge, Dionysus, made the world according to an image of himself in a mirror. The mirror symbolizes the agent which divides the one into the many. Small mirrors can reflect enormous terrains. Scripture is a mirror whose Old Testament reflects the New. In Alain de Lille's *Summa de Arte Predicatoria*, one is admonished to look in the threefold mirror of Scripture, nature, and creatures, and these three are divided into parts. In his *Anticlaudianus*, Reason displays a triple mirror, the source of Jean's carbuncle, in which may be seen the patterns and forms of all things, and Faith gives Prudence a mirror which shows the celestial world of beings and forms. Both of these are derived from the mirror of Providence in Bernard Silvestris's *Cosmographia*, a mirror which never loses an image it once holds, and whose images are the ideas which underlie all nature and all history. Finally, and ultimately, God is a mirror who contains images of all.

Jean explicitly enunciates two of these more speculative concepts of the mirror: first that it has the power to multiply, "E d'une en font il pluseurs naistre" (And they make the many spring from the one—18,177), a power which Nature offers to anyone who understands optics; second that God is the mirror of Nature, and her law (19,896–906). For Jean, then, the mirror is both an emblem of new science, whose properties one can learn from books and which represents an advance of reason over superstition; and at the same time the mirror is a symbol of the cosmos as presented in Chartrian metaphors as diverse, fertile, analogous, and ideal. These two concepts underlie Genius's critique of Guillaume's mirror and his description of the carbuncle in the *beau parc* (20,431–70; 20,525–90).

Genius claims that the Fount of Love in Deduit is murky, so that one who looks to see his reflection there sees nothing. He spurns the magical properties of the two crystals in the Fount: why do they show only half the garden at a time? . . . they must have an imperfection. Jean's Genius seems unaware of C. S. Lewis's interpretation of the crystals, followed by most critics since, that Guillaume's crystals are the lady's eyes—or in Robertson's variation, the eyes of Amant himself. Also Genius argues that without the sun, Guillaume's crystals would show nothing at all. The carbuncle is a jewel both round (spherical?) and three-faceted. It is its own sun, the sun of the garden, which makes time stand still in eternal day. It has two marvellous powers: a man who looks at it and at the water of the Fount of Life (it is not clear whether the actions are simultaneous or sequential, but I think Jean means for us to imagine the carbuncle hanging above the water like a lamp, so that the actions would be sequential) can see reflected all the contents of the *parc* and "les quenoissent proprement, / E aus meïsmes ensement" (know them properly, and likewise in themselves"—20,573–74); and the carbuncle improves the eyesight of the beholder.

The point of Genius's attack is to make distinctions on the basis of Jean's understanding of mirrors, to clarify Guillaume's confusions. If modern commentary can serve as evidence, the relation in Guillaume's account between the reflecting surface of the fount and the powers of the crystals is confused. Jean suspects that Guillaume did not understand, or care to portray, the optical principles of mirrors. Amant's talk about the magical powers of mirrors is superstition based on ignorance: he does not know that a hemispheric mirror, whose equator is on the plane of the horizon (which is how one sees, from above, a spherical crystal lying in a spring), will reflect everything above the horizon; nor does he know, it appears, that a plane mirror, like the surface of water, has entirely different properties. The only mirror which is really magical is God, the Trinity which the carbuncle symbolizes, which makes vision better and allows the beholder to see things, not "a orne" as in the Mirror Perilous, but "proprement." Only in the *beau parc*, in the ideal world, do such Neoplatonic metaphors as reflectivity have reality; the love of Amant and Narcissus is grounded on an illusion, a set of metaphors—rose, mirror—which clarify but do not transcend the human.

We need not conclude that Jean had no respect for Guillaume's poem. Rather he had such great respect for it that he troubled to complete it—the idea that Jean tacked his summa onto Guillaume's feeble romance as a *jeu d'esprit* has little to recommend it. It is true that Jean wrote his poem in another time, in a world in which much had happened; the new science only suggests the changes. But it is inappropriate to say that in the forty years between Guillaume's and Jean's writings man's ideas had changed from a magical to a rational, scientific mentality, or that the separate audiences of the two parts— if the evidence which supports our guesses about these audiences is correct—Guillaume's provincial court and Jean's urbane university, required utterly different kinds of literature. Some change in time and in audience may have inclined Jean toward emphasizing Guillaume's archaism—the earlier poet was certainly outdated, but then all romancers are outdated. But the "Chartrian" Neoplatonism of Jean is similarly old-fashioned. I would extend Wetherbee's point— that Jean modifies and criticizes his source Alain, as a poet is likely to borrow from and attack his own tradition—to Jean's relationship with Guillaume as well. The new kind of allegory in Jean, the "Chartrian" allegory which Wetherbee, following Chenu, calls rationalist as opposed to symbolist, in which metaphors turn out to be, in the realm of ideas, real entities, is in this case a development in literary tradition, not in the history of consciousness.

The third story from mythology told by the narrator himself, the story of Pygmalion (20,817–21,214), harks back to the Narcissus myth: Pygmalion, complaining of his perverse love of his statue, claims he is not quite so foolish as Narcissus. Like Narcissus, he regards an image generated out of himself and is attacked by the god of love. As Amant is linked with Narcissus, so is he with Pygmalion: Jean introduces the story in a comparison of Pygmalion's statue with the last shape of the rose, the enshrined image of a woman. Both images are warmed by Venus. We are not privy to the process of Amant's change, but we are invited to interpret the Pygmalion myth as a commentary on Amant's final state, educated by the instructors of adult reality and the principles of Venus, Nature, and Genius. I would borrow a term from New Testament criticism, "acted parable" (such as Jesus' blasting the fig tree), to describe the relation of Amant's experience to the three myths in *The Romance of the Rose*: Amant's plot, the main allegory, is an acted exemplum.

Gunn summarizes the different kinds of love in the two myths by speaking of Narcissus's love as imagination, and Pygmalion's as the body, its book. Following Gunn, Poirion emphasizes the onset of warmth in Pygmalion's statue, her enlivening under his caresses, his success in the use of hands, of technique, as compared with the visual narcissism of Narcissus. Venus rewards Pygmalion with life because he tried to get life in a being which, originally only a twinkle in his eye, a potential of his craft as sculptor, becomes another person. The *Ovide moralisé* postdates *The Romance of the Rose*, but its "allegory" interprets Pygmalion as God creating and vivifying man, and later marrying his creation as man's holy soul (10. 3,561 ff.); the myth could be read that way within a generation or two after Jean. Love, if properly enacted, can create; oddly enough, this hermetic maxim has a simple basis in human reproductive physiology, and it is just reproduction that Genius has been urging and that Amant is about to perform.

The story in Ovid links the theme of Pygmalion's artistry—art hiding art, the plasticity of wax, the artful lie—to his loving. Jean mentions Pygmalion's name twice before the narration of his story proper, both times with reference to his art. First, in the section describing Nature's struggle with death, the narrator digresses onto the topic of art's (including alchemy's) inability to imitate nature, especially that artifacts cannot live, even when made by such an artist as Pygmalion (16,177). But with Venus's help, or to interpret the myth allegorically, with the alchemy of love, Pygmalion can transmute his statue into a woman. The second reference is in la Vieille's speech: she speaks of the song about Pygmalion as full of lore about beautiful clothing (13,079-88). The bulk of Jean's additions to Ovid, when he retells the story, are long descriptions of the fine clothing Pygmalion decks the statue with, as part of his skillful wooing and his fine dancing and singing before it.

Pygmalion's high art of sculpture can make a statue, but it is his human art of loving another that makes a woman. Before Venus animates the statue, Pygmalion touches it and thinks it lives—only to realize he is feeling the life in his own hands. In this heightened awareness that his beloved is not himself—awareness coming from the sense of touch, not sight, in contrast to Narcissus, Pygmalion practices his art, just as Amant has become a "bon ouvrier e sage" (a good and wise worker"—21,380) in the craft of love. Fleming and

Rosemond Tuve consider the story of Pygmalion an exemplum of sinful idolatry, and it would be except that the statue ceases to be an idol. The transmutation is supernatural—Pygmalion himself suspects that he dreams, or that demonic sorcery has taken place, when the statue is animated—and in the realm of myth; but the interpretation of the myth, that artful loving topples idols, is natural.

The key to the story, and the final link between Pygmalion and Amant, occurs at the end. The newly created woman bears Pygmalion a child, Paphus, for whom the island Paphos is named, who begets King Cinyras, who unwittingly commits incest with his daughter, Myrrha, who bears Adonis from the union after she is metamorphosed into a tree. In short, Pygmalion's hot art has a product, and his lineage enters the passionate and turmoiled world of Mediterranean legend and history. Both Pygmalion and Amant conclude their stories, not with death and metamorphosis, but with the unconcluding generation of humanity.

The divinities, landscapes, physical objects, monsters, and events of classical myths are pure and unanalyzable in their integrity, but set in an allegorical context they become virtually allegory: the relation of Venus to Pygmalion in the old myth is not radically unlike the relation of Gloriana to Arthur in *The Faerie Queene*, once the motive to interpret the myth is presented. Like allegorical narratives, myths are fantastic and free, and the agents and objects in myths can correspond to the projected agents and rationalized objects in allegories (woods of error, anatomized bodies, fountains of life). As rhetoric analyzes the world in terms of language, and so is akin to allegory, so myths analyze the world in terms of narratives, and so are akin to allegory. Mythical expression, as Cassirer puts it, converts ideal differences of significance, such as being mutable or immutable, into ontological differences of being and origin, such as being a divinity or a flower. The same can be said of allegorical expression.

Poirion associates the Narcissus myth with a rite of initiation, a sudden and complete transformation caused by magic, and the Pygmalion myth with education, the progressive, artful change caused by obedience, knowledge, and mastery. Looking back to chapter four, we can compare the two myths to the two stages in Redcrosse's experience represented by the House of Pride and the House of Holiness. The myths of Narcissus and Pygmalion, in these terms, correspond to Guillaume's romance presentation of the inception of love in Amant, and to Jean's satiric view of Amant's training in love. The myths, set as they are within the allegory, are irrational and timeless simulacra of the meaning of Amant's experience, which make the poem most concrete at the places where it is most abstract, like a cold mirror receiving a human shape, or an ivory image rising to life.

CONCLUSIONS

Certain characteristics of *The Romance of the Rose* make it difficult to decide where its authors, especially Jean, stand on critical issues. Some of these characteristics, I think, may be considered flaws. Lewis has not done complete justice to the poem, nor the subject of allegory, by implying that respect for and appreciation of the poem are matters of personal taste; to enjoy a poem assumes the possibility of not enjoying it. Guillaume and Jean, perhaps misled by a temptation to satisfy an audience which admired bulky books, both indulge in a kind of fallacy of imitative form: Guillaume's imitation of the abundance of nature leads him to excessively long descriptions—even when we consider the likelihood that the poem was designed to be absorbed from oral delivery—and Jean followed him in this, adding to it a comical imitation of Nature's prolixity, her rhetoric of abundance, and a presumption that his audience would tolerate limitless quantities of topical (antifraternal) and conventional (antifeminist) satire. Only a heroic intelligence, that of a Dante or a Milton, could maintain consistency and sustain variety over the length of *The Romance of the Rose*. There is a great deal in the poem, but we cannot feel as confident as we can with Spenser that it all tends to the same end and hangs together—that it is unified. We can admire and enjoy the poem, but we should not deem it perfect.

This does not mean that Jean was confused: his opinions are not contradictory, but fall within a normal human flexibility of temper— we do not need to invoke Melville's remarks on consistency. Likewise Jean is a satirist, and it is characteristic of satirists to attack from all sides, like Langland or Swift, leaving their own positions ill-defined, presenting a small, rapidly moving target. Guillaume's poem is incomplete, and Jean's poem does not resolve it, but sets it as a problem, opens it up, worries with it, leaves us a nervous tangle of critical attitudes, alternate theses, new points of view. We have to be content to rough out the general sensibilities which the two poets reveal, to acquire only confidence enough to say "That sounds like Guillaume," or "Jean would not feel that way."

The fact that the poem is composed in two parts not only offers an opportunity for comparative criticism, but demands it. I have several times spoken of Jean as "seeing through" Guillaume. Jean exposes Guillaume's rhetorical form and weighs the meaning of plenitude and analysis. Jean attacks in its lair the tradition of erotic sensibility which Guillaume seems to purvey. Jean disrupts Guillaume's smoothly articulate personifications of the psyche by presenting a bewildering array of allegorical techniques on various levels. Jean sees through to the substance of the garden, and he parodies, reinterprets, and attacks Guillaume's central myth. He rubs our faces in mutability and confronts us with true love. Jean intellectualizes and invokes our common sense; he demythologizes and remythologizes; he claims the right to play an autonomous, self-conscious, modernist language game, and at the same time to preserve the inalienable, simple substance of tradition; he poses as at once a brilliant critic, whose text is Guillaume—as Dante's text is Virgil and Wordsworth's is Milton—and as a simple fabler trying to get on with his story. Jean invents where Guillaume displays.

Two great types lie behind those myths of Narcissus and Pygmalion which sum up the themes of Guillaume and Jean. Guillaume's myth, and his part of the poem, hark back to the Fall: the death in the garden, the new and forbidden knowledge of self which follows upon the naming of things, the origins of the chasm between language and reality. Guillaume's Amant withdraws from time, fancies himself in Eden, and sinks. The Pygmalion myth, and Jean's theme, recollect the Creation: chaotic matter just barely rationalized as hexameral form, nameable things, fertility, temporality, humanity. These are types from the Old Testament: like many Christians, Guillaume creates a world—like chivalric romance—withdrawn from the order of sin and grace; and like many Christians, Jean forces his fictive world into confrontation with the truths of Christianity, but remains —like Boethius before him—in the realm of reason and nature, avoiding the appeal to revelation. Jean's work is not to say how men are saved, but to say, in opposition to the erotic poetic which Guillaume exemplifies, the way the world is. Jean might have argued that

ADORNMENT

acknowledgement of the truth must precede salvation. In both poets, love is that which moves and that which binds; but in neither poet, for very different reasons, is love allowed to stand unveiled, or allegory to become, as it can, the least enigmatic, most direct expression of truth.

Bibliographical Note

The essays on *The Romance of the Rose* to which I am particularly indebted are those by C. S. Lewis in *The Allegory of Love*; Daniel Poirion's stimulating article, "Narcisse et Pygmalion dans *Le Roman de la Rose*," in Raymond J. Cormier and Urban T. Holmes, ed., *Essays in Honor of Louis Francis Solano*, U.N.C. Studies in the Romance Langs. and Lits., 92 (Chapel Hill, 1970), pp. 153–65; Alan M. F. Gunn, *The Mirror of Love: A Reinterpretation of "The Romance of the Rose"* (Lubbock, Texas, 1952); and Winthrop Wetherbee, "The Literal and the Allegorical: Jean de Meun and the 'De planctu naturae,'" and "The Function of Poetry in the 'De planctu naturae' of Alain de Lille," both articles now revised in his book, *Platonism and Poetry in the Twelfth Century: The Literary Influence of the School of Chartres* (Princeton, 1972).

A good summary of recent criticism is Marc-René Jung's "Der Rosenroman in der Kritik seit dem 18. Jahrhundert," *RF* 78 (1966): 203–52. Essential for the background of *The Romance of the Rose* in old French literature are Jung, *Etudes sur le poème allégorique en France au moyen âge* (Bern, 1971); and Hans Robert Jauss, "La Transformation de la forme allégorique entre 1180 et 1240: D'Alain de Lille à Guillaume de Lorris," in Anthime Fourrier, ed., *L'Humanisme médiéval dans les littératures romanes du XIIe au XIVe siècles*, Actes et Colloques, 3, Strasbourg, 1962 (Paris, 1964), pp. 107–44; and Jauss, with Uda Ebel, "Entstehen und Strukturwandel der allegorischen Dichtung," in Jauss, ed., *La Littérature didactique, allégorique, et satirique*, Grundriss der romanischen Literaturen des Mittelalters, vol. 6, tome 1 (Heidelberg, 1968). The full bibliography by Jauss and Ebel of this Grundriss, vol. 6, tome 2 (Heidelberg, 1970), pp. 203–80, should be the starting point for any investigation of medieval French allegory.

The recent edition of the poem by Félix Lecoy in the series, Les Classiques Français du Moyen Age, vols. 92, 95, 98 (Paris, 1966–70) has useful notes.

212

I have been grateful for the translations of Harry W. Robbins (New York, 1962) and Charles Dahlberg (Princeton, 1971).

Useful background works on medieval ideas of love, gardens, and the like, are Lewis's *The Discarded Image: An Introduction to Medieval and Renaissance Literature* (Cambridge, Eng., 1964); Peter Dronke's "L'amor che move il sole e l'altre stelle," *SMed*, 3d ser. 6 (1965): 389–422; D. W. Robertson, Jr.'s *A Preface to Chaucer* (Princeton, 1962), and his "The Doctrine of Charity in Medieval Literary Gardens: A Topical Approach through Symbolism and Allegory," *Speculum* 26 (1951): 24–49; M.-D. Chenu's *Nature, Man, and Society in the Twelfth Century*, sel. and trans. Jerome Taylor and L. K. Little (Chicago, 1968) from *La Théologie au douzième siècle* (Paris, 1957); Anders Nygren, *Agape and Eros*, trans. P. S. Watson (London, 1932–53, New York, 1969) from the Swedish (Stockholm, 1930, 1936); A. O. Lovejoy's *The Great Chain of Being: A Study of the History of an Idea* (Cambridge, Mass., 1936); and Jean Leclercq's *The Love of Learning and the Desire for God*, trans. Catharine Misrahi (New York, 1961) from the French (Paris, 1957). Robert Javelet's *Image et ressemblance au douzième siècle*, 2 vols. (Strasbourg, 1967) can be used by way of its elaborate indexes. Robertson's *Preface* contains extended treatment of *The Romance of the Rose*.

On rhetoric see Ernst Robert Curtius, *European Literature and the Latin Middle Ages*, trans. W. R. Trask (New York, 1953) from the German (Bern, 1948); Edmond Faral, *Les Arts poétiques du XIIe et du XIIIe siècle: Recherches et documents sur la technique littéraire du moyen âge*, Bibl. de l'Ecole des Hautes Etudes, 238 (Paris, 1924, repr. 1971); the fine brief essay on the Nun's Priest's Tale by E. Talbot Donaldson, *Chaucer's Poetry* (New York, 1958); and Richard McKeon, "Rhetoric in the Middle Ages," *Speculum* 17 (1942): 1–32, and "Poetry and Philosophy in the Twelfth Century: The Renaissance of Rhetoric," *MP* 43 (1945–46): 217–34. The recent *Readings in Medieval Rhetoric*, ed. and trans. Joseph M. Miller, M. H. Prosser, T. W. Benson (Bloomington, Ind., and London, 1973) contains selections in English and a bibliography. For full bibliography see James J. Murphy, *Medieval Rhetoric: A Select Bibliography* (Toronto, 1971), and his *Rhetoric in the Middle Ages* (Berkeley and Los Angeles, 1974).

On the idea of the cosmos see René Roques, *L'Univers Dionysien: Structure hiérarchique du monde selon le Pseudo-Denys* (Paris, 1954); Walter Kranz, *Kosmos*, *Archiv für Begriffsgeschichte* 2 (Berlin, 1958); Claus Haebler, "KOSMOS. Eine etymologisch-wortgeschichtliche Untersuchung," *Arch. f. Begriff.* 11 (Bonn, 1967), 101–18; Wolfram von den Steinen, *Der Kosmos des Mittelalters von Karl dem Grossen zu Bernhard von Clairvaux* (Bern and Munich, 1959); and the chapter on the cosmic image in Fletcher's *Allegory*, esp. pp. 128–40.

Bernard Silvestris's *De mundi universitate* is edited by Carl Sigmund Barach

ADORNMENT

and Johann Wrobel (Innsbruck, 1876); trans. Winthrop Wetherbee, *Cosmographia* (New York, 1973); Alain de Lille's *De planctu naturae* is in the *Patrologia Latina* 210, 429–82, and also, ed. Thomas Wright, in *Anglo-Latin Satirical Poets and Epigrammatists of the Twelfth Century* (London, 1872) 2:429–522; and translated by D. M. Moffat (New York, 1908). Badly needed editions of both poems are under way. Alain's *Anticlaudianus* is edited by R. Bossuat (Paris, 1955); translated by William H. Cornog (Phila., 1935) with a good introduction, and again translated by James J. Sheridan (Toronto, 1973). John of Garland's *Integumenta Ovidii* is edited by Fausto Ghisalberti (Messina and Milan, 1933); the *Ovide moralisé* is edited by C. de Boer, Martina G. de Boer, and Jeannette Th. Van 'T Sant, 5 vols. (Amsterdam, 1915–38). On Bernard, see Theodore Silverstein, "The Fabulous Cosmogony of Bernard Silvester," *MP* 46 (1948–49): 92–116, and the learned treatment by Brian Stock, *Myth and Science in the Twelfth Century: A Study of Bernard Silvester* (Princeton, 1972). An important study of Bernard and other writers, esp. of the twelfth century, which can serve with its full bibliography as a prolegomenon to the serious high medieval understanding of allegory, is Peter Dronke, *Fabula: Explorations into the Uses of Myth in Medieval Platonism*, Mittellat. Stud. und Texte, 9 (Leiden and Cologne, 1974). R. W. Southern shows we can speak of a "School" of Chartres only loosely, *Medieval Humanism and Other Studies* (Oxford and New York, 1970).

I refer in the text to John V. Fleming, The *"Roman de la Rose": A Study in Allegory and Iconography* (Princeton, 1969); a fine article by Donald Stone, Jr., "Old and New Thoughts on Guillaume de Lorris," *AJFS* 2 (1965): 157–70; M.-R. Jung, "Gui de Mori et Guillaume de Lorris," *VR* 27 (1968): 106–37; Lionel J. Friedman, "Gradus Amoris," *RPH* 19 (1965): 167–77; Rosemond Tuve, *Allegorical Imagery* (Princeton, 1966), which has a long chapter, "Imposed Allegory," with extended comment on the *Romance*; Paul Zumthor, "Narrative and Anti-Narrative: *Le Roman de la Rose*," *YFS* 51 (1974): 185–204; and Jean-Charles Payen, "A semiological study of Guillaume de Lorris," *YFS* 51 (1974): 170–184.

On mirrors see A. C. Crombie, *Robert Grosseteste and the Origins of Experimental Science* (New York, 1953); Lynn Thorndike, *A History of Magic and Experimental Science*, vol. 2 (New York, 1923), pp. 320, 364–65, 442, 455; Plotinus, *The Enneads*, trans. Stephen MacKenna (London, 4th ed., 1969), 4.3.11–12 (p. 270) and 1.1.8 (p. 26). Three good essays on the mirror in *The Romance of the Rose* are by E. Koehler, "Narcisse, la Fontaine d'Amour et Guillaume de Lorris," in Fourrier's *L'Humanisme médiéval* (cited above), pp. 147–64; Frederick Goldin, *The Mirror of Narcissus in the Courtly Love Lyric* (Cornell, 1967); and Jean Frappier, "Variations sur le thème du miroir, de Bernard de Ventadour à Maurice Scève," *CAIEF* 11 (1959): 134–58. I wrote independently of Patricia J. Eberle, "The Lovers' Glass: Nature's

214

Discourse on Optics and the Optical Design of the *Romance of the Rose*," *UTQ* 46 (1977): 241–62, and am happy to find many points of agreement.

On mirrors and belief in medieval thought see Wilhelm Wackernagel, "Ueber die Spiegel im Mittelalter," *Kleinere Schriften*, vol. 1 (Leipzig, 1872), pp. 128–42; Géza Róheim, "Spiegelzauber," *Imago: Zeitschr. f. Anwendung des Psychoan. auf die Geisteswiss.* 5 (1917–19): 63–120; Julius von Negelein, "Bild, Spiegel und Schatten im Volksglauben," *Archiv f. Religionswiss.* 5 (1902): 1–37; G. F. Hartlaub, *Zauber des Spiegels* (Munich, 1951); Sister Ritamary Bradley, "Backgrounds of the Title *Speculum* in Medieval Literature," *Speculum* 29 (1954): 100–15; Hans Leisegang, "La connaissance de Dieu au miroir de l'âme et de la nature," *Revue d'Histoire et de Philos. Relig.* 17 (1937): 145–71; John A. Stewart, *The Myths of Plato* (London and New York, 1905), pp. 239–40; Eugene Monseur, "L'Ame pupilline," *Revue de l'Histoire des Religions* 26, no. 51 (1905): 1–23; Guido Favati, "Il tema degli occhi come specchio," *Studi in onore de Carlo Pellegrini* (Torino, 1963), pp. 3–13; Albert Wesselski, "Narkissos oder das Spiegelbild," *ArO* 7 (1935): 37–63, 328–50. I have not seen Edmund R. Dimirs, *The Origin and Development of the Fount . . . in Three Works of the Spanish Renaissance* (Athens, Ohio, 1977).

Havelock Ellis gives a historical review of his and Näcke's psychological term in "The Conception of Narcissism," *Studies in the Psychology of Sex*, vol. 7 (Phila., 1928), pp. 347–75. He refers to Freud's important essay, "Zur Einführung des Narzissmus," *Jahrb. f. Psych. . . . Forsch.* 6 (1914), trans. in *Collected Papers*, ed. Joan Riviere (London, 1956), pp. 30–59, and to Rank's "Ein Beitrag zum Narzissismus," vol. 3 of the same journal (1911): 401–26. On theological and popular beliefs about the power and symbolism of mirrors, esp. in the Hellenistic period, see Norbert Hugedé, *La Métaphore du miroir dans les epîtres de saint Paul aux Corinthiens* (Neuchatel and Paris, 1957).

The medieval mythography of Narcissus and Pygmalion is summed up in Thomas D. Hill, "Narcissus, Pygmalion, and the Castration of Saturn: Two Mythographical Themes in the *Roman de la Rose*," *SP* 71 (1974): 404–26. A full account of the tradition of Narcissus is Louise Vinge, *The Narcissus Theme in Western European Literature up to the Early Nineteenth Century*, translated, I believe from manuscript, by R. Dewsnap et al. (Lund, 1967). A good treatment of the reception and allegorization of Ovid is Paule Demats, *Fabula: Trois études de mythographie antique et médiévale* (Geneva, 1973). On the theme in Dante and its background see Roger Dragonetti, "Dante et Narcisse ou les faux-monnayeurs de l'image," *REI* 11 (1965): 85–146. For a detailed critique of the episode in Ovid see Joachim Schickel, "Narziss: Zu Versen von Ovid," *Antaios* 3 (1962): 486–96.

CHAPTER SEVEN

The Natural Woman

The Faerie Queene, BOOKS THREE AND FOUR

... yonder in that wasteful wilderness
Huge monsters haunt, and many dangers dwell;
Dragons, and Minotaures, and feendes of hell,
And many wilde woodmen. . . .

FQ 3.10.40

I feared loue: but they that loue do liue . . .

FQ 3.6.37

The same that oft-times hath
Charmed magic casements opening on the foam
Of perilous seas, in faery lands forlorn.

"Ode to a Nightingale"

HOW much Books Three and Four of *The Faerie Queene*, which I shall call the "books of love," resemble *The Romance of the Rose* testifies both to the advanced reach and influence of Guillaume de Lorris's and Jean de Meun's achievement, and to the extraordinary tenacity of the traditions of love poetry in the European culture from which both poems emerge. Spenser adapts images which inevitably recall the *Romance*: Belphebe's carefully protected Rose of chastity (5. 51–53) ;* the various *loci amoeni*, especially the Garden of Adonis ("There is continuall spring") and the Island of Venus; the strings of love personifications in the House of Busyrane and the Temple of Venus; the magic mirror in which Britomart sees her future husband; Cupid's Ovidian arrows, which appear at one point (11.48) headed with lead and gold; the omnipresent receiving of love's wound through the eye; the cosmic combat against time and mutability through the generation of beings, under Nature's, Genius's, and Venus's tutelage in the Garden of Adonis; the appearance of Ease, the first personification of the masque of Cupid; the appearance of Amoret, in a simile, as like an ivory image (12.20); and the suggestions of body allegory in the topography of the Garden of Adonis and the Temple of Venus. There is the personification of Dame Nature herself, often even more humanized in her feelings than in Jean's poem: in the Garden of Adonis; envying the Witch's skillful creation of snowy Florimell (8.5); proud of Britomart as her paragon of perfection (4.6.24); counterfeiting herself to make the friends, Placidas and Amyas, of the same appearance (4.9.11); and amazed by her own labyrinths on the Island of Venus (4.10.24).

The figure of Daunger as wild man in the masque of Cupid (12.11) looks most like a direct borrowing from the *Romance*, either from the French or the Chaucerian translation; but the poetic world of Book Three—its Neoplatonism, its use of mythology, its conventional language of erotic poetry, its themes of plenitude, love's growth, and mutability—reflects a kindred milieu. *The Romance of the Rose* provided the materials which needed only the poet and the medium to receive their proper form. Yet Spenser's poem sharply differs from

---

* References are to the Variorum edition of *The Faerie Queene, Book Three*, special ed. F. M. Padelford (1934). Canto and stanza citations from other books of *The Faerie Queene* are preceded by the book number. The special editor of Book Four of the Variorum is Ray Heffner (1935).

its predecessor in form—including allegorical technique—and in meaning.

Spenser uses the genre romance, whereas Guillaume and Jean use dream vision and speculum. As the summary of correspondences in the last paragraph shows, it is in the relatively static, pictorial scenes, the gardens and houses, where the influence of the *Romance* is most visible in *The Faerie Queene*. Spenser's choice of romance confines him to those rigid conventions, yet frees him, as we saw in chapter four. Principally the romance form enables him to distinguish clearly between his narrator and his characters, and forces him to discover variety among a few traditional motifs—a condition eminently suitable to Spenser's purpose. We shall see how the genre serves him.

As for the meaning of the books of love, in contrast with the *Romance of the Rose*, they center on the human experience of love and respect that experience, whereas Jean, at least, presents love as worthy chiefly of satire, and centers his meaning on cosmic generation and on criticism of poetic convention. Only the Garden of Adonis, among all the material of Spenser's books of love, approaches the Neoplatonic intellectualization of love we find in Jean, and the Garden, while by no means peripheral to Spenser's purpose, is humanized by its context. Further, Books Three and Four rest more comfortably in the near absence of explicitly Christian ideas, in contrast to the *Romance's* problematic, nervous admission and rejection of Christian categories. The more or less secular Guillaume and the more or less Neoplatonic Jean have not Spenser's vision of human love as a piece of nature already redeemed, or never fallen, already full of grace, and discordant with Christian revelation only insofar as it is corrupt. In consequence, the allegorical signification of Spenser's fiction in these books tends not outward toward an alien and saving ideology, but rather inward to the center of the fiction itself, its human actors—analyzed now, better understood, associated with the physics of the world and the powers of the gods, but still human, retaining even—or especially—under allegorical operations their magic and their grace.

In this chapter I plan to trace the principal themes of the central books of *The Faerie Queene*. Beginning with the observation that the form of the books of love is romance, we see particularly the resemblance to the form of Book One, and examine the topic of love and fame as motives. The virtue of Books Three and Four is love, and the wonder of love is one of Spenser's prepossessions; we will look at the relation of love to the other wonders, magic and art, and inquire into the nature of wonder. Central to the romance venture and the experience of wonder is the character's conventional expression of his feelings of love, the "complaint," in which love and language join. The complaint measures a character's sense of himself: it is interior and liable to narcissistic excess. Counterbalancing the private eroticism of the complaint, which often lays false feelings on the world, is the natural eroticism of the world itself, which Spenser images as the sea. The various aspects of the sea correspond to the aspects of love. Finally the various themes—of romance, wonder, complaint, and oceanic eroticism—merge as we consider the *function* of love, and of the books of love, as a making, a true poetry. We forego Spenser's own sequence of events (which he himself disrupts more radically in these books than elsewhere), but try not to deny the impact which a proper serial reading would have. Likewise we forego a systematic summary of the techniques of allegory used in these books, but we will keep our main subject always in mind.

ROMANCE: MOTIVE AND ANTIQUITY

Long so they trauelled through wastefull wayes,
　　Where daungers dwelt, and perils most did wonne,
　　To hunt for glorie and renowmed praise ....

[1.3]

The book opens with Arthur and Guyon riding through "wastefull wayes." In the first three stanzas the same pair of statements is repeated four times: they are riding along, and they are seeking adventurous opportunities for praise, honor, and glory. The Redcrosse Knight, at the opening of Book One, also rides, but his mission is already determined, and there the first three stanzas—likewise a kind of introduction to the action—immediately open out with reference to Redcrosse's Christian armament and his relation to Gloriana's fairy court. In Book One, the romance world is a pendant on the world of revelation; in Books Three and Four, the world of romance is prior. The books of love will be more purely romance than Book One, and will not come to a conclusion. Spenser displays the qualities of chivalry in these books—the particular excellences and limitations of this kind of fiction and this kind of life—and as usual presents all the variations of the conventions, good and bad. Rather than an encyclopedic account, a mere mirror, Spenser gives us the forms of romance spread out through a plot of adventure, and lets us do the collation.

The ideal chivalric romance tells of a knight without past or future riding aimlessly and doing feats of arms courteously for the sake of fame. Like the voie, the romance is a medieval form in which the movement of the protagonist through more or less significant space grounds the narrative sequence. Book Three leans toward voie in that the knights gaze as much as they battle, but still travel, with its virtues of horsemanship (chivalry) and hospitality, supports the action. Arthur and Guyon travel in company, establishing the norm for the books of love. Especially in Book Four, the ability to travel together without bickering represents a height of knightly concord, which Ate's company cannot attain. When Britomart unseats Guyon, who does better on his feet, in canto 1, Arthur with his customary tact blames the horse and the page who failed to cinch the gear. This kind of courtesy is much abused later in the poem, especially by the bad knights of Book Four who blame their poor show at jousting on anything but their lack of prowess. Braggadocchio, the antiknight, afraid to face Paridell, dismounts in order "something amisse to mend" (10.38), as it were to tie his shoe. The other travel virtue, hospitality, fails when a host makes entrance to lodging difficult, as Malecasta does in canto 1 and Malbecco does later, or when he refuses exit, as Busyrane imprisons Amoret with fire, and Proteus holds Florimell by water. Hence liberation of a prisoner, harrowing, becomes a chivalric deed.

The vice which opposes knightly activism is sloth. The purest—most chaste—antidote to sloth is hunting, and so we see Diana, or her shadow Belphebe, hunting "to banish sloth, that oft doth noble mindes annoy" (4.7.23). The protective, mothering types, Venus and Cymoent, try to enforce sloth on Adonis and Marinell, in the one case pure sloth and in the other the chivalric sloth of unventuresomeness, a romance theme as old as Chrétien's *Yvain*. His sloth makes the Witch's son emphatically a Churl (7.12), and in writing of his love for snowy Florimell, Spencer plays on *idle* as *idol* (8.11).

The motives which inhibit sloth and keep a knight knightly are love and desire for fame, which turn out to be related. Arthur and Guyon "hunt for glorie" (1.3); Britomart moves "to seeke her louer" (1.8). When the narrator addresses his audience directly, he often wants to say that love breeds noble deeds, fame, and heroic aspiration. The Spenserian terms which help to distinguish the virtue of friendship (Book Four) from chastity (Book Three) are "publike" and "priuate" (4.1.19). Public love is concord, and its opposite, personified by Ate, reveals ignobility in the knights around her. Ate's dwelling is "hard by the gates of hell" (4.1.20), where Bellona and Discord lodge in Virgil: she is the Alecto of the Books of Love. Britomart is the paragon of private love; she even claims to Redcrosse that her motive is not strictly love, but desire for "worship," although her true motive, to her embarrassment, slips out (2.6–8). In the House of Busyrane she enacts the power of love to *Be bold*, and the power of fear of defamation to *Be not too bold*. Love and fame, then, implicate each other—we shall see how complete this connection is. Fame can appear as a prior motive, but only for a time, when love takes over; this is the case of Scudamour who first quested for his shield of love and Amoret "to winne me honour by some noble gest" (4.10.4).

The other knightly motive, desire for fame, characterizes the romance world as one in which report replaces law as the normalizer. Christian, especially Protestant, thought has no respect for fame, since it derives from public opinion, and not from the interior attitudes and intentions which He can judge who can know the thoughts of men's hearts. Nevertheless, Christian saints, like George, in their immortal bliss and their public recognition by canonization, correspond in form to the great men of pagan antiquity whose spirit survives, and who are "aduaunced to the skie" (4.3.44) as heroes and enrolled in Clio's "volume of Eternitie" (3.4), the romance Book of Life. The famous provide matter for poets (4.1); and poets reciprocate the favor by eternizing the heroes, as Spenser does for Britomart (2.1–3, 4.1–3) and Florimell (8.43), in order to repair old poets' negligence of heroic women. The sad example of Chaucer's work, devoured by time, only urges our poet to make up the loss and continue the report of Cambell and Canacee (4.2.33–34).

The good characters in the books of love value fame above life (5.45–47, 7.26, 4.1.6), and Marinell's mother practically equates his life with memory of him (4.36). Timias's example shows how even an honorable man can be tainted by bad renown, eventually to be forgotten: "out of all mens knowledge he was worne at last" (4.7.41). Oblivion rewards the unchaste and the cowardly, and to be forgotten is to be in hell, or in the cave of night (6.47). Virgil had personified Fame, and Spenser presents bad fame as monsters, the hyenalike creature "swift as word" who chases Florimell, and the hag Sclaunder who chases Arthur, Amoret, and Æmylia, in both cases because they accepted hospitality indiscreetly (7.23, 4.8.24–36). The slanderers recapitulate the dragon Error of Book One and foreshadow the Blatant Beast of Book Six. In the worst case of slander Argante, who was unchaste *in utero*, attempts to defame God by blasphemy (7.39). These examples of bad fame show why the fear of a woman about to lose her virginity, the final personification of the masque of Cupid which represents the "paines in loue, or punishments in hell," is "*Death* with infamie" (12.25).

Fame refers both to the past and to the future—in this also it differs from law, which attempts to judge a man as he is. Fame is the romance counterpart to the *Heilsgeschichte* of allegories of history. Spenser speaks of fame's extension into posterity in metaphors of breeding and flowering, with love as its root, and of fame as progeny, carrying a name through the ages like a dynasty, a bounty of honor. The Books of Love are books of good breeding. Timias, who is nearly fame personified, is often compared to a flower which flourishes or wilts as his reputation waxes and wanes. In the case of Britomart, fame is borne with her offspring to the famous Queene to whom the poem is dedicated. We shall see how important these metaphors are, but now we should look from the point of view of the present back onto the time of the action in the antique past, when the glorious deeds were done which planted enduring fame.

When in direct address Spenser's narrator is not expounding the motive power of love, or warning the fair ladies in his audience to take heed of his "ensaumples" of chastity, he is most often extolling the virtues of the "goodly usage of those antique times" and regretting their passage. As if surprised, like the Squire of Dames, by the chastity of Arthur and the ladies traveling alone with him, the narrator remarks that the "antique age yet in the infancie / Of time, did liue then like an innocent ..." in which lion consorted with lamb, until the world "woxe warre old / (Whereof it hight)" and beauty was lent to lust (4.8.29–32). Antiquity was a time both of heroic action and of prelapsarian virtue, whose memory poets, like Chaucer, bear; hence to preserve the example of a Worthy (to use Spenser's technical term) is a higher charge than to perform systematic philosophy, and Xenophon, in the letter to Raleigh, is "preferred before Plato."

The moral burden on a storyteller to preserve exemplary histories, to make fame work in the present, lies behind the four genealogical histories given in Book Three. Merlin, as magician (and Spenser as *vates ex eventu*), can record fame in reverse, and tell Britomart of her future progeny. After Arthegall's death, her unnamed son will "represent" her husband to her as "his Image dead"—like a work of art, the child keeps famous memory alive (3.29). The other histories, told like Aeneas's *dolores* at the banquet in canto 9, are those of the Trojan lines of Paris, Brute, and Aeneas. Britomart's ancestor founded the British line, surpassing the "antique Worthies merits" by subduing the giant who dwelled in England. Paridell—whose name, derived from his ancestor, Paris, may suggest that as a crafty lover he is a parody of a paramour, and as a lying historian he is a parody of an epic poet—utterly botches the stories he tells with such "a kindly pryde / Of gracious speach"; the facts he gives are accurate enough, but the moral significance he attaches to them goes awry. He considers Paris the "most famous Worthy of the world," extolling him for prowess, as if unaware of the consequences of his preference for Venus and his rape of Helen. His three-stanza abbreviation of the *Aeneid* is a masterpiece of damnation by faint praise, innuendo, and defamation. Aeneas "for safegard fled"; he "weetlesse wandered"; his people are "sad"; he seems to make war on innocent farmers; he is "constrained" to marry by fate; many "complained" of him; he "hardly" defeated Turnus, his "riuall." Paridell's accounts of Trojan heroism exemplify epic poetry mishandled; along with Busyrane he is the antipoet, the Archimago, of Book Three.

The antiquity of the romance world of *The Faerie Queene* sets it at the distance needed for it to acquire its allegorical significance. In this Spenser's poem differs from *The Romance of the Rose*, which is all set in the corrupt "now," and only wistfully remembers the Golden Age. In "those days" motives were purer, activity simpler, the customs of civilized intercourse more direct, and people easier to judge than now. Men's minds more clearly expressed themselves in action, landscape, temper of humours, families, language, and physical appearance than now in the complicated time of Elizabeth. What then was combat "is now" (that is, "means," for we are bound to translate temporal into moral states) interior choice; what was travel is now intention; what were lodgings and castles are crises, revelations, and temptations; what was prison is mental bondage; what was fame is moral being. Only love remains the same in both the romance world and the modern world it allegorizes. Even in its pure form romance tempts one to make allegorical interpretations; the stylized, fantastic, inventive action, the evidence of unusually firm authorial control in the interlaced plots, and the presence of rootless motives and uncaused consequences, drive readers to look for psychological and sacramental meanings in fictions as unsullied by ideas as Greek myths. In Book Three more than elsewhere in *The Faerie Queene*, in all probability because it was the first planned, Spenser takes advantage of the allegorical potential of romance.

THE WONDERFUL: MAGIC AND ART

All as a blazing starre . . .
At sight whereof the people stand aghast:
But the sage wisard telles, as he has red,
That it importunes death and dolefull drerihed.

[1.16]

The romance knight is a famous lover, and what he meets on his travels are wonders. In second-rate medieval romances, especially those influenced by Eastern lore, the quantity of wonders seems to be the criterion of competence. When an allegorist takes up a conventional literary form, as Spenser takes up romance, he stands back from it and dissects it like a literary critic, augmenting fancy with reason, and bounteous invention with logic and morality. The allegorist presumes that the old fantastic conventions embody the truth, if only they can be under-stood (hypostatized). So Spenser shares with us a simple delight in wonder, which most austere criticism cannot quell, and at the same time a searching investigation of the phenomenon of the wonderful itself, which the poet bodies forth as the activity of beholding. Spenser's concern, to show how seeing wonders affects his characters, reflects the critic's concern to show how wonders affect the reader, just as the presence of books in Book One helped to teach us the significance of words as a phenomenon.

When Florimell goes flying by in the first canto, we do not yet know that she always flies because beauty is fleeting, that she is the special patron of beauty, that beauty in allegory is chastity incarnate, whose natural function is to attract humans to virtue. We only know that she is wonderfully beautiful, like a comet, a "blazing starre" which makes "the people stand aghast" and which needs to be interpreted by a "sage wisard." These references to an audience looking on with amazement signal Spenser's interest in the act of gazing (see 4.32, 6.17, 6.27, 7.14, 8.22, 9.34, 4.1.13). Arthur, Guyon, Timias, and Britomart "gazed after her a while." Then Arthur and Guyon chase Florimell, and Timias chases the "griesly Foster" who chases Florimell, but Britomart "would not so lightly follow beauties chace." Sight has stirred action—it is the first motion, the outer frontier, of the soul—and the consequent action determines the nature of the soul: Arthur's and Guyon's masculine pursuit of beauty, Timias's honorable defense of it, and Britomart's feminine indifference. Only later, when meaning becomes attached to the manner and objects of pursuit, the moral significance of these actions will be liable to judgment.

Love first works through beauty, and so through the eyes with Cupid's arrows. Cupid himself is blindfold, but unveils himself to see Amoret in her deepest pain (12.22): in fact love sees all (10.4), as Amant learned at the Fountain of Love in *The Romance of the Rose*. The crafty lover, Paridell, blinds Malbecco's good eye, and both of Hellenore's (10.5). These bad lovers leer wantonly, like Malecasta (9.23–29, 1.41): for them, sight becomes a sensual sense, a "hungry vew" or "greedie gaze," their fancies are fed, and they roll their eyes mainly at night when God's work of beauty is concealed (4.56). The most active emblem of bad seeing is Corflambo, whose eyebeams fire the heart, and whose "infectious sight" is "full of sad powre" (4.8.39, 47–48). Even chaste women are fascinated, in the etymological sense of that word, by lascivious scenes: Britomart gazes on the image of Cupid (11.49)—the god himself "full proud, himselfe vp rearing hye" (12.23) looks on Amoret. Britomart wonders at and half envies Scudamour and Amoret joined like a statue of Hermaphrodite (12.46, the 1590 version); and the more virginal Belphebe looks on the dead figure of Lust, whose appearance is phallic (4.7.5–7), and "oft admir'd his monstrous shape" (4.7.32).

The most intense gazing in *The Faerie Queene* is Britomart's tour through the House of Busyrane: "That wondrous sight faire *Britomart* amazed, / Ne seeing could her wonder satisfie. . . . The warlike Mayde beholding earnestly / . . . Did greatly wonder, ne could satisfie / Her greedy eyes with gazing a long space, / But more she meruailed . . ." (11.49, 53). The house is a wonder to us, too. Spenser offers it as a puzzle: what could be more fun than trying to interpret Busyrane? Busyrane's name alludes to Busiris, and, as Roche has shown, to "abusion," deception; but it may also suggest the crowded sights of the place, in which the innocent tourist "cast her busie eye" (11.50)—the house is the fraudulent imperium of glutted seeing, the reign of busy eye. Britomart enters the House with steely purpose, and so she is in less danger than was Guyon, whose motive to see the Cave of Mammon was simple curiosity (2.7.20), that interest in seeing rich things which initiates greed; but she is more involved than Marinell at the House of Proteus, at the banquet of the sea gods, who wanders about gawking like a philistine at the Uffizi (4.12.4, 17). The difference is that Britomart sees all, and then acts (12.27), and her action overwhelms, even denies what she sees.

The objects beheld with wonder are of three kinds: prodigies of nature—subnatural monsters or supernatural beauties; magical events; and art. Since Spenser fixes our attention on the act of seeing these wonders, the question arises as to whether the status of the beholder alters the status of the object, and hence what objects really are. Spenser reifies our idiom, that one "makes something" of what he sees if he can "make it out" at all. Let us look at some beholders, holding in abeyance for a while the recollection that we too are beholders. In the next few paragraphs I aim to provide a background for the Busyrane episode, which culminates these themes and fulfills, as it were, the type provided by Malecasta's Castle Ioyeous in canto 1, as the old dragon at the end of Book One fulfills the dragon Error at its beginning.

When Florimell races to the sea she takes a boat in which sleeps a Fisher, who marvels at her beauty when he wakes (8.22–23). He thinks "he yet did dreame . . . or that some extasie / Assotted had his sense, or dazed his eie," but then sees that she is "no vision." His reaction is typical: Florimell and Britomart make people wonder if their vision has gone awry. When Britomart unmasks before a company of knights and ladies, they are "with amazement smit" and hold, in the Chaucerian manner, different opinions "according to each wit": some think "some enchantment faygned it," some think she is the goddess Bellona, some think she wears a "maske of strange disguise"—masks under masks (4.1.14).

Artegall sees Britomart's face for the first time, "and of his wonder made religion, / Weening some heauenly goddesse he did see" (4. 6.22). A man about to be betrothed is not culpable for making religion of his dazzled sight of his beloved; but the Witch and her churlish son make a bad idol of lust in their vision of Florimell (7. 11–15), as subhuman figures idolize the beautiful throughout *The Faerie Queene*. Scudamour releases, de-idolizes, Amoret from the altar of the Temple of Venus when he makes bold love to her (4.10. 48–53), even though he says it "sacrilege me seem'd the Church to rob," but she fearfully remakes an idol of herself when her new marriage comes to its consummation at the House of Busyrane. The point is that women are not enchantments, goddesses, or idols, but natural women. When beholders make them other than what they are, it is the beholders, not the women, who are the mages and priests. Women are not to be shown, are not monsters (Latin *monstrum*, *monstrare*). Snowy Florimell is irredeemably an idol, but she is not a woman (4.5.15). This phenomenon of beholding is the first step of magic-making, which in Spenser's poem, I shall argue, is an allegory of nature or nature corrupted, not of supernature.

Magic may be white, black, or divine. White and black magic formally resemble one another, but differ in that white magic expresses what obtains anyhow in nature, if nature is properly understood, and thus prevails, while black magic attempts to denature, to make idols, like bad alchemy or misguided poetry. The magicians of the books of love are Merlin, Canacee, Agape, Cambina, Archimago, Duessa, Busyrane, the Witch (7–8), Cupid, and Proteus. The first four of this group deal in white magic, the second four in black; but the last two, being gods, fall outside these categories—Cupid leaning toward the white and Proteus to the black. Most of the magicians are shown to have access to the underworld, as did Archimago and Duessa in Book One (3.7 ff., 7.22, 8.37, 9.48, 4.1.20, 4.2. 47), to work with sprites (3.7, 8.4, 9.16), and to use charms, the poetry of magic (2.15, 2.50, 3.14, 7.21, 10.4, 12.31–32, 4.2.35).

Several are shape-shifters: Proteus, Cupid (6.11 ff.), Duessa (4.1.18), and Archimago.

When Britomart looks in "*Venus* looking glas" (1.8), made by Merlin, she first views herself "in vaine," like Narcissus; but then, under the tyranny of "imperious Loue," she thinks about her future husband—the Eve of St. Agnes theme—and sees Artegall's image, as Amant saw the Rose (2.22–26). This is pure white magic, for one idea Spenser insists upon is that loving, "kindly flame," is natural and cannot be gainsaid—that is the point of the Marinell story. So Spenser troubles to speak of the spherical mirror as a "world of glas" (2.19); it is, like *The Faerie Queene*, an allegory of the natural world, a microcosm in which one can see, more clearly than in the busy confusion of life, things as they are. Britomart's initial narcissism is immediately translated into love for Artegall, which is both an allegory and a natural good.

The presence of Archimago in the books of love is minimal: he appears only onče (4.45), abruptly, said to be the agent of Britomart's separation from Arthur and Guyon. It looks, in fact, as if he were an accident left from some earlier draft of Book Three. We are glad to see him, though, working in league with his types, the shape-shifting Proteus, "father of false prophecis" (4.37), the divine *mendax*, and Busyrane with his books, who is chained at the end of Book Three as Archimago was in Book One. Only Belphebe, among the four principal women of the books of love, lacks an attendant mage, perhaps because virginity is nearly supernatural itself. Proteus's and Busyrane's efforts are expended to make Florimell and Amoret untrue to their lovers; if they should succeed, the women would forego natural chastity (Spenser is resolutely monogamous) and become Malecastas or Hellenores. Later we will consider, in both cases, how the women are freed from the dark magicians. The white female magicians of Book Four work with "the powres of nature" (4.2.44, and 4.2.35), rather than of hellish sprites, and their magic cancels out in concord. The black Duessa and Ate, "an incarnate deuill" (4.2.3), are the only successful troublemakers in the books of love, because public discord is a fact of nature.

Spenser demonstrates that magic is what he repeatedly calls it, an art, by showing us the failure of artless charm. Britomart's nurse Glauce tries to disenchant Britomart from loving, with herbs, charms, and rituals repeated thrice, but fails (2.49–51). Spenser's brilliant imitation in his verse of the triple rhythm of magic-making confirms the association of the arts of poetry and of magic which we saw in Book One: the end of poetic song is to fashion a gentleman; and the end of black magical charm is to make a monster, as the Witch makes snowy Florimell out of the elements of Petrarchan love conceits reified—lamps for eyes, gold wires for hair, and so forth (8.5–8). The art which is most fit to behold as a wonder is plastic art.

When Spenser represents a work of art in *The Faerie Queene*, he never leaves it free of implications: its effect on the beholder, its relationship to nature, the meaning of its content, its author's skill and intention, its owner's involvement in it. The ready allegorizing of art gives force to the Renaissance idea of the didactic function of poetry: things which do not instruct do not delight; things which delight also instruct. The interest in the bond between delight and instruction derives from concern with the human will; Renaissance thought wanted to know in what man takes delight and found ethical significance in the answer to the question. Like the arts of magic, the art of making and beholding beautiful objects is serious. Again, the relationships within the poem between the work of art and the humans involved with it bear upon Spenser's notion of the relationships of himself and the reader to his poem.

Bracketing the works of art in the books of love are the work of the poet himself and the work of nature. In the proem to Book Three, Spenser speaks of his inability to express chastity, and likens his limitation to that of a "*Zeuxis* or *Praxiteles*," whose "daedale hand would faile" in the attempt. The only other use in *The Faerie Queene* of this word, which Melville used to describe the boat *Fidèle*, describes Venus's power as pacifier and procreator in nature: "Then doth the daedale earth throw forth to thee / Out of her fruitfull lap aboundant flowres ..." (4.10.45). One of the lovers in the Temple of Venus makes this statement, and it is there that art and nature are harmonized, "and all that nature did omit, / Art playing second natures part, supplied it" (4.10.21). The Island of Venus is a good Bower of Bliss. In between artful nature, represented chiefly by the Garden of Adonis, and the daedale, natural poetry of this special poet, lie the artifacts of the poem: the tapestry of Malecasta's castle and the decorated rooms of the House of Busyrane.

The two touchstone phrases in the first canto of Book Three, I think, are "the image of superfluous riotize" and "makes for him endlesse mone"—the first describing the "rich purueyance" of Malecasta's drawing room, beheld with disdain by Redcrosse and Britomart, and the second describing the lament of Venus for Adonis in the tapestry which decorates that room (1.33, 38). The two phrases bracket the tapestry; we are pulled from distant scorn to awed sympathy and back in five or six stanzas.

The tapestry depicts the metamorphosis of Adonis—only later, in canto 6, is Adonis restored, hid "from the skill / Of *Stygian* Gods" (6.46), as is proper to antimetamorphic allegory—and the flower into which he was transmuted is "wrought, as if it liuely grew." The power to imitate life, again and again in Book Three, determines the skill of an artist (Proem 1–4, 9.30, 37, 39, 51); both snowy Florimell, the most unnatural example of an artist's mimesis of nature, and the motifs in the border of one of Busyrane's tapestries, are described with the same formula, "so liuely and so like" (8.5, 11.46). Spenser presents the possibility that art can rival nature, in order to emphasize the contrary truth, that art is not natural. Art is white, like the "snowy skin" of Adonis in the tapestry, or the "whales bone" and ivory to which Florimell in her flight or Amoret in her torment are compared (1.15, 12.20), or the "white marble" statue at the end of the 1590 version of Book Three; but life is red, like blood, like the blush of Britomart, induced by her amorous battle with Artegall and by her recognition of him as the man who would change her chastity from virginal to sexual (4.6.19, 29). Like the mirror of Narcissus, art in the books of love tempts the beholder to remain static and cold, like itself, to remain fixed in wandering gazing and to forego heroic activity. The works of art are located in bad houses. Only by careful argument does Spenser exempt his own poem from this judgment, in the proem to Book Four.

When we read the story of Adonis woven in the tapestry, we can see no connections between it and the progress of Britomart. It serves as an introduction, but a mysterious one, whose meaning can only be unfolded as we read on to the end of the book. Its mystery exempts it from judgment, but it can nevertheless give a framework for judgment, as is proper to myth. The metamorphosis of Adonis proves to be a sort of a fraud, as we learn in canto 6; love is not so essentially deadly after all. The "sleights" and "art" which Venus uses to entice Adonis, characteristic of Malecasta and magnified in the learned loving of Paridell, have not yet exercised Britomart's chastity.

The "secret shade" in which Venus hides Adonis "from bright heauens vew," the temptation of a lover to be overprotective, as Marinell's mother smothers him, will not affect active Britomart. Like Adonis, Britomart will not let love keep her from adventure— love is her adventure. She will not avoid the wound of the boar, namely sexuality. She is shot at the end of the canto (1.65), and knifed after she looks at Busyrane's House (12.33); but her wounds are light, unlike the wounds of Timias, whose honor, and therefore whose very being, is at stake, pierced in his thigh by an arrow shot by a boarish Foster. Finally, the complaint of Venus, mythically described as an "endlesse mone," will not resemble Britomart's complaint, as we shall see. To summarize, Britomart's love will be venturesome, purposeful, artless, pious, open, chastely sexual, and free; its end will not be flowery death but fruitful generation, the real end of Adonis. Progeny is her best art. The tapestry should not be called an allegory of Britomart's experience, but a myth whose elements Spenser allegorizes elsewhere in the poem—a source of allegory.

In the House of Busyrane magic and art reach their consummation. Britomart's task is to disenchant the house, which, as Roche has pointed out, is a projection of Amoret's fear of sexuality, the "phantasies / In wauering wemens wit" which rush upon her on her wedding day (12.26, 4.1.3). Busyrane's removal of Amoret's heart from her body allegorizes a bad divorce of the affections from their seat, of imagination from sensation—a divorce which, in nature, spells death. Magical art here allegorizes fancy, and when Britomart destroys the fancy by being bold, but not too bold, the house collapses and the little love, Amoret, is released. Idle fancy can make love a black magic, but Britomart forces Busyrane to measure "many a sad verse" to re-verse his charms, to become a good poet (12.36). Britomart's power springs from her heroic grasp of what she is, a natural woman.

The house is described in two cantos, which imagine love according to two different schemes: first mythically in the tapestries, Cupid image, and gold work of the outer rooms, and then psychologically, in personification allegory, in the masque of Cupid. The decorated rooms reveal love in all its variety, its "thousand monstrous formes" (11.51), and its imperium over the gods themselves, to change the unchangeable, and to make the happy weep. At the outset we know the rooms are deceptive when Spenser compares threads of the tapestries to a snake (11.28) and when he describes the second room as "ouerlayd" with gold (11.51). Compare snowy Florimell's beauty, like the work of a "guilefull Goldsmith" (4.5.15), as opposed to Britomart's hair, beyond "goldsmithes cunning," more like the sands on a shore (4.6.20).

The second scheme, the masque, shows love from a human point of view, its private terrors and hopes, and its public consequences. At the center of the masque, at the point in the *gradus amoris* where intercourse takes place, stands Amoret in her torment. Both schemes contain elements of theater, with stage business, as if to make a show for Britomart's benefit, just as Dante was shown paradise, accommodated to his powers of imagination, by a special dispensation: in the tapestry Jove "pageaunts playd" and Cupid strews the ground with "mournfull Tragedyes"; in the masque Ease steps out, "as on the ready flore / Of some Theatre" clad for "tragicke Stage" (11.35, 45, 12.3). Of course the *gradus amoris* itself is presented "In manner of a maske, enranged orderly," the fulfillment of the type established in canto 1 by the six knights of the *gradus amoris* in Malecasta's castle who attack Britomart—Gardante, Parlante, Iocante, Basciante, Bacchante, Noctante (12.5, 1.45). The wonderful showy trumpeting, wind, lightning, earthquake, sulfurous stink, and whirlwind which precede the masque test all Britomart's senses and force her, if she would remain steadfast, to reject as fraud all her perceptions, to depend wholly on what is inside her. Busyrane sets fancy and the senses against knowledge and memory.

When Britomart enters the House of Busyrane through the gate of fire, she senses the numen of the place, and tells Scudamour "so we a God inuade" (11.22). In a way she is right, the house does have power, the kind of power over the imagination which pornographic pictures of monstrous love have over adolescent innocence. Britomart gazes and is wounded because she is a lover, but a novice at love. Some of the spirit of love, its violence and sensuality, fills the rooms and educates Britomart; but to be wholly chaste, she needs to push through the house, remove its spell, and free Amoret.

Spenser deliberately passes beyond the delicacies of conventional love poetry into a region of power and terror. It is as if Spenser were informing his romance audience that this is really love. Fortunately, the terror lies only in fancy, the first figure to appear in the masque of Cupid: the terror is a work of imagination, of art, of magic—a wonder. At the end of it all we return to love in nature, represented in the early version as the union of Amoret and Scudamour, with Britomart looking on, "halfe enuying their blesse" (12.46, in 1590 version). The Hermaphrodite is described as a work of art, but clearly it is a natural phenomenon, only seen as artful: the spell of Busyrane is reversed, and nature now is second art.

We are now, I believe, in a position to answer the question I raised earlier in this section as to what effect the beholders in the books of love have on the wonderful objects which they behold. The beholders create the objects. Magic, artistry, and poetry are allegorical fictions which express the phenomenon of making what one sees. But Spenser avoids any regressive, nihilistic cycle of reciprocity between the creating interiors of his characters and the creatures of the phenomenal world, by setting his trust in the constituents of the deepest soul: its graceful nature, which is inalienable and divinely established, and its natural grace, with which it is filled and which sustains it. The books of love allegorize the processes by which nature and grace become perceptible images and felt events; that is, they allegorize the process of allegory. We have already seen what follows from this complex situation—to allegorize allegory is to negate it, as Britomart negates the unnatural fancies of Amoret by disenchanting the house of Busyrane. As I have suggested, where *The Romance of the Rose* reaches out to cosmic principles of generation, the foundations of the laws of nature, and where Book One of *The Faerie Queene* reaches out to redemptive history and the systematic analogies of the world, Book Three probes humanity in relation to itself only, pure humanity at the border-line between beast and angel.

DE PLANCTU AMORIS

And by his side the Goddesse groueling
Makes for him endlesse mone, and euermore
With her soft garment wipes away the gore,
Which staines his snowy skin with hatefull hew. . . .

[1.38]

The art of love which we have examined is based on language: its images are visual reifications of the conventional idioms and conceits of the early love lyric. The books of love present not only these images, even when they are shocking, but the language itself of the physical sensation of love in its purest form, the complaint. The central books of *The Faerie Queene* contain most of the dramatically spoken poetry of the poem, and share with Book Six a special concern with the uses of poetry, the sister art. The metaphors of complaint yoke, in a conventional way, the emotions of a lover with the objects of nature—complaints are little love pastorals. Hence their process resembles the process of allegory, and a study of them is particulary rewarding for us. As we will notice again, the books of love have allegory as one of their subjects.

After Britomart watches Arthur and Guyon chase off after Florimell, she travels out of the forest and finds the Castle Ioyeous "plaste for pleasure nigh that forrest syde" (1.20). The earlier events of the poem, the unhorsing of Guyon and the flight of Florimell, may properly be called, in Nohrnberg's term, pre-allegorical, but when we reach the castle we reach the realm of meaning and judgment, in which the tapestry of Venus and Adonis is an interlude. The events at Malecasta's castle initiate the allegorical analysis of love as a phenomenon which feels painful to the lover, and seems tender and humorous to an outsider. With Malecasta the pain and the humor abruptly become violence and farce.

Most of the books of love explore love as a pain felt from the inside—Book Three, more than any other book of *The Faerie Queene*, expresses characters' emotions. Before considering the language of the pain of love, we should take Spenser's hint—since canto 1 comes first—and first observe loving as if we were wise, experienced lovers who can hold the business in perspective. From afar we can see love as sinful or funny. The whole story of Braggadocchio, the adventures of Malbecco, the tournament of beauty, the bickering of Ate's troop, the hardships of the Squire of Dames, come to the mind as examples. The best example is the first major one, the Malecasta episode.

The episode consists of four stages: the battle outdoors, the decoration of the rooms, Malecasta's wooing, and the bedroom scene. Like love, the battle is not a fair game: Britomart and Redcrosse will lose—that is, have Malecasta for a lover, be untrue—whether or not they defeat the six knights of the *gradus amoris*. When she knows

more, in a parallel game of fairly similar structure at the beginning
of the next book (4.1.9–15), Britomart solves the game with little
effort; but here, at the outset of her adventure, she must undergo
temptation by Malecasta. Britomart must take part in the game
because the *donnée* of the poem is that she is a lover, and to love means
to risk being unchaste. The description of Malecasta's kindling love
for Britomart, and her ever more outrageous attempts to make her
lewd meaning clear to the knight, who is not only innocent but female,
shows Spenser's ability to go inside a character while also judging
coolly from without. The hot complaints of Malecasta are fraudulent,
like Paridell's feigned distress as a learned lover (10.1–11), deliberately modeled on the excesses of language of the erotic lyric tradition,
and at the same time real, as she is pricked by the fire of lust. She
burns, but the narrator carefully lets us see that the burning is bad.
We are prepared for the culminating farce of the bedroom, which
should be compared with Redcrosse's experiences on his first night.

Spenser's special feat in describing Malecasta's night escapade
is maintaining decorum, handling pornographic materials without
breach of the tone, appropriate to romance, of dignity and moral
seriousness—an achievement we associate with such masterpieces as
the third book of the *Troilus*, *Sir Gawain and the Green Knight*, and,
under Spenser's influence, "The Eve of St. Agnes." Retelling the
story more baldly would help to make the point. Malecasta, panting
and trembling, "with her soft hand" feels under the covers the limbs
of Britomart, warm with sleep. She does not yet know that the
knight is a woman. She removes her scarlet mantle and slips under
the covers "with easie shift," extremely softly. The knight shifts in
bed, realizes she is not alone, and goes for her sword. The lady
shrieks and faints, bringing the assembled audience, essential to
farce, into the bedroom. They (and we) see the lady lying on the
floor; standing over her the knight, in her "snow-white smocke,"
pointing the flaming sword at the lady, panting and confused, angry
and afraid, her own hair disheveled. The lady arouses herself, blames
the knight; Gardante shoots her in the side, ripping that smock—
not a deep wound, it "But lightly rased her soft silken skin, / That
drops of purple bloud thereout did weepe, / Which did her lilly
smock with staines of vermeil steepe." The knight, enraged, wields
her sword "Here, there, and euery where about her," and with the
help of her friend, terrifies her foes. Britomart, we may imagine, tells

Redcrosse, "I want to get out of this hotel *right now!*"—"For nothing would she lenger there be stayd." She is wounded, but it is merely a flesh wound.

In the sensational eroticism of the Malecasta episode Spenser jolts the reader into acknowledgement of the impact of his theme— it is parallel to the disgusting picture of Error at the opening of Book One and the gory death of Ruddymane's parents at the opening of Book Two. The elements of the episode—the romance idiom, the pain of love and its expression as complaint, the association of sadistic violence with love—echo through the rest of the books of love. Where the conventional language of romance, the language which establishes the decorum of *The Faerie Queene*, meets the unconventionally grotesque violence of love, we find the formal complaint of love, the most direct, lyric expression of the psychological state of characters in the poem. There are more complaints in Book Three, especially in its fourth canto, than in the other books; it is an introspective book.

Romances, we have seen, are set in the old days, and Spenser's imitation of the speech of those days is the old language which is still present in common parlance, the language of old saws, proverbs, and clichés: "Through thick and thin," "by hooke or crooke," "Hard is to teach an old horse amble trew," "For who wotes not, that womans subtiltyes / Can guilen *Argus*" (1.17, 4.46, 8.26, 9.7). In Book Four Spenser indulges in rough "battle humor" from old epic and romance convention, speaking of a jousting knight as receiving entertainment, or paying for his efforts with usury (4.1.36, 41, 4.6.10, 4.9.30). We even find the old language of sexual innuendo in the second half of Book Three, the cantos of bad love: intercourse as "seruice" (7.54, 9.5, 7, 10.35), as a ship coming to dock (10.6) or as the ringing of a matins bell (10.48). The archaic, medievalized diction of *The Faerie Queene* has received much comment. The topic requires separate study, but I think Spenser's effort to give his knights old language accounts in part for the strangely narrow and boring discourse of some of his heroes—they do, however, become less proverb-ridden as they learn.

We saw in Book One Spenser's concern with the uses of language, and the theme continues here. Words have power, like "Magick art" (2.15): they can feed a humour (2.12), they can remove the sun and moon from the sky (3.12), they can bring about concord

(6.25, 4.2.2), they can heal (11.13, 15), they can instill grace (4.9.14). Words can be misused for the sake of lust (8.14, 34–35, 4.2.9) or pride (9.32) or discord (4.1.25) or slander (7.23, 4.8.24 ff.). At several points Spenser emphasizes the separation of words from action or reality: Britomart tells Marinell that "Words fearen babes" (4.15). Malbecco acts "As if the word so spoken, were halfe donne" (10.33); of Sclaunder the poet says:

> Her words were not, as common words are ment,
> T'expresse the meaning of the inward mind,
> But noysome breath, and poysnous spirit sent
> From inward parts. . . .
>
> [4.8.26]

Like doffing a helmet or beholding a wonder, the act of speaking in *The Faerie Queene* is loaded with significance. The content of what is said may not be so important as that it is said and the manner of saying it. We are in a world of rhetoric, in which speech is an allegory of expression.

The medium of complaint is language; its content is pain. A motif which Spenser repeats with remarkable consistency at the most sadistically thrilling points of his narrative is the appearance of red blood flowing over white garments or white skin: Adonis's gore and "snowy skin" (1.38), Britomart's "purple bloud" and "lilly smocke" (1.65), the silver-fringed mantles of the sea nymphs and Marinell's "gelly blood" (4.40); Belphebe's "lilly handes" ministering Timias's bloody wound (5.33), Amoret's wound "that dyde in sanguine red her skin all snowy cleene" (12.20), Britomart's second wound, in her "snowie chest, / That little drops empurpled" (12.33). Busyrane's treatment of Amoret's heart, steaming in its silver basin, comes closest to an unhealthy mixture of aestheticism and violent sexuality—as unhealthy as Amoret's thoughts. I suggested before that in the books of love the color red indicates life and white indicates art: loving mingles the two colors, not externally, as Amoret fears, as a bloody wound in fair flesh, but internally, as a blush, or as consummated sex. When we see Busyrane most cruelly "Figuring straunge characters of his art, / With liuing bloud he those characters wrate" (12.31), doing magic with Amoret's life (and making Spenser's meter misbehave), he is enacting a damnably physical version of a verbal complaint. He mingles pain and art, but all too externally, like Æsculapius trying to heal by joining parts.

Marinell's name suggests not only the sea, but a phrase in older English "Marry nill," "Marry ne will," "I will not marry"—he represents such refusal to love as may be found in a wealthy, mother-directed bachelor. He finally is overcome by Cupid, who makes him "learne to loue, by learning louers paines to rew." Physical violence is part and parcel of love, especially newly conceived, unconsummated love; it is an educator, even a pleasure (10.60). But it is important to distinguish the talk about pain and cruelty, talk which is part of the art of love, the language of the lyric tradition, from actual pain and cruelty. Otherwise someone could get hurt. Confusions on this point underlie two important episodes in Book Three, the overthrow of Marinell and the imprisonment of Amoret.

Proteus warned Marinell's mother, who is called Cymoent here (Cymodoce later), that her son should keep away from women because "A virgin strange and stout him should dismay or kill" (4.25). Of course the virgin is Britomart, who nearly does Marinell in. Cymoent misinterpreted the prophecy, and told her son not to entertain the love of women, which the narrator comments is "A lesson too too hard for liuing clay, / From loue in course of nature to refrain." Cymoent feared love, not realizing it was the simple physical strength of a warlike virgin that was to be feared; she "vainely did expound" the prophecy to mean "hart-wounding loue." Cymoent has failed to be literal enough; not knowing that she is a figure in Book Three, she did not know that the talk about love's wounds is likely to be physically enacted in the allegory of fairyland.

Following Roche, we have seen that the House of Busyrane projects into theatrical forms Amoret's fear of loving. The objects and events of the house reify the Petrarchan conceits of love: the beauty of the art and the horror of the torture make concrete the lyricist's oxymoron, "pleasing pain." The reification parallels Dante's projection of the moral being of the dead into the spirits of the afterlife—a gluttonous person becomes the shade of gluttony, as his being and his end converge—with this difference, that Spenser is projecting not real moral being, but only a kind of metaphorical speech, a poetic fancy. So he gives the alternatives: the "phantasies / In wauering wemens wit" that make up the masque of Cupid are "Or

238

paines in loue, or punishments in hell" (12.26)—they amount to the same thing in allegory, since both are grotesque and purified imaginations of suffering. Magic has brought the underworld up to the surface, defended only by a gate of fire, and Amoret has become "like a dreary Spright / Cald by strong charmes out of eternall night" (12.19). Both the wounding of Marinell and the spell on Amoret give us rare glimpses of the process of making allegory, the deliberate confusion of literal event and metaphorical language, and the fictive admission of fancy to the world of the senses. The episodes corroborate a suggestion I made earlier, that one theme of the books of love is allegory itself.

Now, conscious of Spenser's profound interest in language and in the tormented experience of love, we can examine the formal complaints of the books of love. The complaints are examples of the "old" kind of speech appropriate to romance since, like proverbs, clichés, lewd metaphors, and battle humor, the language of complaint is traditional and inherited, the very language of European poetry. The complaints are especially expressive, being "overheard" like lyric—Britomart overhears Scudamour's complaint (11.9 ff.) as Chaucer's narrator overhears the Black Knight's complaint in *The Book of the Duchess*—and hence direct announcements of what a character thinks he feels. The complaints serve the poem as Robert O. Payne reminds us the lyric insets serve Chaucer's *Troilus*, as crucial signals of where a character is and as revelations of the emotional undersurface of the poem. The complaints have a peculiar status, like fiction itself, being true in their directness, but false in that the motives which provoke them are mixed and the language in which they are expressed is borrowed—as Poeana complains in a song "she had learned readily by rote" (4.9.6). Unlike the complaints, for instance, of Book One, those of Fradubio and Redcrosse in the dungeon (1.2.31 ff., 1.8.38), which lament of the horror of their actual state, these are complaints of love whose horrific language is distinct from the way lovers actually are. To love is not as serious as to sin, even though a pattern of wounding and healing attends upon both experiences. A sinner has to find redemption, but a lover has only to ripen.

I will enumerate the complaints in the books of love, then consider the four most important. Several of the complaints are not rendered but only referred to, like Malecasta's "sighes, and sobs, and plaints" (1.53), the "exceeding mone" of the Witch and her churlish son (7.19), the "endlesse mone" of Venus for Adonis, and the memorized songs of Poeana before Arthur makes her graceful (4.9.6, 14 ff.). When Venus, searching for Cupid, hears shepherds complaining of his doings, she smiles (6.15)—so should we. Diana smiles at Venus's "vaine plaint" at the loss of Cupid a few stanzas later. Three complaints, those of Cymoent against the fulfillment of prophecy, Arthur against night, and Timias against dishonorable love, contain various examples of self-deception, excessively violent or sophisticated language, fatalism, and plain bad temper, which help us to read the other complaints (4.36 ff., 55 ff., 5.45 ff.)—canto 4 seems to be the primer of the art. The four major complaints are those of Britomart (4.8 ff.), Scudamour (9.9 ff.), an unnamed lover in the Temple of Venus (4.10.43 ff.), and Florimell (4.12.5 ff.).

When Britomart parts with Redcrosse after the Malecasta episode, she comes down to the sea, where so much happens in the books of love, "Following the guidaunce of her blinded guest" Cupid (4.6), and pursued, we learn later, by Archimago (4.45). She has not doffed her arms, but now, having "fed" her love wound with "selfe-pleasing thoughts," making images of Artegall in her fancy, she sits down and unlaces her helmet. The reader of Spenser knows that she is in a dangerous state. The complaint itself, for the first two stanzas, smacks of danger—of self-indulgence, refusal to face reality in a bland fatalism which Spenser abhors, and a low-grade poetic of easy metaphor and cheap allegory. "Huge sea of sorrow," she begins, drawing, like an allegorical critic, the exterior landscape into her interior, mingling the concrete sea with her abstract sorrow. An allegorical poet may connect his character's inside with his outside, but for a character to do so is a kind of narcissism. Sentiment is dangerously objectified. She compares herself to a "feeble barke" in search of haven; love is her "lewd Pilot" and "fortune Boteswaine." She wallows like Troilus.

But this is heroic Britomart, who knows her destiny. She redeems her complaint by three actions. First she makes a pious vow, promising a "table for eternall moniment" to Neptune if she comes to safety. To submit to a deity is preferable to relinquishing one's self to fortune, as Spenser might have gathered from the successful piety of Pygmalion in *The Romance of the Rose* or from Chaucer's Dorigen, who complains by the sea with a sort of piety in *The Franklin's Tale*. Second, she ceases to complain: "She shut vp all her plaint in priuy griefe." Silence seems to be the right language of love—at the end of the 1590 version of Book Three, we see Scudamour and Amoret joined, and "no word they spake" (12.45). Finally, what she has feared in her complaint is an inability to endure, to remain what she is, a heroic lover. At the end of her complaint, she sees Marinell, the emblem of refusal to love, and puts her helmet on again:

> Her former sorrow into suddein wrath,
> Both coosen passions of distroubled spright,
> Conuerting, forth she beates the dustie path. . . .
>
> [4.12]

In a simile which follows, Spenser compares her conversion of humours to the change of foggy mist into a pouring storm. Poor Marinell could not know how great would be the anger of the knight he meets—that anger has a history of pent-up grief. We see elsewhere this kind of conversion of self-directed concupiscence to other-directed irascibility, as Britomart (twice) transforms her shame at being wounded into wrath, and as the Churl, less pleasantly, having lost Florimell, "his mother would haue slaine" (8.4). The conversion can be bad, but in Britomart's case it produces heroic action, which along with piety and silence corrects her complaint. Here the Venusian Britomart fulfills the epithet, *Armata*, by taking arms against a sea of troubles.

Scudamour has lost Amoret to Busyrane on his wedding day, and Britomart overhears him, seven months later, making "bitter plaintes." They are bad: they consist of impious questioning of God's justice and the reward of righteousness, in quibbling, sophisticated language which may remind us of Troilus's predestination complaint in Book Four of Chaucer's *Troilus*. He grovels on the ground and weeps. We do not yet know that the "deadly torments" which afflict Amoret are real (in one sense, of course, they are not) so the complaint seems excessive. Furthermore, Amoret's torture is specifically that "the sharpe steele doth riue her hart in tway," splits her affections. As we learn, Busyrane's attempt is to make Amoret inconstant—to love Busyrane who allegorizes her own fancy—which is Spenser's idea of love perverted. So Scudamour complains not only that he lacks Amoret's love, but that she loves elsewhere; it is a kind of jealousy. In Book Four Scudamour reveals how he just barely got Amoret in the first place, and here we find him unable to retrieve her. He is a decent enough, but unheroic man, not capable of going through the gates of fire, not bold. He needs medication. Britomart, who has learned how to handle grief, encourages him, first by reminding him of grace and the need to submit to providence, and then by joining her fate to Amoret's, "with her for you dy," acknowledging what is already true (if Amoret dies all lovers die), playing the roles of both harrowing hero and lover, a hermaphroditic blend of courage and grace. She contains Scudamour and Amoret within her, as art or boldness contains magic.

Spenser narrates this complaint first, but Scudamour had complained once before, in the episode at the Temple of Venus where the lovers petition the goddess on the model of Chaucer's *House of Fame*. An unnamed lover breaks forth with an odd complaint, which Scudamour follows with a murmured version of the old wound-of-love theme, begging for "ease vnto my smart." The unnamed lover's complaint (4.10.44 ff.) is really a song of praise, modeled on Lucretius, Boethius, and *The Parliament of Fowls*, rejoicing in Venus's power to make the world smile, to bind the seas in their places (just before Britomart's complaint the narrator had worried about the seas' "deuouring couetize" of the land), to bring spring and the mating season, to generate life, "repayre" the world, and give joy to all. This surpasses piety; we must imagine that Venus grants him love, just as in the *Parliament* Nature granted mates to all the birds, except the aristocratic hawks who know too much about love. The contrast between this complaint and Scudamour's tired lament could not be sharper, but, as we see, Scudamour did not learn, and must thank nature and Britomart that human lovers can be got and kept even by the ignorant.

The last complaint is a sea-complaint like Britomart's, except that Florimell is not by the sea but in it. (4.12.5 ff). Like Scudamour's her complaint is overheard by her (accidental) redeemer, Marinell. Her complaint is good and bad: elements of pain and a death wish

are counterbalanced by a desire to "liue, as louers ought to do," and
she at least tentatively acknowledges the power of the gods, "if any
Gods at all." She cannot act, being imprisoned, but an allegorical
action takes place during her complaint: she gives us, and Marinell,
to understand that it is Marinell, not Proteus, that keeps her prisoner—Proteus is just the agent of her unrequited love. As patron of
beauty, Florimell is by nature a sufferer, not a performer. Her
complaint works, Marinell loves her, and as a consequence she is
freed.

Although I have been selective in discussing these complaints, I
believe the pattern of meaning they present is clear. Complaining,
while appropriate to romance, reveals weakness in the complainer,
an illness which needs to be cured by piety, silence, and action.
Complaint is the source of the sadistic torments of the books of love;
it is incorrect fancy articulated in language, language borrowed
from old poetic traditions. Like magic, and like the simplified psychology of humours—fiery wrath and watery desire—which Spenser
uses, the language of complaint allegorizes the mind; that is, arranges
and expresses in unreal but believable forms what the nature of the
mind is. The good people of the books of love complain when they
reach their lowest ebb—even Prince Arthur grumbles at night—and
barely manage to contain their weakness within the world of language
and not let their imaginings affect their actions. Their bad poetry is
not confused, at last, with the truth; the truth disenchants them.

When a character feels like complaining it is as if he were sick. In
Book One we observed Spenser's expression of moral disintegration
as disease, and his healing word. Here the disease is not sin, for which
the only remedy is grace, but love, which is its own remedy. We find
Glauce unable to heal Britomart with "herbes, nor charmes, nor
counsell," (3.5), and the Witch likewise failing "with herbs, with
charms, with counsell, and with teares" to heal her son (7.21).
Glauce, and Belphebe, cannot diagnose the illnesses of Britomart
and Timias (5.49), and Tryphon, who treats Marinell's first wound
with an Æsculapiuslike outer healing, cannot cure him when Cupid
wounds him anew (4.12.24). Apollo is needed to discern that Marinell
"did languish of some inward thought"; Neptune is needed to free
Florimell from Proteus—Neptune and Proteus being gods of the
same world; and Florimell finally cures Marinell:

As withered weed through cruell winters tine,
That feeles the warmth of sunny beames reflection,
Liftes vp his head, that did before decline
And gins to spread his leafe before the faire sunshine.

[4.12.34]

When he who would not marry joins with Florimell in love, nature revives itself and the books of love are complete.

THE SEA: CHANGES AND GRACE ABOUNDING

Dauncing and reueling both day and night,
And swimming deepe in sensuall desires. . . .

[1.39]

If I were not wary of the old distinction between "allegory" and "symbolism," which arose out of late eighteenth-century poetry and theory, I would feel more comfortable in trying to explain the presence of the sea in the books of love. Then I could say that Malbecco, Busyrane, Corflambo, and Belphebe were examples of allegory, but that the sea is a symbol. We need to make another kind of distinction.

In his treatise on nymphs, salamanders, gnomes, and sylphs, pseudo-Paracelsus conceives of the kind of matter appropriate to each creature as its element, its "chaos"; nymphs breathe and exist in water; salamanders can be heard in their homeland among the flames of Etna. Each of the four elements sustains its species of being. The sea bears a similar relationship to much of the action of the books of love: the ground of the events is water; often when a crisis and a solution are at hand we find water; the ocean seeps into the crevices of the poem. Cymoent's undersea bower

Is built of hollow billowes heaped hye,
Like to thicke cloudes, that threat a stormy showre,
And vauted all within, like to the sky,
In which the Gods do dwell eternally. . . .

[4.43]

The sea has its own sky, its own gods, its own inhabitants, banquets, processions, even its own architecture (8.37). The sea is a second world, a "second nature" like art, adjacent to fairyland just as Britain is adjacent to it, and Spenser speaks of the sea as greedy of the land (4.7, 4.12.6–7). It rivals the other otherworlds, heaven and hell: from her watery prison Florimell complains that heaven "is farre from hearing," and that she lies near "lowest hell" (4.12.6, cf. 4.11.4).

In chapter four, we followed Frye in observing that Spenser virtually used up the material of Biblical typology in Book One. The other books take over great expanses of the territory of Greek mythology, Greek pastoral, Greek romance, even Egyptian and Celtic lore, and the new images of Renaissance Neoplatonism. Books Three and Four more directly draw upon chivalric romance than do the others, and also upon the lore of the sea drawn from classical mythology, from immediate observation, and from literary convention. Spenser has found a new source of matter, never exploited so thoroughly before.

Throughout *The Faerie Queene* Spenser speaks of death, sloth, lust, and wicked carelessness in terms of the sea: a figure is drowned in a sea of wanton bliss, or drowned in deadly sleep, or in a boat carelessly drifting at the whim of fortune. Arthur links sleep, the ocean, and hell in his complaint to night:

> Indeed in sleepe
> The slouthfull bodie, that doth loue to steepe
> His lustlesse limbes, and drowne his baser mind,
> Doth praise thee oft, and oft from *Stygian* deepe
> Calles thee . . . .

[4.56]

The image is of a relaxation of heroic endeavour, a letting go of the necessary grasp on one's own being to sink within oneself, and there to find the "liquid humour," as Redcrosse did at Archimago's house, where the soft concupiscent passion has its source, and where one wallows indulgently and aimlessly. Everyone knows this danger. The sea within devours heroic virtue; this is Britomart's special danger when she complains on the shore. As we have seen, she can transform her potential watery weakness into flaming irascibility, and only the allegorist's control—poetic providence—ensures that the objects of her transformed wrath—Gardante, Marinell, Busyrane—are suitable opponents. Malbecco, to his sorrow, changes the other way. The beginning of his mutations is a shift of dominant elements within him: having saved his money from the flames, he realizes he has lost his wife, and "out of the flames" he "into huge waues of griefe and gealosye / Full deepe emplonged was, and drowned nye" (10.17). Paridell imputes the same unheroic change to Aeneas, who "out of the flames for safegard fled, / And with a remnant did to sea repaire" (9.41), but this is in the nature of a factually correct lie. Florimell discovers how specious the sea's safety is, but she had given up her life anyway (7.25–26).

The sea can dissolve a hero's form of being. In it takes place a boundless chemistry of separation and recombination of elements, as if it were the medium of Empedoclean Love and Strife, Venus and Ate; one of Spenser's favorite similes for combat, after Book Three, is the discordant rage of waves meeting in the sea. That the sea always moves suggests eternal mutability, and that it always changes suggests metamorphosis; it is the home of Proteus, the shape-shifting god. Florimell is the patron of beauty, a shifty virtue which swiftly passes, which deceives, and which depends on the eye of the beholder; for this reason she is particularly liable to the dangers of the sea. Amoret is tempted by torture, but Florimell is tempted by Proteus's changes. He tries kind words and gifts, then boasts that he is a god. She tells him she loves a mortal—he says he will become mortal; she loves a fairy knight—he "drest" himself like a fairy knight; then like a king, a giant, a fiend, a centaur. Finally, he becomes "a storme, / Raging within the waues," perhaps as close as can be to Proteus's real shape (8.38–41). Florimell remains chaste, and refuses "chaunge of loue"; Proteus throws her into prison.

The sea changes Proteus offers have parallels in the sky and on land. The tapestry in the House of Busyrane shows all the gods, driven by love, transforming themselves to seize their paramours. Cupid himself, when he wanders from his mother, is "disguiz'd in thousand shapes" (6.11). When the gods' lovers die they are transformed into flowers, trees, and streams. These absolute changes are reflected in the mental changes in the nonmythical figures: Britomart, Amoret, and Timias in love troubles become like pined ghosts (2. 52, 12.19, 4.7.41); Amoret and Scudamour become like a Hermaphrodite. None of these metamorphoses should be judged wholly malicious; the point of them is to suggest the fluid, potential state of being in love, and the near-formlessness of beginning love.

Spenser presents two alternatives to the random flux of the sea. First is the Garden of Adonis, another place of eternal mutability, whose flowers are metamorphosed lovers (6.45). There forms are impressed upon "moyst complexion" (6.8) by the sunlike, rational author of generation, Adonis, as Spenser learned fron Natalis Comes. There being shifts according to the controlling principles of genetics. The garden rivals the sea in plenitude: it "seem'd the *Ocean* could not containe them there" (6.35). Both the sea and the garden are like death, being places where form is dissolved; but the real death— sin and oblivion, the death of substance—is under the control of the last shape-shifters Duessa and Ate (4.1.18, 31) and their hellish colleagues.

Like his forebear Archimago's, Proteus's power is chastened. When Marinell's mother pleads with Neptune that Florimell should be freed, she and the god enunciate two principles pleasantly reminis-cent of English law: that the prerogative of awarding death is the monarch's, and that a "waift" found on the sea belongs to the king, not the finder. Proteus comes to seem an upstart in the beneficent realm of Neptune, like arrogant Mutability in the realm of Nature, and Neptune commands, not that Proteus be bound, but that Flo-rimell be freed to join Marinell. The flux of love becomes the sculpted rock of marriage.

The waters not only separate, but join. We have evidence in the Harvey correspondence that one of the early pieces of *The Faerie Queene* to be drafted was the marriage of Thames and Medway (4.11), the *Epithalamion Thamesis*. The river marriage should be compared with the abortive wedding of Amoret and Scudamour, narrated at the beginning of Book Four. Scudamour describes Amoret in the Temple of Venus as "all in lilly white arayd, / With siluer streames amongst the linnen stray'd" (4.10.52); she appears rather like the other bride, Medway, clothed in a garment "That seem'd like siluer ... And wau'd vpon ... To hide the metall, which yet euery where / Bewrayd it selfe" (4.11.45; cf. 4.11.11, 25). Spenser tells the marriage of the rivers in lovely stanzas which Coleridge thought must be especially dear to those who know the British countryside— or perhaps the imagination of nostalgia is better than the thing

247

itself. The marriage unbinds in a natural magic all the fearful violence and dangerous changes which have filled the books of love. Unlike, for instance, the catalogue of trees at the beginning of *The Faerie Queene*, the catalogue of the rivers and their gods passes beyond moral categories in a pure delight in natural abundance itself.

Spenser boasts of his achievement at the end of his description:

> O what an endlesse worke haue I in hand,
>   To count the seas abundant progeny,
>   Whose fruitfull seede farre passeth those in land,
>   And also those which wonne in th'azure sky?
>   For much more eath to tell the starres on hy,
>   Albe they endlesse seeme in estimation,
>   Then to recount the Seas posterity:
>   So fertile be the flouds in generation,
> So huge their numbers, and so numberlesse their nation.
>
> Therefore the antique wisards well inuented,
>   That *Venus* of the fomy sea was bred . . . .
>
> [4.12.1–2]

The stanzas themselves abound, and assert for the sea the right to be the first nature of the books of love, the author of love's goddess, just as Spenser asserts his own right to number the waters, to order them into poetry. Spenser's image conceives of the sea as pouring forth its progeny into the rivers of the world, running like the tide up Shenan (4.3.27), with its waves whose "white fomy creame, / Did shine with siluer" (11.41), infinitely generating, full of that wealth which Marinell in his refusal to love can use no more than the impotent Malbecco can use his (4.20–23). The seas obey the single word which moves nature, and like the growing creatures of the Garden of Adonis

> yet remember well the mightie word,
>   Which first was spoken by th' Almightie lord,
>   That bad them to increase and multiply . . . .
>
> [6.34]

Earlier I noted that Spenser follows this word and makes his poem obey love's imperium. When Glauce learns of Britomart's new love, she wonders at her sorrow: "this affection nothing strange I find" (2.40). Mark Rose's essay on Book Three argues that for Spenser and his English Protestant milieu, heroic loving is natural, domestic loving—marriage and children. The books of love are motherly books: we have the overbearing Cymoent, the careful Witch, and Agape, whose advice to her triplets seems to me the most motherly sentence in *The Faerie Queene*: "She warned them to tend their safeties well, / And loue each other deare, what euer them befell" (4.2.53). Glauce and Venus behave like mothers toward Britomart and Adonis. Along with Venus and Diana, we attend upon the wondrous birth of Belphebe and Amoret, after Chrysogone's nine-month pregnancy (6.2–28)—the birth of Argante and Ollyphant is the bad version (7.47—49).

Venus and Diana, like their foster daughters Amoret and Belphebe, are twinned and reconciled in the books of love. Venus tells Diana:

> As you in woods and wanton wildernesse
>   Your glory set, to chace the salvage beasts,
> So my delight is all in ioyfulnesse,
>   In beds, in bowres, in banckets, and in feasts:
> And ill becomes you with your loftie creasts,
>   To scorne the ioy, that *Ioue* is glad to seeke;
> We both are bound to follow heauens beheasts . . . .
>
> [6.22]

As every reader knows, Venus and Amoret are females of that loving which imitates God's "large bountie" (4.59), and Diana's other name is included in Belphebe, whose virginity was planted by God as an "ensample of his heauenly grace" (5.52). But grace and bounty finally cannot be distinguished: Belphebe is bounteous (5.44, 4.8.6), and both Venus and Britomart have "amiable grace" (1.46, 4.10.56). Florimell was raised by the Graces on Acidale (4.5.5), but loves Marinell; the Dwarf calls her the "bountiest virgin" (5.8). Another type of beauty, Spenser's virgin queen, is one "in whose chast breast all bountie naturall, / And treasures of true loue enlocked beene" (4.Proem.4). Grace is manifest in beauty, and especially in the gesture which beautifies without words, the smile. Books Three and Four are smiling books, from the rough laughter of Satyrane and the Squire of Dames to Leda's fearless smile at Jove's pride (11.32) to Venus's and Cupid's smiling numina (2.26, 6.15, 10.5, 4.10.56) to the regal, wise, poetic smiles of Merlin and Neptune, which see through love and bring knowledge to feeling (3.17, 4.12.30). Even we, slothful, unheroic readers of poems, are given the grace to smile.

The books of love redefine grace, after the understanding we acquire in Book One; rather, they show another dimension of grace (as Book Six will show yet another). Grace is not simply virginity, nor is bounty only fruitfulness: grace is the power of nature in love, God's magic operating, especially through women. Part of the grace which expresses itself in love is continence, like the land's containment of the sea. The shore, where waves and sand overlap, marks the beginning of love, which needs both the definition of land and the vitality of the sea. The sea has its bounds, which Spenser calls chastity. At this boundary the divinely promulgated customs of men—here represented by the conventions of romance, an allegory of the natural order of the way things are done—control and humanize and give purpose to natural love. In Book One, multiplicity usually bodes ill, but in the books of love the law and sacrament of men sanctions abundance, as the song and the lights of the fishing boats arrange the night and the sea in Wallace Stevens's poem. The waters of the sea have their proper place in the land in the marrying and endlessly bearing rivers.

The difficulty in naming the technique of allegory which accounts for Spenser's use of the sea may be that the sea comes too close to the land, that it is not another cosmos of being or of moral abstraction to which our cosmos, or the fairy cosmos, can be referred. The sea means all the things love means: it is dangerous, dissolving, deadly; it multiplies and changes; it is mutable but eternal, bountiful and graceful, silent and raging, devouring and begetting, wayward, careless, violent, a sleep and a forgetting, but an endlessly inventive memorial of how things come together. In it nature and grace are one. It resides in the universe of nature with a reality and a presence which is unspeakable. We can be grateful that Spenser turned his *Epithalamion Thamesis* into his books of love, as we are that Coleridge's plan to poetize the physical elements withered away into the *Rime of the Ancient Mariner*.

CONCLUSION: MAKING A WOMAN

But to faire *Britomart* they all but shadowes beene.

[1.45]

When critics write about great poets, they often draw upon the poet's own language for their terms. It would be difficult to write about Spenser without such special words as "sad," "blandishment," "recure," "kindly." However, the vocabulary in *The Faerie Queene* which describes allegory can be misleading. The repeated terms, "patron," "blazon," "shadow," "figure," "express," "ensample," "mirror," "paragon," "type," "veil," which the narrator sprinkles through his proems, as well as his direct addresses to the reader, are by no means univalent—I hope such terms as "type" and "express" bear various connotations to the readers of this book. But they do tend in one direction; underlying them is the assumption that an abstraction, especially a virtue, has a particular form which Spenser makes manifest in the analogous forms of his fictional events and characters, that the patron of a virtue unveils it by exemplifying it in action. Of course this kind of allegory meets us everywhere in *The Faerie Queene*, most clearly in the simple personifications. I wish now to examine two examples of more complex allegory of this sort, and then by way of conclusion to consider another method of allegory, which I consider more interesting and more profoundly moral, if less obviously so, the kind of allegory which this chapter has attempted to understand. Our labor heretofore allows me to summarize.

My first example is the scheme of the allegorical analysis of love. At several places the narrator calls on us to see that his theme is love in its variety: "Wonder it is to see, in diuerse minds, / How diuersly loue doth his pageants play" (5.1). The poem itself is a theatrical wonder. He speaks of "all three kinds of loue" (4.9.1). We are to view the spectacle of the different forms of love as Britomart views the tapestry of Busyrane. The narrator continually makes distinctions, between the "sacred fire" of love and the "no loue, but brutish lust" (7.15), or among love of blood-relations, of paramours, and of friends, or among types of bad love like Paridell, Druon, Claribel, and Blandamour—"So diuersly these foure disposed were to loue" (4.9.21).

The good sort of love—chaste, pious, constant, heavenly, bounteous, courteous, natural, beautiful—has its exemplars and its bad counterparts, as if to fill out the scheme: the unchaste Malecasta, the blasphemous Argante and Ollyphant, the inconstant Hellenore and Paridell, the hellish Duessa and Ate, the impotent Malbecco, the slanderers, the black magicians, the idols, the ugly. A few characters, among the most interesting, exemplify the transition from one sort of love to another or problematic states in between— Marinell, Poeana, Scudamour, Satyrane—and a few seem to sum up bundles of characteristics which are represented piecemeal in the minor characters: Britomart, Busyrane, Proteus, and Braggadocchio. Some signs remain in the poem of what appears to have been an intention to have Arthur and Archimago represent total virtue and total vice. I suspect I am not alone in thinking that the stories which blazon friendship—those of "Telamond" and Amyas— too obviously spring from an attempt to fill out the scheme, to portray *agape* and *philia* as well as *eros*, and do not possess the vitality of the rest of the books of love. This kind of allegory, which may be considered a presentation of the branches of a theme, surely helps to account for Spenser's enormous inventiveness.

My second example is really part of the first: the particular scheme of analysis of virtuous love. Others have treated this topic thoroughly, so I need only make a few remarks. The four good women of the books of love—Britomart, Amoret, Florimell, and Belphebe—each have all the trappings of a full-fledged allegorical being: we come to know their history, their education, their speech, their homes, their futures, and their behavior in a variety of crises. They represent bounty, beauty, and virginal grace, summed up in Britomart's heroic chastity (see 4.7.2). They dwell in the crucial locations of the books of love: Florimell at the fairy court and under the sea; Belphebe in her earthly paradise in the retired forest; Amoret in the Garden of Adonis, the Temple of Venus, the House of Busyrane—and Britomart has her run of fairyland, and is at home in Britain.

Among the qualities these figures share is their femininity. Although Spenser indulges occasionally in the old antifeminist conventions (1.51, 3.17, 8.8, 9.7), his avowed purpose is to right the wrong poets have done women. But the division of virtue and vice does not coincide with the division of female and male: for Argante's female lust we have Ollyphant's male (11.4). We see both Mars and Hercules, in love, transformed, shedding "womanish teares" (11.44,

12.7), and we see, in the sheath of the Temple of Venus, behind the veil of the mystery of love, on a "brickle," hymeneal pedestal, a hermaphrodite (4.10.41, cf.12.46, in the 1590 version). Spenser makes women his heroes partly, I think, to get new matter (as he used the sea) and perhaps to shock, as Shakespeare wanted to shock in the Sonnets, if Frye is right, and partly because the transition from maidenhead to womanhood (6.28) is the crisis of chastity, where humanity meets nature and culture. Finally, though, he writes of love among humans, not among women. The reconciliation of male and female in the figure of a hermaphrodite exemplifies the coalescing, atoning, marrying form of many of the events of the books of love, the joining of two spirits in one flesh: they are epitomized in the heroine of Book One, which is itself, after all, a book of love in another key.

These examples show Spenser doing in the books of love what we might have expected from reading Book One, expressing the analysis of a principle. Other kinds of allegory likewise echo the technique of the earlier book. The allegory of the projected interior continues to work—Amyas and Æmylia plan to meet each other and meet Lust and Corflambo instead. There is large-scale revelation, but in the books of love this is not final and apocalyptic, but is placed in the middle—the Garden of Adonis—because love is human and mediate, continuous with history and time. The revelation is not given to the principal hero, who loves without knowing absolutely, that is, she remains human, uncanonized. We find simple personification, architectural and topographical symbolism, genealogical allegory, and even vestiges of a Christian typology in a few passages, which I leave to the reader to consider (5.37, 6.3, 11.18, 34, 4.Proem. 4, 4.9.8). All these kinds of allegory require a double reading, first to get the plot, and then to say, "This happens because ... "; "Florimell flies because ... "; "Timias is wounded because ... "; "Scudamour bypasses Daunger because .... "

Books Three and Four also present a kind of allegory which is specific to them. In chapter four I touched upon the dynamics of Book One, on the graceful movements, controlled by the narrator, of suspension of judgment, laughter, tact, and buoyant goodwill. As I have noted, these movements are central to the books of love, because they are about love, which is just such a movement. Love unmoving becomes self-indulgence, cowardice, sloth, and narcissistic death. I have suggested that the allegory of the books of love returns to human nature, rather than reaching out, referring, to cosmic physics or sacred history; the same reason accounts for this—love, which is human nature. Finally, I have observed that a theme of the books of love is allegory itself, that they allegorize—and hence, in a way, negate—allegory. Again, the cause lies in the nature of love. Like allegory, love is a connecting point between the sacred and the profane, between the abstractions of the mind and the concretions of objects, between the presence of mystery and the everyday. Love is a gap in human affairs—like dreams, ecstasy, magic, sacraments, poetry, birth, and death—which reveals the transcendent, and shows the link between this world and the other.

We name the process by which matter takes form, love: it is a making, a poetry. The movement from self-pleased narcissism to creative pygmalionism, the movement, rather blind, of Amant in *The Romance of the Rose*, underlies the most important episodes in the books of love. We have seen that any sort of sensory projection of the mind, any beholding, can make an object; but love has the special power to make a human being. When the Witch creates snowy Florimell, she exercises incredible power. To make a man is the didactic purpose of an allegorical poem, according to Spenser ("to fashion a gentleman"), and any poet who aims to present a character must make him (or, as in this context we should add, her). In an allegory of love, the making of men is the subject as well as the purpose of the poem.

Of the several ways to make a human being, the books of love present all. One can be born, as it were, immaculately—virtually new-created like Adam or Christ—as are Amoret and Belphebe. One can be generated out of a historical line of progeny, like Britomart. One can be "made" in cultural memory in one's fame or reputation, like the Worthies, the heroic women of antiquity, or like Artegall, whose fame precedes him like an image in a mirror, and whose image will follow him in the person of his son—we have seen how Spenser yokes fame and progeny. One can be made by change, like Poeana humanized by grace, or Britomart and Amoret made women from maidens. These makings have evil counterparts, as always: snowy Florimell has a monstrous birth out of bad language and witchery; Argante and Ollyphant spring, coupled too early, from Titanic incest; Hellenore at her first opportunity declines

254

from womanhood to lechery—she is made in another sense; Amoret makes herself an idol; Duessa and Ate seem human by hellish illusion; Paridell springs from a rotten tree of Trojan history; and Braggadocchio acquires a nasty reputation.

In the extraordinary case of Malbecco, we are permitted to watch a man being un-made, or "dismayde," as he passes from an unsettled submission to his rising humours through several similes in which he is compared to a goat, a bear, a ghost, a snake, into an "aery Spright," and finally into a simple personification: he "forgot he was a man, and Gealousie is hight." This is one way personification allegory can come into being, by an absolute reduction of human beings until they become only language. Malbecco becomes what he is in fact, at the outset, a "cancred crabbed Carle" (9.3), doubtless shaped like a crab—as shades take shapes; his character is reified and then abstracted. His next appearance will be as Milton's Satan, who shifts his shape and squats at the lady's ear. Allegory can do this to a man, but it can also make a character "so lively and so like" that we find ourselves responding as if to real humans in real life.

The kind of making Britomart finally is empowered to perform is giving birth to children. A few years after Spenser's time, Ben Jonson was to write a poem in which he claimed that his son was his best poem. Spenser may have shared this sentiment; his constant critique in *The Faerie Queene* of art as a snare and a delusion anticipates a query about the status of poetry which we think of as peculiarly seventeenth-century, or modern. The answer lies in legends (things that ought to be read) like Britomart's, where what it means to be human is analyzed into polarized alternatives: to be a monster or a god, vicious or virtuous, natural or gracious, perceiving or creating, ignorant or knowing, intent or active, private or public, a creature of the sea or air or fire, a product of history or a maker of the future, finally, a real thing or an artifact. The books of love present the crossroads of humanity as articulately and as clearly as has perhaps ever been done; what makes them wonderful is Britomart, who, analyzed to pieces, comes out at the end as nothing other than human. She is completely made: Spenser has loved her as she loved Artegall, venturing forth until image became reality; or as he hated Malbecco. We leave our world when we read the poem, just as Britomart journeys to fairyland from Britain, but we return somewhat changed; something is born in us.

255

Bibliographical Note

The general books on Spenser listed in the note appended to chapter four need not be named again here, except to note the authors of treatments of special interest for the books of love: Roche (book-length), Rose, Nohrnberg, Hamilton, Hankins, Alpers, Nelson, Sale, Hough. Much of C. S. Lewis's *Spenser's Images of Life* (Cambridge, Eng., 1967) is devoted to Books Three and Four.

Harry Berger, Jr., has written a series of stimulating articles which I hope will eventually be collected: "*Faerie Queene*: Book III: A General Description," *Criticism* 11 (1969): 234–61; "The Discarding of Malbecco: Conspicuous Allusion and Cultural Exhaustion in *The Faerie Queene* III. ix–x," *SP* 66 (1969): 135–54; "Busyrane and the War between the Sexes: An Interpretation of *The Faerie Queene* III.xi–xii," *ELR* 1 (1971): 99–121; "Two Spenserian Retrospects: The Antique Temple of Venus and the Primitive Marriage of Rivers," *TSLL* 10 (1968): 5–25.

In *The Allegorical Temper* (New Haven, 1957), Berger examines Guyon's curiosity of vision, as I have tried to examine Britomart's. I allude to Robert O. Payne, *The Key of Remembrance: A Study of Chaucer's Poetics* (New Haven and London, 1963). Rosemond Tuve treats the relation of Spenser to *The Romance of the Rose* in her *Allegorical Imagery*, pp. 280–83.

Articles of special interest are Alistair Fowler, "Six Knights at Castle Joyous," *SP* 56 (1959): 583–99, and earlier studies cited there; J. Dennis Huston, "The Function of the Mock Hero in Spenser's *Faerie Queene*," *MP* 66 (1969): 212–17, a fine study of Braggadocchio; Helen Cheney Gilde, "'The Sweet Lodge of Love and Dear Delight': The Problem of Amoret," *PQ* 50 (1971): 63–74, and "Spenser's Hellenore and Some Ovidian Associations," *CL* 23 (1971): 233–39; Richard A. Lanham, "The Literal Britomart," *MLQ* 28 (1967): 426–45; Lesley W. Brill, "Battles that Need Not be Fought: *The Faerie Queene*, III, i," *ELR* 5 (1975): 198–211; Donald Cheney, "Spenser's Hermaphrodite and the 1590 *Faerie Queene*," *PMLA* 87 (1972): 192–200; A. Kent Hieatt, "Scudamour's Practice of *Maistrye* upon Amoret," *PMLA* 77 (1962): 509–10; John Steadman, "Spenser's House of Care: A Reinterpretation," *SRen* 7 (1960): 207–24; and Judith H. Anderson, "Whatever Happened to Amoret? The Poet's Role in Book IV of *The Faerie Queene*," *Criticism* 13 (1971): 180–200. For background to Paridell's bad Aeneas, see Meyer Reinhold, "The Unhero Aeneas," *C&M* 27 (1966): 195–207. I regret finding only as I read page proofs Gordon Braden's fine article, "riverrun: An Epic Catalogue in *The Faerie Queene*," *ELR* 5 (1975): 25–48.

CHAPTER EIGHT

Blighting Words

HAWTHORNE'S "RAPPACCINI'S DAUGHTER"

She who has once been a woman, and ceased to be so, might at any moment become a woman again, if there were only the magic touch to effect the transfiguration. . . .

Would not the earth, quickened to an evil purpose by the sympathy of his eye, greet him with poisonous shrubs, of species hitherto unknown, that would start up under his fingers?

The Scarlet Letter

But O, selfe traytor, I do bring
The spider love, which transubstantiates all,
    And can convert Manna to gall,
And that this place may thoroughly be thought
True Paradise, I have the serpent brought.

DONNE, "Twicknam Garden"

HAWTHORNE'S allegories derive from a Romantic tradition of gothic romances of horror, exemplified by the tales of Hoffman and Tieck—whom Hawthorne probably read—in which fantastic fragments of folklore and superstitious religion provide the material for a new investigation of the psyche. The imagination, in which the human soul splits, projects, and sympathizes with shadowy figures of men and animated objects, resembles the Renaissance idealistic cosmos of spirit and analogy. Demons, no longer credited by literate men, leave their Spenserian caves of sin, illusion, and oblivion, and step onto the stage of fiction as primary agents who, once acknowledged, cannot be dispelled. The archimago gives way to the Drummond light. Spenser could regain, under these conditions, his ascendancy for a writer like Keats; the forms of myth and enchantment again could flow into poetry, but in a new epistemological status, wholly disbelieved but wholly present, seized upon and remade in a polemical, embattled mood.

In Spenser's time, Sidney wrote that poets do not lie because they affirm nothing; but the Romantics could feel that poetry is the principal way to truth—that what the imagination seizes as beauty must be truth, and the recollection of imagination is poetry. In its simplest guise—its too simple guise—this idea could pose a conflict between scientific and imaginative knowing, a conflict unthinkable in the Renaissance, but made possible by empirical psychology in the tradition of Locke, and the abolition of the "idols" of the idealistic cosmos. Since there is something unconsidered and facile in opposing empirical science to imagination, I will simply assert that the opposition more readily suits satire, perhaps Byronic satire, than visionary poetry. So some of Wordsworth's poems, in which he reduces his powerful epistemology to this stark polarity, are of the second rate. "Rappaccini's Daughter" is an allegory of the painful relation, in Romantic thought, between knowledge and love.

LAMIA

Keats's *Lamia*, which I intend to examine as an analogue to Hawthorne's tale and as an example of Romantic allegory, suffers from too simple an opposition of scientific and imaginative knowing. Its tone wavers unsteadily between the tough, satiric irony of Dryden's *Absolom and Achitophel*—the model for its prosody, and the source of its opening lines—and the melting, purple synaesthesia of Leigh Hunt or Swinburne. The alternations of tone may well be deliberate, an effort to capture the double point of view we need to understand the poem, but as a solution to a poetic problem they are unsuccessful. It is not good Keats; and therefore we can the more freely exploit it for ideas at the service of Hawthorne, as a poet's easier work often sheds light on the inclusive, radiant poetry of his prime.

Keats drew the story of the lamia from Burton's *Anatomy of Melancholy*, as if to reveal to us the link between Romantic and Renaissance imagination. The plot is simple: a serpent demon, a lamia, assumes the form of a woman and seduces a young Greek, Lycius. Lycius's sapient mentor, Apollonius, reduces her to her original form by browbeating her; she vanishes; Lycius dies. The story can be interpreted as a psychological allegory, in which a projection of the passionate and aesthetic nature of a man seduces him, until a projection of his rational, scientific nature unveils the delusion, destroying the other projection and ending the man's life. An issue which we investigated in the last chapter, the significance of beholding, takes precedence in *Lamia*; and love, which can join the divided forces of the mind and heal the split between matter and spirit, is omitted— here knowledge is disintegration and death.

Keats introduces two complicating elements which salvage the poem from the barren ideology which my summary suggests. First is the introductory story, in which the lamia helps Hermes find a nymph whom he desires, in return for the god's favor of giving her a woman's shape. The story begs the question of its relation to the central plot. I find several connections. Keats opens the poem emphasizing that the setting of *Lamia* is among the classical haunts of nymphs, satyrs, and Olympian gods, and not the medieval and Renaissance world of fairies. Yet Spenserian touches are scattered through the poem, in language ("in self despite," "made moan") and in setting (the house which the lamia constructs has a "faery-roof").

In fact the poem bridges the gap between the mythical world and the fairy world; that is, between the world of unconscious ideal and the problematic world of the allegorized powers of the human soul. Hermes takes his nymph, untroubled by moral considerations, because they live in a world of myth outside of time: "Nor grew they pale, as mortal lovers do." The only changes which enter Hermes's world are external—whether the nymph will be visible or not— but in the world of Lamia and Lycius, the moral, teleological world, metamorphosis and death occur. Keats reiterates the idea that the lamia, her house, and her love are products of Lycius's imagination, as it were dreams—he wakes "from one trance ... into another"; but Hermes's nymph, who suddenly appears like a dream, is real, "or say a dream it was, / Real are the dreams of Gods. ... " Keats's special territory as a poet is the place where dreams and reality meet.

The second complication of the story is our uncertainty about the value we should place on the principal characters. Initially we assume that a serpent demon, a lamia, is not good, and that the protecting human, Apollonius, is a beneficent savior. She is of Swinburne's world of coy seduction, masochism, willfulness, and deceit; he of Dryden's world of reason, temperance, wisdom, and tough insight. But we cannot rest our judgment here.

Lamia, first of all, seems to become human and to draw our sympathy. When she assumes a woman's shape by Hermes's power, she changes in a frenzy of sharp torture: "She writh'd about, convuls'd with scarlet pain" as if she were experiencing the pangs of birth, entering the human world by the human method. We know that the "serpent prison-house" is her original form, but we are almost led to think her lies ("I was a woman") are true, that she was originally a woman—like Milton's Adam, who becomes serpentine in gesture after the fall. Keats lavishes attention on her rainbow brilliance as a serpent, and she becomes a beautiful woman, in whom the colors remain mingled in "That purple-lined palace of sweet sin"; beauty is beauty, and Keats fails if he does not make us feel the beauty of Lamia. If this is seduction and deceit, it may be worth it.

More obviously, Keats makes us critical of Apollonius. He is called a sophist, and characterized as jealous of Lamia's hold on Lycius. His "cold philosophy" itself receives the narrator's criticism—it will "clip an Angel's wings ... Unweave a rainbow, as it erewhile made / The tender-person'd Lamia melt into a shade." The hint here becomes actuality, as Apollonius "absorbs" from the lamia-woman her rainbow of colors, making her a "deadly white"—in anticipation of some of Melville's color symbolism. Apollonius stops the music, and the dream house collapses like Busyrane's.

Apollonius and Lamia even share some attributes. Her loving, like Paridell's, is scholarly:

Yet in the lore
Of love deep learned to the red heart's core:
Not one hour old, yet of sciential brain
To unperplex bliss from its neighbor pain. . . .

Both scientists are unperplexers, makers of distinctions. On his part, Apollonius with his bald head, his fixed cold eye, his "lashless eyelids," seems very like a snake—Lycius accuses him of being possessed. As Apollonius and Lamia begin to merge as serpentine scientists, there is less to choose between them. When Lycius cries, "Begone, foul dream," we cannot tell whether it is Lamia's or Apollonius's vision which he would exorcize.

His choosing constitutes the meaning of the poem, and *Lamia*'s fatal weakness is a failure to render the chooser, Lycius, in sufficient detail. When the lamia returns to serpent form, his more or less valid recognition of her as what she is causes her to vanish, and the inrush of knowledge brings death to him. Lycius is accidentally the agent of the climactic actions; the other characters are, in the allegory, parts of himself. But we have too little representation of the human state in its perplexed, woven form. Lycius's love is specious and shallow at the outset. A more powerful fiction would need to pose Lycius looking and loving more deeply and seriously—Lycius barely steps out of myth, into the unconsciousness of the Narcissus stage of loving. I would speculate that Keats saw this problem as he worked on his poem, and killed Lycius off as he turned to his other projects.

"RAPPACCINI'S DAUGHTER": POINTS OF VIEW

Like *Lamia*, and unlike Book Three of *The Faerie Queene*, Hawthorne's "Rappaccini's Daughter" tells of failed love. The title character, Beatrice, is, like Lamia, poisonous. (The pseudomedical topic was in the air in America; Holmes's *Elsie Venner* was to be the best-known example. The motif is connected with our other kind of allegory: Alecto envenomed Virgil's Amata—*Aen.* 7.349–56.) Her would-be lover, Giovanni Guasconti, is the "center of consciousness" of the tale—the Jamesian term fits, because James learned the craft of point of view from tales like this of Hawthorne—and like Lycius, Giovanni, influenced by a scientist, loses faith in his beloved and causes her death. The role of Apollonius is played, so to speak, by the rival scientists, Rappaccini and Baglioni. The issues of beholding, of different kinds of knowing, of the relation of science to art and nature, are common to both tales. But Hawthorne expands the range of reference, chiefly by allusion, far beyond what Keats attempts, and in so doing complicates those relations of knowledge and of state of being which are the special material of allegorical interpretation. The story's density and complexity require us to examine it in close detail; first I will refresh our memory of its plot.

Giovanni Guasconti comes to Padua from Naples to take up studies at the university. The time of the action may be guessed as during the Renaissance, perhaps the late Renaissance. His lodgings in Padua adjoin the garden of the physician Rappaccini, who breeds poisonous flowers on the theory, we learn, that "all medicinal virtues are comprised within those substances which we term vegetable poisons."* Giovanni sees Rappaccini's daughter, Beatrice, in the garden, and comes to know her and love her after his fashion. The youth is warned by a colleague of Rappaccini, Professor Baglioni, a friend of Giovanni's father, that Rappaccini has used his daughter, and is now using Giovanni, as part of his experiments. Beatrice has so acclimatized herself to the poisonous atmosphere of the garden that she, it appears, becomes poisonous herself. As the tale progresses, Giovanni has evidences that he, too, is becoming poisonous.

As Baglioni presses his warnings, he gives Giovanni a vase containing an antidote and encourages him to administer it to Beatrice. In the last scene in the garden, she confesses that her father's science has estranged her from mankind, and Giovanni gives her the "antidote." Rappaccini, at this point, explains that he has given his daughter, and now Giovanni, marvellous power, the ability to kill with a breath, for which they should be grateful. The antidote overwhelms Beatrice, and as she dies Baglioni, who has been looking out on the garden from a window, calls out to Rappaccini "in a tone of triumph mixed with horror."

Each of the principal characters in the tale, as well as the narrator, would interpret its events in a different way. The simplest understanding is that of Rappaccini himself, but we are never allowed a

---

* I quote from the reprint of the 1883 Riverside Edition of Hawthorne, edited by Hyatt H. Waggoner, *Selected Tales and Sketches*, 3rd ed. (New York, 1970).

direct glimpse of his motives and feelings until the last scene. There he appears as a gothic horror madman, who sacrifices his daughter for the sake of science in the gruesome belief that she would want "to be as terrible as [she is] beautiful." He is, as Baglioni calls him, a "vile empiric," and his function in the story is so mechanical that his own conclusions about the significance of what takes place are of little consequence. Like Archimago, Rappaccini establishes the donnée of the tale—his daughter is poisonous—and having set the action in motion he retires to appear only at the end, announce his inhuman idea, and end "thunderstricken" at his daughter's denial and death. Rappaccini is an allegorical agent, a representative of a certain moral position—science as power—retired from the arena of choice and judgment like a god or a devil.

When we consider Baglioni's interpretation of the raw events just summarized, we touch on complexities of value judgment from a slightly more sophisticated point of view. Baglioni appears as a jovial, warmhearted man in opposition to the cold Rappaccini, and his attitude toward Giovanni is avuncular and paternalistic. Their relationship, then, implies the problems of surrogate father and son. In this case it is clear that Baglioni protects his status with care and considers himself a rival of Rappaccini, not only in the medical profession, but as Giovanni's guardian from an evil potential father-in-law. He mentions that Rappaccini is as learned as any member of the profession in Italy, "with perhaps a single exception," doubtless himself. The narrator warns us that Giovanni would have taken Baglioni's grudging account of Rappaccini's work "with many grains of allowance" if he had known of the "professional warfare" between the scientists. Baglioni thinks of Rappaccini as trying "to snatch the lad out of my hands," as an academic is likely to be jealous of his students, and he vows to "foil" Rappaccini.

In short, Baglioni, like Keats's Apollonius, cannot be considered a disinterested witness to the events. His very offer of an antidote is suspect, and we find ourselves thinking that it is only his word, which the narrator accepts, that the fluid is an antidote at all. His final posture in the tale, looking out of Giovanni's own window onto the garden, just as Giovanni looked out on Rappaccini and his daughter at the beginning of the tale, is presumptuous meddling, verging on peeping; and his gloating over Rappaccini's discomfiture, which amounts to gloating over Beatrice's death, appears to be as amoral as Rappaccini's behavior. The problematic character of Baglioni prohibits us from interpreting Giovanni's dilemma as an allegorical conflict between cold and warm science.

Beatrice's view is more complicated, but still not complete. She knows that Giovanni can see evidence of the poisonous atmosphere she exudes, but she begs him to believe only what she says—the "outward senses" may lie, but her words are "true from the depths of the heart outward." The experiment to which her father submitted her made her lonely, and her love for Giovanni made her recognize her loneliness and discover happiness. She seems innocent, like an infant, and her hurt when Giovanni curses her for drawing him into the poison lets her accept her death easily. She admits that she is "the horrible thing" Giovanni calls her.

As Beatrice dies she tells Giovanni, "Thy words of hatred are like lead within my heart; but they, too, will fall away as I ascend. Oh, was there not, from the first, more poison in thy nature than in mine?" This judgment is the most powerful so far: she recognizes that Giovanni has failed her, and that her physical poison finds its counterpart in his character. These words hint at an essentially allegorical interpretation: in this tale, the physical fact of poison reifies a poison normally found, outside of fiction, in such expressions as "a poisonous atmosphere" (of envy, egotism, greed, jealousy, etc.) or "she is poison" (she terrifies me; I should not love her). At the moment of her death, Beatrice understands the relation between her fantastic physical poison and Giovanni's all too human meta-phorical poison. Beatrice's character raises questions which we need to examine further in relation to matters beyond her knowledge, but her own insight goes far enough to prohibit us from interpreting the story simply as a conflict between empirical scientific knowledge and loving intuition.

Giovanni shares with the narrator the primary point of view of the story. Nearly all the action is seen through his eyes, and his thoughts are openly revealed. His consciousness is the locus of the main problem which the tale presents—doubt. Most of his performance in the first part of the story is looking, especially through his window, and assembling evidence about Beatrice and the garden as his interest grows. Hawthorne takes care to present the objects which Giovanni beholds in the most ambiguous manner, so that the first pages put the reader through a bewildering maze of alternating interpretations.

Giovanni associates Beatrice with the purplest, most poison flower; the narrator draws back, and suggests that Giovanni saw "mysteries" in the garden because of the influence of the light of the declining sun. In the daylight Giovanni inclines toward "a most rational view of the whole matter," setting aside his "wonder-working fancy." Beatrice embraces the dark shrub, and Giovanni sees that drops from the flower kill a lizard. Again, the narrator suggests that Giovanni has had too much wine, and also that he "could scarcely have seen anything so minute" from that distance. An insect flies near Beatrice and dies; the narrator assures us that Giovanni's "eyes deceived him." It "seemed to Giovanni" that a bouquet quickly wilts in her hands; the narrator tells us he could not have seen the fading flowers at "so great a distance."

These incidents show the narrator communing with Giovanni's own dark thoughts and rationalizations, and counterpointing his judgments. It turns out that Beatrice is poisonous and of course the narrator knows this, according to the convention that a writer sets down his story after the fact. But the narrator joins Giovanni in ignorance and "uneasy suspicion," seeming to avoid the facts. This again is conventional, the skillful storyteller's withholding of information in order to maintain suspense; but I will argue that the ambiguity of Giovanni's perceptions has further meaning, that his alternating moony fancies and daylight rationalizations actually affect what he sees.

Returning to Giovanni's interpretation of the events in which he participates, we find him more and more fascinated with Beatrice and unable to suspect her when he is in her presence. When he is alone, or being warned by Baglioni, he doubts her: "hope and dread kept a continual warfare in his breast." His doubts are darkly described: "horrible suspicions that rose, monster-like, out of the caverns of his heart" and "dim suspicions which now grinned at him like so many demons." For a time the doubts are repressed as "the shapeless half ideas which throng the dim region beyond the daylight of our perfect consciousness." He senses a pressure to allegorize his interior. We should compare Glauce's remark to Britomart, "Or why make ye such Monster of your mind?" He splits Beatrice—"It mattered not whether she were angel or demon"—so that her double nature corresponds to his doubled heart. His love fails to integrate either his beloved or himself, to see her as a man sees a woman. His thoughts are, metaphorically, poison, and his breath reifies the metaphor: "Again Giovanni sent forth a breath, deeper, longer, and imbued with a venomous feeling out of his heart: he knew not whether he were wicked or only desperate." The spider at which the breath was directed dies.

His utterances, allegorized as his poison breath, his "blighting words" as the narrator calls them, contrast with Beatrice's unsullied conversation, which the narrator compares with a new, Edenic fountain, fresh, sparkling, and brilliant like the fountain in the garden. Giovanni struggles, for a time, with the venom in his system, but when he finds himself blasting flowers and killing spiders he gives himself up for cursed and takes the darkest view, which Beatrice confirms. We have no access to Giovanni's thoughts when Beatrice dies; the story we have been reading works out these thoughts, commenting on Giovanni through the narrator, and enlarging our moral perspective by presenting objects and references of which the narrator himself is unaware.

The narrator of "Rappaccini's Daughter" intrudes his own judgments with clarity and force. He speaks as Giovanni's alter ego, expressing as fact what the young man only dimly and fitfully perceives. Not as brilliantly focussed as the narrators of *The Scarlet Letter* and *The Blithedale Romance*, still he is of their kind, and makes critical judgments on the tale. As we would expect, his perspective is that of a humanitarian and an older man, who can speak of "the tendency of heartbreak natural to a younger man." His principal critique is that Giovanni's head is split off from heart: " . . . the fantasy of a young man's brain, only slightly or not at all connected with his heart"; "Guasconti had not a deep heart"; his vanity is "the token of a certain shallowness of feeling and insincerity of character"; he has "bitterly wronged" Beatrice with his blighting words; he has "that cunning semblance of love which flourishes in the imagination." Beatrice, on the other hand, "was capable, surely, on her part, of the height and heroism of love"; later, more emphatically, "the real Beatrice was a heavenly angel. Incapable as [Giovanni] was of such high faith . . . . " We cannot doubt where the narrator stands, and his insistent judgments force us to consider a strange possibility—that if Giovanni had loved Beatrice more deeply and with higher faith, the poison might have left them.

The narrator reads the physical venom allegorically as a metaphor of the lovers' relation. If the narrator were an actor in the tale, we must imagine him exorcizing the curse as Britomart exorcises the House of Busyrane, by returning metaphorical language to its place, outside the physical world. The key passage is this one:

> Besides, thought Giovanni, might there not still be a hope of his returning within the limits of ordinary nature, and leading Beatrice, the redeemed Beatrice, by the hand? O, weak, and selfish, and unworthy spirit that could dream of an earthly union and earthly happiness as possible, after such deep love had been so bitterly wronged as was Beatrice's love by Giovanni's blighting words! No, no; there could be no such hope. She must pass heavily, with that broken heart, across the borders of Time— she must bathe her hurts in some fount of paradise, and forget her grief in the light of immortality, and *there* be well.
> But Giovanni did not know it.

If Giovanni had not blighted the flower of his love, we understand, "ordinary nature" would be granted him; but he makes Beatrice a demon in the garden and an angel in heaven, never a woman. What Beatrice is physically opposes what she is morally; the failure to reconcile this division is Giovanni's. The passage is weighted with irony as it alludes to another Beatrice and another fount, but these are matters beyond the view of the narrator. We have examined the characters' ambiguous and conflicting ideas of their actions; now we must perform interpretations of our own.

OTHER EDENS

In his sketch "The New Adam and Eve," Hawthorne sets an innocent pair in Boston on the day after the abolition of man in order to test the human arts—institutions, learning, customs—against uncivilized nature. We need such a fantasy to see how corrupt we are because, he writes, "It is only through the medium of the imagination that we can lessen those iron fetters, which we call truth and reality, and make ourselves even partially sensible what prisoners we are." When Giovanni comes to Padua, he is given, through the superhuman agency of Rappaccini, just such an imaginative experience, and he has the rare opportunity, normally available to men only through the medium of fiction, to choose whether to accept the reality which his imagination grasps or the ordinary reality of this world. Giovanni acts, in this sense, as a reader of fiction—he is "one of us"; hence our confused, uncomfortable feeling when the narrator becomes increasingly critical of him.

Giovanni is a new Adam in a new Eden. Eden is another world, parallel to ours and present in our imagination, in which the original knowledge, the original power of naming and worshipping, the original choice, are presented pure, stripped of the sophistication of history. In "The New Adam and Eve," the couple make the right choices: they are "satisfied to be" and "content with an inner sphere which they inhabit together." As they explore the artifacts of civilization and the profusion of nature, they decide what to incorporate into their new life and what to pass by as distasteful and counter to the intuitions of their hearts. They choose, at least on the first day, to depend on nature, to seek God, and to love one another. Giovanni chooses otherwise.

He enters Padua as an outsider. He is young, Neapolitan, and of Greek appearance, and therefore closer to the original fount of experience, the south and the east, than the professors with whom he mingles. The newness of things offers him a rare perspective, so that he can compare the garden with the city around it in unusual freedom from convention. "The young man rejoiced that, in the heart of the barren city, he had the privilege of overlooking this spot of lovely and luxuriant vegetation. It would serve, he said to himself, as a symbolic language to keep him in communion with Nature." His task, like Adam's (and like the reader's), is to decide which elements of the language of the garden are natural.

So far I have suppressed Rappaccini's responsibility for his own garden, and I mean to go further along this line. Beatrice tells Giovanni that "this garden is [her father's] world," and later she shocks him by mentioning that her father "created" the central shrub. Rappaccini is the God of the garden, "that Eden of poisonous flowers," but it is only confusing to conceive of him as other than an evil parody of the God of *Paradise Lost*, who leaves the gardeners free by retiring from it. Rappaccini cannot even touch his creation, whereas Beatrice embraces it passionately, like a sister. For Giovanni the garden becomes "the whole space in which he might be said to live"; it is his language, his Eden, his responsibility. Giovanni and Beatrice stand in the garden "in utter solitude." The garden is constructed by magic, and whether it is to be considered natural, or taken for an alternate nature, depends on a human decision. Rappaccini's relation to the garden corresponds to an author's relation to a fiction: the author need not be held responsible for a particular reader's response.

Hawthorne alludes to another isolated world, the island of *The Tempest*, which also resembles Eden:

> The tinge of passion that had colored Beatrice's manner vanished; she became gay, and appeared to derive a pure delight from her communion with the youth not unlike what the maiden of a lonely island might have felt conversing with a voyager from the civilized world. Evidently her experience of life had been confined within the limits of that garden.

Beatrice resembles Miranda, a *tabula rasa* whose nurture has been so carefully isolated and controlled that her nature shines through, although it has been physically corrupted by the anti-Prospero, Rappaccini. Her isolation makes her character a scientific study, as if she were an experiment in human design or a figure in allegory, abstracted from the contingencies of human association. *The Tempest* —and more recent isolation romances, like Conrad's *Victory* and much recent science fiction—share this feature. In Hawthorne's tale, however, it is the "voyager from the civilized world," the Ferdinand, who draws our attention; Giovanni, the emissary from earth to the green space, must judge it as our representative.

Elements of the garden stand at a remove from the natural world because they are works of art. The marble fountain is in ruins; but the living species, the young couple and the plants, are both artifacts of Rappaccini, who is like "an artist who should spend his life in achieving a picture or a group of statuary and finally be satisfied with his success" in forming the pair. The plants "shock" both the narrator and Beatrice, "by an appearance of artificialness indicating that there had been such a commixture, and, as it were, adultery, of various vegetable species, that the production was no longer of God's making, but the monstrous offspring of man's depraved fancy, glowing only with an evil mockery of beauty." The plants are bastards like those which Perdita scorns in *The Winter's Tale*; they are *natura innaturata*, or art. Giovanni's responsibility is doubly complicated. First, the nature which he "reads," especially Beatrice, must be sorted out from the art imposed upon it (again we recall our burden as readers). Second, he himself, made artificial, venomous, by Rappaccini's science, needs to unperplex his own consciousness in order to see clearly. Time will not distinguish art from nature for him, as it has distinguished the natural fountain from its artful basin; Giovanni's decision will be momentary and eternal. The symbol of Giovanni's decision, the vial of antidote wrought by Cellini, both precipitates the conclusion of the tale and suggests the quality of Giovanni's choice—he has set art against art, and finds destruction instead of solution.

The two largest heterocosms to which Hawthorne alludes are the antique world of Vertumnus and Pomona and the Christian afterlife of Dante's Beatrice. The statue of Vertumnus in Rappaccini's garden recalls Ovid's account of the successful suit (involving mendacity) of a goddess in a garden and works in the tale as the story of Hermes and the nymph works in *Lamia*, by pointing to an unperplexed, direct, pagan, and natural kind of loving which is not available to humans. Hermes appears early in Keats's poem, and Vertumnus appears early in Hawthorne's tale, just as the comparable myth of Venus and Adonis, a love troubled only by nature itself in the form of a boar, appears early in Book Three of *The Faerie Queene*. None of these myths presents utterly uncomplicated love, but they point toward an ideal of eternal and guiltless enjoyment.

The allusions to Dante likewise suggest a love beyond Giovanni's grasp, but in this case the fault is Giovanni's. The Neapolitan attains only that state of infatuation followed by treachery which the Florentine reached before his vision (Dante confesses he was untrue to the memory of Beatrice). But Dante met his Beatrice again, when he was purged and renewed like a new Adam, at the top of the mount of Purgatory in the Earthly Paradise, whence she led him to his celestial vision. Giovanni kills his Beatrice and turns the garden to hell, like Donne's speaker in "Twicknam Garden," an Adam and serpent at once. He cannot go "leading Beatrice, the redeemed Beatrice," back to the natural world; but he could have hoped she would redeem him.

Just as Hawthorne sought, in this and others of his tales, to introduce us to another world—strange, foreign, antique, bathed in the
moonlight and covered in the moss of romance—so Giovanni encounters a new world, placed in the very heart of the old, as if it
were the unacknowledged center of civilized Padua. He responds to
it in all the wrong ways: he tolerates art in Eden, tries to be a Prospero
to Rappaccini's Prospero, and contributes to the adulteration of
Beatrice; he is transformed, not with redeeming love and final vision,
but with venomous matter.

THE SENSE OF LOVE : SEXUALITY AND IDEALISM

So far we have examined two kinds of allegory in "Rappaccini's
Daughter." The first, the reification of the ethical metaphor "poisonous," derives from the difference between the clichés of language
and the actuality of things. The second kind is typology, the assumed
relation between the carefully isolated garden with its inhabitants
and the vision of Eden, filtered through the various Edens of Pomona,
Dante, and Prospero, as corrupt or artificial. Both allegorical meanings expand the dimensions of the tale to include absolute, primal
moral significance and issues which touch upon man's deepest nature.
A third kind of allegory, the veiled reference to sexuality, reminds us
of the old theory that allegory conceals.

Hawthorne gives us the clue to this enigma in the person of old
Dame Lisabetta, who leads Giovanni to a "private entrance into
the garden" by way of obscure passages, just as old Angela brought
Porphyro, "Stol'n to this paradise," to Madeline's chamber in "The
Eve of St. Agnes." Porphyro intended a sexual conquest; Giovanni's
similar intentions are suppressed and confused. The *hortus conclusus*,
in the commonplace figure, symbolizes maidenhead—we find Giovanni "forcing himself through the entanglement of a shrub that
wreathed its tendrils over the hidden entrance," in the sort of
anatomical allegory Spenser had used and Melville was to use.

Our awareness, and Giovanni's partial awareness, of his sexual
desires, come slowly. Giovanni first enters the garden—after some
time spent only *gardant*—and he converses with Beatrice.

271

Ever and anon there gleamed across the young man's mind a sense of wonder that he should be walking side by side with the being who had so wrought upon his imagination, whom he had idealized in such hues of terror, in whom he had positively witnessed such manifestations of dreadful attributes—that he should be conversing with Beatrice like a brother, and should find her so human and maidenlike.

It is when he ceases to converse with her as a brother and behaves as a lover toward a maiden that the poison enters the relationship. They walk by the shrub and Beatrice says she had, for the first time, forgotten its presence. In a courtly gesture, Giovanni makes as if to pluck one of the purple flowers; she shrieks, catches his hand, and exclaims, "Touch it not!" The scene would make sense if we substituted the rose of chastity for the poisonous flower. We learn that her touch of his hand, which he discovers leaves a purple print, is the only contact they ever have, "so marked was the physical barrier between them." She arouses a "fever pitch" of feeling in Giovanni: "she had at least instilled a fierce and subtle poison into his system. It was not love . . . nor horror . . . but a wild offspring of both love and horror . . . ."

The lovers' fears have different motivations. We understand Beatrice's fear as like Amoret's, as natural enough, if excessive; what is wanting is a Scudamour or a Britomart to exercise the boldness which gets the nod from Venus or which disenchants. Giovanni fails to assume this charge. He fears Beatrice as Alexander the Great learned to fear the woman whose "love would have been poison—her embrace death." Hawthorne gathered this story, which is repeated by Baglioni, from Sir Thomas Browne; its more immediately sexual meaning points to the suppressed content of "Rappaccini's Daughter." Hawthorne uses sexuality in a formal way; he interests himself in the formal relationship of matter to spirit, of natural impulses to human reason and will. Spenser has taught us that, in properly attuned love, sexuality and reason are in harmony, like matter and spirit. The force of natural will involved in sexuality brings an immediate and passionate response to a metaphysical problem.

"The Maypole of Merrymount" and *The Scarlet Letter* trace Hawthorne's concern with the transformation of attitudes toward sexuality in and out of the more or less spiritual state of marriage, and his concern with the consequences of sexual commitment as a paradigm of man's commitment to his own dual being, half angel and half beast. Giovanni's fear of his sexuality, the monster he makes of his own mind, allegorizes his fear to acknowledge what he is, a human being of matter and mind. The fear is poison. He fends off his nature with a mental construction, as some pagan sculptor enclosed the fountain, or as Cellini wrought the vial which encloses the antidote. Giovanni tries to counteract Rappaccini's art—Hawthorne gives the term "art" its inclusive older sense—with a borrowed art of his own, but he should have responded to nature with nature, have seen the fountain of running water in the corrupt vessel of Beatrice, the flower of her beauty which supports the poison. The objects, from one point of view, are associated with decadence and death, but from another point of view they are the furniture of paradise.

The narrator, speaking of Giovanni's mingled love and horror of Beatrice, remarks, "Blessed are all simple emotions, be they dark or bright! It is the lurid intermixture of the two that produces the illuminating blaze of the infernal regions." This lurid intermixture may not be blessed, but it is a favorite lighting effect of Hawthorne's, a harsher version of the moonlight, twilight chiaroscuros which are his element. The dim glow of romance may be analyzed, when the demons are closer to the surface, into its parts—glaring light and blackness—as in "The Celestial Railroad" or "The Birthmark." In "Rappaccini's Daughter" the lurid intermixture resides only in Giovanni's heart, but an analogous confusion in odor, another medium than light, affects the atmosphere of the tale.

Baglioni seems to smell the poison in Giovanni's apartment, but Giovanni denies it:

" . . . nor, I think, is there any fragrance except in your worship's imagination. Odors, being a sort of element combined of the sensual and the spiritual, are apt to deceive us in this manner. The recollection of a perfume, the bare idea of it, may easily be mistaken for a present reality."

Hawthorne can use odor because of the metaphor of poison and can reinforce his theme that what is perceived is altered by the perceiving faculty. The sense of smell, easily confused, weak in "memory," displays the power of mind over matter and raises doubt about immediate perception itself. The problematic relation between odor and the sense of smell constitutes a good proof of Romantic idealism.

We can set the problem in terms of the pair of myths in *The Romance of the Rose*, those of Narcissus and Pygmalion, which underlie Hawthorne's tales "Monsieur du Miroir" and "Drowne's Wooden Image." At one point Hawthorne puts Giovanni before his mirror, "a vanity to be expected in a beautiful young man" but "the token of a certain shallowness of feeling and insincerity of character." When he sees that a fresh bouquet of flowers has drooped in his hands, "Giovanni grew white as marble, and stood motionless before the mirror, staring at his own reflection there as at the likeness of something frightful." Giovanni is narcissistic, uninitiate in love, and his incapacity to love Beatrice is poisonous; he projects his own poisonous doubts and fears onto her, as onto a mirror image—"he fell down grovelling among earthly doubts, and defiled therewith the rare whiteness of Beatrice's image."

His development is arrested in narcissism; unlike the carver Drowne in the other tale, he cannot break out of himself to add spirit to his art and to bring Beatrice to life. He grows white as marble before his mirror because the failure to bring life, as Pygmalion did, into one's creation—the failure to see and love another as an other—is a failure to live. If Pygmalion had not succeeded in bringing the statue to life, he would have become a statue himself, like Narcissus, merging into his own image in death. This choice appears in "Egotism; or, The Bosom Serpent." At the end of that tale, Roderick, whose "diseased self-contemplation" takes the form of an internalized serpent, is saved at a fountain side by his estranged wife, who has the grace to make him "forget [himself] in the idea of another." The serpent leaves him. Giovanni, like Roderick, carries within him the venom of self-knowledge, the knowledge of sin; but Giovanni does not find the antidote, knowledge of another, love. Beatrice holds a better position, wishing, as we can imagine Eve having wished, "I fain would rid myself of even that small knowledge."

It is helpful to turn to still another tale for a related theme, which also has a curious connection to *The Romance of the Rose*. I refer to the Great Carbuncle, in the tale of that title, which has marvellous power:

... a radiance was breaking through the mist, and changing
its dim hue to a dusky red, which continually grew more vivid,
as if brilliant particles were interfused with the gloom. Now,
also, the cloud began to roll away from the mountain, while,
as it heavily withdrew, one object after another started out of
its impenetrable obscurity into sight, with precisely the effect
of a new creation, before the indistinctness of the old chaos had
been completely swallowed up.

Like Jean de Meun and Spenser, Hawthorne follows the old lapidary
tradition that a carbuncle generates light out of itself. Here we find it
dawning, creating the landscape like God, forming an Eden. However, the various seekers after the carbuncle make it their own: each
has his own purpose for the jewel, and each defines its meaning
according to his own idea of the truth. As pure, self-generating light,
the carbuncle is wholly object, wholly other, wholly responsible for
informing the rest of creation; it is the center of an essentialist universe.
As the object of a quest, it is pure subject, wholly internalized,
reconstituted in each seeker's mind; it is the name for a set of intentions in an existentialist universe. Comparison with Melville's Drummond light is inevitable: the Drummond light is not self-generated,
but powered by new technology, and it is compared to fictional
characters, not to the creating deity. Of both lights it could be said
"Everything starts up to it," like the jar in Tennessee in Stevens's
poem. Both light and jewel symbolize the possibility that the center
of the universe can be shifted to create new worlds, especially new
moral worlds, in which it is man's responsibility to fix the center.

The analogues to the Great Carbuncle in "Rappaccini's Daughter"
are the central fountain and the shrub, a configuration which recalls
the *beau parc* of *The Romance of the Rose* and is based ultimately on the
description of Eden. The fountain sparkles "into the sunlight," and
the purple flowers, again and again, are called gems. The flowers
glow; one which Beatrice plucks "almost glimmered with the dazzling
effect of a precious stone." The shrub "seemed enough to illuminate
the garden, even had there been no sunshine." Giovanni observes an
"analogy between the beautiful girl and the gorgeous shrub that
hung its gemlike flowers over the fountain" which is expressed in
terms of light:

275

Her spirit gushed out before him like a fresh rill that was just catching its first glimpse of the sunlight and wondering at the reflections of earth and sky which were flung into its bosom. There came thoughts, too, from a deep source, and fantasies of a gemlike brilliancy, as if diamonds and rubies sparkled upward among the bubbles of the fountain.

The water is new, Edenic, and somehow both reflects and radiates light.

Giovanni lives under two suns. One is the everyday sun. He feels "a little ashamed to find how real and matter-of-fact an affair [the garden] proved to be, in the first rays of the sun. . . . " This sun wakes him, one morning, "to a sense of pain"—the first glimmering that Beatrice's touch is poison. The other sun is the shrub, and its analogue is "the pure light of her character," which alters everything: "she glowed amid the sunlight . . . positively illuminated the more shadowy intervals of the garden path." There are several hints that while Giovanni is "basking in the Oriental sunshine of her beauty" he is dreaming. Once, arrested in the street by Baglioni, he "stared forth wildly from his inner world into the outer one and spoke like a man in a dream." In this dreamy inner world, we have noticed, he carries his own source of light, "the illuminating blaze of the infernal regions."

The alternate systems of illumination, like the alternate worlds superimposed upon the garden, compel interpretation and choice. Revelations are plural and merely partial; they depend on where Giovanni stands or the light in which he considers things. Either the broad sun which lights Padua or the gleaming jewel of Beatrice and her flowers is the reckoning point on which his astrolabe fixes to determine the orientation of the world and its true geography. The last resort of light resides inside himself, and we have seen that it is composed of glare and gloom, that it is not a good light to read by.

CONCLUSIONS

In this chapter I have used, with a layman's imprecision, a philosophical term whose ambiguity suggests a link between the modes of allegory of the Renaissance and of the romantic poets. Let me simplify in order to polarize a general condition. "Idealism," in the Renaissance scheme of things, refers to the Platonic conception of special entities which lie behind the sensible world and give it shape. The Ideas are "intelligible" but not visible; they can be imagined to reside in a mythical heaven, but in truth they are philosophical constructions found necessary to account for such concepts as sameness and difference or unity and multiplicity, or to assert the order of the world in spite of the irregularity of phenomena. Romantic idealism likewise feels a need to account for the intelligible scheme underlying the confused tangle of sense impressions. In both periods the descriptive power of mathematics, which seems to penetrate the darkest secrets of the universe, gives evidence of an elegant and simple form underlying phenomena. But Romantic philosophy—the Continental philosophy which grew out of Leibnitz and Kant—reconstitutes the ordering Ideas as mental entities, categories of thought. The Platonic forms are abolished, and new, interiorized forms are conceived of either as limitations on man, as arbitrary but ineluctable channels of perception and rationality, or as freedom for man, giving him responsibility for what exists in the world. In this rough distinction, for a Renaissance thinker the Good would be the divinely substantiated Idea which makes sense of various good phenomena; but for a Romantic thinker the Good has no such existence, but can only be thought of as the adjective applied to an action upon the judgment of an individual. Both idealisms degrade matter to the status of a function: in the older system, to a function of the eternal Idea; in the more recent system, to a function of the mind.

Some consequences of this shift can be detected in the Romantic poets and their successors. The most powerful, creative faculty of the mind, which is by definition the imagination, whatever that is, transcends all else. In the extreme view, avoided by nearly everyone, the imagination stands alone—this is solipsism. The room for doubt of the validity of phenomena, of moral judgments, or of anything, is enlarged in proportion as the individual mind is felt to be limited. Words are distrusted as arbitrary constructions placed upon phenomena which lump all good things into a category, the word *good*, when the category has no objective existence. The science of psychology best reveals the change: we think of Renaissance psychology as the discovery of physiological materials, such as humours, in their relation to spiritual entities, such as the intelligences represented by the stars; whereas Romantic psychology is the study of perception, sensation, language, dreams, memory, learning, "association of ideas," of the furniture and operation of the mind.

We have seen that Renaissance idealism supports allegory by posing the analogy between concrete phenomena and spiritual truth. The later concept of mind did not yet exist; the human faculties were conceived as the meeting place of nature—the outside world and the physiological equilibrium which reflects the outside world—and grace, the divine presence which is granted to humans. I think if Spenser could have understood what I mean by the word "consciousness," the absolute, inalienable core of my self which is prior to reason and perception, he would have denied its existence, or more likely, he would have explained to me that I referred to the image of God which exists at the center of my being. Renaissance allegory is simply the exposition or expression, in its most direct fictional form, of the systematic correspondences of the things of this world and their fulfillment—their final intelligibility, justice, authentication, cause, and resting place—in grace.

Romantic idealism likewise supports allegory. The notion that existence is privately generated takes form in fictions in which a center of consciousness (not a necessity in pre-Romantic fiction), usually a particular character, causes by his behavior and perception the events and objects which surround him. When Beatrice shrieks, forbidding Giovanni to touch a purple flower, she flees, and Giovanni notices that Rappaccini has been watching them. In the strict and extended view of Romantic idealism which the poets could explore, Giovanni caused the appearance of Rappaccini; or, to look at it from another point of view, we are expected to interpret the appearance of Rappaccini as if it were a consequence of Giovanni's mental state—namely, his sense of the poison involved in love.

These two widely different grounds of allegory, these two idealisms, can take precisely the same fictional form. Sansjoy can be interpreted as projected out of Redcrosse in just the same way that Baglioni can be interpreted as projected out of Giovanni. The difference is that Sansjoy really is a part of Redcrosse—the knight is divided within himself—who might as well be expressed as a humanoid opponent. A being like Sansjoy exists in real men, outside of fiction. But Baglioni is a figment: if a man carried around within himself such notions as Baglioni represents, we would say he was deluded, that he lived in fiction. Outside of fiction, a Romantic thinker would deny the existence of a being like Sansjoy as part of the mind—the mind does not come in parts. We do not have wars of virtues and vices within us, but schizophrenia; divisions within us are considered immature or pathological, fictions of accommodation and self-protection. Our integrity is not achieved by the unity of nature and grace in revelation, but by the acknowledgment of the fictional status of nature and grace, and the consequent revelation of our self as a unity. For a Romantic, Archimago, the creator of illusory beings who confront the struggling soul, is not independent, but is the self.

I think it is fair to say that, with regard to these issues, Hawthorne is a knowing reactionary. He focussed the matter at its crucial places, at the sense of sin, and at love, where men are most conscious of themselves and of the problematic relation between themselves and the outside world. A story like "Egotism; or The Bosom Serpent" contains representations of three different states of consciousness: first, people satirized as unaware of sin; second, Roderick conscious only of sin (which is comparable to Narcissus loving only his own image); and finally, Herkimer and Rosina, who bring Roderick to the saving consciousness of love, beside the fountain which symbolizes the unity of nature and grace. Roderick's sin, however, is self-consciousness itself. The story expresses as a development what Hawthorne considered a constant human condition: the need for the terrible consciousness of the arbitrariness of the world and the self's responsibility for it, balanced by the attendant or consequent need of love, a willing commitment to another.

When we speak of love here, we refer not to affection or passion but to the mere acknowledgment that another, independent consciousness exists. This is the hardest love. No reason can be given for maintaining such a love: Kierkegaard called it absurd and compared it with Abraham's absurd faith. At his best moments, I believe, Hawthorne accepts that faith in all its difficulty. When he writes at second best, he either assumes the faith too easily or too easily rejects it; he turns mawkishly sentimental or fashionably dark. At his best Hawthorne rewrites Spenser for the modern world.

Keats does not address the issue squarely in *Lamia*, but only provides the materials for direct treatment. Lycius never really loves, or he loves tentatively and in delusion. He has not been purged by consciousness of sin, hence he scarcely knows himself; much less can he acknowledge, in any profound way, his beloved. He lives in a dreamy, pagan, subjective world of childlike eroticism and imperious egotism, a Busyrane world. When Apollonius confronts Lamia, Lycius understands himself at last—his soul is analyzed in front of him—and he passes out, like Narcissus, in a self-recognition which spells the end of his enchanted ignorance. There is no room for self-consciousness in a mythical world. Let me state the problem again. One might love, as Hermes does in *Lamia*, without self-consciousness; such love can even be considered an ideal. But humans are such that the process of loving, or the onset of love, arouses self-consciousness. For humans, the knowledge of self amounts to the knowledge of sin; it is alluring, and it tends to obliterate the existence of everything but the self. A real love, if it can exist, must possess this knowledge and love anyway.

Hawthorne presents the problem in the clearest possible way. Exotic, "romantic" as the setting is, "Rappaccini's Daughter" stands squarely in the Christian world; "perhaps" a former occupant of Giovanni's lodgings had a place in Dante's Inferno. Unlike Keats's old Corinth, the Christian world has room for its fallen. Giovanni enters this world with a curiosity, inspired by a healthy sexuality, equalled only by his readers' curiosity, inspired by other motives. The space of the main action emphatically constitutes an "other world" for Giovanni, in which his actions and speech bear, with unusual clarity, a heavy burden of responsibility. He is a new Adam, entrusted with the old freedom and the old choice; he is a new Ferdinand, who can participate in Beatrice's brave new world, or give it up. When he reaches that terrible state of consciousness and inchoate love which Narcissus and Lycius before him reached, Giovanni retreats, unlike them, at his own risk; he is liable to damnation.

Giovanni considers the garden "a a symbolic language to keep him in communion with nature." Beatrice asks him to trust her words, not what he sees. When Giovanni realizes his situation, he addresses Beatrice with "blighting words." He has never reached out to Beatrice, to the source of the fountain of sparkling words which she pours forth. When the story reaches its climax, and the dreamy ignorance of Giovanni, his wordy unbelief, collapses into knowledge, he falls silent. His fiction, his allegory of poison and magic, ceases. In other, more positive tales, Hawthorne shows us the aftermath of such crises of love. Generally, in their new consciousness the lovers find themselves inhabitants of a new society, happy or grim, or in society transformed by a new vision: "Young Goodman Brown," "The Maypole of Merrymount," *The Scarlet Letter*, "The New Adam and Eve." We do not know what becomes of Giovanni after his fall. Perhaps we can imagine him, like the Mariner, telling his twice-told tale to others, so filling it with allusions, metaphors, turns of phrase, symbols, and intruded judgments that the knowledge he acquired will be accessible to anyone who listens. The interpretation of the garden may not be as difficult at second hand.

Bibliographical Note

The best studies of *Lamia* are those of Earl R. Wasserman, *The Finer Tone: Keats' Major Poems* (Baltimore, 1953); David Perkins, *The Quest for Permanence: The Symbolism of Wordsworth, Shelley, and Keats* (Cambridge, Mass., 1959); Walter Jackson Bate, *John Keats* (Cambridge, Mass., 1963). I owe the comparison of Lamia's colors to the "whiteness of the whale" to Michael Stillman; and I believe Robert Langbaum, who taught me most of what I know about Romantic poetry, noted Apollonius's serpentinism. An interesting study of the background is Nai-Tung Ting, "The Holy Man and the Snake-Woman: A Study of the Lamia Story in Asian and European Literature," *Fabula* 8 (1966): 145–91.

"Rappaccini's Daughter" has been much studied; for a good review of criticism see Nicholas Ayo, "The Labyrinthine Ways of 'Rappaccini's Daughter,'" *RS* 42 (1974): 56–69. Ayo says the text of the forthcoming Centenary edition will not vary significantly from the old Riverside. The best general accounts are those of Roy R. Male, *Hawthorne's Tragic Vision* (Austin, Texas, 1957); Hyatt H. Waggoner, *Hawthorne: A Critical Study* (Cambridge, Mass., 1955, rev. 1963); and Richard Harter Fogle, *Hawthorne's Fiction: The Light and the Dark* (Norman, Okla., 1952, rev. 1964). Most interpretations focus on the question of which of the principals holds center stage, on how the Eden material works, and on the reliability of the various points of view. They can be located by use of the MLA bibliography.

The connections, which are not conclusively demonstrated, between Hawthorne's tales and the works of Keats, Hoffman, and Tieck, are examined by Hubert I. Cohen, "Hoffman's 'The Sandman': A Possible Source for 'Rappaccini's Daughter,'" *ESQ* n. s. 18 (1972): 148–53; Norman A. Anderson, "'Rappaccini's Daughter': A Keatsian Analogue?" *PMLA* 83 (1968): 271–83; and Eberhard Alsen, "Hawthorne: A Puritan Tieck: A Comparative Analysis of the Tales of Hawthorne and the Märchen of Tieck," Indiana diss., 1967 (*DAI* [1967] 2199A). This last I have not seen.

The sexual implications of the garden are noticed everywhere, but particularly in Richard B. Hovey, "Love and Hate in 'Rappaccini's Daughter,'" *The Univ. of Kansas City Review* 29 (1962): 137–45; Oliver Evans, "Allegory and Incest in 'Rappaccini's Daughter,'" *NCF* 19 (1964): 185–95; and Frederick C. Crews, *The Sins of the Fathers: Hawthorne's Psychological Themes* (New York, 1966). The background to the poison motif is sketched by Jackson Campbell Boswell, "Bosom Serpents before Hawthorne: Origin of a Symbol," *ELN* 12 (1975): 279–87; who leads us to look back again to Alecto.

Of more general studies which shed light on the tale, I note again the books by Feidelson and Matthiessen mentioned in the note to chapter five. R. W. B. Lewis has brilliantly summarized the meanings of Eden for Americans of the period in *The American Adam: Innocence, Tragedy, and Tradition in the Nineteenth Century* (Chicago, 1955). A fine, brief glance at mirrors and narcissism in Hawthorne is in Malcolm Cowley, "Hawthorne in Solitude," *A Many-Windowed House* (Carbondale and Edwardsville, Ill., and London, 1970). On Hawthorne's attitude toward allegory see John O. Rees, Jr., "Hawthorne's Concept of Allegory: A Reconsideration," *PQ* 54 (1975): 494–510; and John E. Becker, *Hawthorne's Historical Allegory: An Examination of the American Conscience* (Port Washington, New York, and London, 1971).

CHAPTER NINE

Without a Counterpart

KAFKA'S *The Castle*

What in the midst lay but the Tower itself?
   The round squat turret, blind as the fool's heart,
   Built of brown stone, without a counterpart
In the whole world.

BROWNING, "Childe Roland to the Dark Tower Came"

The crows maintain that a single crow could destroy the heavens. Doubtless that is so, but it proves nothing against the heavens, for the heavens signify simply: the impossibility of crows.

KAFKA, *Reflections*, 29

Imagine someone using a line as a rule in the following way: he holds a pair of compasses, and carries one of the points along the line that is the 'rule,' while the other one draws the line that follows the rule. And while he moves along the ruling line he alters the opening of the compasses, apparently with great precision, looking at the rule the whole time as if it determined what he did. And watching him we see no kind of regularity in this opening and shutting of the compasses. We cannot learn his way of following the line from it. Here perhaps one really would say, "The original seems to *intimate* to him which way he is to go. But it is not a rule."

WITTGENSTEIN, *Philosophical Investigation*, 237

SPENSER affirms, and Hawthorne sometimes affirms, that salvation comes to man if he can sustain a knowing relationship to himself, to nature, to history, and to God by the agency of grace and through the medium of love. The dissolution of any of these relations dissolves manhood itself, and leaves man empty and alone, adrift in ambiguity, in a vertigo of arbitrary sensations and disconnected reasons. The mode of allegory could pose these relations, of man's interior to the outside world, of events to history, and of human development to divine providence; in fact allegory simply expresses these relations in most immediate fiction. The sin of pride, in Spenser's age, is the arrogation of an improper place in the scheme of relations; but as we have seen, for Hawthorne and for a dominant tradition of Romanticism, a new pride, not always considered a sin, is the denial of the validity of the relations themselves in what Hawthorne called egotism or diseased self-contemplation.

Kafka's land surveyor, *Landvermesser*, crosses a bridge and enters a world in which this idealistic dismeasure, *Vermessenheit*, is taken for granted as a condition of existence. The consequences for the tradition of allegory are extreme. The old forms of relationship, which Kafka remembers from his reading of literature, and which K. manages to perceive because of his special consciousness and his special vocation, present themselves with naked, tantalizing clarity, so that *The Castle* has all the outward signs of classical allegory, but K. is estranged from them. It is not quite accurate to say that *The Castle* is formally an allegory, but contains no real "other"; rather, the other stares K. in the face—there is simply no "bearing across," no metaphor, no medium of transition like analogy or love, to connect K. with the other. The image of the bridge proves misleading. In this chapter I try to describe how allegory can operate under a condition of self-criticism, in a novel whose theme is the impossibility of connection with the other.

THE SHELL OF ALLEGORY

The pilgrim arrives at a city. The castle appears on the horizon, difficult of access. Within the frame of these antique figures, Kafka constructs an urbanized system which displays the outward and visible signs of classical allegory. From the most exterior view, *The*

Castle assumes the shape of the allegories of history which we examined in part one, and the allegories of love we are treating. As an allegory of history, it commences, not *in medias res*, but at the end of things, in the New Jerusalem itself, across the bridge. By a simple inversion, the intruder now is not the *mendax*, but the *verus vir*, K., surrounded by mendacious persons. Like the passengers on Melville's *Fidèle*, the villagers are confidence men; but they are more ominous, being ignorantly confident of their righteousness of belief, like children, rather than greedily confident of their material shrewdness. For a moment let us put off consideration of the novel as an allegory of love as we fill in a few of the details of the alluring appearance of traditional allegory.

K. enters the novel on foot in search of something, as a pilgrim, or better, in the alternate medieval form of the quest, as a knight—the vaguely feudal administration of the castle recalls the Middle Ages. He is a pedestrian knight like Spenser's Guyon. Like Sir Gawain in the English romance, after a "long, hard journey" ("die lange, schwere Reise"), he enters into a bedroom relationship with the mistress of a powerful man.* As Gawain's goal is nearer than he knew and as Redcrosse's first adversary, after Error, is closer to home than he was aware, so K.'s castle is right at hand, somehow nearly indistinguishable from a village, a "miserable little town" ("ein recht elendes Städtchen") as K. is "disillusioned" ("enttäuschte") to see (487). As James Rolleston observes, it is here at the beginning that K.'s quest is nearly accomplished, only to fail as K. attempts to establish "normal" links with the castle. Like Don Quixote—the analogy is Marthe Robert's—K. blurs the sense of a goal for the sake of the quest itself. Pilgrims are drawn to their goals in passive submission; knights actively quest, but are liable to be misled. K.'s vocation suggests that he is still more active, empowered not only to seek his goal, to act, from Pepi's point of view, as "a hero, a rescuer of maidens" ("ein Held, ein Mädchenbefreier—739), but also to survey his goal, to measure it out as a service to the public. An official surveyor cannot get lost. K. is a knight of reason, who fixes

* *Das Schloss*, published in *Franz Kafka, Die Romane* (Berlin, 1966), p. 546. This accessible text of *Das Schloss* (pp. 481–814) is based on the standard edition (New York, 1946). Further references to the novel will be enclosed within parentheses in the text. For other documentation and references see the note at the end of this chapter.

the coordinates of the world according to the science of his profession; he performs the Romantic function of the artist—to orient, to judge, to lay out boundaries, to impress his mind on the landscape.

The castle itself resides where it should, if the name of its count is any indication, "Westwest." One takes his final rest there. The west has always suggested death; the words *Schloss* and *Klamm* share a sense of confinement. Frieda wishes she were with K., forever, in a grave "deep and narrow" ("tief und eng"—603)—her name means peace. Near the end of the novel, Pepi offers K. a place for the long winter in her "dark, narrow maids' room below" ("dunklen, engen Mädchenzimmer unten—754). If Wilhelm Emrich and Ronald Gray are right in their speculations, the conversations about clothing at the end suggest death. The last character to appear, in the uncompleted but probably nearly complete novel, the consumptive Gerstäcker, bears a name which might mean "spear-sticker," as if he were drawing K. to his end, a tubercular death-in-life like Kafka's own. If *The Castle* were an allegory in the classical tradition, we could without hesitation interpret the castle as the place of revelation, of theophany, which in modern times has been relegated exclusively, for believers, to the moment of death. On the morning of the last day of the novel as we have it, an official imitates a cockcrow (725), and K.'s file, perhaps, is torn up, as if it were a Day of Judgment. The castle is, properly, unlocated in the geography of the earth; Frieda's references to Spain and the south of France, where she would like to go (602), come as a surprise, much like the French place-names which Guillaume de Lorris included in the account of his unlocalized garden. The castle exists in a specialized world, like Spenser's fairyland, in what Walter Benjamin called Kafka's "*complementary* world," the world of allegory and revelation. The castle's world is an inverted *locus amoenus*, a shabby town with short days, short summers, snow and mist, eternal fatigue, and very little outdoors. Our allegories of love have all taken place in gardens, but this one will act itself out in a sick city.

The castle actually enters K.'s line of vision only three times in the novel. The appearances are puzzling and raise questions, but they do not necessarily preclude the existence of the castle or its potential meaning as the heavenly residence of truth. K. first looks "up" ("empor") at it in the first paragraph of the novel. Unlike the New Jerusalem, which may be invisible because it is clothed in its own radiance, the castle is concealed in mist and darkness, with no light to intimate ("andeuten") that it is there. K. simply gazes up into a void, which is either an appearance of or a fiction of emptiness ("scheinbare Leere"). The second view (486–88) has more substance. K.'s prospect is distant—he seems to approach as we read, stands still as if to consider it with better judgment ("mehr Kraft des Urteils"), and finally is distracted ("zerstreut") by the teacher, so that he, and we, never quite take in the view. The main impressions are that it first appears to tower "free and light above"; then it, disappointingly, begins to look like a miserable village—K. remembers his hometown. Finally, its single tower, not a church, has windows which shine in the sun, "somewhat insanely" ("etwas Irrsinniges"), and is topped by broken, irregular battlements, as if designed by an anxious or careless child, and as if a depressed ("trübseliger") inhabitant, who should have been imprisoned in the top room of the house, had burst through the roof. So ends the tradition of the *specula*, the watchtower of Reason in classical allegory. The shifting nature of appearances and the cloud of bizarre interpretations which K. intrudes between us and what he sees make us uneasy about rendering any objective judgment.

The final look at the castle (567–68) takes place at twilight on one of those very short days; as we watch, the castle begins to dissolve ("aufzulösen"). This time K. compares the castle to a person who gazes "free and unconcerned" ("frei und unbekümmert"), as if he were alone, and the gaze of the observer, K., could not fix on the castle person, but slides away. The longer K. looks, the less he discerns. K.'s perception does what a certain kind of allegorical interpretation does: it dissolves the object into a set of meanings. We begin to feel that K. is an allegorist in a world which refuses to admit the correspondences necessary for allegory. Given this kind of description, we resign ourselves, as indeed all the characters in the novel do, to thinking of the castle not as a visible edifice of stone and plaster, but as an ineffable substance, like God—an organization.

The problem with the castle organization is that it is obliged to include everything; it represents a metaphysical conundrum whose political counterpart is totalitarianism. In fact, the castle's work can never be complete, no single administrative act can be accomplished; Bürgel asks, "Who could, alone, even if he were the hardest worker, keep together on his desk all the material related to even the smallest case?" Yet the work of the bureaucracy makes sense only in view of its completion. Ionesco says, "What has no end, is absurd." Its task is to measure—K. dimly understands that his vocation usurps this task—and it needs all the facts before it can measure; but the facts are infinite and continually growing. Emrich draws our attention to the parable of Poseidon, which lays out this theme with Kafka's usual clarity and humor. The sea god administers the seas, and is continually reckoning figures, trying to keep account of his domain. The task keeps him endlessly at his desk; he has scarcely seen the sea. He only hopes that, when the world ends, he will have some free time in which to take a "little tour" of the waters. The objects under his charge overwhelm him in their infinite facticity; the phenomena of the seas can never attain the status of universal being—they merely become, and are desperately calculated by their own divinity.

So the castle. The officials are charged to establish and keep account of the order of the village, and since each villager's life presents them with infinite detail they are swamped with paperwork. Surely their comic frustration resembles the endless, irresolvable burdens of adjudication in the legal office of an insurance company. If K. did not, by his resolute courage, attract our serious sympathy, the novel would amount to a metaphysical joke on certain problems of infinite regress, problems to which the reflective nature of consciousness seems inevitably liable. The tumbling columns of bundles of files represent the material of the Book of Life, with which at some putative end point judgment will be made.

Austin Warren suggests that the castle hierarchy "provides, negatively, for deferment of responsibility or infinite regress." When the village administrator ("Vorsteher") asks K., "How should I know all the sons of all the under-castellans?" we sense that the number of officials is infinite. Only a letter distinguishes the name Sordini from Sortini (or dirt from fate); perhaps the names of the officials use the set of all the combinations of the letters, like the books in the Library of Babel.

The castle officials are arrayed in hierarchies, reflected in the pathetic hierarchies of status in the village—chambermaid versus tapstress—with "control officials" ("Kontrollämter") who seem to cut across categories, like internal auditors in a commercial enterprise, to keep the operations in tune and to maintain consistency in the general principles and methods of work. The official hierarchy serves as a mediating series between the will of the highest and the laborers in the village. The twin problems of mediation, which concerned Dante and Plato, are: how can any given level of a hierarchy communicate with any other (do mediators need mediators?), and how can mediation come to an end (if mediators infinitely recede, how can there be a "highest will," a final deity?). This issue borders the concerns of religion and of philosophy, in the one mythologized as angelology, and in the other mysteriously operative in the logic of infinite series and the mathematics of the calculus. Kafka inescapably alludes to angelology by presenting the lowest of the hierarchy, the messenger ("Bote") Barnabas, in shining raiment, with uncanny speed (504), even though this *angelos* ("messenger") is later revealed as a sorry fraud. The name of the head of the castle, Westwest, reduplicates itself as if to suggest that even it could extend indefinitely.

At this point we should gather up the strands of interpretation which we have already touched, because they are all tentative and deliberately inconclusive. The usual kind of allegorical interpretation which we have been making misses the point of the novel. We have noticed that the castle conforms to an inverted ideal of the New Jerusalem or the *locus amoenus*, that its administration recalls the mediating powers of religious myth, and that it presents the structure which a figure of truth or death, an apocalyptic figure, would present in a classical allegory. Kafka's executor, Max Brod, left the criticism of *The Castle* with versions of these observations, which are after all patent; Brod has been criticized, unfairly, for not going beyond what he obviously intended as a bare introduction to the novel.

The bulk of printed interpretation of *The Castle* has centered on the question of what the castle represents, that is, what metaphor might best be substituted for Kafka's metaphor. The most usual is God, especially Kierkegaard's God: Herbert Tauber says "Officialdom is the impenetrable executive of Providence." Walter Sokel, who carefully studied Kafka's whole corpus, understands the castle as, among other things, a generalization of Kafka's contorted conception of the father, the father figure as power figure, in an alliance of power with the submissive villagers. A political reading interprets the castle as the totalitarian state, empowered not so much by its own militia as by the abject consent of its subjects. Some autobiographical speculations have compared Frieda to Milena, one of Kafka's mistresses during the period the novel was under way, and Klamm to Milena's competent, distant husband. Many of the published psychoanalytical interpretations have been irresponsible; the likeliest reads the castle as the oppressive, guilt-inducing superego —this correlates with the idea of the castle as father. Emrich's interpretation is perhaps the most general along these lines. I take him to mean that the castle and its officials represent both the superego and the id, both that which is universal because it is transcendent, a necessary entity to complete metaphysical specula- tions (the ontological proof of God), a universal of the sort mathe- matical science has discerned, and that which is universal because it is inescapably natural—the instincts, the sexual drive, the will to survive. The castle stands for these universals in opposition to the individual human—K.—who wants to be a private person and to be free, to be an "I," in Emrich's and Sokel's terminology.

All these interpretations have some justification, and it is easy enough to extrapolate from them, and to feel confident in asserting that the castle represents the power and ground of existence and judgment—that which is final. Its menacing character has its source in its absoluteness; an individual like K. must feel threatened with emptiness and alienation if he refuses to acknowledge it, if he avoids connection. Benjamin says Kafka's world is a swamp of polarities: K. must oppose himself to the castle. This is the typological inter- pretation of the castle; it all springs from the idea that the castle is a counterpart of the New Jerusalem.

These matters may be clarified if we approach the allegory from another direction. We have become accustomed by now to reading allegorical figures as projections from the psyche of a single con- sciousness—a method which runs into serious problems when it coincides with German idealism—and also to reading allegorical situations as reifications of otherwise harmless metaphors, as liter- alism. The former technique has been applied wholesale to *The Castle*. Gray noted that Pepi's name is the nickname of Josef or Josefine in a German dialect, that K. calls himself Josef at one point, that the hero of *The Trial* is named Josef K., and that Pepi in her pathetic ambition is a kind of alter ego of K. Many critics have interpreted the assistants, in one way or another, as projections of K.'s childish ambition or his libido, his raw nature. The ambiguous descriptions of the castle have drawn readers to consider it a projection as well. The castle might be created out of whole cloth by K. in his need for a ground and a controlling power, just as he may have fabricated his "call" as a land surveyor; or it might be merely a projection of the village and its villagers, a grotesque parody in which the highest, a shabby, bestial facade, amounts to the best that men in this world can conceive—as Frederick A. Olafson puts it, a projection of the villagers' moral immaturity. People get the kind of god they deserve. Sokel and others compare the professional roles of the teacher and the messenger to K.'s vocation and to Kafka's. Donald Pearce interprets Frieda as K.'s *anima*, the incarnation of his repressed humanity; the landlady as his accusing conscience; and the assistants as his psychic automatisms, his instincts.

The situation of German literature in Kafka's time supports these interpretations; the idea of characters as expressions which emerge from a central consciousness gave its name to a prominent literary movement. But Sokel especially warns us that, although the term "expressionistic" suits Kafka's earlier work, *The Castle* in fact presents persons who properly lie outside the scope of K.'s consciousness, that Frieda and Amalia and the rest reflect K.'s thinking as humans reflect one another, not as fantastic projections. In *The Castle* Kafka was concerned with social as well as metaphysical problems. We have immediate access only to K., but other consciousnesses are about, constantly pressing us to be skeptical about K.'s judgments.

The same strictures apply to another kind of allegorical interpretation, which works well when applied to an early work like "The Metamorphosis" but which is inadequate for *The Castle*, namely, the view of the action as the reification of a metaphor. The names of important officials, "Klamm" and "Erlanger," and the pun involved in *Landvermesser*, suggest that the idea of reaching out for something, of grasping, underlies the action; the snowbound, dark, alien setting suggests the metaphysical problem of emptiness; the jaded language of bureaucracy suggests the failure of communication. But as Stanley Corngold says, in an interpretation of "The Metamorphosis," "The ontological legitimation for asserting analogues is missing in Kafka, who maintains the most ruthless division between the fire of the spirit and the principle of the world. . . ." In all the interpretations we have considered so far, the analogies ultimately disintegrate. The presence of allegory is felt everywhere, but the links of one thing to another never solidify. As Benjamin says, Kafka offers "a sort of theological whispered intelligence dealing with matters discredited and obsolete." Heller seconds this opinion: "Kafka represents the absolute reversal of German idealism." A world without an absolute cannot sustain allegory of the traditional kind; the fragments of old allegory simply float free without meaning. Kafka may be too modern to have recourse to the imagination as the absolute.

Yet Kafka avoids what might seem inevitable under these conditions, a disoriented and fragmented story, so relentlessly frustrating that no reader could bear it. His problem is to avoid the sort of radical diffuseness which Langland, in different ways, barely avoided, as we saw in chapter three. Kafka can hold his story together because of his reliance on another tradition than Expressionism in German literature of his time—Naturalism, the attempt at a fiction of scientific historicism. This school taught Kafka to rely on detail; hence springs his oddly Dickensian humor. We can imagine Kafka constructing episodes by inserting a scientific rationalist into a bizarre situation, K. into the village, just as we imagine Spenser constructing his episodes out of the materials of revelation and the theory of correspondence. It is Kafka's continual leaping from concrete detail to metaphorical abstraction, without the mediation of historical "types" of characters, of generalizations which arise out of social consciousness, which Lukács sees and dislikes. Lukács writes, "Modernist literature thus replaces concrete typicality with abstract particularity"; Kafka is his "modernist" bogeyman. Although his negative evaluation need not be conceded, Lukács's analysis is correct— typicality and typology are not the resting places of an interpretation of *The Castle*; we have to look at the links and relations themselves, freely and without the canon of authority or the convention of the typical.

THE MEDIA

The physical objects mentioned in the novel, with only a few exceptions, receive lovingly detailed attention, if scarcely any ordinary "description." Most of them appear to be media of communication between K. and the castle, or memorials of former communications. Several of these are pieces of paper of which the protocol of Momus may be taken as typical. Klamm's "village secretary," Momus (named for the god of raillery), seconded by the hostess of the Bridge Inn, Gardena, urges K. to submit himself to an interrogation in order to complete the protocol, which may contain a hostile and detailed account of K.'s activities. (Kafka deleted, but preserved among his papers, a clearer explanation of the contents of the protocol.) Gardena claims that the protocol is K.'s only hope of a way to Klamm, at least that it is "perhaps a kind of connection" ("vielleicht eine Art Verbindung"—582). Momus tells K. that Klamm will never read the protocol, but again the landlady urges that it represents an important relationship, because it was written up in Klamm's service, and Klamm therefore consents to its existence, "And how can something have Klamm's consent, if it is not filled with his spirit?" K. declines to be interviewed.

The term "protocol," like its cousins "agendum," "memorandum," "file," "document," or "correspondence," suggests just those vague pseudoforms of bureaucratic discourse which serve a purpose opposite to their apparent intent. They correspond in officialese to genre in fiction, but rather than ordering and articulating, they obfuscate, because they are redundant, tedious, and amorphous. Neither Klamm nor K. can stand protocols, but Klamm consents to them, whereas K. demurs. None of the forms of communication offered by the castle has any use; K. nevertheless is almost unique in refusing to cooperate with these forms, even if they are filled with the spirit of official consent. To the villagers and to that incarnation of the village spirit, Gardena, K.'s refusal has the negative, mean quality which, for a Christian, characterizes a religious person's refusal to accept the Bible, as if Bunyan's Christian were, for arbitrary, fickle reasons, to pay no heed to Evangelist's scroll.

The other documents in K.'s life are the letters he receives from Klamm, the correspondence concerning his job which took place years before his arrival, the letter, described to him, which Amalia received from Sortini, and the files ("Akten") which the officials keep—files presumably held together with paper clips ("Aktenklammern"), which could be a source of Klamm's name. Facts on paper acquire a peculiar validity in legal as well as religious contexts, so Kafka takes care to inauthenticate these documents: their sources are more and more obscured, their equivocal meanings subjected to rabbinical discriminations, their content negated by exquisite logic. K. is not alone in twisting the significance of the writings; one recent critic has found himself able, for instance, to deny that Sortini's letter is obscene, on the grounds that Olga's witness to its contents is defective. As with everything else that bears the form of fact in *The Castle*, there is room for doubt about the documents. We almost feel relief when a servant tears up the file which K. arbitrarily surmises is his own, perhaps sealing his doom (730). As readers we find ourselves suspending disbelief in these documents in order to maintain the integrity of the story; we are put on parole.

Of parallel status are the telephone communications early in the novel. I have not investigated the phenomenology of phone calls in 1920, but we might guess that the technical difficulty of placing calls and understanding the rasping voices made the whole operation more fictional in those days—the receiver would have to fill in the gaps of what he actually heard by the constructive powers of his mind, just as the watcher of old movies has to smooth the nearly discrete freezes of action to create the illusion of continuous motion. K. hears the hum of children's voices, singing as if trying to pierce deeper than paltry hearing, and the village administrator tells him that this hum is the only real and trustworthy thing he hears—all else, the voice of the man with the speech defect, is deceptive. "There is no fixed telephone connection with the castle" ("Es gibt keine bestimmte telefonische Verbindung mit dem Schloss"—497–98, 544). The confused, musical sound which K. hears suggests angelic harmonies, like the ravishing music of paradise in the opening pages of C. S. Lewis's version of Bunyan, *The Pilgrim's Regress*; but at the same time it is the buzz ("Summ") of a faulty telephone connection. K.'s telephone conversation, naturally, is a farce of tangled identities of speakers ("So who am I?" asks K.) and disconnected cross-purposes of speeches; Gray terms it a parody of prayer.

Finally, K. has access to the castle through another medium, pictures. In the first chapter he sees a portrait, as he learns, of the Castellan (485–86). When he first saw it, he thought it was only the dark backing of the frame from which a painting had been removed, but this second, closer look reveals the human figure. K.'s altered perception arouses the suspicion that he had repressed the figure before, or that he is fabricating it now. The portrait seems to be all frame and backing, without substantial representation, like the novel.

Another picture in the novel seems to depend for its form even more on the interpretation of the observer—Gardena's photograph of the messenger whom Klamm sent to call her for the first time (549). The picture is a medium of recollection and depicts a medium, an official messenger, in the act of performing what he is wont to do, leaping.

Gardena shows K. the photograph proudly, as her evidence of her special relationship with Klamm, and playfully—K. is to guess what it represents. K. first sees a young man, lying on a board, stretching and yawning. With prodding, K. sees that the board is a rope, that the youth is leaping, and that the yawn is strain: "his mouth is open, his eyes shut, his hair fluttering." The difference between the first interpretation of bored fatigue and the second of vigorous effort represents just the difference between the weary state of village life, to which K. slowly succumbs, and his initial active effort.

The alternate interpretations display how flimsy the science of interpretation is. The messenger's leap, if that is what it is, surpasses in vigor any other activity in the novel—Kafka resembles James in minimizing action. The leap surely recalls Kierkegaard's "leap of faith," the courageous motion required to bridge the gap between the individual and transcendence, between Gardena and Klamm, or the gap between appearance and reality which interpretation tries to bridge. But the tentativeness of the leap, its representation in an old photograph of dubious meaning, requires a leap of imagination to be accepted as such—it carries no more authority for a skeptical mind than does the New Testament for a nonbeliever. The photograph delineates what leaping would be like if leaping existed, but the evidence is inconclusive—it may be a yawn. This is Kafka's variation upon Kierkegaard. Visual representations of events, in *The Castle*, carry no more meaning than garbled messages or fleeting memories; they are forms without content, pure objects.

In addition to these objects of communication, K. meets several persons who are related to officialdom, the messengers and liaison officers. They, too, are mediators. We can look at them in the order which the officials themselves would approve, the order of their "competence" ("Zuständigkeit") in the case of K. I reserve treatment of the most competent (because the least), Bürgel, for a later section.

First, Barnabas is as competent a messenger as K. is a land surveyor, or Josefine a singer, or the Hunger-Artist an artist—all of these figures display the outward forms of their vocations with meticulous precision, but in substance are mere desperate impostors. In a figure like Barnabas we see the old *mendax* type, the liar and deluder, the imposer of fictions, degenerated into a buffoon—more pathetic than Melville's confidence man because ignorant of his own lie. Like an angel he bears messages to K., but as we read, the messages disintegrate, and we finally learn that Barnabas has seized this office in a grim effort to save his family from their relentless misery. As a bringer of messages, Barnabas symbolizes the role of the artist, the "son of consolation" (Acts 4:36); Sokel observes that Barnabas and K. are mirrors of each other. Barnabas, too, lives in exile—he mediates nothing.

Another link between K. and officialdom, the pair of assistants sent to him, much more effectively represent the will of the castle. They are kafkesque: irrational, comic, childish, sometimes frightening. They, too, as Gray has shown, reflect K.'s own activity in exaggerated form—while he peers through a peephole, seeking ocular connection with Klamm, they make telescopes of their hands like children (519). Unlike Barnabas, the assistants are essentially alien to K. and to us. Whereas Barnabas becomes warmer and more human, the assistants become cold, are driven outdoors, and are finally rejected when they reveal that their mission had been to encourage K. to take things less "seriously" ("schwer"—689). The two lines of interpretation of the assistants which have been put forward, like the two general views of the castle itself, can be joined: the assistants are both projections from inside of K.—of his libido, his erotic and destructive instinctive energy—and emissaries from the world of nature (this is Emrich's view), the cold world of law and impersonal determinism with which K. contends. Libido and universal nature are one; in the Middle Ages both could be called Amor.

The media, both as objects and persons, distinguish themselves as relatively close to or removed from K. Barnabas and the paper documents are within his ken, and fail to connect as they prove to be fraudulent messengers. The photograph, the telephone, and the assistants slip out of K.'s reach as they appear more authentic. We have no sense of the castle and its administration except by way of these media, but the lack of verifiable *Verbindung* draws our attention to the media themselves in a distracted condition which is the condition of Kafka's world.

As in the philosophy of existence, we can look only at phenomena rather than at substances. Everyone who reads Kafka has noticed the resemblance of these frustrating relations to the situation of a textually based religion like Judaism. K.'s problem is hermeneutic; as Benjamin puts it, Kafka sacrifices truth for the sake of its trans-missability, its Haggadic element. K. cannot know the castle, but he can know its emissaries, so he sets himself the hero-commentator's task of understanding them fully, linguistically, logically, with all the powers which reason and a skeptical sense of human nature can bring to bear. He is like a rabbi, or like us when we discriminate the meanings of the Name of Klamm. The only principle of interpretation available to K. is allegory, but he must read the allegory with the conviction that the analogical, systematically mediated cosmos, sustained by divine power, does not exist: the other is simply other. When K. encounters the irritable, slightly sadistic village teacher, who distracts him from his first attempt to reach the castle, he confronts the harshest parody of himself in the novel. We should now turn to K. himself, "der ewige Landvermesser" (498).

THE HERO

If K. is not an impostor, he behaves like one. Throughout the novel his vigor of action steadily diminishes until he reaches near stasis, like the constant K in a chemical formula of equilibrium. His peculiar Gogolian combination of pettiness and ambition smacks of a careerism and a narrow-mindedness which are repellent. He exploits people; he has the humorless suspiciousness of a paranoid; he is essentially idle. Marthe Robert describes him as, from the point of view of village and castle, a sordid parvenu adventurer. If Melville's metaphor of the Drummond light were applied to him, he might be counted as one of those characters to whom everything starts up. But people and objects circle around him not because of any powerful vision or strength which he possesses, but because of his self-centeredness, in which we readers are involved because of the exclusive point of view of the narration. K. exhibits that minimal form of integrity, a sense of his rights. Like the medieval questers, Langland's Will and Dante's Dante, he is curious, somewhat importunate, and possessed of a strong will guided only by the superficial mechanics of reason. In short, K. is one of us.

We feel sympathy for K., however, beyond what we would expect from identification, which Kafka restrained by changing the person of the narrative from first to third. Assuming for the moment that what K. wants is worth having, we must grant that his exertions recall the endeavors of a hero. He stands out as a figure of movement and color against a gray screen, the twilight snowscape. His spirit seldom flags in spite of exhaustion and apparently insuperable obstacles. Like a hero, he alone can give value to what he does; he persists steadfastly in a situation of utter isolation. Where Hawthorne's Giovanni, or even Spenser's Britomart, had responsibility thrust upon them, K., like Redcrosse, seizes responsibility and spurns the loophole of egress from the village. What Sokel calls K.'s heroic realism stands first among his qualities, his refusal to be turned aside from his quest by the specious claims of religion, of sentimental affection, of community consensus, or even of his own ideas as they are proved false, one after another. Like a classical hero he has his weapon and his nation to defend: his weapon is the shield of logic, and his nation, as Frye describes it, "the common contemporary types of tragic irony, the Jew, the artist, Everyman, and a kind of sombre Chaplin clown"—the nation of modern man.

We assumed that the goal of K.'s quest was worthwhile; given that, he may be called a hero. He is not Aeneas, not even Yvain, but he behaves heroically in the terms of the world he lives in. Like many characters in fiction, he can best be defined by what he loves. But what does he want? Kafka makes this the most obscure question of all. The change Kafka made in the opening scene of the novel deepens this obscurity. In the original version K. burst upon our attention with aggressive fearfulness like a secret agent, but in the revision he assumes a sort of bewildered, passive cunning which scarcely seems directed toward a goal.

The modern response to Kafka suggests the hypothesis that K. wants to be himself, to find and fill in peace his place in the scheme of things. I think the generality of this hypothesis springs from the allegorical character of *The Castle*—otherwise we might wish to say only that K. wants to be land surveyor for the castle. Even so, there is a contradiction built into K.'s desires, as can be seen in a comparison of two critic's statements about Kafka. W. H. Auden speaks of K. as a letter wanting to become a name, a self with a vocation. Sokel (here following Emrich) says that in Kafka's work the truth emerges by the defeat of the protagonist's consciousness, that "consciousness hides truth" and "the end is always the revelation of truth in the defeat of self." Sokel thinks of K. not as a letter wanting to become a name, but as a reduction, an abbreviation of a name like Klamm. These contrasting statements derive from two different views of what a "self" is: Auden's (and it is generally Auden's) that a self is a creature expressing its nature in its vocation in the world; and Sokel's (the sense one acquires from continental existentialism) that a self is an entity uniquely conscious, in rebellion against the world. *The Castle*, perhaps alone among Kafka's works, poses both these ideas of the self, and a double desire which emerges from them. K. tries to authenticate himself and the castle both at once, as if he were aware that only in reciprocal relation can either exist in mutual peace. More than any of the works' we have considered, *The Castle* is an allegory which depends upon our understanding of a particular character. K. represents us by being especially concrete.

Brief consideration of three episodes which are turning points of K.'s understanding can sketch for us the curve of K.'s will and its vicissitudes. They are all moments of heightened desire followed by distraction: K.'s memory of his home and the churchyard wall (505–506); the scene in the courtyard at the Herrenhof (571–75); and K.'s conversation with Bürgel (709–21). The episodes increase in difficulty.

With K.'s advent into the village, we are plunged into the action; since we receive little information about his past, his reminiscences about his childhood come with unusual force. While K. thinks Barnabas is leading him straight to the castle—his mental distraction is realized in his journey—he recalls an event that delineates, in little, his relation to the castle. In his home town the boys would try to climb the high wall surrounding the graveyard of a church. The point was not to get inside—a gate provided easy access—but to conquer ("bezwingen") the wall. One morning "the still, empty square was flooded with light—when had K. before or afterwards ever seen it like that"—K. climbed the wall "with surprising ease" ("überraschend leicht"). "No one was greater than he, here and now." A severe teacher, passing by, made K. get down; he hurt his knee descending; but the feeling of victory seemed to him a thing which would last forever ("für ein langes Leben einen Halt zu geben").

It is difficult to say what makes the scene so poignant: the bright sunlight on the scene of isolation, with the graves near at hand; the image of the boy with his flag and his victory, derived from no accomplishment or gain except the overcoming of an imaginary obstacle; or the boy's capacity to hold his sense of triumph in spite of the teacher's frown and the physical pain. The memory is of lonely triumph, the reward of a hero. His climbing the wall as a boy, before he was fully conscious, suggests that the ambition of ascetic and athletic grasping toward an inconsequential goal is innate in K. That the climb is frivolous in the eyes of the world merely reinforces its importance: boys are taught that heroes stand alone. The stuff is adventure; the claim on us is the claim of a Conrad figure, of romantic striving. The one triumph, achieved as if by magic under the confirmation of the bright sunlight, fixes K. for life in the desire to attain the highest. In the contrast between this archaic saint and wholly modern, tired, compromised society of the village, the novel finds its comedy and its pathos. K.'s cunning and worldly wisdom only cover over this core of desire; his social maturity covers over an adolescent (not infantile) will to be free, alone, and on top. K.'s mask is vulnerable.

When K. hopelessly waits in the Herrenhof courtyard for Klamm to come to his coach, he encounters another of those few objects in the novel, a bottle of brandy. The brandy should be considered among the media of communication. K., snuggled indolently among the furs in the coach, smells the brandy, and it seems as fondling ("schmeichelnd") as praise from a friend. He drinks, and suddenly the liquor is transformed ("verwandelt") into a drink fit for a coach-man. The courtyard bursts into (electric) light, and K., startled and guilty in his regressive repose, springs up and spills the brandy on a fur. The scene concludes with K. waiting still, standing in the darkened courtyard, and some of the most powerful phrases in the novel: "It seemed to K. as if they had broken off all relations ['Verbindung'] with him, and as if he were indeed freer ['freilich freier'] than ever before ... ; but —and this conviction was just as firm—as if at the same time there were nothing so meaningless, nothing so hopeless, as this freedom, this waiting, this inviolability ['diese Freiheit, dieses Warten, diese Unverletzlichkeit'']."

Gray's suggestion that the spilling of brandy hints of masturbation points in the right direction. The infantilism which the taste of brandy confirms is already present in the very idea that Klamm might come to K. The sweet, flattering smell of the brandy encourages K.'s pipe dream, and the glare of the lights shatters it, leaving the guilty consequences on the fur. Waiting, remaining in isolation and in stasis, leaves the hero utterly free and utterly out of touch. K. "wrenched himself out of" his regressed condition and, for the first time in the novel, enters a room simply because "he wanted to see people." He is not Prometheus: if he climbs the castle wall, it will be in the company of others. The avenue of retreat into his own body, the womb of comfort, leaves him in a darkness whose lonely freedom terrifies him.

Another kind of freedom tempts K. in his nocturnal conversation with a minor official, Bürgel. As in the other scenes, K. here ambitiously reaches for contact with the castle at the same time he succumbs in fatigue (and rum) and collapses into himself. Bürgel (perhaps "guarantor," and a hint of "little castle") is the secretary of Friedrich (kingdom of peace), and Bürgel's very "incompetence" in the case of K., as he explains, makes him the best hope of a true *Verbindung* which K. will encounter: his title is "Verbindungs-sekretär." Bürgel's first serious remark about K.'s condition reveals a common sense which in *The Castle* is unique: "That is amazing . . . you are land surveyor and have no land surveying to do." K. responds to Bürgel's offer of help with a smile. Bürgel seems to him an innocent with respect to his complicated difficulties—and K. for the first time assumes a posture of weary bureaucratic wisdom over against this naive and sanguine official, as their roles are reversed. Bürgel goes on to explain the situation in detail: the accidental applicant to an incompetent official does reverse the role of power; the applicant under the circumstances of night and surprise finds the official uniquely vulnerable; the official must treat the night applicant as a private person; and finally, the sudden compulsion on the official to grant the applicant's wish makes the official himself free, as he no longer functions as an official—hence the official organization is torn apart ("zerreisst"), as both the lowly official and the applicant can take on enormous power. By the time Bürgel explains all this, K. is fast asleep.

Earlier, halfway through Bürgel's discourse, K. nods off into a strange half-sleep, in which "word after word struck his ear, but his cumbersome consciousness ['lästige Bewusstsein'] had shrunk, he felt free, no longer did Bürgel hold him, only from time to time he groped out toward Bürgel still, he was not yet in the depths of sleep, but he had plunged in." K. considers this loss of consciousness a victory, and dreams of a celebration in which someone raises a champagne glass in his honor. As he slips deeper into his dream, the struggle and victory over consciousness is transformed into a fistfight with a naked bureaucrat who looks like a Greek god. K. advances successfully and relentlessly against his foe, who every so often lets out a squeal like a girl. The bureaucrat finally vanishes, leaving K. alone in a large room. K. sees the champagne glass broken on the floor, tramples it, is pricked by the shards, and wakes up, feeling sick like a child. At the sight of Bürgel's bare chest a thought occurs to K.: "Here you have your Greek god! Drag him out of bed!" Bürgel continues his lecture, and at some point K. dozes off again.

If Sokel is right, that for Kafka only when consciousness collapses can the truth emerge, this dream, which begins as a celebration of the loss of consciousness and enters into the complete unconsciousness of total sleep, should be the key to the meaning of the novel. But, *natürlich*, as Kafka would say, this revelation of truth is couched in the enigmatic, parabolic form of dream narration, and will not easily yield its secret—how could it be otherwise? Kafka's truth is parable. The dream has elements of the other sequences we have been examining: the sense of victory later ridiculed, the feeling of freedom, the regression into childhood, and the sudden rupture, like the hurt knee and the spilt brandy, of the champagne glass. Prior to any effort at complete interpretation, one might say of the dream that it presents in compressed form some themes of heroism and antiheroism which we now can assert are central to the meaning of *The Castle*: the illusory and guilty character of human triumph; the loneliness of freedom; the embarrassing, too human relation between adulthood and childhood; and, most generally, the imposture of consciousness.

I think the objects in the dream, the bureaucrat ("Sekretär") and the champagne glass, cannot be interpreted but only talked around. The breaking of the glass suggests the Jewish wedding ceremony, as

302

well as the German cornerstone-laying ceremony and the wonderful unshattered glass of Goethe's *Elective Affinities*. Like a hymen, it is broken to make a new thing; its associations are with a sacrament of institution and with sex. Perhaps its connection here with a sense of victory and a welcome unconsciousness means that K.'s liaison with Bürgel will bear more fruit than the liaison with Frieda. And if Bürgel is like a Greek god, he squeals like a *Mädchen*. K.'s victory wobbles between a Titanic upheaval and a farcical sexual conquest. *The Castle* will come no closer to theophany than this. This is where the paradox of dream as revelation and dream as enigma ends: when one is unconscious, asleep, he is at the same time nothing but consciousness, the outside world being cut off. To a dreamer the meaning of things amounts to no more than vaguely controlled private intentions—his god is the child within him. In Emrich's terms, K. is now at his most private and personal, at the same time he is in touch with the most universal.

K. leaves Bürgel's room with a smile and shows some signs of sympathy and humorous self-knowledge in the remaining fragments of the novel, but we cannot speak of a clear change in his character. Nothing suggests that he has come closer to the castle, or into a better relationship with the villagers. If he, and through him we, have learned anything, it is a small thing, a kind of resignation and a gathering of forces within a smaller circuit, as if they had been overextended. The dream of gods and women merely bemuses K. Olafson best sums up the status of K.'s heroism: he avoids both the Nietzschean "pathos of Promethean moral heroism" and the Kierkegaardian "pathos of faith 'quia absurdum'" and he realizes "the moment in religious life in which the moral consciousness 'prises itself off the world' [as in a true dream] and recognizes itself for the first time in all its vulnerability and precariousness." The media fail K., and he is left only with this self.

K.'S LOVE

Only Gustav Janouch can attest to the accuracy of the rather humorless aphorisms which he attributed to Kafka, but one of them serves our purpose:

We attempt to set our narrow world above the infinite. Thereby we disturb the rhythm of things. That is our original sin. All phenomena in the cosmos and on earth move in cycles, like the heavenly bodies, it is an eternal repetition; man alone, the concrete living organism, runs a direct course between life and death. For man there is no personal return. He only follows a declining path. So he breaks the cosmic order. That's original sin.

A Greek interpretation of a Hebrew idea, which we have seen before: it is Alain de Lille's idea of the complaint of nature. To speak of flowers and animals as selfish is nonsense, but those private, personal desires which arise out of some mysterious region of the free human self hinder the mechanism of the cosmic eros.

In *The Romance of the Rose*, Amant seems at first a naïf member of the dance of love, but under Jean de Meun's cold eye he is revealed as the autonomous, eccentric human that he is, whose love for the rose just barely fulfills universal Nature's demand for plenitude in a world not yet given grace. Britomart is tempted to separate her human love from the high concord of Christian nature, but she is filled with the grace of British history, and as if by fairy magic she brings her passionate love into harmony with the lasting cycles of generation, while Florimell and Marinell and the waters of Britain recreate spring. Hawthorne's Giovanni fails to align his infatuated self with the natural and universal love offered him by Beatrice; for Hawthorne in this tale, the poison of voyeurism—the artist's dilemma—pollutes the well of grace. For neither Amant nor Giovanni does the image of the beloved ever step out of the mirror as it does for Britomart; our male lovers remain narcissistic.

This last paragraph, and the last three chapters, describe a property which I would include in a general account of the character of allegories of love. This is the property of testing the love which humans bear toward each other, especially sexual love, against divine love, whether it be the cycling eros of the pagans or the saving grace of the Christians. By its modes of analogy, its constant suggestive pressure toward the universal, its reciprocal appropriation of metaphors of the sacred and the profane, allegory can bring under rigorous scrutiny the behavior of humans in love and judge the meaning of the most deeply felt and defining experience.

The Castle is unique among Kafka's works in presenting directly the action of love. We think of Kafka's central characters as bachelors, perhaps newly engaged, but strangers to women (until the publication of the letters to Milena and Felice, the same was said of Kafka himself). In *The Castle* Kafka narrates two relationships which, like the various love stories of the middle books of *The Faerie Queene*, fill out the scheme of possibilities for a lover. For Kafka there are only two: the thwarted love of Amalia and Sortini, and the love of K. and Frieda.

Tauber drew attention to the parallel with the story of Amalia which seems inescapable, Kierkegaard's analysis of the Abraham story in *Fear and Trembling*. The disgusting Sortini demands of Amalia that she "suspend the ethical," to love him simply because he is of the castle. She refuses, and the pathetic consequences of her refusal, as Kafka spells them out at length, are among his most powerful writings. The opportunity which Amalia refuses is to link herself, as Gardena and Frieda had done, selflessly with the castle in its aspect of erotic power. In this view, the castle officials resemble archaic divinities, despotic and transcendent. That Kafka presents them as farcical in no way qualifies Amalia's courage or righteousness —she is righteous but not faithful in terms of village religion—and to interpret her refusal as an erroneous defense of virginity made absolute, as Sokel does, seems to me to miss the point of her long story. Kafka needs Amalia's story at its most painful, as tragic farce, to serve as contrast and explication of the story of K. and Frieda.

Frieda abandoned Klamm for K., and at the end, neglected by K. (as he admits), returns to her liaison with officialdom in the person of Jeremiah, one of K.'s assistants. In contrast with Amalia, who never relinquished her self, Frieda attempted, with K., to acquire a self, but gave it up.

K.'s affair with Frieda begins in earnest on the floor behind the bar of the taproom outside Klamm's office in the Herrenhof, with a passage which stands alone in literature:

> Then she started up, as K. remained quietly in thought, and began to pull at him like a child: "Come, it's suffocating under here!" They embraced, her little body burned in K.'s hands, in an unconsciousness from which K. tried ceaselessly but vainly to escape they rolled a few feet, hit dully against Klamm's door

and lay in the little puddles of beer and other trash which covered the floor. There hours passed, hours of breathing in common, of heartbeat in common, hours in which K. continually had the feeling that he was losing himself or that he had gone farther into an alien land than any man before, an alien land in which the air itself had a different composition from the air of home, in which one might suffocate from alienation, yet in whose senseless allurements one could do nothing but go further, lose oneself further. [517]

And the next morning:

There they lay, but not so surrendering as the night before. She sought something, and he sought something, raging, contorting their faces, boring their heads into each other's breast they sought, and their embraces and their tossing bodies did not make them forget, but reminded them of their obligation to seek; like dogs desperately pawing the ground, they pawed into their bodies; and helpless, disillusioned, grasping at last for happiness, they drew their tongues over each other's face. Fatigue finally quieted them and made them thankful to each other. [520]

No more than K.'s dream can these passages be interpreted, but the same themes, here in erotic form, recur: the frustrated aspiration, the association of heroic quest with childishness, the isolation of freedom, and the glories and dangers of unconsciousness. The same physical action at one time is sublimed into alien, perhaps angelic air, and at another time sinks into the bestial—both are "allurements" ("Verlockungen"), temptations like the castle itself to draw K. and Frieda out of what they are. Like the dream, the lovemaking evokes an old tradition in allegory, only to invert it. K. and Frieda for a time are at one ("gemeinsam"), in unmediated relationship, but in the Kafka paradox their achievement occurs in unconsciousness and cannot be dragged into the light of their strictly human reason. It remains merely recollection in their days together. Frieda seems partially aware of this when she offers K., by implication, joint death as a substitute for satisfactory love—another form of unconscious *Verbindung*.

At the end K., too, is aware of his failure. Having failed to warm his woman into life, to live with her, as Pygmalion was able to do, as a creature substantially other rather than as a projected image of himself, he retires into himself in mild resignation. Gray considers the style of K.'s last conversation with Pepi almost a parody of the adverbial Kafka style of qualifications and false starts (like the style of parts of *The Confidence-Man*), simply early draft stuff, which Kafka later would have revised and strengthened. I think, to the contrary, that Kafka's final style reflects a new situation, that K.'s mind has sunk into a wash of endless discriminations and self-incriminations, as his activity slides into an almost purely reflective and interpretative mode without choosing or movement.

With Pepi, K.'s female mirror image, he reaches his wisest and bitterest self-knowledge:

> "I don't know whether it is like this, and my guilt is not wholly clear to me, yet when I compare myself with you [Pepi], something of this kind appears to me, as if we both had struggled too hard, too clamorously, too childishly, too crudely to obtain something which is easily and imperceptibly won with, for example, Frieda's calm and Frieda's matter-of-factness—we with our whining and scratching and tugging, like a child tugging a tablecloth, obtaining nothing, but dragging down the whole splendid show, putting it forever beyond reach; I don't know whether it is like this. . . ." [757]

The child's irresistible will to have the fine objects ("die Pracht") frustrates itself. If the objects were ever to come within the child's reach—Kafka told Brod something like this would have concluded the novel—the event would be merely fortuitous, beyond will or interpretation, a matter not so much of love as of chance. We can want the world to conform to our allegories, but it may refuse, we may have to leave it alone, inviolable.

For Kafka, love is consciousness, and hence self-destructive; but love is also unconsciousness, the perfect freedom of alienation, the self-othering which would be a living allegorizing, which is too terrifying for a human to sustain. One of Kafka's parables illustrates the paradox, a parable put, like an allegory, in terms of a division of the soul. I give the Muirs' translation:

The Spring

He is thirsty, and is cut off from a spring by a mere clump of bushes. But he is divided against himself: one part overlooks the whole, sees that he is standing here and that the spring is just beside him; but another part notices nothing, has at most a divination that the first part sees all. But as he notices nothing he cannot drink.

Bibliographical Note

Because the critical writing on Kafka has the proportions of the kafkesque, this note will be particularly selective. There are full-length bibliographies, as well as the general serials, especially that of the *MLA*. I should first of all acknowledge my debt to the good translation by Willa and Edwin Muir, Eithne Wilkins, and Ernst Kaiser (New York, 1930, 1958; London, 1953).

The most comprehensive among the good studies of *The Castle* are those of Walter Sokel, *Franz Kafka—Tragik und Ironie: Zur Struktur seiner Kunst* (Munich and Vienna, 1964) of which pp. 391–500 treat *The Castle*, and Wilhelm Emrich, *Franz Kafka* (Bonn, 1958), trans. Sheema Zeben Buehne as *Franz Kafka: A Critical Study of his Writings* (New York, 1968). Sokel has summarized some of his ideas in brief form in a pamphlet, *Franz Kafka*, Columbia Essays on Modern Writers, 19 (New York, 1966).

The fullest studies are by Ronald Gray, *Kafka's Castle* (Cambridge, Eng., 1956)—his opinions differ somewhat in the essay on *The Castle* in *Franz Kafka* (Cambridge, Eng., 1973); Klaus-Peter Philippi, *Reflexion und Wirklichkeit: Untersuchungen zu Kafkas Roman "Das Schloss"*, SzDL, 5 (Tübingen, 1966); and Richard Sheppard, *On Kafka's Castle: A Study* (London, 1973). Too little noticed is the stimulating essay on *The Castle* by Marthe Robert, *L'Ancien et le nouveau: De Don Quichotte à Franz Kafka* (Paris, 1963), pp. 175–311. (I have not seen the English translation by Carol Corman, Berkeley and Los Angeles, 1976.)

Collections of essays on Kafka often present the better German essays in English. Among these are Ronald Gray, ed., TCV *Kafka: A Collection of Critical Essays* (Englewood Cliffs, N.J., 1962), which includes two fine essays

to which I refer: Erich Heller, "The World of Franz Kafka," repr. from
The Disinherited Mind (Cambridge, Eng., 1952) and Austin Warren, "Franz
Kafka," repr. from *Rage for Order* (Chicago, 1948). I quote also from Heller's
essay on *The Castle* in his *Kafka* (London, 1974), pp. 107–38. Angel Flores
and Homer Swander, eds., *Franz Kafka Today* (Madison, Wisc., 1958) has
a full bibliography, and contains the essay by Donald Pearce, "The Castle:
Kafka's Divine Comedy."

Peter F. Neumeyer, ed., *Twentieth-Century Interpretations of "The Castle"*
(Englewood Cliffs, N.J., 1969) contains the brilliant essay by Frederick A.
Olafson, "Kafka and the Primacy of the Ethical," repr. from *HudR* 13 (1960):
60–73. The journal *Mosaic* 3, no. 4 (1970) devoted an issue to Kafka, which
contains the essay by Stanley Corngold, "Kafka's 'Die Verwandlung':
Metamorphosis of the Metaphor" (pp. 91–106). This essay is now available
in Corngold's book, *The Commentator's Despair: The Interpretation of Kafka's
"Metamorphosis"* (Port Washington, N.Y., and London, 1973). Likewise the
CRB devoted an issue (no. 50, 1965) to Kafka, which contains the quotation
from Ionesco that I borrowed (p. 4). Finally, Angel Flores edited an early
collection, *The Kafka Problem* (New York, 1946), which also contains a version
of the Warren article.

Other essays which I draw on are the pair of chapters on Kafka by Walter
Benjamin, *Illuminations*, ed. Hannah Arendt and trans. Harry Zohn (New
York, 1968); W. H. Auden, "The I Without a Self," in *The Dyer's Hand and
Other Essays* (New York, 1962), pp. 159–67; James Rolleston, *Kafka's Narra-
tive Theater* (Univ. Park, Pa., and London, 1974); and the first two chapters
of Georg Lukács, *Wider den missverstandenen Realismus* (Hamburg, 1958),
trans. John and Necke Mander as *The Meaning of Contemporary Realism*
(London, 1963) or *Realism in our Time* (New York, 1964).

The words allegedly spoken to Gustav Janouch are recorded in *Conversations
with Kafka*, trans. Goronwy Rees (New York, 1971) from *Gespräche mit Kafka*
(1968). Frye on Kafka is from the *Anatomy of Criticism* (Princeton, 1957). The
epigraphs are from Kafka's "Reflections on Sin, Pain, Hope, and the True
Way," from *The Great Wall of China*, trans. Willa and Edwin Muir (New
York, 1946) and Ludwig Wittgenstein, *Philosophical Investigations*, trans. G. E.
M. Anscombe (Oxford, 1953, 1958). "The Spring" is quoted from *Parables
and Paradoxes* (Berlin, 1935; New York, 1937, 1946–58). Now Anthony
Thorlby has written thoughtfully about what I fitfully perceived when I
selected the epigraph from Wittgenstein, in "Anti-Mimesis: Kafka and
Wittgenstein," in *On Kafka: Semi-Centenary Perspectives*, ed. Franz Kuna
(London, 1976), pp. 59–82.

Conclusion

IN his essay "Figura," Erich Auerbach reminds us that the word "type" originally meant nearly what printers mean by it today, the impress of a forming shape, like a seal, in a receiving material like wax. The early ambiguity as to whether it is the mark of the imprint or the molding device (which itself had to be shaped) which is the "type" was resolved in generality: the type is the shape, outline, form, the "figure"—whether conceived as a stamping device or a design which has been stamped. The processes implied by the early Greek usage of the term—sealing, printing, carving, molding, hammering on an anvil—all imply the capacity to duplicate a form accurately. Both the forming device and the formed material conform to a third thing, a desired figure, which someone wants to see repeated. The desire for repetition may simply be a desire to save labor—as in book-printing—but it may also be a desire to assert authority, as is the case with a royal seal, which can command insofar as its imprint can be recognized as the authentic form of the royal power. The seal is the medium for the recognition of power.

In the introduction I suggested that reification allegories may be viewed as hyperbolic and fantastic expressions of what is "typical" of someone or some situation. When Æmylia, lusting, encounters Lust, or when an angry character meets Furor "in middle space" (*F.Q.* 2.4.32), what is typical of their characters (at least for the time) becomes reified. In an allegory, when a character conforms to a moral type, the conformity becomes visible in a monstrous shape as the type enters the fiction. As in typology, in which a fiction repeats, especially in its structure, an "old" story, so in reification allegory a fiction repeats, in monstrous characters or situations, an essential, usually moral, characteristic, a form of the soul. The business of reduplication, which underlies both typological and reification allegories, is the principal technique of allegories; the idea of a repeated "type" is common to both. So allegorists are fascinated with mirrors and books. The reduplications are of two kinds: those in which the plot of a story imitates another plot, and those in which an external phenomenon imitates an internal one, in a fictional person.

Among the things which overt repetitiousness implies is constancy, even an inhuman fixity. The predictability of allegorical plots and allegorical characters seems contrary to the arbitrariness of the events of the world and the human capacity for change. But the allegories we have studied focus carefully on the process of change. The near stasis and repose of the central figures of *The Castle* and *The Confidence-Man* are exceptions which prove the rule, since both those works deliberately contravene the tradition of allegory. Doubtless change inheres in any narrative plot, but in an allegory, where so much seems rigid and secure, where plots and characters seem predetermined in their conformity to type, change stands out like a moving figure on a stationary ground.

The forms of change in allegory are endless, from simple motion across a significant landscape to metamorphosis. Two fundamental plots orient the changes in the allegories we have been considering: in the allegories of history, the motion toward, or failure to attain, the City of Peace; in the allegories of love, the motion toward, or failure to attain, marriage. Both Jerusalem and holy matrimony are constituted as stable conclusions where change will cease. All of the allegories we have studied, because they are true to the imperfections of the world, conclude with instability: the city is not quite attained; the marriage is postponed, the engagement broken, or the union noticeably imperfect.

One great allegory has it both ways. Dante attains the resting place in vision, but constantly reminds us of his distance from it as he writes his vision here in this world. Remaining Dante in the flesh, the poet at his bench, he is changed entirely in his vision. His poem is the imprint of his vision as he traces, as best he can, with his pen the flight of his mind. We find nowhere else, I think, such conscious-ness of fiction as fiction, of vision as allegory. In the very awareness of his distance from paradise, he is set free in it.

Let us take one moment of Dante's journey as an example. In canto 22 of the *Paradiso*, Dante ascends to the sphere of the fixed stars, and has a "Scipio vision" of our earth, the "little threshing floor which makes us so ferocious" ("L'aiuola che ci fa tanto feroci"). The nature of the place could not be more determinate: it is a specific sphere, and like all the circles of Dante's system, has its particular characteristics. Dante lights among the stars of Gemini, his natal constellation, and acknowledges the stellar influence which gave him his genius "whatever it may be" ("qual che si sia, il mio ingegno"). It is an image of allegory: astrological influence is nature's purest case of the correspondence of mind and matter, of the way physical beings can conform to psychic entities. When Dante is with his own stars, we understand him to be discovering his own essence, displayed as an allegorist can display things, visibly.

The fixed stars constitute a turning point in the poem because from them Dante can look down upon the lower heavens and the earth, and he can look up to see the crystalline sphere, the boundary of the natural and the empyreal orders. As Dante discovers his own natal character, he sees the other heavens, the seven planets, in their kindest relationships, as parents and children: the moon is Latona's daughter; the sun, Hyperion's son; Mercury and Venus are referred to as the children of Maia and Dione; Jupiter is Saturn's sun and Mars's father. From his place, Dante now can see the complex motions of the planets, the variations "of their Where" ("di lor dove"), but his new knowledge of physics is submerged under his deeper knowledge of the mythological relationships of things, and his still deeper knowledge of the loves and wars of human families.

"With my sight I returned" ("Col viso ritornai"), he says, to look upon the earth. The pilgrim has visions like the poet. He smiles in high contempt at the "low semblance" ("vil sembiante") of the earth and hopes, in his last address to us, the "lettore," to return again, after his vision closes and he dies. For now, for six cantos, he will wheel in his constellation, becoming a turning point himself, in his final preparation to see the real turning point, the "punto fisso" at the center of the intelligible universe (as Satan's flanks are the center of the sensible universe). When Dante looks down again, in canto 27, to see the "little threshing-floor" and the "mad track of Ulysses" ("il varco / folle d'Ulisse"), he still wheels among the Twins; then he is rapt to the crystalline. While among the stars, he is examined by the apostles on the theological virtues, as if to confirm his readiness for final knowledge.

In Paradise, as he mounts the spheres, things grow greater and more brilliant, and Dante's rhetoric insists increasingly on its incapacity to describe what he sees: "one cannot refer to the passing beyond the human in words" ("Trasumanar significar per verba / non si porìa—1.70–71). As he reaches his place in the stars, however, Paradise seems no longer to expand, but to diminish, to be refined. There is a hint of this just before he whirls to the stars: the music of Saturn is silence before it turns to thunder (21.58, 142). In the stellar garden of the Church, there is a music so sweet that our sweetest earthly song would sound like thunder compared with it (23.97–102). When Peter appears he makes Dante's pen leap rather than describe his song: the colors of our speech, even our imagination, are too vivid (24.25–27). Twice Dante sees so clearly that he sees nothing: when he sees St. John (25.120), and when he looks at the "triumph" which plays about the fixed point and little by little is extinguished from Dante's sight (30.10–13). The point itself is so small that the smallest star we can see from the earth would seem a moon beside it (28.19–21), even though it paradoxically encloses that which seems to enclose it (30.12). Duration of time contracts and collapses like sound and light and space. Beatrice is silent only instantaneously as she watches the fixed point—only as long as the sun and moon are held "balanced" on the horizon at one moment in the year—and she speaks of the creation of the world as a flash of light: "From its becoming to its entire being there is no interval" ("dal venire / all'esser tutto non è intervallo"—29.1–6, 25–27). Here and elsewhere in *Paradiso* Dante turns to a calculus of infinitesimals to express the ineffable. The fixed point would have no dimension. In the "light intellectual, full of love" ("luce intellettüal, piena d'amore"—30.40) Dante feels himself rising beyond his own visual powers. St. John had told him that he must "sift with a finer sieve" ("a più angusto vaglio . . . schiarar"—26.22–3), and at the very last vision, in a final image of diminished refinement, gazing with his own mind (like God) "fixed, immobile, and intent" ("fissa, immobile e attenta"—33.98), the thing he sees is transformed, "sifted out" ("travagliava"—114).*

Dante has a "physical," if supernatural, explanation for the inversion of phenomena from aggrandizement to diminishment. Beyond the crystalline sphere, the universe is arranged as it really is, in concentric circles which diminish toward their center, the fixed point which is the Godhead. As one moves from the natural center, the earth, to the fixed point, one first experiences the enlargement of the spheres; then, in the Empyrean, where things appear as they are, the spheres diminish. In spite of this inversion, the intelligences of the spheres, the orders of the angels, maintain their proper order, so that the highest order, the Seraphim, inhabit the largest natural sphere, the crystalline, and the smallest empyreal sphere, the closest to God. Dante's mind, and our minds, are brought to conceive of this spatial paradox through love and intelligence, by her "who imparadises my mind" ("che 'mparadisa la mia mente"—28.3). The imagery of infinitesimal size and duration, of silence and blindness, attempts to speak of the unspeakable in the language of a mind imparadised, a mind which sees things the way an allegorist writes them. The new sensibility which Dante acquires begins in the midst of his natal constellation, the source of his original sensibility as scholar and poet. As part of the Twins, Dante himself is fixed, relative to the stars, but wheeling relative to the earth; in several senses, the vision which begins in canto 22 may be called a turning point.

The human being moving through the repetitive landscape and the predetermined temporality of plot admits of the change within fixity which characterizes allegory. We have seen that allegorists depict the world *intelligibly*: there is some plan which accounts for phenomena, some ideas to be expressed. But it is typical of humans to lack intelligence. In the great, perfected allegories—the *Divine Comedy* and *The Faerie Queene*—part of the "other-speech" is narrative irony, since a human person, the central character, is ignorant of a rationalized landscape and rhetoric which we can see. The progress of the central person is toward knowledge, and allegories approach the mythical when the protagonist at last sees what we see. The

* John Freccero calls my attention to these sifting images.

change of mind, the conversion (*metanoia*), nearly becomes metamorphosis. Dante says he was "made within as Glaucus was made by tasting the herb which made him companion of the other gods of the sea" ("tal dentro mi fei, / qual si fè Glauco nel gustar dell'erba / che 'l fè consorte in mar delli altri Dei"—1.67–69), but the change for Dante was only *dentro*, only mentally did he grow gills for a new element. Metamorphosis in allegory remains mental and visionary, and the hyper-articulate landscapes of allegory collapse with the onset of knowledge.

Plato's term for allegory is "under-meaning," *hyponoia*. We have seen that allegorists express their hyponoia by typology and reification, most extremely by the display of the universe according to mental coordinates and the display of events according to the plot of the Bible. Dante's poem is the purest allegory. The pathological state which overmentalizes the world, which aligns things, in a parody of idealism, in terms of categories of intelligence, we name with another Greek term, paranoia. In an allegory, the world is in a good conspiracy in that it teaches us about ourselves and God. The tragedy of *The Castle* and the bitterness of *The Confidence-Man* are felt because the elements of the conspiracy are present with all their paranoid terror, but the conspiracy is hollow at the core—it is all talk, no crime has been committed, nothing revealed. In the positive allegories of Dante and Spenser, a character changes, undergoes metanoia, so as to conform to the truth of the world in knowledge. Yet he does not metamorphose; he remains within the world, as Redcrosse or Dante, lightened by his knowledge and hoping to return.

Index

Terms associated with allegory are listed under the word "Allegory," and references to the Bible and scriptural exegesis under "Bible." Otherwise this is an index of authors and anonymous works.